TALKIN' SOCIALISM

Mary Harris ("Mother") Jones and J. A. Wayland talkin' socialism in Girard, Kansas, c. 1911. Courtesy of Virginia Lashley.

TALKIN' SOCIALISM

J. A. Wayland and the Role of the Press in American Radicalism, 1890–1912

Elliott Shore

 UNIVERSITY PRESS OF KANSAS

© 1988 by the University Press of Kansas
All rights reserved

Published by the University Press of Kansas (Lawrence, Kansas
66045), which was organized by the Kansas Board of Regents and is
operated and funded by Emporia State University, Fort Hays State
University, Kansas State University, Pittsburg State University,
the University of Kansas, and Wichita State University

Library of Congress Cataloging-in-Publication Data

Shore, Elliott, 1951–
  Talkin' socialism.
  Bibliography: p.
  Includes index.
  1. Wayland, J. A. (Julius Augustus), 1854–1912.
2. Socialists—United States—Biography. 3. Socialism
—United States—History. 4. Socialism—United States
—Periodicals—History. 5. Press, Socialist—United
States—History. I. Title.
HX84.W4S56 1988   335'.0092'4 [B]   87-37255
ISBN 0-7006-0352-2

Alternative Cataloging-in-Publication Data

Shore, Elliott, 1951–
  Talkin' socialism: J. A. Wayland and the role of
the press in American radicalism, 1890–1912.
Lawrence, KS: University Press of Kansas, copyright 1988.
  Illustrated with photos, facsimiles, and cartoons.
  PARTIAL CONTENTS: The one-hoss philosophy. -The
Coming Nation. -The Appeal to Reason. -Advertising the
socialist dream: radical publishing at the turn of the
century. -Strike. -The second Coming Nation.
  1. Wayland, J. A., 1854–1912. 2. Socialist editors—
United States. 3. Socialist periodicals—United States—
History and criticism. 4. Socialist Party (United States)—
History. 5. Appeal To Reason—History and criticism.
6. Coming Nation—History and criticism. 7. Advertising
in socialist periodicals. 8. Newspaper publishing—
United States—History. 9. Radicalism—United States—
History. 10. Radical publishers and publishing—
United States—History. 11. Warren, Fred.
12. Union-busting—Kansas—History. I. Title. II.
Title: Talking socialism.
335.00973 or 071

British Library Cataloguing in Publication Data is available.

Printed in the United States of America
10 9 8 7 6 5 4 3 2 1

For Sandy

Contents

List of Illustrations

Acknowledgments

Teachers, librarians, friends, and colleagues helped me to write this book. At Bryn Mawr College, where I wrote the dissertation upon which this work is based, Barbara Miller Lane and Arthur Dudden were my two most influential critics. Alfred Rieber, Ralph Flood, Howard and Martha Balshem, Rosamond Putzel, and Phil Yanella all helped shape my early thoughts on the *Appeal to Reason*. Librarians throughout the country—Sandy Berman, Jim Danky, Joe Zucca, Sandra Taylor, Anita Lingle, Barbara Tucker, Dorothy Swanson, Ed Weber, and Tom Whitehead—helped to find materials and provide support for my research.

Criticism of parts of the manuscript from Jane Caplan, Colin Sparks, and Sean Wilentz refined my thinking. Kathryn Meyer, Gail Malmgreen, and Nick Salvatore read the manuscript closely and provided suggestions that were instrumental in clarifying my argument. Milton Cantor's criticism helped to sharpen my focus, even though I didn't incorporate all of his suggestions. Mari Jo Buhle's comments improved the final manuscript, and I warmly appreciate her enthusiasm for the project. Ken Fones-Wolf helped encourage me from the beginning to the end to such an extent that just saying thank you is not enough.

I have been fortunate in the last three years to work at the Institute for Advanced Study, where I have benefited from the kindnesses and criticisms of a number of visiting scholars, among them Lawrence Cremin, Linda Nochlin, Susan Mosher Stuard, and Elizabeth Hill Boone. Above all, I'd like to thank Joan Wallach Scott of the institute's faculty for her close reading of this book, especially in the key middle chapters, where her critical comments helped make explicit the theme of the book.

Time and money, as J. A. Wayland would understand, were essential. Time was provided by Temple University; money, by the Max L. Richter Fellowship of Bryn Mawr College; and both, by the director of the Institute for Advanced Study, Harry Woolf. J. A. Wayland's granddaughter Virginia Lashley and his youngest daughter, Edith Wayland Stephenson, were generous with their time, their memories, and their photographs. Gene DeGruson, of Pittsburg State University, helped to provide information and photographs. Joyce Good, Betsy Luff, Lisa Nunes, and Denise Diamond helped produce various drafts of the manuscript. Lynda Emery and Mark Darby at the institute supplemented the excellent work of the editorial staff of the University Press of Kansas.

1
Introduction

The decade between 1890 and 1900 was a period of unusually rapid cultural change. Most of the first generation of leaders of the socialist movement and many of the rank and file grew up in the United States of the Civil War period, steeped in producer ideology and Republican politics. Largely native born and watching their world slip away, many turned away from the Republican party and towards the new parties of the 1880s, which began to address the growing inequities in society, before moving to the Peoples party in the late 1880s and, finally, to the Socialist Party of America after 1901. Significant among these leaders is a large group of country editors, mostly men, who ran small, one- or two-person operations that chronicled life in small-town America. They were all boosters, booming the virtues of their own towns, trying to attract business and industry, while waging ideological warfare on the local Democratic paper. They were a mobile group: struggling to stay in business, they moved from town to town in search of better prospects. Those who became socialists were certain that the Socialist party promised a solution that was consonant with the basic tenets of the American political tradition.

Culturally and ideologically they remained Americans rooted in the fundamental concepts of business and the booster spirit. They measured a person's worth by financial success. Suspicious of theory, hardened to politics through nitty-gritty local struggles in the press, country editors stood geographically and intellectually at the middle of American society, and many would become the editors and proprietors of radical papers. In the 1880s and early 1890s, they would turn local weeklies into populist papers. Deadlines, a shortage of labor, and the dearth of capital would force them to continue to use "patent insides," preprinted inside pages of a four-page sheet that had already been prepared with news and advertisements for patent medicines, while on the outside pages they presented local news with a populist punch.

These editors became the practical men and women of American socialism. They and—from the overwhelming evidence—most other

Americans had little use for refined theoretical political arguments of any kind. Rather, they wanted their politics to work for them as Republican or, for some, Democratic politics had done earlier. They also wanted their papers to succeed financially, seeing in such success an endorsement of the efficacy of their work as educators for socialism. The more subscribers, the more machinery, the more staff—and for some—the more advertising they could get, the more successful they were, and the more successful the movement appeared to be.

Modern periodical publishing came of age between 1880 and 1920. These years saw the first mass-circulation newspapers and magazines, wire services, and distribution companies. Many things made this development possible: advancing technologies, spreading industrialization, the growth and concentration of population in urban areas, and rising literacy rates. At the same time, populism and socialism—the most widespread and popular radical movements of the end of the nineteenth century in the United States—came of age and drew their strength from the very factors that allowed the development of modern publishing. The task of spreading information about these movements, in an attempt to convert the public from traditional political solutions to new and radical ones, fell to populist and socialist newspapers and magazines. To be successful, these publications followed the pattern of development pioneered by their more traditional publishing colleagues.

These editors did not live in isolation. They could not escape the transformation of the 1890s. Advertising changed as America's culture became a mass one. The creation of demand had been associated in the previous century only with the patent-medicine industry; by the turn of the twentieth century, advertising was helping to create national markets for all manner of products. With advertising came changes in the economics of newspaper publishing. Previous advertising practice usually involved a small notice in the paper that a local business had received a new shipment of a familiar product and announced its price and availability. The income from this kind of notice helped newspapers, but most of their money came from subscribers. By the turn of the century, the ratio had changed dramatically; advertising now led all other sources of income.

Advertising was the kind of cultural phenomenon that forced socialist editors and publishers to take sides. One could hardly ignore an ad that promised the good life and was placed next to a story about wage slavery. Advertising, perhaps most starkly, pointed up the multiple contradictions inherent in striving for a democratic, peaceful socialist transformation in a mass consumer culture. Advertising's siren call showed a way out of daily problems, and its revenue was needed to float all manner of socialist publications; those who didn't take it cut themselves off from money needed to expand, and to attract more subscribers. If socialist publications did take it, they took with it a whole style of commercial speech that directly undercut the message of the movement they embraced.

Mass culture was unthinkable without mass communications. With national product advertising to support them and freed from the technological limitations of the hand press, handmade rag paper, and hand-set type, newspapers and magazines sought greater audiences. They burst forth with editions in the hundreds of thousands of copies from web presses, using rolls of pulp paper and printing from plates that were swiftly set on Linotype machines. Country editors grew up as this was happening, and some adapted to this new reality. They became the advance men and women for the socialist future, bringing word of the movement to the marketplace of a mass consumer culture. Here, in the mass-media marketplace, wage workers, the middle class, and farmers would weigh the merits of socialism against the competing claims of religious papers, trade-union papers, and the papers of William Randolph Hearst and Joseph Pulitzer. American socialism, as recent scholarship has shown, was intensely American and public, and the people who brought its news to the public were shaped by American values and competed for success in a new American culture. What they brought to the struggle and how market forces shaped the struggle constitute the subject of this book.

The heart of the largest publishing enterprise of American socialism was its founder and guiding spirit, J. A. Wayland. Wayland founded a number of midwestern county-wide weeklies and radical newspapers between the 1870s and the first decade of the twentieth century; his associate Fred Warren oversaw Wayland's flourishing business between 1904 and 1914. Almost alone among radical publishers, Wayland faced squarely the apparent contradiction of attacking society through its own conventional institution, the newspaper. Although he often chafed at the need to do business in a capitalist world while agitating to overthrow it—on two occasions he tried to create his own radical economy separate from established society—he still made the necessary compromises to stay in business. Warren, a generation younger than Wayland, grew up with mass-market magazines and saw more clearly than did Wayland the irrationality of using capitalism to finance the fight against it. Yet he also made the choices necessary to keep in public circulation the papers that he controlled. Those choices meant accepting advertising from large corporations, producers of patent medicines, and promoters of get-rich-quick schemes; fighting unionization at the printing plant; and indulging in sensational journalism and in heavy-handed subscription schemes. The *Appeal to Reason*, the flagship paper of the Wayland/Warren empire, which was based at Girard, Kansas, was the most successful institution of the socialist movement in the United States and the one national weekly newspaper that unified the movement from coast to coast. As such, the contradictions manifested by socialist goals and capitalist realities were magnified at the *Appeal*. At the *Appeal* we can glimpse the intersection of Socialist agitation and American mass culture.

How the paper operated in its daily routines and how practical business problems affected positions that the paper took in regard to various issues are crucial questions in light of the contradictions that an idealistic paper or party must face when involved in practical politics. The effects of competition among weekly socialist newspapers and the *Appeal's* place in the general publishing world bear on the question of how the *Appeal* tried to promote socialism by using popular techniques. The news stories that the *Appeal* chose to report after the turn of the century, its proclamations of honesty and forthrightness, and the effect of financial success on the organization are all elements of the story.

There is an impressive scholarly literature on labor history and the history of American socialism. The parties and their leaders have been treated, as have the role of women, blacks, and immigrant groups; regional variations in socialism; and the relationship between socialism and trade unions. But the studies, even those using social history techniques, rarely turn those techniques on the institutions that socialist men and women created. We have learned from the past generation of scholars about the composition of the working class, its ethnicity, and the experience of women, in the contexts of work-place and family experiences. It is a basic tenet of social history that the economy, the society, and the culture help to construct class and individual responses to change. In a period of developing mass culture, the question of communications, specifically of the press, should also be addressed. By looking at the key newspapers of the socialist movement and at the men and women who created them and made their living from them, and by asking questions about advertising, labor organizing, family background, gender relations, institutional structures, and business practices, this book seeks to understand better the nature of the appeal that socialism made to a mass audience.

Nick Salvatore has shown that the principal strain of American socialism, as typified and exemplified by the life of Eugene Debs, comes directly from the mainstream of American culture.[1] Salvatore locates Debs as a citizen of small-town midwestern America who naturally embraces an American socialism that harks back to the deepest chords of the American spirit of reform and renewal. The present work seeks to push the argument further. With the work of Salvatore and such others as James R. Green and Mari Jo Buhle as a starting point, we can ask what further elements of the republican ideology bear on the American socialist movement.[2] For example, if American socialism can be seen as a logical extension of the battle for preserving individual freedom by controlling the rapacity of corporations, then what about the almost universal but contending belief in "doing business"? As James Oliver Robertson puts it, "Almost all of the post Civil War reformers were in favor of traditional American business, of the freedom of the entrepreneur, of the independence Americans had long thought could be found in the marketplace by business activity," even while they were afraid of big business. "Almost all of them felt there were great advantages to machinery, industry, railroads, and the 'efficiency' or the 'progress' that seemed to come with big business," even while they felt that the power and wealth were poorly distributed.[3] Debs's early career working at the local dry goods company in Terre Haute, Indiana, may have helped to push him towards socialism, but it also indicated a healthy respect for the American tradition of success through entrepreneurship. J. A. Wayland, editor of the *Appeal to Reason*, the largest and most influential of all socialist publications, repeatedly reminded his readers that the *Appeal* was first and foremost a business enterprise.

American cultural distinctiveness was manifest in the people who worked in socialist publishing. Wayland and his successor, Warren, were the two most prominent journalists associated with the paper, but a number of other even lesser-known men and women also shaped its role in American publishing history. Most of them shared a common background with Wayland and Warren: they had been born in the Midwest between 1855 and 1875, had been Republicans before turning to populism and socialism, had edited country weeklies, and had suffered in the depression of 1893. Above all, these men and women shared a belief in the efficacy of political action, even as they came to view the old parties as morally bankrupt. They believed that the American political system was flexible and could prosper through radical change, and they expected to win.

The most formative influence in their lives took place during the 1880s and 1890s, when the "culture of political revolt," which had grown up through the Midwest, the South, and the Southwest, flourished. People throughout these parts of the country organized lecture exchanges, cooperatives, and self-help groups to bring about fundamental economic change, all of which culminated in the People's party. It was a time of "democratic promise," in the words of Populist historian Lawrence Goodwyn, when people perceived a chance to take control of their economic and political lives.[4] The men and women who worked at the *Appeal* shared this vision of radical change and tried to realize it through a socialist program. Their lives form a subtheme of this study.

This book follows the life of J. A. Wayland and the development of his newspaper and real-estate businesses while it also examines his political and philosophical development. It begins with a discussion of his early career, moves to an analysis of his thought, follows him and his first successful radical newspaper, the *Coming Nation*, into the Ruskin, Tennessee, commune that he founded. At Ruskin, Wayland encountered the first of a series of contradictions that help us to understand the complexities of pursuing radical reform in America; there, it was the clash between sound business practice and cooperative decision making. Forced out of the cooperative village, he founded the *Appeal to Reason* and faced the choice between a disciplined socialist party and an all-embracing one. Chapter 5 marks a divide in the study, by looking generally at the radical press in the context of American publishing and by exploring the impact of advertising on the various choices for the management and operation of these enterprises. A strike of the workers at the *Appeal* provides the background against which the various forces that went into the creation of the movement and its press are examined. Here the questions of socialism and unions and of women and capitalism are explored. The last three chapters examine how the issues that were only partially resolved by the strike were worked out, in the stories that the paper published, in the community that the paper helped to create in Girard, Kansas, and in the fate of the paper, the movement, and the individual editors and publishers.

In 1913, after the Socialist party had reached the peak of its electoral success, the official historian of the *Appeal to Reason*, in hyperbole that was typical of the style of the newspaper, wrote: "The history of this wondrous paper *is* the history of American socialism."[5] While this statement is in some sense an exaggeration, in others it is not at all. In the general context of the publishing world and the socialist movement, the present study gives central place to the *Appeal* as a vehicle by which the various aspects of American socialism can be examined in a fresh manner, seeking to observe, through the institution of the newspaper and the people who worked in it, the intersection of American culture and American radicalism.

1

J. A. Wayland

To be brief, he "landed" me good and hard. I saw a new light and found what I never knew existed. I saw what the increasing dullness meant and went into the financial study so thoroughly that the result was, I closed up my real estate business and devoted my whole energies to the work of trying to get my neighbors to see the truths I had learned.

— *J. A. Wayland*, Leaves of Life

On November 10, 1912, three days after the Socialist party's greatest electoral showing, Julius Augustus Wayland walked up the stairs into the bedroom of his handsome and large home and put a bullet through his head. Only fifty-eight years old, publisher of the most influential radical paper in America, wealthy and respected in his community, he was mourned by many of the half-million readers of his paper. For weeks, letters poured into the office of the *Appeal to Reason* in Girard, Kansas, from every part of the continent. Men, women and children spoke of the trust they had placed in him and of the profound impact he had had on their lives. The letters came from dirt farmers, small manufacturers, housewives, lumberjacks, and teenagers. Their disbelief and anguish spoke of the hopes that a part of America had for a more just society. For them, Wayland represented the man who fearlessly spoke the truth and fought for their interests. "We have lost the great pioneer of our cause. To him we owe more than any one person in the movement."[1]

Wayland is one of the "lost men of American history." Although he was of central importance to a large group of disaffected and radical Americans between Reconstruction and the First World War, he has been passed over in the popular history of the United States. He assumed center stage both in the history of radicalism and in the history of publishing; he was also one of those few Americans who rose from poverty to prosperity in the Horatio Alger tradition. To his friends he was larger than life; to his enemies—even those who attempted to ridicule or belittle him—he was still a force to be reckoned with. His experiences, dreams, thoughts, and hopes characterized those of many contemporary reformers. His life reflected the prospects for radical change in America.[2]

The few Americans today who have heard of Julius Augustus Wayland associate him with the *Appeal to Reason* and Girard, Kansas. To those who remember the times before the First World War or who have heard or read about early radicalism, the "Lil Ole Appeal," as the paper was affectionately known, brings to mind the struggle to establish the Socialist party, or Eugene Debs's editorials or perhaps just midwestern American radicalism. But few remain who truly remember the paper, the people, or even the place whence it came. The Temple of the Revolution, which was built to house the paper, has burned down; the presses that churned it out disappeared long ago; and almost all of the people who subscribed or worked for the paper in its heyday are now gone. Except for personal memories and archives cherished by the local heirs of southeastern Kansas radicalism, Girard appears forgetful of this element of its past history as a publishing center.

The *Appeal* was published by and for people who objected to the course being charted by American society. It was an angry paper, a partisan paper that spoke for the cares and hopes and for the frustrations and dreams of people who were united in their desire to change what they saw into a curious mixture of what could be and what they believed once was. There are no monuments, no postage stamps or coins, and no historic plaques to proclaim the nobility of the attempt. What Wayland and the others did is viewed as essentially unimportant because these disaffected, unsatisfied, and questioning people were not successful. American heroes who pass muster have many of the characteristics of the people of the *Appeal*, most notably Wayland, but the *Appeal* worked for what was then a somewhat unpopular cause and is now even considered downright un-American.

Yet the socialism that the *Appeal* practiced and preached was part of the American experience, as deeply rooted as were the radical revolutionary principles of '76, the ideal of Jeffersonian democracy, or the abolitionist movement. The United States has had problems with its radical heroes in recent times; they have either been sanitized, when their accomplishments were too important to ignore, or ignored, when they proved unsuccessful or premature. Thomas Paine has been sanitized; he is remembered as the author of *Common Sense*, but his work on the radical Pennsylvania constitution has been almost completely forgotten, as has his later contribution to the French Revolution. And Jack London, whose socialism was an essential ingredient in his work, is celebrated mainly as a writer of adventure stories. His radicalism has been washed away by a marina shopping complex that bears his name in his hometown of Oakland, California, and by a museum exhibit near his last home, which presents his life without mentioning his socialist politics.

Wayland and the *Appeal* have been largely ignored, dropped from the popular consciousness of American history. But Wayland's life, his publishing career, his successful real-estate and later manufacturing operations, his beliefs in freedom, and his fears of concentrated power in the hands of monopolistic industry and its governmental allies—all place him and his readers squarely within the American tradition. What Wayland did—and did better than most others—was to help to knit together the disenchanted against forces that were fundamentally altering American institutions. He was a conservative radical: he wanted to harness industrial power in American society for the good of the many, but in a mixture of old and new elements that constitute the unique blend of indigenous American radicalism.

Wayland's family, of whom he liked to boast, was of American Revolutionary stock and Virginia ancestry. In the late 1840s the family moved to Versailles (pronounced Ver-sāles), Indiana. The youngest of seven children (four boys and three girls), he was born on April 26, 1854, four months before a cholera epidemic killed his father, a sister, and a brother. The family was unable to keep the grocery store that his father left, but did manage to hold onto the small house in which Wayland grew up. His mother, who never remarried, was the sole support of the family; she took in sewing and washing for a living. Brookey, as young Wayland called himself in his "Dairy" (diary), stayed in Versailles, the seat of Ripley County in southeastern Indiana, close to the Kentucky and Ohio borders, until he was seventeen. His one surviving brother enlisted in the Union Army, and that departure left the family impoverished during the Civil War. They appear to have existed just above the subsistence level. James Tyson, a schoolmate and lifelong friend, who was also a partner in Wayland's later printing operations, remembered that Wayland was a typical boy whose principal interests were marbles, checkers, swimming, and collecting nuts. He was particularly fond of picking blackberries. While still young, he had to take small jobs, which brought his school career to an early end. He spent less than two full years in school; then he worked at bailing shingles and helped out in a printing office. Tyson particularly recalled that young Wayland was sneered at by Versailles people who had more money. He remembered Wayland promising: "Jim, I'm going to make enough money to buy a whole pack of them!" Frustrated in his attempt to find work as a carpenter, Wayland tried printing as an outlet for his ambition.[3]

Two weeks before his sixteenth birthday, Brookey was apprenticed to the printing trade, starting as a printer's devil, or "rolling boy," on the *Versailles Gazette*, a local weekly, at $2 a week. For six months he worked as an apprentice, using all sorts of stratagems to get the regular printer, M. H. Thompson, out of the office, so he could practice setting type

Wayland's first office, at the Versailles Gazette *where he apprenticed for six months, was located on the ground floor of the Masonic Hall. Courtesy of Virginia Lashley.*

and designing pages. Wayland began to print the paper himself when the regular printer decided to take a vacation. After a month or so as a fill-in printer, he demanded the combined wages of the former devil and the printer. He was turned down, so he left the job to someone who would work for less. His first independent job, which came in the fall of 1871, lasted for only two weeks, when he left because of a wage dispute. Then he worked a short stint at Lawrenceburg, seat of the adjoining Dearborn County, on the Ohio River. Soon Wayland took off again, taking his first steamboat ride on the Ohio River as a cabin boy on the *Ben Franklin* to Louisville, Kentucky, and looking for better-paying printing jobs. When he found none, he worked several runs on the *Robert Burns* from Cincinnati to Memphis in the spring of 1872, seeing the sites of Civil War battles and being taken by the beauties of the Mississippi River, except for one eyesore, Cairo, Illinois: "This is one of the most filthy cities of its population in the country. Its streets are unpaved, and miserably muddy all the year." At the end of one run, he looked for work in Memphis; though he was not successful, he "noticed that Southern people are more friendly than Northern people."[4]

In his limited journeys from home, Wayland never ventured far from the Ohio River or the mid Mississippi. His experience was similar to that of a growing number of artisans in many fields, but specifically of tramp printers. Never without a job for too long, these semiskilled practitioners hustled from town to town, working for a time to replace the previous printer or filling in at a job shop that had a temporary rush of work. By 1885, a little more than ten years after Wayland's stint, 40 percent of the members of the International Typographical Union were on the move from town to town. It is probable that during his trips Wayland met a number of the printers and editors who were to work with him in the future.[5] Apparently Wayland was not a member of the union, and he was to tangle with it on several future occasions.

Young Wayland finally did land some more printing jobs, but he still looked for other work. In the summer of 1872, while working on a local paper in Versailles, he prepared to teach school the next winter, even though his own formal schooling was so slight. This eighteen year old, between steamboat and printing jobs, did a lot of odd jobs, yet he had leisure time as he moved back and forth from one house to another, enjoying the company of his male and female friends. From Wayland's diary, one gets the sense that the printer's trade then consisted of half-days and long days of intense work, alternating with enforced idleness because of lack of copy or, more frequently, no paper on which to print. In his early shops, there seemed to be only enough type to set two pages of the typical four-page paper at a time—usually the two outside pages first. Job printing—that is, announcements, invitations, handbills—seems to have been at least as important as printing the newspaper itself.

When there was no work at the shop, Wayland took off, picking berries, going to socials, or attending meetings of the one formal organization of which he was a member and later an officer, the IOGT, the International Order of the Good Templars, a Christian temperance group. He seems to have been conventionally interested in religion; he attended the odd service, prayer meeting, or Sunday School. His diary shows no evidence of introspection, and his reading was minimal: American history texts and newspapers that printing shops got in free exchanges. His home life was also conventional—once when his mother was sick, he tried to cook for himself, with indifferent success, and was relieved when she took over the chores once again.[6] The young printer was conscious of differences in status, as his friend Jim had remarked. Joining in the local celebration of Grant's reelection in November, 1872, Wayland was not amused when the "one-horse men" started to make speeches. "A noticeable instance of how aristocracy will cling to each other was illustrated this evening. One of the 'bon-bons' of this place went and got some matches for a 'fast one' of her class, who was so drunk that he could not get them himself."[7]

After a few years of knocking about, Wayland acquired enough experience and managed to scrape together enough money to buy out the owner of the *Versailles Index*, in partnership with his printer friend M. H.

Thompson. The two had managed to put together enough money to promise to pay $685 to buy the paper. By working there since the previous August at $33.33 per month and then, in January, 1873, advancing to $10 a week, they had come up with the rest of the security for their note from the newly elected Republican officials in town. Wayland and Thompson's first issue of the paper, which they renamed the *Ripley Index*, came off the press on February 6, 1873. It was the first of many that Wayland would control in his forty-year publishing career. Wayland was very proud of the first work he wrote for their own issue of the paper; he was scrupulous about accounting for his money; and he was determined to succeed.[8]

Wayland, at nineteen, began his first reform program shortly after starting the *Ripley Index*. The paper's predecessor had been virtually ignored by its habitual readers; advertisements had gone unchanged for ten years; and though steady readers no longer paid for renewals, the editors continued to distribute the paper. Wayland and Thompson did it over completely. They formed one paramount rule, one that would remain with Wayland from Republican through Populist through Socialist days: No papers on credit. He trimmed down the list of people who received the paper to include only those who had actually paid for it, and he forced those who had been cut off to pay one year in advance before renewing deliveries. Although the going was difficult for the pair of new owners, they managed to make it through the first year (the Panic of 1873 began two months after they took over) by printing notices of sheriffs' sales. The two rejoiced whenever they were given such a notice to print, for they received a high fee for their work.

Copies of Wayland's first newspaper have not been located, but one issue of another paper of his from the same period has survived. The *Bugle*, from Osgood, Indiana, a small village a few miles up the road from Versailles, shows Wayland and Thompson to have been boosters, happily noting that the railroads were booming—a dubious report in a year of panic—although they did caution that the railroad owners were becoming a powerful influence. This small weekly used black dialect humor and, in one of its columns, a standard stylistic device common to country papers: reporting local news fact by fact in sentences each of which is a word or two longer than the one before, thus giving a pleasing look to that page of the paper.[9]

Neither the *Index* nor the *Bugle* was enough to sustain them both, however, and Thompson left in mid 1874, selling his share to Wayland for a silver watch and $25. Wayland struggled to keep the Versailles paper afloat; in the course of his attempt, he discovered two further important business rules: buy cheap, sell dear; and diversify. The opportunity came through selling one of the new sewing machines that came on the market with the lapsing of Singer's patents. The White Sewing Machine Company offered to sell him machines that normally retailed for $65.00 either at $16.50 per machine or at $16.25 per machine if he would give the company a free advertisement. When Wayland learned that he could make more money selling the machines than advertising them, he set himself up as a sewing machine salesman. Advertising for himself in his paper, he sold them to local people for half of the going price, thus making almost 100 percent profit on each sale. By 1877, he had made enough money to pay off his debts and still save over one thousand dollars. He earned the respect of one of his contemporary country editors, who thought that Wayland must have been a born financier because it was a miracle to make money from a country paper.[10]

If the picture of Wayland as a determined young businessman with conventional views is correct, he could probably only think of marriage after he had become somewhat independent financially. He started to refer to a particular young woman in his diary only shortly before the two of them decided to marry. Wayland was twenty-three years old in 1877, when he and a local girl from Osgood, Etta Bevan, decided to elope. From October fifteenth to November seventh, Wayland and his bride took a whirlwind three-week wedding trip, which started off badly when the groom failed to get the marriage license on October fifteenth, the "day set for being matrimonied." He dashed around the county and "took an hour and fifty pounds of knuckles and patience" to awaken the deputy clerk at Versailles; he finally got a license a day later. After mislaying the license, the couple were "linked together" in Lawrenceburg and set off on their honeymoon.

The young couple "put up at [the] Louisville House [at] $4 each day. Had a magnificent bridal chamber and set off in the morning for Mammoth Cave." They "took lunch and started to [the] cave—9 miles—[from Cave City] over the worst road and in the worst old stage that ever decked American highways. . . . After supper, poorly cooked and well charged for we . . . shortened our clothes and started for the grandeur of this subterranean wonder, following an elderly coloured guide. Words nor letters can do justice to the awful grandeur of the cave. After about four hours travel we emerged again in the outer world over which long had hung the sable mantles of darkness. Wearied with the exercise, sleep soon soothed the weary limbs."[11]

The two then took off for Cincinnati, stopped back in Osgood for their things, and started out west, following Horace Greeley's advice, to "grow up with the country."[12] The first stop for the newly married couple was Harrisonville, Missouri. About thirty miles south of Kansas City and lying within twenty miles of the Kansas border, this was, like Versailles, a county seat. The Waylands chose Harrisonville because Etta had relatives there. J.A. went first, and upon arriving, he "loafed about town trying to buy part" of a printing office, and after a week, he "purchased a half interest in the *'Courier'* of James E. Paine for $700 and paid $500 by check on [a] bank and $200 by [a] note due in 60 days." Wayland "fixed up for housekeeping . . . at $6.00 per month." Within a month, he and his new partner purchased the building in which the office was located "for $1000 paying $500 cash and $500 note due in 12 mos at 10% interest and secured by a deed of trust on the said building." A couple of days later, Wayland "sent money for fare [from Indiana to Harrisonville] for Charley," Etta's brother.[13]

Obviously, Wayland controlled more money after his wedding than he seems to have made from printing, and it seems clear that some of it came from his wife's family. One indication is the almost constant presence throughout his life of his two brothers-in-law, Charley and Harry Bevan, in the Wayland household. Both Bevans seem to have helped out at the printing offices and Harry would become a partner and later purchase his own papers; Harry helped to bring to a head the contradictions that would surface when Wayland became a socialist publisher who retained the sharp business practices learned during this period of his life. Wayland's boyhood friend J. H. Tyson, who was a rival for the hand of Etta Bevan and later became a favorite of Wayland's children, also lived with the family for a time when it moved further west. He also joined in several of Wayland's ventures.[14]

By the age of twenty-three, Wayland had grown into a self-assured man, ready to seek his fortune and already the head of a somewhat extended family. Along with the capital that he had saved from his first printing successes and with the boost from his new family, he must also have gained some maturity during his tramping days. He stepped into an interesting situation at Harrisonville. Wayland was a confirmed Republican, but his *Cass County Courier* was the leading local Democratic organ in a largely Democratic town in the largely Democratic state of Missouri. Though probably he had made some prior arrangements to purchase the paper, the local Democrats opposed this Indiana Yankee. It made for an eventful ten months, especially since he also became the postmaster of the town, a political appointment from the new Republican administration.

Wayland used methods that had worked in Versailles and Osgood. "Depending solely on the people for support, we intend that every subscriber shall feel he is getting more than his money's worth in taking the Courier," so the editor forced his readers to pay for the paper a year in advance. By the third issue of his tenure as co-owner, Wayland was offering $125 in premiums for new subscribers, on the order of what the *Kansas City Times* was doing, or so he claimed. Within six weeks, he decided that a good selling device would be to publish all of his subscribers' names, as an inducement, one supposes, to those who also wanted their names in the paper.[15] "To please all, however, is an undertaking we never have and never intend to assume. . . . Our paper will be partisan . . . steady, unremitting service to the principles of the Democratic party."[16]

It was an exciting life that Wayland chose in the late 1870s and early 1880s. The attraction of the West was strong; sparsely populated areas seemed to beckon with new opportunities for making a name and a fortune. The Midwest and the West were dotted with small towns where competing weeklies were published. The warfare between these Republican and Democratic sheets was furious. Proprietors of the papers were ready to trade partisan insults whenever they could. Partisanship was the distinguishing feature of the press in general throughout this era, to which the claims of objectivity that characterized the mass media by the middle of the next century would have appeared baffling. Technological advances also brought with them lower prices for materials and less labor to publish papers. New presses were on the way that could completely outmode the entire plant of a country shop.[17]

The late 1870s and the early 1880s were times of rapid expansion in the Missouri county press. From thirty to sixty new publications appeared each year, although many of them failed. At the end of the Civil War, there was a real lack of local newspapers: between 1869 and 1881, the number of localities with at least one newspaper jumped from 104 to 201. The state was gaining rapidly in population, despite the temporary slowdown caused by the Panic of 1873. These papers, ironically, became more local in emphasis at a time when technology was making it possible to gather national news rapidly, for there were only a few big-city papers that could afford to take advantage of the telegraph and the railroad or to place reporters in other localities. The county papers, except for the very largest, could not afford even the cost of correspondents. So local news, especially politics, was the subject of papers such as Wayland's.[18]

The Republican-turned-Democrat revealed his foremost concern, not with such issues of the day as problems attendant on the ending of Reconstruction or with the problems of blacks, but with the national debt arising from the Civil War. Debt in general seemed to haunt Wayland; it was a question he took quite personally; it was evident in his ledgers, his diaries, and the records of his real-estate transactions; and it remained the central isuse, whether he was publishing a Democratic, Republican, real-estate, Populist, or Socialist newspaper. A second, but related, theme, immediate to most issues of the *Cass County Courier*, was the concern to boost the local economy, as he had done in Osgood. "The local newspaper is of superior interest to all classes" when it does such things as advocate the building of roads to Kansas City to help farmers avoid the necessity of using the railroad to ship goods and thus save money.[19] A quarter of a century later, in another county seat, but with a socialist newspaper, Wayland would advocate local initiative and local ownership of an interurban line to compete with the monopoly-owned railroads. A third aspect of the mature Wayland that is evident in these early publications is his skill as a paragrapher, the dominant style of that period in county newspapers: the ability to present his arguments in concise units across the front page.

Although these characteristics run through his journalistic career, Wayland was uneasy about conducting a Democratic paper, which he was doing probably because it was the only paper available for purchase when he came to Harrisonville. Eventually, he was commissioned by the Republican leaders of Cass County to set up a Republican paper instead, which they agreed to finance. He began publication of the *Cass County News* in 1878 and again succeeded. More outspoken than before, he "made it hot" for the local Democratic politicians. Wayland was the sole proprietor of this paper. Although he published the *News* out of the same office that he jointly owned with his erstwhile partner on the *Courier*, Wayland's paper was not as handsomely produced. Partisanship, not typography, was important to him. In the second issue he reassured his Republican backers: "Republicans need not fear the *News* being consolidated with the *Courier*. We couldn't be a democrat if we desired, and after a trial of ten months and utter failure, we vow we shall never have such a desire. If we are not able to make a success of a republican paper here, we shall migrate to a place where we can."[20]

Wayland's work on behalf of the Republican party of Missouri was rewarded by political recognition from the administration in Washington. After intensely lobbying for the job, he had been appointed local postmaster by President Hayes in 1877. In perhaps the most corrupt election in U.S. history, "Rutherfraud" had achieved the presidency through the force of soldiers who were still stationed in the reconstructed South.[21] It was a fitting climax to the centennial year, which saw a disgraced President Grant leave office after the celebration of material progress in the grand centennial show in Philadelphia. The politics of the period had hardened into the regional rivalry between North and South that would characterize the two parties into the twentieth century. The Republican party, by 1876, had turned its back on blacks and was concentrating its campaigns, as it was to do until 1890, on running against the South by waving the bloody shirt. There were few issues in these elections, as complacency settled into the two parties; but small stirrings of change were taking place. In Indianapolis, not far from Wayland's hometown, the Greenbackers were holding their first convention.

"The convention of greenbackers on last Saturday had the opportunity to do good things for the country," according to the revived Republican editor, but it had failed because the Greenbackers hadn't driven the crooks out of the new party. More importantly, Greenbackers were very rigid ideologically, refusing to cooperate with any but those who identified themselves "absolutely" as Greenbackers. Wayland would have preferred a situation in which the new party officials would have approached Republicans to come to the convention and would have run unified slates in those areas where there was a chance to beat the Democrats. Wayland, however, recognized the legitimate fear that Republicans in Democratic strongholds might have of being swallowed by the Greenbackers:

> The people may for a time be led away by false theories of government and become intoxicated with newfangled ideas, but they must at last return to a proper understanding of the necessities of the community and the duties and privileges of citizens. Those of us who believe that the republican party is the proper exponent of these rights and privileges can not afford to abandon our organization and professions to be swallowed up by a party antagonistic to us in principles merely for the sake of beating an old enemy.[22]

At the age of twenty-four, Wayland had two principles—opposition to rigid ideologies and the fear of losing one's principles for temporary political gain—that already, like the fear of debt and the booster mentality, were guideposts in his thinking. Meanwhile, his understanding of the political ferment around him was limited to the possible political capital that the Republican party could make out of it or to the purely practical consequences for his business. During the Panic of 1873, which brought riots and dislocation, Wayland had celebrated when he had received bankruptcy notices to publish. Antimonopoly thinking and the rise of the Granger movement and of the Knights of Labor did not dislodge Wayland from his solidly mainstream, Republican orientation. It took more than a decade after the antimonopoly parties got going for Wayland to be moved.

The *Cass County News* "made it hot" for local Democrats, while it succeeded on Wayland's business principles. Unable to rely on the "extortionate advertising patronage of the Court House ring" for the public notices, such as bankruptcies, which had benefited him in Versailles, he depended upon the support of "honest taxpayers"—that is, Republican voters. It took a year to get five hundred subscribers, and he was close to his goal of a thousand in less than two years. His issues were largely the same except that now he was attacking the Democrats: "The democratic party of today has no principles that it respects, no traditions that it reveres," he quoted approvingly from the leading Republican paper in Missouri. Wayland's mudslinging at the Democratic party's mismanagement of local government, however, caused him embarrassment when his former partner charged that Wayland had purchased his postmastership for $200 from a Kansas City attorney who had connections to the Hayes administration.[23]

Wayland associated economic stagnation with the Democrats, and he needled Missourians about the sluggishness of their state's economy in comparison with that of neighboring states, asserting that under the Republicans, northern capitalists had poured money into Missouri, prices were high, land was high, and taxes, though relatively high, were inconsequential. Kansas, Colorado, and Nebraska were doing much better under Republicans than Missouri was now doing under the Democrats. In what must really have disturbed local Democrats, Wayland recommended for Missouri the *New York Herald*'s plan for Kansas—namely, encouraging black migration into thinly settled parts of the state. "And by the way, there are several colored towns in Kansas which are thriving wonderfully, and speaks well for what the colored man can do when he has a chance."[24]

Wayland stayed in Harrisonville for about three years, but the Bourbon Democrats rebuffed the young Yankee from southeastern Indiana, who had first tried to join them and then to beat them. He resigned his postmastership and sold his paper, though he retained some income-producing property; and he and his wife returned to Versailles shortly after the birth of their first child, Jon Garfield, who was named for the Republican president-elect in 1880. The reasons for leaving Harrisonville could probably be found both in the increasing hostility of the community and in his improving financial position. According to accounts that were made public only after his death, Wayland was at least twice subjected to death threats arising from his position as an outspoken Republican country editor in a border state. Emerging as the hero of both recorded episodes, he stood down a mob that had "roped him round the neck and talked lynching" and, during a second encounter, either spat in the eye of a sheriff and another mob or, unarmed, "merely reaching for his hip pocket," bluffed his way out.[25]

Wayland's return home, however, was not what he expected. He had big plans to surprise the Hoosiers by introducing the newest cylinder and job presses into the town. He repurchased his old office by buying out the stock of the company that was publishing the local paper, and

Wayland and his first wife, Etta Bevan Wayland, in December, 1883. Courtesy of Virginia Lashley.

in March and April, 1882, he also tried to publish the *Illustrated Comic Hoosier*, a dialect and country-humor paper that was printed on pink stock and laced with ads for job printing and giveaways to subscribers. But nothing could revive his enthusiasm for Versailles. This time, after again "clearing up several thousand dollars," he set out for the West, arriving in Pueblo, Colorado, in the spring of 1882, a committed Republican with more than $5,000 in capital. He would leave Pueblo after ten years, to return to a town just a few miles from his birthplace, a committed socialist with $80,000 in gold and government securities.

In Colorado, Wayland's Republican politics and business sense met modern industry and radical economic theory. In Pueblo, Wayland developed the curious amalgamation that is the essence of American socialism. Continuing to grow up with the country, he again chose a county seat and once again started up a weekly newspaper with old friends from Indiana. But Pueblo was no rural county seat. It was becoming a modern manufacturing and distribution center, the "Pittsburg of the West." Between 1880 and 1893, Pueblo's population increased 1,000 percent, from less than thirty-five hundred to more than thirty-five thousand people. According to the 1890 census, it was the most rapidly growing city in the United States, a good choice for a family that wanted to grow up with the country.[26]

Pueblo was located at one of the centers of the silver- and gold-mining industry of Colorado, which, after the abortive rush of the fifty-niners to Pike's Peak, was developed with capital supplied from the East. The mines were sunk deep, and it was necessary to use smelters to free the metals from the ore. Prospectors quickly became miners and laborers in smelters, working for the "interests" of the East instead of for themselves. Frontier towns became congested mining slums, more like eastern factory towns than like western outposts.[27] Railroad rivalries, fueled by eastern capital and played out locally by small business interests, pitted one Colorado town against another. In Pueblo, which was established in 1859 as a mining camp, boosters desperately attempted to make their town the sole railhead for the rich mines of Leadville and Cripple Creek, and marked Denver as their main rival.[28] Steel grew in importance. A locally sponsored mill had become, by the early 1890s, a battleground for Edward H. Harriman and John D. Rockefeller.[29]

In spite of the opportunities that Pueblo offered to a man with some capital, Wayland and his friends Lon Hoding and J. H. Tyson did not succeed immediately. Wayland's partners sold out, and so did he after two years, to work as a job printer. He claimed that his local paper had nearly bankrupted him, and he sold some of his Missouri property for funds to tide him over. The new job-printing business prospered quickly, in spite of having a shop with just one small press, only a few fonts of type, and several competitors who were much better equipped. Since Wayland's first success in 1877, he had ceased to work as a printer, but he was forced, in 1883 or so, to "don an apron" again and go to work "with a desperation born of necessity."[30] He called his business the "one-hoss print shop."

Wayland kept this "plebeian appellation," which may have been an asset in drawing business, "although in four years' time the business grew to occupy a brick block of its own full of presses of the best make."[31] The one-hoss printer found other ways to make a living, which soon far surpassed the $100-a-week profits from the shop. While building his plant, and a house with non-union labor,[32] he discovered the profitability of real-estate speculation in booming downtown Pueblo. He made $2,000 on a piece of property on which he intended to build his larger shop and $3,500 on another, for which he had advanced only $100 in cash. With these profits, he soon devoted full time to his speculations, turning the printing business over to others while retaining the controlling interest. He didn't limit his speculations to Pueblo and its environs: he traveled widely, speculating in New Orleans, Fort Worth, and Jackson-

Wayland with Otto Thum in Pueblo in the mid 1880s. Thum was a boyhood friend and fellow printer. Courtesy of Virginia Lashley.

ville.[33] Most of Wayland's activity was centered in Colorado, however; and his speculative successes were not surprising for someone who had sufficient capital in a state (admitted in 1876) whose population had grown from thirty-four thousand in 1860 to more than four hundred thousand in 1890.

Exploitation was the business of the times.[34] The railroads were outlets for British capital, which was funneled through eastern financial houses; and the railroads exploited cheap immigrant labor from both Europe and Asia. More capital was given to them by the federal government in the form of land grants, which were in turn used as inducements to get people to settle in the West and to use the rail lines. Transcontinental freight was not sufficient to turn a profit for a line, especially because many roads were competing for the trade. The amount that could be made out of local rates was normally the difference between success and failure. Miners were slightly better paid in Colorado, but their cost of living was high. Farmers found it difficult to make ends meet on small farms, and they overextended themselves with easy money, which had accumulated in savings built up since the disastrous Panic of 1873. The huge movement of people (especially into Colorado—more than fifty thousand in one year in the mid 1880s) led to crisis: the bubble burst in western Kansas in 1887, in Nebraska in 1891, and in Colorado, as well as in the rest of the country, in 1893.[35]

During the 1880s the penetration of the West by big capital and the resultant reshaping of the lives of hundreds of thousands helped to fuel a resurgence of radicalism. The seesawing of the economy, the restrictive currency, the crop-lien system in the South, the foreclosure of farms, the disappearance of crafts, and the rise of large-scale enterprises—all affected too many lives not to provoke a reaction. In Chicago, anarchists, led by recent German immigrants, were agitating with some success for an eight-hour day. The Knights of Labor and the American Federation of Labor developed and grew rapidly. The former was a mixture of secret society, labor union, and labor movement; while the latter was organized along craft lines. The southern and western farmers started to organize themselves into cooperatives; and the Farmers Alliance gave voice, through its Lecture Exchange, to the growing chorus of resistance to the moneyed few, who, it seemed, manipulated the lives of others at their own convenience.

Wayland was either unconscious of this movement or it left no impression on him. He later recalled about this period that he "was a radical Republican and as ignorant as a new born babe."[36] He had not been aware of the underlying social problems that would lead to the emergence of the People's party from the National Labor Union (1871), the Greenback party (1876–84), and the Union Labor party (1888). Rather, he saw these parties as another form of traditional politics, not as the expression of deep-seated unease with the direction of American life. In the orthodox view of political history, partisan loyalty was so strong among both Democrats and Republicans that angry voters organized third parties rather than cooperate with the opposition.[37] In fact, there was no room for reform in either party, both of which were wedded to class interests that ignored the condition of the uprooted and the indebted. The major parties lost Wayland's allegiance at the end of the 1880s.

Wayland's radicalization was an important milestone in his life, as it was for countless other socialists. Conversion from conventional thinking to a socialist perspective had a powerful spiritual component.[38] Repeatedly, people found the way to socialism, not, as one might expect, through the personal experience of economic exploitation and the sense of powerlessness and outrage that this would cause, but rather through conversation, reading, and argument, at least according to those who were articulate enough to record their experiences.[39] Wayland's move to the left, like that of Eugene V. Debs, served as an important example to the members of the movement because it had an educational value in its retelling. Five slightly different versions of the radical editor's conversion survive: three that Wayland wrote; a fourth, which was published by a friend during Wayland's lifetime; and a fifth, by another colleague just after his death.[40] The conversion took place in two parts: first, Wayland recognized his ignorance; then, he found knowledge.

In a casual conversation in a railway smoking car out of New Orleans, Wayland remarked to a fellow traveler that there must be a lot of duplication in railroad construction. This was presumably in 1889 or 1890. Wayland's companion happened to be an important railroad lawyer, who sneered at Wayland's and the public's ignorance of the basic facts of life for the railroad industry. He pointed out to Wayland, in a highly condescending manner, that the highest expense for the railroads was, not building, but rent. His manner antagonized Wayland, who closed his mind to the lawyer's explanations. But as Wayland retold it, the railroad man "not only called me an ignoramus; he proved his case and made me register a vow to get an education on the subject."[41] The education came in Pueblo.

Wayland's plant was doing some printing for a group of striking railroad workers in 1891. As he was "sauntering down Union avenue . . . one June evening, I approached a small group of men talking the commonplaces of the day, in front of William Bradfield's shoe shop."[42] Wayland brought up his conversation with the lawyer, remarking that he now thought that the government should own the railroads, "having experienced as a shipper the iron heel of extortion"; but he did not win the argument that ensued. After the discussion had ended, Bradfield handed Wayland a pamphlet that explained the situation in economic and political terms.[43] Wayland's education continued through several books and pamphlets, provided by the shoemaker, who had been born in England; none of the material even mentioned the word socialism. At last, Bradfield gave Wayland the *Cooperative Commonwealth*, by Laurence Gronlund, which was clearly a socialist work.[44] Upon seeing the word written on the title page, Wayland is reported to have thought: "Until that moment, the word had been associated in my mind with conspiracies and assassination. I thought of it as something about like a 'Black Hand' society. When I saw the word, I was tempted to throw the book away. Then I thought I might as well find out what it was anyhow and decided to sneak the book into the house and read it 'secretly.' "[45] At another time, Wayland recalled: "To be brief, he [Gronlund] 'landed' me good and hard. I saw a new light and found what I never knew existed. I saw what the increasing dullness meant and went into the financial study so thoroughly that the result was, I closed up my real estate business and devoted my whole energies to the work of trying to get my neighbors to see the truths I had learned."[46]

This is the popular account of the making of Wayland the socialist, who was to guide hundreds of thousands with his publications and hundreds through personal acquaintance along the same trail. Without denying the essential accuracy of this tale, though it was doubtless embellished for purposes of advancing the cause, there were concrete economic reasons which helped to push Wayland down this path in 1890, rather than in 1887, when he had read the newly published utopian novel by Edward Bellamy, *Looking Backward*.[47] It was becoming increasingly evident to Coloradoans that the individual had little control over his life. According to historian Melvyn Dubofsky,[48] the economic and social change that produced American radicalism in the late nineteenth century was nowhere so rapid and so unsettling as in the mining West. It seemed to small businessmen and miners alike that Colorado was little more than a colony. A contemporary newspaper had editorialized: "Colorado in proportion to its population . . . is more largely dominated by corporation influences than any other state."[49] The Republican party in Colorado was to an even greater extent than elsewhere a creature of big business interests, which went virtually unchecked as long as the benefits were spread thickly enough. As the economy started to decline in 1889, especially after the failure of the Baring mine in 1890, creditors began to liquidate their holdings in Colorado and elsewhere. Not only did miners and railroad workers suffer, but so did owners of small businesses who depended on their trade.[50]

Caught in the middle, these business people had to choose between supporting the unreliable mining and railroad interests, which were centered in New York and London and responded to world market conditions, or the working people, to whom they were close personally and on whom they were just as dependent. Wayland found himself squarely in the middle of this dilemma. He was not alone in choosing the side of the workers.[51] His investments made him acutely vulnerable to the slightest change in economic trends. He was too modest an entrepreneur to be able to make policy: his capital was too small, and it was invested in a place that could quickly become a ghost town if the price of silver were to plummet. And from what we already have seen of his writings, he had an intense belief in individual autonomy. It would have been difficult for him to ally (or continue to ally) himself to the "interests," after arriving at a new understanding of their nature, their manipulations behind the scenes, and their making of financial decisions that denied access to knowledge that would allow individuals to make real choices. In spite of the hopes that local Republicans had for him as a mayoral candidate, Wayland denounced them. The one-time real-estate speculator and printer had moved into the ranks of the opposition.[52]

There appeared to be a number of possibilities for the future course of American society in 1890. The triumph of corporate capitalism was not yet complete, and the memory of the Civil War and of Lincoln was still fresh for many—a memory that had its strongest popular appeal as a triumph of good over evil. Colorado was a small enough place for people to know one another and to define a common enemy. Together with the beliefs that education could change people and that simple reforms could lead to justice, the manifestation of populism in Colorado, as elsewhere in the country, brought enthusiastic support. The belief that times could improve and, possibly more important, that things had been better in the past and could be good again made for fervor. What happened in Colorado was different to some degree from the populism of the Farmers Alliance, but it was not just a wave of support for free-silver coinage; it was a deep-seated, highly motivated revolt against capitalism.[53] Though it was not socialism, it was the only anticapitalist political movement in Colorado, and as such it drew the support of socialist radicals.

Gronlund's book, which was published in Boston in 1884, made sense of the economic uncertainty that Wayland was no doubt feeling. It was the first attempt by an American socialist, himself a Danish immigrant, to explain Marxism to the average person.[54] It was not a completely faithful translation of the philosophy; it deviated most sharply on the doctrine of class struggle, the existence of which Gronlund refused to recognize. In spite of the obvious instances of class conflict all around him in the mining camps, Wayland followed suit. Gronlund emphasized the trend toward the concentration of capital, the inevitable reduction of wages, and the hopelessness of such schemes as profit sharing, cooperative factories, and an inflationary currency. He saw the movement towards organized labor as a necessity, but insufficient as a tool to battle the plutocrats. The ideas that the unions did foster, such as the eight-hour day, were doomed to fail; the only salvation for the working class was socialism, which was inevitable because the established order was falling to pieces.

Learning his way from the pamphlets and books that the shoemaker provided and from the conditions that he saw around him, Wayland plunged feverishly into the political work of organizing against the interests of foreign capital and in favor of local control. His method was to use the printing press and the spoken word in the service of a political party. Turning to the local Populists, organized in Colorado in 1891 out of the remnants of the Independent party, with recruits from the Farmers Alliance and various labor and reform groups,[55] he was at first rebuffed as an opportunist. He somehow convinced local party members of the sincerity of his convictions, contributed heavily to the campaign fund, and began to work. His chief contributions were his money and his expertise as an editor. His own establishment was printing the *Colorado Workman*, which was owned privately and was the chief local organ for the party. He took control of the paper as an unpaid editor, renamed it the *Coming Crisis*, and as he recalled: "I made it as hot as I knew how, and increased its circulation from a few hundred non-paying subscribers to 2,700 paid ones in nine months."[56] For the month before the 1892 election he also bought two columns in a local paper, the *Pueblo Evening Star*, at $10 a day. His work in Pueblo included reprinting leaflets and spreading them throughout the town while speaking on street corners and buttonholing business acquaintances to advise them of his change of heart.

Wayland used his column in the *Pueblo Evening Star* to reprint columns from the *Coming Crisis* and to attack the Republican paper, the *Colorado Chieftain*. A few weeks after Wayland's column began to appear, the editor of the *Pueblo Evening Star*, a Democratic paper, announced for the Populist ticket. Wayland's views were sharply stated, with the conviction of a new convert to the cause:

> There is a conspiracy of silence on the part of the leading press of this country, and the money question is studiously avoided. They know they are not to discuss it without causing the people to investigate, and to investigate is to leave exposed the most heinous conspiracy to rob the people of their liberty, by robbing them of their property, that was ever concocted in the brain of man. . . . The people are to be soothed with various reasons as to the hard times, like a dentist distracts the attention of a child until he gets hold of a tooth, but all the time the people are losing their homes, their farms and their businesses, while the drones in the human hive are living in luxury off the toil of the dupes. It is the case here in Pueblo. There are scarcely a dozen business houses in the city that are not slaves to the banks, and could be closed out by them, and the banks assure the people there is plenty of money.
>
> . . . The [Pueblo Republican] club does not dare advise its scholars to read the books we are distributing. Ignorance needs only one side.[57]

Although the *Star* became a populist organ, it stopped short of supporting Wayland all the way. In an editorial, "The Star and Mr. Wayland," the editor noted:

We find it necessary to occasionally take issue with Mr. Wayland in his Coming Crisis articles which appear in the Star. . . .

Hardly any one need be told that every religious and political movement has its enthusiasts who run far ahead of the rank and file of the main body. With Mr. Wayland's theories in many respects we have nothing to do. . . .

The mission of the People's Party, if it really has laid the foundation of a new party, is that of the Free Soil party in '55 and '56.[58]

But J. A. responded the next day by defending radicalism: "Every progress, every improvement has been made by men who were not satisfied with things as they found them."[59]

Wayland became a force in Pueblo politics, helping to arrange a visit of the Populist presidential candidate, James B. Weaver, and the fiery Populist orator Mary Elizabeth Lease to Pueblo in August for a campaign rally. The enthusiastic crowd was disappointed that Wayland was not able to accept the gratitude of the Populist supporters in person.[60] Statewide he mailed off one hundred thousand copies of each of the money-conspiracy pamphlets that were in current vogue: *Ten Men of Money Island* and *Seven Financial Conspiracies*.[61] The results of the 1891 local elections were so heartening that the Democrats sought a fusion ticket with the Populists in 1892. Wayland's advice, perhaps pivotal in the state party, was against fusion. The tide was running in favor of the Populists, and their fortuitous link with the advocates of free-silver coinage provided enough extra votes to give them a surprising gubernatorial victory. The new governor, Aspen journalist Davis H. Waite, a firm believer in the entire Populist program, was in an unenviable position, because the Populists had not carried the state legislature and because many of their voters had not fully understood that the nature of their program was to reform the industrial world, crush monopoly, and fight the privileged. Waite announced: "Is it not the truth that for thirty years the two old parties have been legislating for the creditor class? It is true and turnabout is only fair play. We must have the needs of the masses for our polar star. It is the greatest good for the greatest number that must lead us upward and urge us onward."[62]

Waite's election led to two years of ineffective rule, during which he failed to change the direction and the nature of the economy in Colorado with the feeble power of a state government that was hostile to Populist ideas. Wayland did not wait around to see the fruits of his work. He had already been making plans to leave Colorado even before the Waite campaign began.[63] Wintering in Florida, Wayland became convinced that the panics in other western states, as interpreted through his new understanding of the economy, were signs of an impending depression. He quickly returned to Pueblo and plunged into a fever of panic selling of his real-estate holdings and his printing business, turning the receipts into gold. He had begun to sell out as early as 1889. Property in Harrisonville that he had bought for $1,000 in 1877 and $600 in 1879, he sold in 1889 for $1,500 and $700, respectively. One property in Pueblo almost doubled in value—$1,400 to $2,750 from 1882 to 1892; another tripled, from $3,500 in 1887 to $10,500 in 1889. But on some of the properties he sold last, he just broke even.[64]

Preaching silver and hoarding gold, Wayland recalled with relish the way he gave "the gold standard men . . . a taste of their own medicine." He also tried to get business acquaintances to join him in selling out. They refused, as they were more than a little annoyed by his transformation from a fellow Republican to a leader of the opposition. They offered him bets on the outcome of the election, several at $100, which he happily took and won.[65] The apparent efficacy of the propaganda campaign that Wayland waged on behalf of the Populists, combined with the unreliability of real-estate speculation as a way of making a living, made the thirty-nine year old into a full-time editor again for the next decade.

With his wealth in gold, he returned to Indiana for the third time, in February, 1893, convinced that a national propaganda sheet, filled with his newly acquired knowledge of politics and economics, was just what was needed. His connection with Colorado, his home for a decade, was never completely severed. He retained property there, and he returned there a number of times for summer vacations, kept contact with numerous friends he had made, and managed to convert several of his former business associates to socialism. Wayland explained his return to Indiana as an attempt to place himself in the center of the country's population, near such industrial "centers as Chicago, St. Louis, Cincinnati, Cleveland and other places where I expected to get the circulation. My ideal was then a circulation of 10,000 a week. That sounded very large to me. I knew that I had enough money to run it several years even if it did not pay."[66]

Wayland became a socialist in politics, but it is crucial to keep in mind that his personality had been shaped by the early circumstances of his life and especially his success in business. Throughout his life he remained largely what he already was: a real-estate speculator and a sharp businessman who used his talents to advance the cause of American socialism. This was the man who returned to Indiana from Colorado in 1893, tall and slender, with a wife and four children: Jon, thirteen, who had been born just before they left Harrisonville; Olive, eleven; Walter, nine; and Julia, an infant. The father and husband was a trifle stoop-shouldered, with a medium complexion, moustache, and glasses. He wore an expression that has been characterized as a pleasant frown. When meeting Wayland for the first time, one young admirer said he looked to him a little like his own idea of how Lincoln must have looked. Wayland was known as an agreeable companion to his small circle of friends. He was devoted to cigars—without four a day, he claimed, he was impossible to live with. His favorite form of relaxation, at which he was quite skilled, was playing whist with his neighbors; and he felt that whist was a way to really get to know how other people's minds worked. But most important to him were his family and his home life; and his sense of what these meant was extremely conventional.[67]

Outwardly, Wayland appeared to be hard-hearted and vindictive, according to one of his closest associates, because he was unable to give expression to his innermost feelings.[68] Another associate found him "not sentimental outwardly."[69] Wayland had a quiet voice, a quick intellect, and a firm manner. Those people in the movement who would meet him later and record their feelings all seem to have shared a sense of expectation in meeting him. He inspired many with feelings of loyalty and trust; at least one colleague, who had severe differences with him, nevertheless remarked on his personal magnetism and explained: "*I trusted Wayland on the spot.*"[70]

"Talkin' socialism" had become Wayland's favorite pastime, either with fellow stalwarts in the movement or with people he was trying to "convert." Mary Harris ("Mother") Jones, a union organizer who became close to Wayland, recalled the many times when they "used to set up at night and talk" about Voltaire, Victor Hugo, and Thomas Paine.[71] He would often stop work to talk to visitors who came to his newspaper office. He lent his books, especially to younger people who he felt still had a chance to change their thinking; and he continued to buttonhole people on the street, as he had in Pueblo. These activities he carried out face-to-face; Wayland was unlike other socialist propagandists of the day in that he refused many invitations to go on the lecture circuit. His reticence was coupled with the refusal to have his picture taken for public use. He seems also (although the evidence is somewhat contradictory) originally to have wanted to publish his newspapers anonymously. As he became better known, at least in socialist circles, he traveled under the alias of J. A. Willson, a family name. He even attended socialist conferences as an unrecognized spectator. This behavior may have indicated some reluctance to be allied publicly with the cause that he was championing with his pen.[72]

Wayland was sloppy in his work habits, unable to find addresses in the clutter of his desk, and allowed himself to be interrupted by a steady stream of visitors. He seems not to have kept a record of his correspondence, discarding letters after he answered them and not keeping copies of his own replies. The records he did keep were those of business transactions, which he jotted down in a notebook that he always kept on his person. He used the same book to record his thoughts, which he turned into the little paragraphs that graced the front page of the newspaper. Writing was easy for Wayland; he once told an interviewer that he could knock out an entire front page in a morning. He did it at a desk, with a set of Ruskin's works at his elbow, to which he referred often for inspiration.[73]

Wayland, called J. A. by his co-workers, was not a meticulous man, like the more highly educated and more refined members he would meet in the socialist movement. He stood solidly in the middle of the country, with middlebrow tastes and habits, although as he got older, he taught himself enough German to read newspapers, and he relished trips to the city to see plays, hear operas, and, later, attend films.[74] He liked his simple pleasures, and he prided himself on his ability in real-estate speculation and on his trading skills in general. He was the quintessential self-made man, soon to be surrounded by a growing and admiring staff. Wayland was a man who had prospered under the existing system yet said he wanted to change it.

Wayland brought more than gold and securities from Pueblo, Colorado, to Greensburg, Indiana. This mature man's life was shaped by more than twenty years of working, writing, and doing business throughout the Midwest and the West. Although he was radicalized in the Centennial State, especially in Pueblo, the Pittsburgh of the West, his basic assumptions had changed little from the time when he was a young editor on the make. His attitudes, prejudices, and pet ideas came through his socialist period of intense study of about two years. He was frankly scared of being in debt, recalling the bitter years of poverty and the social slights he endured as a child. He did not like ideological rigidity, but he would not relinquish basic principles for the sake of temporary advantage. Politically, this translated into supporting a party that held true to its beliefs yet was flexible in interpreting them, while refusing to fuse itself into another party that might only temporarily share its goals. Above all, he was a savvy businessman, who renounced speculation from time to time in order to conform with his new allegiance but who never lost the taste for it; and he was a white American, whose definition of family and home was indistinguishable from that of nonradicals of his time.

During 1892 and 1893, Wayland shut himself up in his study after supper until one o'clock in the morning every night except Sunday, to read whatever radical literature he could get his hands on.[75] He turned this study into a "One-Hoss Philosophy," which was eclectic, rambling, all-encompassing, and sometimes contradictory. The One-Hoss Philosophy owed much to Wayland's Colorado environment, his early life and career as a printer, his success in Colorado politics, and the atmosphere of populist reform. Of the books he read, Gronlund's and Bellamy's loom large, as they did for most radicals and reformers during the 1880s and 1890s. But what sets Wayland somewhat apart in America was his reliance on the English philosopher, art historian, aesthete, and social critic John Ruskin. Of all the works that Wayland studied and later offered for sale through his publications, the most important to him were Ruskin's. Ruskin exerted a profound influence on the radical editor. Wayland wanted to emulate Ruskin's own ten-year career as the editor of a radical paper: "O, that I had even a small part of his wisdom with this paper [the *Coming Nation*] and its forty times as many readers [as Ruskin's *Fors Clavigera: Letters to the Workmen and Labourers of Great Britain*]. But those who had studied Ruskin can see an echo of his writing in all these columns, for his mind is my inspiration."[76] It is to Ruskin the social philosopher that we must look as one of the sources of Wayland's thought if we are to understand the assumptions that informed the columns of the most widely read series of radical publications in American history.

2
The One-Hoss Philosophy

But let me tell you one thing, and tell it to you in italic sentences *that this is the beginning of the* FIRST *struggle for* ECONOMIC FREEDOM *that has ever agitated the governments of mankind.* . . . Books, not bayonets, pamphlets, not pistols, paper, not powder, speeches, not swords.
—*J. A. Wayland*, Coming Nation, *1894*

Just prior to the Panic of 1893 and one day before his thirty-ninth birthday, Wayland published the first issue of the *Coming Nation* in Greensburg, Indiana. All of the early influences on him are evident in this four-page paper. Even printer's devices, the masthead, the title, the terms under which the paper could be purchased, the titles of the articles, and the nature of the subscribers reverberate with the One-Hoss Philosophy. The tag line of the new paper read: "For a government of, by, and for the People as outlined in Bellamy's *Looking Backward*, abolishing the Possibility of Poverty." A column by Tom Watson, the influential southern Populist leader, appeared near an excerpt from Ruskin. The newly elected Davis H. Waite of Colorado was the second subscriber. One of the ears (the boxes at the ends of the masthead) contained Bacon's exhortation: "Read, not to contradict, but to weigh and consider"; the other ear proclaimed "Advocate Right Everywhere."

It was all there: Lincoln's republicanism; American socialist thinking through Gronlund and through Bellamy's nationalism; Colorado and southern populism; a commitment to the American ideals of democracy and abolitionism; an abiding belief in the efficacy of education and in promoting socialism through boosterism. This paper would be self-sustaining, untainted by advertising; and it would be cheap, published by an American with an endearing monicker that promised rustic simplicity and individualism in his socialism. Written in Wayland's own style, the *Coming Nation* was the first in a series of publications that triggered a unique phase of American publishing and left an indelible mark on the nature of Gilded Age radicalism.[1]

It is difficult to isolate the influences on Wayland's thought. The One-Hoss Philosophy partakes of a wide range of experience and attempts to bring together elements that are sometimes antagonistic to one another. Nowhere does Wayland neatly summarize his ideas; rather, they emerge through the content of the weekly paper, in which the pressure of deadlines always limited reflection and consistency. "Philosophy" is too grand a word and too explicit to apply to the amalgamation that emerged from Wayland's pen. One is hard pressed to define the nature of his thought—it is certainly not a consistent system. The One-Hoss Philosophy was more an informed sensibility, a working set of assumptions to be employed to bring about a growth of consciousness leading to a change in social conditions. It was Wayland's brand of socialism.

Because socialism has always seemed alien in the United States, Wayland had to fight against those who recoiled at the very mention of the word. In Wayland's writing, socialism blends into the established tradition of dissent and protest, a tradition that often managed to shape the nature of the American experience. His socialism grew out of the American tradition of protest, rather than out of that introduced ready-made from Europe, a foreign implantation, as its detractors long characterized it. For J. A. Wayland, socialism was a means to control the forces that were threatening his America. He shared with many people the prejudices and ideas of mainstream American thinking. For him and others, socialism was just the next practical step to get America going in the right direction. And he spoke his radicalism in the language of county newspaper paragraphs—humorous, biting, sentimental, and uncompromising:

You can hire two men one day for two dollars now. Formerly you could hire but one man one day for two dollars. Are men depreciating?

The school book trust is now plucking the pockets of foolish working people who prefer the old tickets and private enterprise to voting for men who want the state to print and furnish books to scholars as it does school houses, desks and teachers.

Wheat is selling at 32 cents in Utah. Wheat gamblers live in palaces. One busts occasionally but the farmers do not move into his palace—another gambler does that. And the farmers are pretty solid for the same good old tickets. I'll tell you what, fellow citizens, this is the greatest, grandest, freest country on the globe and our people are the most intelligent.

Mayor Leech, of Mt. Pleasant, Iowa, at an old settlers' meeting, made some telling comparisons between the conditions of the pioneers then and now. Monopoly had robbed the men who had transformed a wild into a beautiful place, of all title to the results of their labor. He well said that the children of the pioneers would have to solve the question their fathers had left them—and they would do it.[2]

Socialism means social harmony—and perfect social harmony means the millennium. There are many who pray for the Millennium, for "on earth as it is in heaven"—who do all they can to prevent its being realized. They are not intentionally bad or hypocritical—they are simply ignorant of what it takes to have the prayer realized.[3]

In a very real sense, Wayland embodied the typical American socialist reformer of the turn of the century. A study of several hundred reformers of Wayland's period finds that they were for the most part "substantial, middle-class Americans with deep feelings of social right and wrong." The study "reinforce[s] the theory that the reformer was essentially of middle-class, native origin with Anglo-Saxon ancestry . . . with an interest in, a sympathy with, or an actual advocacy of socialist ideas which covered a range of Utopian to Marxist." Those in the group who specifically identified themselves as socialists have many of the specific characteristics of Wayland's life; nineteen of the thirty-four in the sample made journalism their career, and those middle-class socialists who "rose from the laboring class" were born "in a small urban center . . . and received a few years of public school education."[4]

When Wayland established the *Coming Nation* in 1893, he was perfectly placed to bring together the several strands of dissent that were growing in the United States. He had participated in a successful Populist campaign in Colorado, helping to elect a governor on the first try; he was an experienced publisher of weekly newspapers, making money where many failed to break even; and most important, he had capital to invest. The *Coming Nation* and, later, the *Appeal to Reason* became the leading papers of American radicalism. During the first ten years of their existence, no other paper could claim anywhere near the readership that Wayland amassed; and in the following ten, his paper reached unprecedented numbers. In a period when print dominated communications, Wayland dominated socialist publishing.

In the beginning, Wayland was the link between the growing Populist and the small socialist movements. After the Populist party joined the Democrats in 1896, he provided a haven for disaffected Populists who felt they had been deserted by their own party. Even after Wayland relinquished control of the *Coming Nation* in 1895, his ideas still motivated the new editors. His success was born of good timing, a sense of what was important to disaffected Americans who were ready to dissent; it was also due to his commercial know-how. From 1893 to 1912, when American radicalism exerted its greatest influence, he was talking to more people than anyone else. They read what he thought; they supported his truths by subscribing to his paper. He helped to provide financial support to the leader of the American socialist movement, Eugene V. Debs, whose basic vision was Wayland's as well. Wayland influenced the "Golden Age of American Socialism" at least as much as any other single figure.

Wayland's thought is confusing, but it seems to have evolved from four sources. The first could be called a composite of basic beliefs in American institutions, Jeffersonian and Jacksonian ideals, the abolition movement, a deep affection for Lincoln and an abiding faith in democracy, accepting much of the heritage of the producer ideology. The second component is populism, the populism that Lawrence Goodwyn has described as a "movement culture," which people developed through self-education "that grew out of their cooperative efforts." This crucial aspect of Wayland's thought was, again to quote Goodwyn, "a people's movement of mass democratic aspiration."[5] Third, Wayland had his socialist beliefs, which came from the Americans Gronlund (a Danish immigrant) and Bellamy. Fourth, welding together all of this and forming Wayland's world view, is his reliance on Ruskin as his intellectual guide. This last aspect of the One-Hoss Philosophy sets it further apart from the thinking of Wayland's contemporaries. All of these influences merged and came into conflict with the conventional assumptions that Wayland had received as an American growing to maturity during the last half of the nineteenth century.

Wayland was a confident man, sure of his own perceptions and his ability to transmit his view to his fellows. He believed in democratic means of reform. He was staunch in his defense of American ideals and was reactionary in his social and racial thinking.[6] But above all, he saw that the faults of American society were economic at base. He hit out in paragraph after paragraph against what he saw as unfair and to show how people could change things:

I was looking out of the window of a flying train into the darkness of a cold and stormy night. Across the window pane rushed a camp fire—there was barely time to discern the outline of a human being, crouched down over the fire in an effort to keep from freezing. He was an American Voting King, who, out on those wind swept plains, miles from a town and perhaps any habitation, was engaged in a very real struggle—a hand to hand conflict with death in two forms—that of freezing and starvation. Yet, strange as it may seem, he was getting only what he had been voting for at the ballot box. He didn't know that he was voting for that of course, but then you know "Ignorance of the law excuses no one."[7]

You know I was a republican, and was taught that "competition was the life of trade." But right here I find in a Republican paper "Safe companies combine—the great concerns combine to prevent disastrous competition." That sounds just like a real socialist argument. Wonder how long it will take for the working people to catch on and combine at the polls, the only place they can combine, and elect men who will go these robber trusts one better and have the government take and operate them for the benefit of all the people instead of the few? But then these working people are so queer. They like to compete with each other to see which can work for the least wages, instead of organizing like the postal system, the fire departments, the police or other public employees. "Disastrous competition!" Rich, coming from a g. o. p. organ, isn't it?[8]

If nine-tenths of a hive of bees gather and bring in all the honey, why should the other tenth control that honey to the exclusion of the working bees? If such a proportion is ridiculous for bees, why not for men? Have men less sense than bees? If so, why so?[9]

When William Bradfield transmitted his love of Ruskin to Wayland, he could scarcely have anticipated the profound impact Ruskin would have on Wayland's thought. Ruskin's echoes in Wayland's career are numerous and would be consciously acknowledged by Wayland. Ruskin's ideas shaped the way Wayland incorporated the other influences on his radical thought. Ruskin's works supplied the central curriculum when Wayland, coming to his task as a relatively old student, worked at renewing his education with a fierce determination. The first number of the *Coming Nation* contained a three-column extract from his mentor. Subsequently, Wayland frequently reprinted Ruskin and advertised for sale, in the columns of the paper, *Fors Clavigera, The Two Paths, Time and Tide, A Joy Forever, Wild Olives,* and *Sesame and Lilies,* alongside standard Marxist and Populist texts. When circumstances forced Wayland to relinquish the *Coming Nation* and start over with a new paper, he turned immediately to Ruskin for copy and possibly for moral support, reprinting *The Veins of Wrath* and "On Just Wages" in the first two numbers of the *Appeal to Reason* in 1895. But more important than such obvious reliance on Ruskin for material to fill out the weekly quota of copy are the ideas that became part of the One-Hoss Philosophy.[10] As Wayland told one colleague at the turn of the century, that is "simply Ruskin turned into the language of the common people.[11]

Ruskin has inspired people across a broad range of social, political, and artistic fields of interest. He encouraged the Pre-Raphaelite painters; he was an early champion of J. M. W. Turner; he was a friend of William Morris's and informed the work of Oscar Wilde and Arnold Toynbee. His influence can be found in the Bauhaus Movement and in the writings of Proust, Bergson, and Gandhi.[12] Although one can read some reform suggestions into Ruskin's earliest essays on art, it was only after 1860 that he wrote on political economy. His ideas on politics, like those on art, are complex, contradictory, and interwoven with ideas on all other aspects of human existence. His writing is digressive to the point of distraction. According to one Ruskin scholar, "He wrote whatever came into his head, gives us the stream of his consciousness and mingles straight socialist propaganda with art criticism, chapters of Marmontel, arguments about glaciers, a recipe for Yorkshire goose pie, prose poems addressed to St. Ursula, animadversions against the South Kensington system of art teaching and fragments from an unfinished biography of Sir Walter Scott."[13] Such was Ruskin's *Fors Clavigera*, the periodical whose goal of educating the workingman inspired Wayland.

Ruskin's politics grew out of a desire to put into practice his ideas about art. Not content only to dream about an art that would satisfy him, "he strove to realize the good and the beautiful in the actual world—to build the Tabernacle of God among men." His irregular letters to the English working class were one way of fulfilling a debt he felt he owed to the common man, to lift some of his burden of misery, and to alleviate the suffering he saw, suffering that made him feel guilty and slowed his other work. In these letters, though he rambles, his writing is fierce and uncompromising. He lashes out at those who fail to see that he is right. He called people a "mob of money begotten traitors" whose religion is "the rottenest thing" about them. What these people were supposed to see lay buried among the other subjects that were dear to Ruskin, but the ideas were consistent with the social and political theories that he expounded in such earlier works as *Unto This Last, Munera Pulveris*, and parts of *Sesame and Lilies.*[14]

Ruskin made the most succinct expression of his ideas near the end of the life of the periodical *Fors Clavigera*. All social problems arise from "the pillage of the laborer by the idle"—the idle included landlords, soldiers, lawyers, and priests. And the letters were meant to spur workers into originating a movement, in alliance with any "trustworthy element in the higher classes," which would do good in the sense of enabling people to work hard and well; to feed, clothe, and shelter themselves;

and to "please people with arts, or sciences or any subject of thought." Specific premises and prescriptions are scattered about in *Fors Clavigera*: the nation is not really prosperous; relief will not come from the government; the people themselves should become landlords and capitalists, instead of dispossessing current landlords; there should be agricultural and technical schools set up for the people. Although relief would not come from the government, Ruskin nevertheless assigned large powers and responsibilities to the state: to provide the necessities of life, which included education; to organize labor and to provide raw material; "to abolish abolishable filth, the first process of education"; banning such mercenary professions as preaching, lawgiving, and fighting; and limiting the number of but maintaining scholars, painters, and musicians. In Ruskin's view, the state would be enjoined from importing food—if there was not enough, people would be sent out to colonies. All would have to work for a living and such work should be hard work, for machinery drawn by steam would be almost completely prohibited.[15]

These are some of the ideas and measures Ruskin promoted in his *Letters to the Workmen and Laborers of Great Britain*, the subtitle of *Fors Clavigera*. Some of them Wayland adopted; some he altered; many he ignored. But the sensibility behind these measures was more important to him, as was the method of explaining and distributing his ideas. Something of Ruskin's style, stripped of the majesty of his prose and produced without the erudition of its expounder, came to Wayland.

Ruskin's social critique is the elaboration of this idea: "Government and cooperation are in all things and eternally the laws of life. Anarchy and competition eternally, and in all things, the laws of death." According to James C. Sherburne, Ruskin knew better what he opposed than what he supported, since he always worked intuitively, utilizing the Romantic tradition, in which he matured, to inform his social and political thought. Ruskin was excellent at getting to the heart of the "matter, gaining a sound grasp of first principles and organic relationships." But "he is much less capable of the slow, step-by-step testing of propositions which the scholar and scientist endures." Ruskin's technique was to restate, preach, and apply the principles that he developed very early in his life.[16]

The danger for Wayland, in imitating Ruskin's style, was that he was acting on assumptions that Ruskin had come to without proof. The personal flavor of Wayland's writing can also be traced partly to Ruskin. According to Sherburne, the flamboyant style does not detract from Ruskin's arguments: "The reader feels that Ruskin, with his blocked paths and intuitive brilliance, is there on the page. There is no game of hide and seek, no pretense." Again from Ruskin, Wayland could probably trace his own reluctance to draw in detail the implications of his vision. Ruskin contented himself with the outlines, making specific but disconnected suggestions; but he left the theory building more to the imagination than to rigorous, detailed formulas. "He propounded no theory so specific and rigid that it can be definitely rejected."[17]

Ruskin's uncertainty about the method of reform, as seen in the obvious contradictions in his specific measures, follows in large part from the nature of his thought. Sometimes he called for revolution; at other times he preferred voluntary gradual action. At times the workers would need his leadership; at other times, as mentioned, he called on the workers to become their own capitalists. Much of his thought is authoritarian in the extreme. One can find him railing against the servility of the people: he opposed democracy, believing that only the wise should rule. Liberty, Ruskin thought, was not essential to human happiness. Ruskin thought that if you weren't smart enough, you should leave the thinking to others. Authoritarian ideas, typical of many Victorian reformers, are also found in Wayland's thought.

This extraordinary mixture of compassion and discipline, of the love of art and authoritarian measures that could bring a new age into being, produced a faith that education would enable people to see the light. It would cure public distress and save the human race. It should be moral education, to make men "thoughtful, merciful and just." Through education, the people would be ready to bring about Ruskin's vision of their future. The desire to educate was the single factor that inspired Wayland to publish his own paper, which he aimed at the working class, to teach them economics and politics. Ruskin's thought on education touched this point—namely, that all should understand how the product of their work was used and controlled. But more important, education was the primary motivation of human beings, the reason for existence. Wayland, throughout his career, continually preached that you could do no better than to "empty thy purse into thy head." His efforts were directed at getting people to read in order to learn what was wrong and what they could do about it.

Wayland was not alone in advocating a belief in the power of education in the United States. At least since the abolitionist movement, radicals had believed that education was the key to radical change in the United States; it was the unifying faith that had fired the Populist lecture network. The truths propagated by a myriad of reformers, in Wayland's view and in that of hundreds of his colleagues, would change the world once they were understood and assimilated by the majority of working people. This belief was reinforced by Ruskin's work.[18]

Ruskin was only one important influence on Wayland. It is only necessary to read one or two of Wayland's paragraphs to be convinced of his location in the mainstream of American beliefs. He loved to remind his readers that he was "an American of revolutionary stock,"[19] and one could always read in him the commonly held beliefs that the Republic the founding fathers had launched was the right idea, as was the attempt to ensure basic freedoms through a written constitution. But the time of innocence had passed: the train of progress was off the rails, and freeborn Americans should do something to get it going back in the right direction. The free-labor republicanism that Eric Foner has described is the linkage that Wayland made when he compared 1860 to 1893: "The arrogance of the slave power—the power of the property class to make money out of the labor of others—is duplicated today . . . in grander style off the labor of others—wage slaves. . . . Will the millions who hold the power open their eyes to the plain facts and cease to vote for their own enslavement? Will another Lincoln rise up to lead the people to the abolition of wage slavery? I think the time will produce the man."[20]

He had been a Republican and had given it up, not only because he saw some basic truths in socialism or because he was convinced that his past beliefs were wrong, but also because of the hollowness of Lincoln's successors. What had appealed to Wayland in the Republican party was its morality, the justice of the antislavery movement; what repelled him was the political reality, once it was made clear to him, of a party in power, rewarding its friends and existing for business interests. He himself had reaped the advantages of the venal side of the Republican party; now he wanted to return to the earlier, more righteous period. His heroes were Americans: Paine, Jefferson, Jackson, Greeley, and Lincoln. He believed that through the action of democracy, policies could be changed and wrongs could be righted. In his mind, there was a direct connection between this lost America and the coming Socialist America.

As the masthead proclaimed, he was for a government of, for, and by the people. This was the kind of government that could achieve such great things as abolishing slavery. Wayland had lived through the Civil War and had seen the quick initial electoral success of the Colorado Populists; he thus had learned that changes could be made with the ballot. Just one generation separated the victory over chattel slavery and the new battle against a new form of slavery; there was nothing in his experience to show him that victory was not possible again. America was a land of promise, a virgin land, with an idyllic past and a correctable present. Wayland had the optimism of a successful entrepreneur who had realized the possibilities for making his own fortune. He now wanted to make sure that this individual success would be generalized, and it seemed to him that if things didn't change, success would become impossible for all but a very few.

These feelings of Wayland's may have been even more important an element in his radicalism than his understanding of Ruskin; whenever there appeared to be a contradiction, Wayland would assert them. For example, he could describe accurately and in detail the abuses of the present election system. He could show how corrupting and how powerful business interests could be in the political system and then confidently assert that all that was needed in order to change things was to win at the ballot box. His belief in American democracy was basic to his belief in the progress of American society. It was such a strong belief that it prevailed in the face of relentless proof of an opposing reality. This tension was unconscious, and it allowed the most difficult problems in his "One-Hoss" beliefs to remain unresolved.

Bellamy's thought influenced Wayland in ways that reinforced much of what he understood from Ruskin, emphasizing a belief in the perfectibility of American institutions. *Looking Backward* portrayed a future perfected without undue violence, a future society that had peacefully and thoroughly worked out the problems of the concentration of industry and the continual abasement of the individual. In that society the monopolies came under public control: "In a word, the people of the United States concluded to assume conduct of their own business, just as one hundred years before they assumed the conduct of their own government, organizing now for industrial purposes on precisely the same grounds that they had then organized for political purposes."[21] Bellamy's vision of this future society shared many of the authoritarian features that informed Ruskin's vision: there would be an army of workers providing service, and there would be state control of almost all phases of life. Life, as in Ruskin's writings, would be played out within fairly restricted lines, in a controlled society. Bellamy wanted to replace the chaos of history with a final and concrete image of the future. This new life would be a moral one.

This is indeed a conservative vision of change: Bellamy himself saw the work of reform as a counterrevolutionary measure devoted to maintaining the Republic against the onslaught of control by monopolies. In Bellamy, as in Ruskin and in Wayland and others of a similar radical stamp, anarchy was to be rooted out in politics, in production, in social relations. As one critic explains, "for Bellamy, enlightened authoritarian direction is the natural response to the wasteful diffusion of power and wealth that he saw around him."[22]

Wayland, though he had read Bellamy, had first worked in political action in a Populist election campaign. Lawrence Goodwyn boils down the notion of populism that motivated Wayland's quest for social change:

[Populism's] animating essence pulsed at every level of the ambitious structure of cooperation: in the earnest probings of people bent on discovering a way to free themselves from the killing grip of the credit system ("The suballiance is a schoolroom"); in the joint-notes of the landed, given in name of themselves and the landless ("The brotherhood stands united"); in the pride of discovery of their own legitimacy ("The merchants are listening when the County Trade Committee talks"); and in the massive and emotional effort to save the cooperative dream itself ("The Southern Exchange Shall Stand"). The democratic core of Populism was visible in the mile-long Alliance wagon trains ("The Fourth of July is Alliance Day"); in the sprawling summer encampments ("A pentecost of politics") and, perhaps most tellingly, in the latent generosity unlocked by the culture of the movement itself, revealed in the capacity of those who had little, to empathize with those who had less ("We extend to the Knights of Labor our hearty sympathy in their manly struggle against monopolistic oppression," and "The Negro people are part of the people and must be treated as such").[23]

In Wayland's thought, the populist ethos cut across the intellectual stimulus from Ruskin and the conservative utopian influence of Bellamy. Populism informed Wayland's economics and his personal style; it also sanctioned many of the prejudices that he would reveal in the One-Hoss Philosophy, providing the cement that would bind it together. The Omaha Platform, of July, 1892, the basic document of the People's party, called for specific measures under the rubric of these major ideas: that the forces of labor were now united, that wealth belongs to the creators of wealth, that the government should own the railroads, and that there should be a safe, sound, and flexible currency. Some of the specific proposals included a call for postal savings banks, the eight-hour day, and the graduated income tax. Wayland, in a remark that might indicate the essence of his thought, said that "all there is of *Spirit* in the Declaration of Independence or the Omaha Platform is socialistic, but neither represents all of socialism."[24] The money question was of course a key one, in that it had drawn much additional support to the core of more radical demands for public ownership.

Wayland's economic thinking and his more theoretical underpinnings derived much of their force from questions about silver and money in general, questions that everyone seemed to be discussing in the eighteen nineties. Since the so-called steal of 1873, an economic scandal that symbolized the corruption of the government, silver had been a talisman that had drawn together the forerunners of the Populists, as a symbol of the antieastern and antimonopoly establishment fever that gripped most people in some way. William Harvey's *Coin's Financial School*,[25] a publication that Wayland had bought and distributed in prodigious numbers, taught its basic lesson of inflationary money through simple blackboard lessons. Silver was a way to stop the American people from falling into one of the two fates that the Omaha Platform feared: you became either a tramp or a millionaire. The Populists were going to restore the government to the "plain people" who were heading down the road to tramphood.

Those plain people had been Wayland's associates at the *Colorado Workman*, which he subsequently took over and where he may have first worked with Mrs. Mary Elizabeth Lease, one of the most outspoken symbols of the Populists.[26] Some of the Populist spirit must have rubbed off on Wayland, especially the beliefs in working-class institutions and the efficacy of education. The "democratic promise" of the new movement, in Lawrence Goodwyn's phrase, "generated new possibilities of individual self-respect and mass aspiration."[27] The Alliance Exchange movement, the grass-roots source of Populist power, placed a premium on exhortation, education, and uplift. Wayland had done a good deal of his own exhorting in Pueblo, by buttonholing passers-by on the streets and fellow passengers on the trains and by sending out vast numbers of unsolicited tracts during that first Populist campaign. After the successful election of Populist Governor Waite in Colorado, Wayland had encouraged the new governor to start "talkin' socialism":

> By pushing the campaign of education with papers and books, Colorado can be carried in '94. But it will require concerted earnest action. You can bank on Pueblo. It is the best educated town in the U.S. All it requires is one or two influential, active citizens to keep exhorting the people *all the time*. If you will put *three* well-posted socialist speakers, (they need not mention socialism) in Denver *three months*, and have speakings [sic] in the labor districts, you can surely carry Denver. The cost would be insignificant if spread out among a dozen or two members. There are many able men who would come for a trifling pittance. Denver is the best field in the state to work.[28]

The down-home atmosphere of the One-Hoss Philosophy was populist in nature. The popular economics came from the money theories that were part of what Goodwyn calls the Populist "shadow" movement, a movement that adopted some of the remedies that the Populists advocated without the underlying assumptions that informed them.[29] The sensibilities of the One-Hoss Philosophy and its form of presentation came from Ruskin and to some extent from Bellamy, but the basic socialist underpinning Wayland derived from Gronlund's *Cooperative Commonwealth*. Informed by Wayland's basic belief in American forms of democracy, the One-Hoss Philosophy derived the following from

Gronlund: (1) The economy was unstable and was increasingly being controlled by fewer and fewer large capitalists; (2) unions were ineffective in checking this power; (3) a political party could be constructed to appeal to a large number and a broad range of people; (4) electoral success was within reach; (5) people could be educated to the truths of socialism through the written and spoken word; and (6) through political action, a new age, a "Coming Nation," could be brought into being, which would combine the freedom of pre–Civil War America with the unknown wealth that the new technology could bring.

The nature of the One-Hoss Philosophy, then, is close in many ways to the development of Debs's thought, as articulated by Nick Salvatore. Almost contemporary with one another, Wayland had become radicalized in the West, as a businessman who had learned from Ruskin and Gronlund and who had seen with his own eyes corporate capitalism in Colorado; while Debs, back in the center of the country, had risen from employment on the railroad to a position in a fair-sized firm and ultimately to prominence as a labor-union official. If one were to compare their positions, they would probably be furthest apart on labor issues; and in human terms, Wayland was much less prone to emotional reactions to human suffering, for which he castigated Debs when the two worked together on the *Appeal to Reason* after 1907. While Debs made his thought known through speeches all over the country, Wayland reached his audiences through the growing circulation of the country's most popular political paper. The two would be linked together for the five most productive years of American socialism, from 1907 to 1912, when their two forms of communication worked together most closely: Wayland as publisher and financier and Debs as associate editor and chief subscription hustler.

The business of publishing a successful newspaper informed the message that it proclaimed. As we have emphasized, Wayland was as much a successful speculator as he was a newspaperman, and the business side of producing his radical papers placed Wayland in a quandary. Sharp business practice seemed to be the antithesis to the goals of a humane socialist publication. Wayland sensed the contradiction and turned to Ruskin for help. The publication and distribution of *Fors Clavigera* were unique to Ruskin, for he wanted to put into practice his remedies for reforming corrupt business practices. The published price of a book was not always representative of what the public paid for it, primarily because of the wide difference in discounts given to various booksellers and the willingness of these booksellers to undercut each other. Because Ruskin believed in "fixed prices, cash down and confessed profits," and because he abhorred advertising, he set about selling his books in a new way, a method that antagonized the booksellers, who subsequently boycotted his works.[30] His remedy was to become his own publisher and to charge a fixed price to the public and to booksellers, allowing no discounts or credits and, except for sending a few free copies to the press during the first years, engaging in no other form of advertising. As the idea passed the stage of ridicule, it was modified to the point where Ruskin set a fixed price for the sale of his works and a fixed discount to the trade, thus ensuring that his works would be available everywhere at the same price. This eventually became the practice of the modern publishing industry, breaking down only in the 1970s. These basic business formulas were incorporated into the sale of the *Coming Nation*.

In practice the One-Hoss Philosophy was the weekly outpouring of Wayland's facile pen. He borrowed the rambling style of the *Fors Clavigera* from Ruskin, as well as its tone—an impatience with people who did not learn. "Get your eyes open and dethrone the oppressor" was the first and one of the mildest injunctions with which Wayland challenged his readers.[31] The sense of superiority, the knowledge of being correct, came from his mentor. As the years wore on, Wayland's exasperation with people who failed to learn his truths would rise. But at the beginning of his experiment to publish a nationwide propaganda organ to educate the working class to the truth as he saw it, he reached out expectantly from the small town of Greensburg, Indiana, twenty-five miles from his birthplace at Versailles, in the hope of attracting a readership in the not-too-distant cities of Cincinnati, Cleveland, Indianapolis, Chicago, Pittsburgh, and St. Louis. He secured the names of correspondents of the existing labor and reform papers and, as a way of advertising, sent each of them a bundle of ten papers to distribute. The paper itself took no advertising; the yearly price was set at an unusually low rate for a weekly, fifty cents. At the start, the expenses and receipts, as well as the names of new subscribers, were printed each week. The publishing ideas were clearly consistent with those of Ruskin.

Wayland's capital did not have to carry the paper for long, because in six months the paper was breaking even and in seven it showed a profit. The paper was extremely well received, not (significantly) in the industrial cities, but in the towns and the countryside, especially in California. Wayland had to discontinue the practice of printing the lists of new subscribers, for they were soon taking up almost a fourth of the paper. They had served, however, to prove that the circulation was real, and they put many reform-minded people in touch with one another. An American subcommunity had found a national organ.[32]

The most salient feature of Wayland's work, the one thing that he is noted for among all his critics, is his ability as a paragrapher. He was able to reduce any question, news item, or philosophical argument to a paragraph, usually less than 150 words in length. Rarely did anything that Wayland wrote extend beyond one column. The first page of his paper was cut into bite-sized chunks of information that were complete stories in themselves; they did not lead to the next paragraph or story. Each paragraph, no matter how small, was a finished story, complete with a moral; and it usually ended with an exhortation to change things, to learn more, or to wake up. Or it ended with a ringing profession of faith and hope in the future. The theme throughout the early issues of the paper was one central to Ruskin: producers were not getting a just return for their labor; even though they made the food and the clothing, they were ill-clad and starving. The solution was to use the state, through taking political control, to devolve the ownership of the means of production and distribution onto the people. This last point was one that Ruskin might have objected to, but it would fit in nicely with the socialism of Bellamy and Gronlund. Wayland quotes Ruskin directly on the nature of work and says that the real object of work should be love, not money. Ruskin and Wayland had as their goal to free people so that work could be its own reward.[33]

Wayland, like most nineteenth-century reformers, commented often in the *Coming Nation* on the similarity of chattel slavery to white wage slavery.[34] This afforded a good example of the interplay of Wayland's ex-Republican beliefs, his Ruskinite views, and his share of mainstream American prejudices against the black man. Chattel slavery, in Wayland's estimation, had definite advantages over the current wage slavery, for at least the black slave was protected against unemployment and depressions and provided with the rudimentary necessities of life. Although the chief purpose of this theme was to point out the low state to which the supposed free American had fallen, the repetition gives one pause. The same kind of thinking is found in Ruskin and has a long history in the writing of nineteenth-century economists. Ruskin thought that black workers in the tropics were much better off than their white counterparts in industrialized nations.[35] This touch of authoritarian paternalism, although used for effect, lingers in the mind of the reader.

As for the black man himself, Wayland's prejudices reflected those of white Americans in general. Though tempered somewhat by his economic views, he would still advocate segregation so that blacks could develop at their own more relaxed speed. Wayland summarized his opinions on blacks and socialism in this fashion: "There will be no question when Socialism prevails—colors will be separated by custom, not by law, and the crime the black man did [raping a white woman in Ohio] would not have been committed for lack of opportunity."[36] Other races, such as the Chinese, would be similarly segregated under socialism by the votes of workers in individual factories, who could and probably would decide to exclude them. Socialist America would effectively reduce immigration through Wayland's brand of nativism, which ran deeply through the opposition parties from the founding of the Workingman's party in 1877 by the Irish-born demagogue Denis Kearney, who agitated equally against the rich and the Chinese, to the Populists, whose anti-immigration and anti-Semitic policies have long stirred historians.[37] "They come in now by the millions, with or without your consent, because the private owners of industries can hire them cheaper than you want to work for. . . . Chinamen might come, but Chinamen would not be able to work without your consent. . . . Private ownership of industries mixes up the races, reducing blacks, whites and yellows to a common level, while socialism would separate the races and lift them all to the highest level of which each is capable."[38]

Wayland held similar prejudices about Jews and about the place of women in society. He had no compunction about reprinting material that stereotyped the capitalist as a fat hook-nosed friend of the Rothschilds.[39] Later, he attempted to describe his own ideas in more detail and concluded that though Jews were no better or worse than any other group, they were better in business than other folks but were incompetent as warriors. He saw the Rothschilds as having foisted on the world a system of finance that caused misery, but he saw it as their retribution for the awful murders during the Crusades. He tempered this statement by saying that when the Jews became reformers, they did great work, as did the greatest reformer, Jesus Christ.[40] But three weeks later, he published a rabid anti-Jewish article on the nature of Zionism, claiming that Britain was "Jew-governed."[41] His opinions on women, like those on the place of blacks, did not receive much space in the earliest issues of the paper, except when Wayland was discussing his plans for an experimental commune. As we will see in the next chapter, woman's proper place was in the home.

These issues were subsidiary to the main theme of what the white working class should be doing and thinking. Echoing Gronlund, Wayland repeatedly spoke about the futility of strikes and the utility of the ballot. This was the time of some of the most violent labor disputes in the nation's history—Haymarket (Chicago), 1886; Homestead (Pennsylvania), 1892; Pullman (Chicago), 1894—not to overlook the mining battles that Wayland had witnessed in Colorado. Wayland's views on this question were probably partly responsible for the ambivalent regard of city workers toward the paper.

These views on labor's key weapon may have derived from Wayland's own position as an employer of labor. Writing during the Pullman strike, he saw the whole episode as merely a lesson that demonstrated his theme, although he, of course, sided with the workers. When the strike was over, he felt that Debs, who Wayland had early and often predicted would eventually lead the forces of reform, had learned the same lesson.[42] Two weeks later, Wayland remarked: "The Haverhill shoemaker strike has failed, adding another to the long list of lessons to labor that striking is not the right way as long as it votes capitalist tickets."[43] On a report of the troubles at the Homestead steel mill, he remarked: "The working people vote for parties that uphold private property and then try to upset the ownership by brute force. They will not succeed. . . . Ideas can change the world, but brute force and ignorance, never."[44]

Labor unions and political action seemed always to be combined in Wayland's mind. Take a front page paragraph from 1898:

> The failure of the engineers' strike in England has been a great educator. It has shown the men that it will be necessary to go into politics and get the laws changed as well as to hold labor unions in order to fight the capitalists. It has taken many years to get this idea into the heads of the workers, and much punishment, but the ideas grow rapidly now that it is once started. It is a lesson that American labor unions will have to learn sooner or later, and the longer they shut their eyes to it the longer they will have to suffer.[45]

Wayland's reports on current events were not newsworthy; he went to press the week before the Saturday that the publication was dated, and thus had no access to the latest news. He had no reporters; he relied on other papers that he received through the mail. His comments took the form of editorials after the fact, like those on Pullman and on Coxey's Army: "But let me tell you one thing, and tell it to you in italic sentences *that this is the beginning of the* FIRST *struggle for* ECONOMIC FREEDOM *that has ever agitated the governments of mankind.* . . . Books, not bayonets, pamphlets, not pistols, paper, not powder, speeches, not swords."[46]

All people who worked with their hands would be affected by industrialization, and all would have to react:

> The independent shoemaker has been displaced by the shoe factory, and has now become a slave to the capitalists; the "village blacksmith" has degenerated into a mere repairer of factory work; the weaver has met the same fate; the carpenters are merely machines to put into place work of the great factories, and do a little choring; printers are tasting the beauties of trying to compete with machines. . . . The backbone of the nation is the farmer. He has remained conservative and taken no notice of the changes going on all about him. But he is doomed [Bonanza farming will make him a tenant]. . . . It's coming and I am glad of it. It will bring a change.[47]

Wayland differed strongly from Ruskin in his views on industrialization. Wayland welcomed the steam engine and the gasoline
engine, and he later championed the infant airplane industry. Unlike
Ruskin, who wanted to preserve handicrafts, thus idealizing the medieval
laborer, Wayland thought this kind of technological change was good,
as long as it brought a change in social consciousness. In a rare foray
into the realm of more abstract thought, Wayland expanded on the idea
that pain was the motivating force of history. In one of his longest articles, he argued that people do things out of the necessity to alleviate
pain:

> I believe I am right when I say that pain has produced all the prog-
> ress made by the human family. . . . Pain caused early man to seek
> shelter. . . . Pain of isolation produced the desire for companions,
> hence communities. . . . Had not such men [as President Cleveland]
> appeared in the arena of life, and committed the monstrosities of
> bad laws, I believe the progress of the human family would have been
> retarded a thousand years. . . . I feel confident that the violent leaders
> of the nation in favor of capitalism are doing 90% of all work for
> a better system. . . . The people would never have listened, never have
> read, never investigated but for the pain the actions such men pro-
> duced. This pain is the salvation of the race.[48]

Writing much of the original copy for a weekly publication forced
Wayland to reveal his thoughts on a range of topics, much as his mentor
had done in *Fors Clavigera*. The paper made the statements and sentiments of the "One-Hoss" editor more accessible and brought the
readers into his personal view of things. He was, for example, not against
prohibiting the sale of intoxicating beverages, but he thought that the
prohibitionists were attacking an effect of social dislocation, not a root
cause.[49] He shared the widespread assumption that big cities were vice-
ridden and unhealthy places in which to live: Chicago he called a
"cesspool of corruption."[50] Wayland was also given to hero worship, favor-
ing Tom Watson and Eugene Debs as the leaders of the Coming Nation.[51]
Spiritualists came in for a good word: "It is claimed that there are thirteen million spiritualists in the United States. The growth of belief in
this theory is one of the wonderful phases of this age. While not accepting the faith, I find them as a rule advanced thinkers and liberal in their
views."[52] Postal savings banks were a pet reform that Wayland advocated
early and often. He at first refused to use the banks, and he resorted to
money orders, drawn through post offices, to "save" large sums of money,
another echo of Ruskin, who railed against interest and usury.

To Wayland and to many others in the movement, the post office, along with public schools, libraries, and municipally owned utilities, were all examples of incipient socialism. Chiding a correspondent who criticized these views, he replied: "He [the correspondent] doubtless learned to read in a socialistic public school, went to a socialistic letter box over a socialistic . . . street to mail it, had it carried to the [office] by a socialistic letter-carrier and delivered to me by a socialistic postal system."[53] In a paragraph he neatly summarized his views:

> Rural free delivery is being put into operation all over the country by the postal department in order that farmers may have the benefit of mail facilities every day instead of losing time to go to the postoffice. See the immense saving in time and labor this effects. This is the Socialistic way of doing things and every time the old party administration stumbles onto a Socialistic idea they make a ten strike with the people. But private profit stands with a club at every step of the way. In this case it is the poor dear little merchant who don't want it because the people can then sit in their own homes, send one or two thousand miles for goods and get them delivered at the door cheaper than the little one can sell them for. Hence he is wroth. He would rather have 200 or 300 farmers compelled to hitch up and come to town so that he can skin them. But the little retailers days are numbered. The competitive system has the seeds of dissolution within itself and it is practically dead today.[54]

The position that Wayland took on the postal system was symptomatic of a side of his thinking for which he was attacked by the more rigorous socialist thinkers of the period; it also showed the sloppiness to which he was prone, no doubt accentuated by weekly deadlines. In fact, rural free delivery was not in any sense a socialist notion, unless the word loses all meaning. It was pushed upon the government by large retailers, led by John Wanamaker, for precisely the reason that Wayland adduces: it would help to kill off the small retailer by enriching the mail-order houses and growing department stores. Whatever ancillary benefits there were did not detract from the real reason that the "old parties" supported it.

Nevertheless, the argument that the postal system was socialistic served Wayland by getting people to think about the "public" sphere and about state involvement in a more creative fashion—precisely the difference between an indigenous radicalism and a disciplined party concerned with the exegesis of texts, which would come to stifle the American socialist movement after Wayland's generation had passed from the scene.

This all-inclusive notion of what socialism would mean in America caused Wayland to be knocked around from both sides. From 1893 to 1895,

Wayland was walking the line between organized socialism, limited chiefly to a small, heavily Germanic Socialist Labor party (SLP), and the People's party. He supported the Omaha Platform of 1892, which in his eyes was virtually a socialist platform, and he printed it in the paper alongside the SLP platform. For this, he was attacked from the Populist right, who accused him of trying to deceive their supporters by injecting "socialistic poison into the families" of good Populists. "You pretend to be a Populist and print a populist paper, yet you are teaching doctrines as far removed from Populism as the depths of Hades are from the glimmering hilltops of Zion."[55] Earlier, he had tangled with Daniel DeLeon of the SLP, who had condemned the Populists as a bourgeois party of small farmers. Wayland replied that "all of the Populist leaders and all of the followers are as true and earnest socialists as you Eastern chaps and by election returns stood by those principles better at the polls."[56]

When, by 1898, another party, the Social Democracy, which was more akin to Wayland in thought and make-up than was the heavily German SLP, began to make some headway, he, harking back to his earliest political instincts, saw principle, not party, as paramount:

I have several inquiries as to which party to support—the Socialist Labor Party or the Social Democracy. The *Appeal* is not a party organ. It is not your business to take anybody's advice in this matter but to use your own judgment. The trouble with people is that they have always been too lazy to investigate for themselves and have depended on others to do it for them. Get the methods and tactics of both parties. Study them and then use your own judgment. Personally I want to see them both go on making converts to socialism. When a strong socialist sentiment is created all over the country the members will come together and no set of leaders will be able to prevent it. I rejoice to see the success of each.[57]

Although these political questions would become more important as the decade wore on, when he would ultimately lash out against the rigidity of the SLP, the outline of Wayland's thinking, however fuzzy the details, was pretty clear. He was attempting to pull together the greatest number of the disaffected, uniting many strains of dissent under the umbrella of what he called socialism. As we can see, that umbrella was extremely large, and Wayland could either wink at or be unaware of the contradictions that he sanctioned. Earlier he had turned to Populism, not only because it was the only radical party then, but because he saw in it, with his newly opened radical eyes, one manifestation of the rest of the people's "gettin' their eyes open." Future details could remain fuzzy at that point, because it was important just to learn the basic truths of the One-Hoss Philosophy.

Wayland always returned to education. The belief in change through education—so strong in Ruskin, among the Populists, and in the mainstream of American culture—is the one theme that was most important to the One-Hoss Philosophy. Education is information. Perhaps for this reason, Wayland saved his greatest scorn for his competitors in the capitalist newspapers and for the people who believed what they read in them. His relationship to these newspapers was a curious one because, like everyone else, he relied on newspapers for news but used their contents as straw dogs in the hundreds of paragraphs he wrote in which he treated the contents of newspapers ironically. The standard press was essential, if only to point up his own valiant effort. He was moral; he looked to structural causes for events; he carried only that news which educated people; he was answerable only to himself for editorial content.

The capitalist papers, on the other hand, were immoral; they reported current events with no regard for underlying causes, carried sensational rather than useful material, and pandered to their advertisers. He called them the papers of the "plutes," the subsidized press. He railed against the newly reorganized Associated Press and against the news companies that controlled distribution in the cities and that would not handle the *Coming Nation.* "There were wise men when there were no papers and books cost a fortune. . . . The ignorance of today is the creation of the newspapers more than anything else. [Papers are like Roman Circuses.] Papers are cheaper than the circus and you pay the bill besides. . . . Every base idea, every false impression you have is traceable to the vileness and villainousness of the daily press in the pay of the monopolies of this country . . . stop reading the vile press of America and you will be wiser."[58] Elsewhere he included Congress for good measure: Congress and the capitalist press are both hopeless. One should make it "a policy to utterly ignore them." Wayland saw himself as trying to nurture a spirit "of independence and self-reliance which will wean the mass of men from their blind reliance upon papers published in the interests of special classes and which are paid special pleaders for the preservation of their class privileges."[59] Compare this to Ruskin's comments that the press was nothing more than so many "square leagues of dirtily printed falsehoods" and the Parliament, "a mouldering toy."[60]

Wayland pointed to specific sins of the press whenever he could. During the 1893 political campaign, he noted that in the Ohio gubernatorial election, one would not know from reading the daily press that there were any other candidates beside the Republican McKinley and the Democrat Neal. There was no mention of the People's party candidate, Brackett.[61] Wayland's indictment of the Associated Press was made on the basis that it would further weaken the freedom of the press because it would tend, by its very nature, to crowd out more substantial and more controversial articles.[62] When the daily press did find space for articles on topics such as socialism, "it is never," according to Alfred Shenstone Edwards, then the foreman in the composing room of the *Coming Nation,* "with an intention to inform the people of the benefits of socialism that the apologists for the present inadequate and brutal system write about it, but always with a studied and sometimes quite subtle purpose to mislead and deceive. Your average daily newspaper editor writes what he must write or lose his job. His misrepresentation of progressive ideas . . . must be proportionate to the growth of such ideas and the strength of such movements. Otherwise he is no longer serviceable to the class whose 'interests' are imperiled." Edwards concluded the article with a quote from Benjamin Harrison, once publisher of the *Indianapolis Journal:* "We must make the poor content and the rich secure."[63]

The force of the arguments made under the name of the One-Hoss Philosophy, as is clear from this last example, was often marred by obvious overstatement and the tendency to paint conditions in bold colors. Motives and causes were clear-cut to Wayland and to those whom he permitted to write in his columns. Accuracy was often sacrificed to make points, a tendency that was typical in the journalism of the period. Sometimes this inaccuracy could be traced to poor sources, which were almost invariably the standard press that Wayland attacked. But in many cases it was due to Wayland himself, who was perhaps too sure of his world view and was engaging in speculation that was just plain wrong. One example of Wayland's overdone style is his report of the bankruptcy of Mark Twain in 1894, which he must have read about in one of the papers of the day. Wayland concluded from his evidence that "Twain's genius made money and another who did not make the money has it without giving Twain anything for it."[64] Wayland did not take into consideration how Twain had lost the money—by engaging in the speculative business of backing new typesetting machinery—or why he had lost it— the result of Twain's own greed and ignorance. Although this kind of inaccurate generalization was prevalent throughout the popular press of the time, Wayland's inattention to accuracy and his willingness to jump to the most radical of conclusions, even on the slimmest of pretexts, would come back to haunt his publishing business in more prosperous times.

The One-Hoss Philosophy consisted of elements taken from Ruskin, from populism, from the experiences of a publisher and real-estate speculator, from the traditions of American dissent, and from beliefs in social progress and the power of education. It was propounded in a folksy way by a self-assured autodidact who was in a position to make himself heard. His ideas fell on fertile ground. Wayland's *Coming Nation* prospered, and it led its owner deeper into the American experience with radicalism, towards a tradition that has held continuing interest for every generation of American dissent: the commune. The lure of the quick fix, the practical experiment that would prove to all Americans who wanted to be shown that socialism could work and could work immediately, inspired Wayland to build the Cooperative Commonwealth with the paper that would educate the masses.

3
The Coming Nation

> It would surprise you if I printed the name of the president of a large manufacturer in Boston, Mass, who sends in subscriptions with "cooperation" on the corner of the letter. If you think there are no men of means and ability watching this movement, you are deceived. In fact, those who are doing the best work are men making money under the present social anarchy but are disgusted with it.
>
> —*J. A. Wayland*, Coming Nation, *1894*

In 1893, the first year of the publication of the *Coming Nation*, Wayland often described what he was thinking. In a typical passage, a front-page paragraph, he answered his various critics:

> I have several kicks at the typographic and other errors in the paper. Thank you. That shows you read the paper, anyhow. Maybe I don't write the purest English. Society robbed me of my school days, by forcing me to drudgery or starvation. I've tried hard to improve myself mentally in the last few years and may write passable English after awhile. But I think my statements are plain enough. To other inquirers let me state that the one-hoss is nearly forty years old, an American of revolutionary stock and has the right to do all the kicking against the infernal tyranny of capitalism that he pleases.[1]

His English was more than passable: it was witty and idiomatic, one of his strongest assets. Though the paper repeated the same themes, his style kept it from boring the steady reader.

A typical edition began with a page containing short paragraphs, which ranged over whatever topics had come across Wayland's desk during the previous week. In each small story, Wayland articulated conclusions and morals (for those who, he thought, might not draw conclusions themselves). The second page was almost invariably given over to reprints of his favorite authors, such as Ruskin, Bellamy, Gronlund, Henry George, Henry Demarest Lloyd, or some of the lesser reform writers, such as Stephen Maybell or the Reverend F. M. Sprague. On occasion, the second page was used, as the third page was, for longer articles on current topics, usually reprints. The fourth page often had more of the same paragraphs as the first, occasionally an article by a staff member other than Wayland, and small notices of publications that were for sale or news from other radical periodicals. Short reprints from the rest of the reform press and letters to the editor—"Shot and Shell from the *Coming Nation* Postal Card Battery"—could be found as a small column, on either the third or the final page.

This was the paper's format from 1893 to 1896. There were some typographical errors, but they were so slight that a reader accustomed to the sloppiness of a modern newspaper would probably not notice them. It was printed on the cheapest newsprint, the type was extremely small, and there was no attention to the quality of the printing or even the rudiments of design. At the start, the local printer in Greensburg handled the presswork until he had to choose between getting out his own paper or concentrating solely on Wayland's demand for more copies. The printer naturally chose his own paper, which soon failed; and Wayland took over the printing in his own shop, using a two-revolution Campbell press, for which he paid the startled salesman in gold, holding to his practice of avoiding the banking system. By the twenty-fifth week, Wayland's circulation had nearly reached his original goal of ten thousand subscribers, and he was almost breaking even. He started to project plans in dollars and cents, with the minute attention to detail that was not only a hallmark of the radical press but was also characteristic of the American press and Americans in general. Wayland's self-congratulatory tone and infectious enthusiasm come through in this front-page celebratory plan:

> I have demonstrated that a weekly reform paper at 50¢ a year, without advertising, can be made profitable. With the present facilities, I can handle 40,000 weekly, with economy. When it reaches that figure it will require a web perfecting machine that will print 10,000 folded papers an hour ... [$7,000 for the press]. With it, a circulation of 250,000 can be handled. That circulation can be had within three years but not at 50¢ a year. It will require 25¢ a year and 15¢ for 6 months. I can make that [change with?] 40,000 regular subscribers. Paper can be bought cheaper, making a savings. I estimate with such a circulation, paper and postage for 52 copies will cost 15¢, and the 10¢, the difference between 15¢ and 25¢ a year will pay the employees necessary to do the office work and pay them fair wages.[2]

This plan and similar plans that Wayland promoted in future years had a double effect. The first was to impress the readers with Wayland's sincerity and to interest them in helping the enterprise. The second result, which would be important to the fate of the paper and the direction of the movement, was to link the circulation of propaganda directly to the fortunes of radicalism in the United States. Wayland repeatedly claimed that educated voters would bring about the millennium. All one had to do was to get the right information to them, wake them up, and they would do the rest. This link proved to be the key both to the success of the paper and to the frustration of a movement that could not convince a majority, no matter how many books, pamphlets, leaflets, or copies of newspapers it could print and distribute.

In 1893, many people were just trying to stay alive. It was the first great depression in modern American history, part of a business cycle that was showing more and more frequent and devastating swings from prosperity to crash. There was both unemployment and deflation. The Populists had chalked up impressive totals in national and local elections. Ferment was all around. Wayland's visions of success in moving this mass of discontent to social action seemed possible, for his paper had quickly gone to the fore of the radical and Populist press of the time.

He was proud of and pleased with his decision to leave Colorado and return to Indiana. He told Colorado's Governor Waite:

> I am so tied down I can't get away at all. My office is without competent assistants. But it is a howling success. I feel confident of 25000 inside the first year. I had no idea that I could strike the hearts of so many people. If I desired to make money I have a picnic, but I shall spend in the cause of equal freedom all the profits in the business.
>
> The profits this week were nearly $10 a day, and I havent got started yet.[3]

Wayland thought his subscribers were mostly Populists, in spite of his open endorsement of socialism; and he was probably right. A later colleague said that the audience consisted of "typical Americans"— Protestants living on farms or in towns of less than ten thousand people, who went to public schools and read country weeklies—although Wayland had hoped to attract an urban audience.[4] That he did have many Populist readers was made clear when the publisher of the leading Populist paper, the *Non-Conformist* (which had passed from its original owners to a rich farmer who wanted to combine his paper with the *Coming Nation*) offered Wayland its editorship, an annual salary of $5,000, and half of the profits. Wayland "was having too much fun to change playgrounds," as he put it himself, so he refused the offer. He had other ideas for the *Coming Nation*.[5]

Wayland was in a hurry to change things, so he decided to accelerate the pace by showing people what could be done through practical experiment. The fact of his own success in building the paper was no doubt partly responsible for his decision to show the American people what socialism meant. He had not gone into publishing with the object of making money, which he already had in abundance; yet he was making money. He came up with a scheme to reinvest the profits from the paper in an experiment that would prove the practicability of his radicalism. In a statement that he kept in type for at least six months, he repeatedly published a summary of his views called "A Cooperative Village: He lives in vain who lives not for the good of all" (see app. 1), in which he propounded the idea of a commune based on the *Coming Nation*.[6]

The town would supply everything that the rich had: good schools, free libraries, parks; and it would provide security in the form of permanent employment. The funds for the founding of the town would come from the *Coming Nation*, which, Wayland hoped, would make a profit of $23,000 a year when it reached 100,000 readers. That money would buy 3000-4000 acres, and anyone who sold 200 subscriptions for the paper would be eligible to be a charter member.

The nature of the scheme, the slightly superior tone in which it was set forth, and the close attention to practical details are all evocative of the One-Hoss Philosophy. Wayland had to defend himself against those who thought what he was doing was impracticable. He pointed out, in the plan and in answer to a critic, that capitalists do similar things all of the time; but with typical irony he wrote that if the workers would toil for the benefit of the rich, wouldn't they be happier doing it for themselves?[7] He pointed out to another critic that the Standard Oil Company was a successful corporation, proving that cooperation could succeed![8] He claimed that his reading on the history of cooperative communities had shown him how to avoid failure by keeping wages equal, making everyone a director, and never going into debt. "If your by-laws are right, you will succeed. If wrong, a few men will soon have all you have made."[9] He waxed enthusiastic over the prospects, too, because they were being endorsed by wealthy people around the country: "It would surprise you if I printed the name of the president of a large manufacturer in Boston, Mass, who sends in subscriptions with 'cooperation' on the corner of the letter. If you think there are no men of means and ability watching this movement, you are deceived. In fact, those who are doing the best work are men making money under the present social anarchy but are disgusted with it."[10] Here Wayland again reveals some assumptions that inform his actions. The ability to succeed in business is a measure of a person's worth.

The attempt to create a utopia, although Wayland's form of it was rather unusual, was true to a general intellectual style that had held sway in America almost without interruption from the earliest days of the Republic.[11] The virgin country had always seemed to afford the possibility for perfection. Building cooperative settlements had proved to be one of the stabler industries in American history. In the 1890s alone, at least thirty-four colonies were started, many, like Wayland's, inspired by the utopian thought of Bellamy.[12] The commune idea was also one of Ruskin's ideas: he had set up the Guild of St. George, an attempt to put into practice some of his thoughts on the nature of utopian society and to which the publication of *Fors Clavigera* was directed. The guild aimed at worker resettlement and land reclamation in an attempt to reconstruct an agrarian society, but it succeeded only in holding a few acres of ground and a couple of cottages and in building a museum.[13]

Wayland's utopia was designed to be much more practical and industrial. At the heart of the scheme was the money-producing *Coming Nation*—the centerpiece which was supposed to attract other industries. Wayland announced that a plant from Mizpah, New Jersey, which manufactured overalls, was ready to join in; and it was already being run on cooperative lines.[14] He had big plans for the colony. He added a column called "Cooperative Village Jottings," in which he recorded his musings about the project: the colonists would make all of their own clothing; no children would be starving at Christmas; there would be a fruit cannery for the women and a park for recreation in the center of town, complete with a palatial Swiss-style summer residence for all.[15] "When we get settled in the colony I expect to do as extensive and fine printing as Harper Bros. We shall have just as fine material and knock out as elegant work. I have already some ten publications to start with."[16] It was Wayland's version of utopia, which he would supervise from the columns of his newspaper.

On Wayland's road to paradise, the paradoxes abound. In a brochure that Wayland circulated about "A Cooperative Town," he ran these two sentences together: ". . . with this one principle, that no member shall have more power or influence in the organization than any other, other than the balance are willing to concede him for his purity and knowledge. This is one principle that I shall insist on." It was Wayland who was setting the ground rules, Wayland who was putting up the money, and Wayland who was dreaming the contradictory dreams: "When the title is acquired, the grounds shall be at once [provided with] water service, sewers, lights and power at the least possible expense. Yes, power, for all wives will have small dynamos for doing much work that is now done by 'elbow grease.' " Wayland was going to make women's lives easier for them, within the context of their traditional roles. But women would also receive equal pay for equal work and would have an equal voice in the workings of the settlement.[17]

It is easy to see now that Wayland's plan had little chance to succeed. Even at the beginning, there were problems that might have stopped a less optimistic person. Some of the prerequisites that Wayland had set were never fulfilled. The most important, perhaps, was the fact that the circulation of the paper never did reach the magic figure of one hundred thousand. Even so, the search for land was begun, but it did not go well. Several sites were suggested and rejected, not by a committee, as envisioned in the plan, but by Wayland himself, often in conflict with the opinion of his agent. There were worse problems with the staff, which had grown by the end of the first year to include seven full-time people, in addition to Wayland's brother-in-law Charley Bevan. Wayland was paying a wage of $12 a week to each person, and he estimated that he was making about $8 a week on their labor. That money was supposed to be going to the colony, but it remained under Wayland's control. Of the staff, the most important was A. S. Edwards, whom Wayland brought to the paper in early January, 1894, from Minneapolis, where he had been active with the Knights of Labor as a speaker and writer. Edwards was made foreman of the composing room; he also wrote several articles (signing them "One in the Printery') and was highly praised by Wayland in May, when Edwards's name was added to the masthead as associate editor. Edwards proved to be a powerful critic of Wayland's methods.[18]

Two months after Edwards's promotion, Wayland precipitated the move of the paper to a location near Tennessee City, Tennessee, to land that his agent had previously reported as being poor, and abandoned Edwards and some other dissident staff members. Wayland then introduced more changes into the plan for the colony. The prerequisite for families who wanted to join after the charter group had been formed was no longer two hundred subscriptions; it was now $500 in cash. The reason for moving out in July was not made clear at the time, but the whole situation in Greensburg had become untenable for Wayland. He and his family, at least according to his own account, had become the target of growing hostility from their small-town neighbors.

Even more important was a full-scale staff revolt, led by Edwards, which culminated in a suit against Wayland for the staff's share in the profits of the paper. The immediate cause of the suit may have been Wayland's decision to accept the poor land in Tennessee. Wayland probably did so in order to speed up the process of removal and also because it was cheap. Edwards's name was removed from the masthead, again without public explanation; and unknown to readers, Edwards and his fellow claimants

The first Ruskin settlement, Ruskin, Tennessee. From the American Fabian *(New York), vol. 3, no. 4 (April, 1897), p. 1.*

were fired. In July the first colonists, who were not aware of the hidden maneuvering, began to arrive at the backwoods location, with Wayland and the press following soon after. Edwards stayed behind in Greensburg to launch a new paper, *Freeland*, in the same month that Wayland left. The new paper limped through its first year of publication, while the *Coming Nation* continued to flourish, at least in terms of its circulation.[19]

Wayland called the colony Ruskin.[20] It began inauspiciously: there was a staff crisis, and a new paper was competing with the *Coming Nation*. Some colony members from the start suspected that Wayland, in order to get a reduced price, had made a deal to "boom" the land with the Chicago-based land syndicate that owned most of the area. By bringing in settlers, the remaining land would, of course, grow in value. Wayland did not reveal all of these problems at the outset, thus setting a bad precedent for the paper and for the readers. Wayland's stated reason for publishing was a shared sense of outrage at existing conditions, a sense of the need for reform that he shared with his reading public, reform that would come only with complete candor and the responsibility to tell the truth to the reader. Wayland had told his readers that he used the first person singular because he spoke only for himself. If they didn't like what he wrote, at least they knew where he stood. The publication of subscribers' names and the disclosure of the financial condition of the paper on a weekly basis were other ways to tell the readers that they could trust the One Hoss. He was not taking any advertising, he was depending on the readers to support the endeavor, and the readers were repaying him with their trust.

Wayland was not keeping that trust. He never fully admitted in public what the conditions were at the time of the founding of the colony and only reported what happened later in the history of the colony in a desultory fashion.[21] And he never mentioned what happened between him and Edwards. Wayland's ostracism in Greensburg, which a later memoir gave as the reason for starting the colony, was kept from readers, who were busy collecting subscriptions or, later, the $500 necessary for a family membership.[22] When he left the colony after one year, he was again less than candid. He complained privately to the Chicago reformer Henry Demarest Lloyd about what he thought was really going on at Ruskin, but he waited to make charges in his new newspaper, the *Appeal to Reason*, until six more months had passed. Wayland may have been acting out of fear that the movement would suffer from washing its dirty laundry in public and from a Victorian sense of restraint, but indeed he must also have been concerned about his own part in the drama. Wherever the blame lies, and it appears to lie at Wayland's door, this conduct was not consistent with the aims and goals of a radical movement and a radical newspaper, which were to usher in a new age.

A. S. Edwards was not so reticent. His first issue of *Freeland* contained a detailed indictment of Wayland's character, business practices, and ethics. Although from an obviously interested party and a hostile one at that, it was the most complete critical account of Wayland that was ever published. As such, it deserves a close look. Edwards claimed to be speaking for himself and two other staff members who had withdrawn from the enterprise. He charged "that there has at no time been, nor is there now, any promise of real cooperation under J. A. Wayland's management." An example that Edwards gave to prove his contention was an incident involving wages and ownership. One staff member was promised profit sharing; later, this promise was amended to a share in the business and the understanding that the employee's contribution to the paper would be recognized as his ticket to Ruskin. But Wayland later assigned ninety-seven of the one hundred shares of the paper to his wife and gave only one share to the staff member, who was then paid off at its face value of $30, instead of the $1,000 that Wayland himself had claimed as the actual value of the stock. Edwards characterized Wayland as someone who would turn away from Ruskin colony "a penniless man with the heart of Christ and the brain of Plato to make room for a natural fool with $500." Edwards further claimed that Wayland lacked the education to be able to cooperate successfully, that he took advantage of his staff, that he was money mad, and that his chief aim was the appearance of always being right. Edwards pointed out instances of false statements in the *Coming Nation:* Wayland said that he had given the office to the association, though the Ruskin Cooperative Associa-

A stock certificate in the Coming Nation Publishing Company, in the name of Mrs. Etta B. Wayland. Courtesy of Virginia Lashley.

tion did not yet exist, and that he had ten publications to begin work with when they got to Tennessee, but these existed only in Wayland's imagination, according to Edwards.

Edwards showed that people who did the same work in the office were paid different wages. He said that Wayland told other Greensburg people that those who did not cooperate with him according to his ideas would be bought out and would then work for him. Edwards pointed out that Wayland had bought out a business that had been organized by his brother-in-law and another staffer after it started to show a small profit. Edwards claimed that Wayland had wasted large sums of money, especially by purchasing an expensive press (probably the one that he boasted he had bought with gold) that did not work. Lastly, Edwards took credit both for naming the colony and for writing its bylaws.[23]

These allegations, both petty and serious, ring true, especially when they are compared with the course of subsequent events. But it should be kept in mind that Edwards himself was not free from suspicion, especially because within a year he would take over the *Coming Na-*

tion. Some of the charges sound like pure spite, but others, especially those that detail Wayland's labor practices and his desire for control, seem accurate. The two men had different backgrounds: Edwards came out of the labor movement, while Wayland came to socialism through study and as an employer, which no doubt affected the way the two looked at things. Both appealed to H. D. Lloyd: Edwards for money to keep his struggling paper *Freeland* afloat, and Wayland, to condemn Edwards as a scoundrel who still owed Wayland the money that he had borrowed to bring his family from Minneapolis to Greensburg. Edwards's allegations, though made publicly, were probably not widely read at the time. Even if they had been, they probably would not have deterred prospective colonists from arriving at Ruskin and staying. Many had no other place to go, because of their investment and because of the lack of opportunities. There was unprecedented unemployment in the country as a result of the Panic of 1893. Labor unrest was manifested by the Pullman strike in Chicago, which was put down harshly and violently by the federal government, and by marches on Washington by armies of the unemployed.[24] Wayland stayed at the colony exactly one year, although he was gone for a while during the first month and again in March, 1895, when he was traveling.[25] It was a tempestuous year which featured at least two struggles over control of the colony's chief asset, the newspaper.

None of the problems was publicized in the paper, following the custom that Wayland had already established. To the outside world, it seemed as if all was well in paradise. It is not easy now to get at the truth of what happened during that first year, and it is even less easy to do so for the ensuing six years of the colony's existence. From the participants in the life of the colony, there are at least six different versions of the conflicts that led to its dissolution.[26] The crisis that most people write about was not the Wayland "problem"; it was the eventual splits, which caused lawsuits that brought about the windup of the Ruskin Cooperative Association's affairs in Tennessee. Whatever its faults, however, Ruskin proved to be a formative and vital part of the lives of many people, and even as late as 1961, the question of what caused its downfall was still agitating the mind of the last living adult member.[27]

The choice of the site, everyone agreed, was bad. The land was virtually untillable, and its one apparent asset, its extensive timber holdings, was not of commercial grade. It was located near a town—actually an incorporated city—Tennessee City, Tennessee, about sixty miles west of Nashville. Though virtually deserted, the town did have a post office and a railroad station, the two requirements for publishing the paper. The colony was incorporated under Tennessee law as a stock company, organized under a mining and manufacturing charter, with charter members contributing either $500 or its equivalent in goods or subscriptions. Each family received one share of stock for the husband, and most wives got an additional free share. The company, known as the Ruskin Cooperative Association, elected Wayland president by a vote of the twenty-seven male members who constituted the charter group. By fall, there were about one hundred residents and sixty thousand subscribers to the paper.

The colonists did not have an easy time of it. Those who had come first were apparently city dwellers, most of whom were artisans by profession. The earliest arrivals had erected a plant for the paper, which was installed in August. There was a shabby hotel, built by the Chicago developers, where some of the colonists, especially the printers, were housed to be near their work. Most stayed in roughly built shanties, which were erected on the colony site a few miles from the town. These homes were made out of green lumber, which shrank as the weather turned cold. The cracks in the walls were filled in with back copies of the newspaper.

The first crisis came over the ownership of the paper. Apparently, Wayland told the shareholders in October that he was giving the association "all the material and goodwill of the *Coming Nation*, the building and money."[28] The minutes of the October 31 meeting—shareholders were meeting weekly at this time—hinted darkly at unspecified recriminations between Wayland and another member of the colony.[29] In late November the proposal was made that all male members fill out time slips.[30]

Under the original law of incorporation, there was a question of whether the association could actually own and publish a newspaper. Wayland then proposed, on December 26, that he lease the publication from the association for $50 a month and take on the existing obligations, which included $10,000 in unfulfilled subscriptions and a payroll of $150 a week. According to the official history of the colony, and this is partly borne out by the minutes, the colonists felt that they could not do without Wayland, so they accepted his proposal by an overwhelming vote. Three members, including the one whose fight with Wayland was mentioned in the minutes, promptly made known their intention to resign, and others soon followed their example. Instead of yielding the colony $23,000 a year that Wayland had predicted when the paper hit the one-hundred-thousand circulation mark, the *Coming Nation* was now paying the colony only rent and wages.[31]

Ruskin continued to sustain itself through the addition of new members at the price of $500 a family, while the *Coming Nation* continued to appear regularly. The final crisis for Wayland and his family came in July, 1895. Outwardly, the only indications of trouble were two articles: one in May reported that people who left Ruskin "telling tales may have left because they were not prepared to work hard"; another in June said Wayland was annoyed because "much of [his] time has been called to colony affairs." Two weeks later, the *Coming Nation* reported that the business manager had quit the printery and had moved to the construction unit. For the next two weeks the "Notes from Ruskin" column was not printed, and then, on July 27, a short statement announced that "by mutual consent, Mr. J. A. Wayland has severed his connection with the *Coming Nation* and the Ruskin Cooperative Association." The next week brought this pair of explanations:

GOOD BYE!

With this issue my association with *The Coming Nation*, child of my brain and heart, ceases. I will not worry you with what has led up to this severance. As I have not been informed who will be my successor, I cannot, therefore, introduce him or her. As to my future course, it is not definitely mapped out, but as soon as I can find a suitable location and create a medium for my pen, you will find my little banner in the thickest of the fight for economic liberty of the masses, and exhorting your hearty assistance.

SALUTATION

The sudden retirement of Brother J. A. Wayland from the Ruskin Cooperative Colony and the editorship of the *Coming Nation*, is an event that will occasion surprise among the readers and friends all over the country.

Thousands of enemies of socialism will triumphantly exclaim "I told you so" "Ruskin is busted" "It's always the way with colonies," and so on.

We wish it distinctly understood that Ruskin is not "busted." That *The Coming Nation*, though it will no longer bear the imprint of J. A. Wayland's genius, and readers may, possibly, miss the caustic style of "One Hoss," yet the paper will continue to be the exponent of true socialism, with the added advantage that its conductors will be PRACTICALLY as well as *theoretically,* socialists.[32]

The immediate cause of Wayland's exit was the colonists' claim to ownership of the $5,000 printing press. This demand was almost certainly instigated by A. S. Edwards back in Greensburg.[33] After demands and counterdemands, Wayland, his wife, his brother-in-law Bevan, and Bevan's wife left Ruskin. The deal that they agreed to turned the paper over to the colony in return for several thousand dollars, to be paid by January, 1896. Their claims on the association (either $2,000 or $3,500) were paid off by January, 1896.[34] Edwards arrived on the next train, took over the paper without missing an issue, and was voted into the association without having to pay the $500 initiation fee.[35] The paper changed very little. A letter from the *Non-Conformist* was published in August, along with several others, which said that their authors had examined the last issue closely to see if the *Coming Nation* had deteriorated and found that it had not.[36]

Nor did Wayland miss a beat. Within a month of his removal, he had started a new paper in Kansas City, Missouri, the *Appeal to Reason*. But the *Coming Nation* refused to die. Edwards continued to carry on Wayland's practices in almost every way, and the *Coming Nation* continued to be more successful than the new *Appeal to Reason* for the next two years. Wayland refrained for a while from commenting on the *Coming Nation* in his new organ, probably hoping that the paper and the community would fail, so that he could regain control.

Only once during the two years that the *Coming Nation* was in the ascendance did the two papers quarrel, and the fight was caused by the fact that the colony managed to pay off its debt to Wayland in January, 1896. This upset and surprised Wayland, who claimed that the colony had many members who wanted to leave but who were waiting to be paid and that the public was being fooled into thinking that the paper was being run cooperatively.[37] "It has degenerated into a mere confidence game."[38] The *Coming Nation* responded by answering the charges in some detail, accusing Wayland of trying to ruin the colony.[39] At the time, the circulation of Wayland's *Appeal* stood at fifteen thousand; the *Coming Nation* had from two to four times as many readers.

The colony limped into 1896 and began to prosper. Ruskin retained the initial land purchase, but it also bought more land several miles away in a fertile valley, which, in addition to providing good farming, had two large caves, which were suitable for cold storage and for some recreational and manufacturing activities. The colonists erected permanent buildings at the new site, including an impressive printery, which still stands. New members continued to be admitted. The circulation of the paper remained respectable, although it dropped Wayland's practice of printing the weekly totals. The colony purchased new type, cleaned up the design of the paper, and started to commission articles from outside correspondents. But the *Coming Nation* retained the essence of the One-Hoss Philosophy, with Edwards doing a convincing imitation of Wayland's paragraphs, although he emphasized cooperative living more than political action. This change in tone would grow stronger as the century drew to a close.

The height of the colony's fortunes, and of the paper's influence, was reached in the spring and summer of the following year, 1897. In April

The entrance to the Grand Cave (left); the Grand Cave serving as a warehouse at the second location of the Ruskin Cooperative Association (right). From Scientific American, *vol. 81, no. 6 (August 5, 1899), p. 89.*

the colony printed a fourth-anniversary issue (dated from the first issue of the *Coming Nation,* not the founding of the colony), which contained a history of and a celebration of Ruskin. It also included a detailed account of the differences between the colonists and Wayland, which it managed to discuss, in addition to the founding and first two years of the paper, without once mentioning Wayland's name.[40] The crops were good, and the annual local celebration of Independence Day, which area residents had long held in the big cave on the colony site, was sponsored there by the colonists and drew unprecedented numbers. The paper engineered the first national conference on cooperation, held in St. Louis. The conference endorsed a national organization, the Brotherhood of the Cooperative Commonwealth (BCC), which the Ruskin Association had founded in August, 1896. Its stated aim was to foster socialism through the idea of colonies.[41] Also that summer, the cornerstone of the Ruskin College of the New Economy was laid in an impressive ceremony featuring an address by H. D. Lloyd. Ruskin was riding high. It was probably the most closely watched of all the socialist experiments of the time.[42] It seemed to be in excellent financial health. It had attracted Debs, then the most popular figure in radical circles because of his role in the Pullman strike; and it celebrated his release from Woodstock Jail in November, 1895, with a special edition. The *Coming Nation* provided one of the main forums for Debs after his conversion to socialism in January, 1897, and it welcomed him as the national organizer of the BCC.[43]

That was what readers saw in the paper. In fact, the picture was not so rosy. From the start the colony's financial situation was hopeless. Only the addition of new members and their infusion of capital, the profits

of the paper (which were probably not high), and perhaps most important, a constant stream of gifts from outside supporters kept them going. They had started several small manufacturing industries, such as
making brooms, chewing gum, and cereal coffee; but these products probably cost more to make than they returned in income. Crops were grown
for variety, but staple items such as grain, potatoes, and beef had to be
purchased by the carload.[44] As long as new members came in, as long
as the public continued to support what it thought was a highly successful socialist experiment, and as long as there were not too many
mouths to feed, things could appear to be sound. The leadership turned
down requests to perform more difficult but more remunerative work,
such as using their steam laundry facilities to do work for a nearby college or growing celery as a cash crop for winter sale in the north. The
debt on the new land remained a constant threat to the security of the
community, as spare cash was diverted away from payments to what
many considered frills instead of improving the self-sufficiency of the colony in agricultural areas. A standard feature of the paper, the "Colony
Notes," appeared faithfully each week and informed the public of the
progress of the colony. Without a hint of discord, and written in an engaging style by the colony's physician, the Notes put many in the outside
world on an intimate basis with the colonists, allowing the former to
share with the Ruskinites their communal life, without having to deal
with the realities of backwoods living and without knowing what was
really going on.

Things started to unravel in the winter of 1897/98. With new members
coming in continually, some brought new ideas, in addition to their $500.
One small group advocated anarchism and "free love," or at least discussed them favorably. The paper published articles that, while not actually advocating anarchism, at least discussed it rationally.[45] Editor Edwards was drawn into this group. Ironically, almost three years to the
day after Wayland had made his first demand for control of the paper
at Ruskin, Edwards made a similar demand. The leaders were hostile
to this move, and Edwards lost the fight. Therefore he and the "anarchists" left the colony in the spring of 1898, ostensibly on a vacation and
subscription-gathering trip. At about the same time, the colony leaders
were silently burying the idea of Ruskin College (they were probably
afraid of losing influence within the colony if a number of students and
professors came to town). The leaders diverted funds that the colony had
been collecting for a college building fund.[46]

Edwards never returned, though the colonists had not heard the last
of him. Herbert Casson, the leader of the Lynn, Massachusetts, Labor
Church, was engaged to succeed Edwards as editor. His entrance into
Ruskin had been prepared by the articles that he had written almost

Herbert N. Casson. From the American Fabian
(New York), vol. 4, no. 1 (January, 1898), p. 1.

weekly for the paper. At about the same time, the feminist editor and
writer Lydia Kingsmill Commander also came to Ruskin to begin a
women's column. Her column, along with another column for children,
which was edited by Casson, marked a fresh departure for the paper. But
most of Edwards's and Wayland's influence remained. A number of articles, or letters, were still published on visitors' impressions of Ruskin.
Municipal ownership, which had merited a special issue under Edwards,[47]
got another from Casson.[48] "Direct Legislation," an idea that had wide
support in the reform press, remained a feature column. The paper continued to publish commissioned pieces and an occasional column that
appeared in Populist newspapers, "Musing of the Mossback," which was
edited by Bige Eddy, a witty resident of the Northwest. Commander's
column was clearly the greatest innovation: for the first time, women's
issues were expressed regularly in the context of a general radical paper.
Wittier than either Edwards's or the somewhat ponderous Casson's,
Commander's writing drew much comment. When Casson was in-
capacitated with typhoid fever throughout the fall of 1898, Commander

edited the paper. As a result of her influence, the *Coming Nation* published a special women's issue in early 1899.[49]

By the end of 1898, however, there were some signs that the paper was deteriorating in quality and in circulation. A special issue on Ruskin was essentially a reprint of the 1897 number.[50] The paper had always previously managed to avoid even the mention of circulation difficulties, but now they became front-page news.[51] Casson did not like the hard conditions at the colony. His attack of typhoid fever soured him, as did the food and the nature of the accommodations. Although he had early aligned himself with the anticollege group, he soon fell out with those who had invited him to come as editor. The winter of 1898/99 brought all of the contending forces to a confrontation. The old charter group, which had held power until that winter, found itself outnumbered. It was pressed to provide shares for the wives of the later members, as it had done for the first group of wives. The charter of the association made it subject to suit by any of its stockholders, and both sides took their cases to court. In the midst of this strife, Casson left, taking Lydia Commander with him, after a festive wedding at the colony. It was probably the last occasion to celebrate.

While the Cassons were throwing themselves into the reelection campaign of Toledo's progressive Mayor Samuel M. ("Golden Rule") Jones, former editor Edwards joined the charter group in filing the suit that brought the whole issue to a head; it revived the old charge that the colony could not legally publish a newspaper. The suit went on to repudiate the socialist principles upon which the colony was founded. Edwards and his friends defended themselves on the grounds that the new leaders of the colony were bankrupting it and that this was the only action that they could take to salvage what they could before inevitable insolvency. In fact, neither side was looking out for the best interests of Ruskin; people on both sides saw the colony as a way to exercise power and to live out their own dreams. A court-appointed receiver wound up the affairs of the colony, which had almost nothing to show after five years of work.[52]

The majority of the group decided to start over again. They drafted new bylaws, renamed themselves the Ruskin Commonwealth and scraped together enough money to buy the *Coming Nation* and some of the cottage industries that they had been conducting. They joined forces with another failing colony and moved to its land in Georgia. Starting over again in the fall of 1899, the leaders who had lost the suit against the old charter group proved their incompetence: they planted the wrong crops, thus defying both local advice and pleas from the most recent arrivals—those who had the least education, capital, and knowledge of socialist principles but who had the strongest desire to see the colony succeed.

As the colony started to fail for the second and final time, the quality of the paper also declined. Special articles disappeared, the number of subscribers plummeted, and the pages were filled with matter clipped from other papers. With half of the colonists who had come to Georgia scattered, a last faction took over the paper in early 1901. These people were the first to make public in the pages of the paper the whole story of the failure of the Ruskin experiment in the "Secret History," and they openly reported what was currently happening in a thoroughly revised "Colony Notes." Unfortunately, the revelations were the best thing that they wrote: the paper went from bad to worse. A last-ditch effort to save the paper from the hands of creditors, who were moving in to seize what was left of the colony's assets, was made by selling it to a group of local businessmen. But that also failed, as had an experiment with advertising conducted during the preceding year. On July 27, 1901, the last issue of the Ruskin Commonwealth's *Coming Nation* was published. The colony's affairs were wound up completely by September. The *Coming Nation*, however, would soon rise again (see chap. 7).

It is no wonder that the Ruskin Colony has had so many different historians with so many different points of view. Each has tried to see it as noble experiment somehow gone wrong, and all have found ready scapegoats. None of the people involved in Ruskin wanted to question the basic assumptions of the charter or even the reasons for starting the whole thing in the first place, because that would have called into question their own judgment. Wayland produced the incredible statement that the colony had failed because there were no more nonsocialists around to convert to socialism, so they had resorted to attacking one another. His friends pointed to the experience as an important one for the socialist movement because it drove the idea of communes out of Wayland's system. This kind of reasoning assumes that the Ruskin Commonwealth actually put some form of socialism into practice. In reality, the colony was not much more than an attempt at paternalistic capitalism, one that had more in common with company towns than with any other kind of organization. Wayland himself had no intention of changing his way of life; he opposed the introduction of any communal features. It was not until after he had left that the colonists were able to build even a communal dining room. The last group of colonists was the only one that defended Wayland's attempts to control the paper and the colony because they shared with him the conviction that the subsequent leaders of the colony were incompetent managers. But even allowing this reasonable explanation of Wayland's actions, one wonders to what extent he ever intended to cooperate at all. Perhaps he just wanted a pleasant place to live in, where he would be respected as the patriarch, writing the paper, basking in the love of his captive work force, and proving that socialized industry could work, without changing conventional social relationships.

Attempting to build a backwoods utopia, which was removed from the benefits of capitalism, making inferior products, and living in substandard housing, Ruskin was the antithesis of a socialist ideal, which would bring modern productive capacity under the control of the people for all to share. Ruskin was an undercapitalized town with one major industry. Conflict over control of the colony and the newspaper served to point out weaknesses in the people who had made it their life's work to reform American society. The pettiness, poor management, and rank hypocrisy that surfaced should have given pause. Even granting the notions that Ruskin was practicing socialism and that Ruskin was not just a mistake, many should have been led to conclude that it would not work. Granting the opposite assumption—namely, that socialism is not possible on a small scale in a capitalist environment—then the judgment of these leaders of the American movement should have been severely questioned. Only once, and unconsciously at that, did later editors of the *Coming Nation* come close to recognizing in print the problems shared by Wayland, Edwards, Casson, and, by extension, the supporters of their papers. Unfortunately, the editors could not, without calling into question their own and the movement's existence, make the connection to what they themselves were doing. In replying to a criticism of Ruskin made by Casson, which Wayland published in the *Appeal to Reason* about a year after Casson had left the colony, the *Coming Nation* concluded: "Casson is not a fakir. He is an impulsive, active propagandist. Everytime he reaches a new conclusion, he is cocksure it is the absolute truth, and he wants to tell the whole world about it. He now BELIEVES colonies are a failure, so he states it as a fact."[53]

What was said of Casson could also be said of Wayland. Wayland had once been sure that colonies were the right way; then he had learned by experience that they would not work. This change in policy did not discredit him in the eyes of his readers, and he tossed off the whole incident in the first *Appeal to Reason* by remarking: "We all make mistakes when we are weak and ignorant, but let us not linger with them when we discover them." Wayland went right back into the field by publishing the *Appeal to Reason*; Edwards went right back into the field as editor of the *Social Democratic Herald*, the paper of the Milwaukee socialists; and Casson went right back into the field by campaigning for progressive reforms in Toledo, Ohio. Wayland was to make more mistakes on the way, most of which would fall into the same categories as the Ruskin experiment. Tied as he was to the culture in which he was brought up, he relied on instinct to guide him; but this often clashed with socialist principles. The problem with making mistakes, for a radical socialist editor, was of a greater magnitude than for a newspaper that just attempted to report current events. For a movement that claimed to have the answers for the country's economic and social problems, the repetition of errors would surely work to discredit what was supposed to be a scientific theory. Wayland's first big mistake—colonization—was to be repeated in a bigger way a few years later by Eugene Debs. Many had taken that road before J. A. did; it was almost a badge of experience in the movement. Wayland would now turn his attention fully to political action.[54]

4

The Appeal to Reason

The one-hoss at no time contemplated supporting anybody whom the democrats would nominate on any kind of platform. . . . It [the *Appeal*] feels that from now forward it can do more good by supporting a purely socialist party than any other course. There were conditions when it could do greater good in supporting the people's party, but since it died the field of socialism is the place to do effective work. . . . A small section of earnest men is of more worth than a large following of a heterogeneous aggregation of uneducated voters.

—*J. A. Wayland*, Appeal to Reason, *1896*

Mary Harris ("Mother") Jones, a union organizer and folk hero of the socialist movement, has left the only eyewitness account of the founding of the *Appeal to Reason*. Writing thirty years after the event and mixing up the dates a little, Mother Jones recalled that she had declined an invitation to join the Ruskin Colony when it was being organized because she felt that communes succeeded only when they were led by strong religious figures. When Wayland left the colony and went to Kansas City, Missouri, in August, 1895, Jones found him despondent. She and three white-collar workers urged Wayland to start another paper, and one of them suggested the title "Appeal to Reason."

Wayland demurred: "But we have no subscribers." Mother Jones said she would get them. After Wayland had produced a limited first edition, she took copies to Omaha and sold subscriptions to nearly every young soldier at the federal barracks and to many others at the Omaha City Hall. She gathered "several hundred subscriptions all together and the paper was launched."[1] According to another, though secondhand account, Wayland wanted to call the newspaper "Wayland's Weekly," but he was dissuaded by an old German socialist who said: "Give it a name that in time will be better known than the man who made it."[2] The first issue of the *Appeal to Reason* was published on August 31, 1895, in Kansas City, Missouri, from the Radical Cigar and Book Store. In addition to Mother Jones's help, a Philadelphia social reformer, Dr. Charles Fayette

Taylor, bought forty-seven hundred subscriptions to distribute to physicians throughout the country.[3]

Even with these boosters, Wayland was not in a strong position. The *Coming Nation* dominated the field of socialist publishing, and the Populist press was reaching its peak. In most ways, the *Appeal* had little to offer to the reader who already subscribed to the *Coming Nation*. At the beginning of the *Appeal*'s life, there was almost no difference between the two newspapers. Both supported direct legislation, a panacea for the ills of society, which, they believed, would help usher in socialism by allowing the people to write their own laws. Both papers used columns by Eltweed Pomeroy, a New Jersey industrialist who edited his own direct-legislation newsletter and provided columns on the subject to a number of socialist and Populist newspapers. Both papers employed Wayland's paragraph style, both supported Eugene Debs, both subscribed to the One-Hoss Philosophy. The *Coming Nation* was well established, so it had no need to drum up circulation the way that Wayland, who was starting over from scratch, had to do. One of his first campaigns was to "Spread the Light" into the nation's barbershops. Again he looked forward to the magical one-hundred-thousand circulation that he had envisioned for the *Coming Nation* but had never reached.

The circulation did not come during the first year, one of dismal failure for Wayland; it did not rise above twenty-five thousand. Wayland admitted having lost about a thousand dollars after six months. He even offered commissions to people who solicited subscriptions, but without noticeable success. Probably in an effort to save on rent, he moved the office to Kansas City, Kansas, in October, 1896. He discontinued his practice of printing information about circulation. Finally, on October 24, he announced that the paper would suspend for a week because attention had to be given to building up the number of readers. At the bottom of the last page of that issue, he printed this cryptic note: "I am a printer, editor, solicitor. Do you need either, or all three? If so, write me and we'll not let wages be an obstacle. Best of references. Situation in a country town preferred." There were no issues of the *Appeal to Reason* for the next three and a half months.[4]

There was more to Wayland's initial failure than the competition from the *Coming Nation*, although that was a big factor. As the *Coming Nation* improved in design and content, the *Appeal* seemed to weaken. Wayland may just have been biding his time, waiting for Ruskin Colony to fail. But when it did not, and especially when it paid off its debt to him in January, 1896, his heart went out of his effort. During that first year, the *Appeal*, instead of its usual contents, included long letters, reprints from other publications, and republished material that Wayland

MAKES A WILD THREAT.

The Journal at Dothan, Ala., says that if ever the Socialists elect a president and senate and house they will not be permitted to fill the places—that the men who own property will at once begin to shoot, hang and imprison every Socialist. The poor fool who wrote that did not stop to consider that the propertyless outnumber the property class ten to one—but they do. And that men who announce that they will not abide by the majority or even the plurality but kill rather than submit, are public enemies that better deserve a prison than editing a paper. Still, they are harmless, as they haven't sense enough to convince any person that murder is better than legal order—except a very few. But it shows what fools uphold a social system that has robbery for its basic principle. The editors of that paper are poor; their paper shows it; they are simply as I was thirty years ago—a poor country printer who thought that if my party did not get the offices so I could hold the county printing that the U. S. would soon cease doing business. They will get wiser with time and Socialist agitation.

A typical one-hoss paragraph.
Appeal to Reason, *January 2, 1904.*

had long since used in the *Coming Nation*.[5] A general feeling of dejection pervaded the paper, especially just before the suspension.[6] The problem could also be traced to the first political crisis that the One-Hoss Philosophy had to face. The issue was one that Wayland had successfully straddled for at least five years, since he first had been converted to socialism. Before the summer of 1896, Wayland could support both populism and socialism. Now that the Populists were moving towards fusion with the Democrats over the issue of the free coinage of silver, he had to make a choice. It was not easy for him. The One-Hoss Philosophy seemed to be capable of transcending everyday politics and of supporting not just one party but, rather, the cause of socialism in its differing manifestations. This Wayland shared with Ruskin in his advocacy of generalities, making it difficult to pin either of them down to any one doctrine which might eventually be discredited. But for a long time, Wayland, along with Gronlund, had advocated political action.

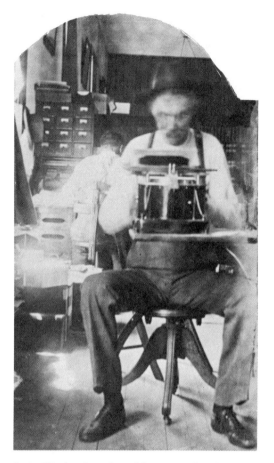

J. A. Wayland at the addressograph, 1898.
Courtesy of the J. A. Wayland Collection,
Pittsburg State University.

Schemes such as colonization, which had failed in the editor's mind, or direct legislation, which he had supported off and on for more than a decade, did not answer the question of whom to vote for. He often challenged his working-class readers who engaged in strikes but who voted for capitalist parties to change their ways. If you should not vote for the Democrats or the Republicans and if the ballot box was the way to the cooperative commonwealth, should you vote for the People's party or for the Socialist Labor party (SLP)?

For a socialist the answer should have been obvious. But Wayland had supported the People's party since its inception and only hesitantly had given his support to the SLP. He was not alone in his hesitation. (Gronlund, for one, was a member but quit in disgust; Herbert Casson was kicked out.) Much of it had to do with the nature of the party and its leader, Daniel DeLeon.

A Columbia University lecturer in international law during the 1880s, DeLeon was a native of the Dutch West Indies, was a veteran of the Nationalist Clubs, and was active in Henry George's campaign for mayor of New York City in 1886. In 1890, DeLeon converted to Marxism, joined the SLP, and in 1891 took over the party's English-language newspaper, formerly the *Workman's Advocate* and now the *People*, which aimed at broadening the base of support for the mostly German and heavily Jewish party. DeLeon, who claimed he was from a wealthy, aristocratic Spanish family, was almost certainly of Jewish origin. He had spent time in Europe, was fluent in several languages and had a good grounding in several subjects aside from the law. He had been a practicing attorney in Texas and had edited a Spanish-language newspaper for Cuban revolutionaries in New York during the 1870s. A quick study, he used his abilities as a lecturer, editor, and translator of German classics to become the leading Marxist theoretician in the United States.[7]

His medium was the SLP and its paper. The party and the *Workmen's Advocate* were the legacy of the first international workers' movement, remnants of the First International, which Marx had transferred to New York and which later expired in Philadelphia in 1876. The party in New York was tiny, and DeLeon used the new *People* to turn this small group (at its height in the 1890s it had eight thousand members) into a strict Marxist revolutionary organization. DeLeon was a fanatic. He, probably more clearly than any of his colleagues, felt the need for absolute adherence to the science of Marxism, of which he became the chief American expositor. The *People*, which had previously been filled primarily with light articles, became a stern teacher of party theory. DeLeon adopted many of the techniques of European Marxists: contempt for rival theories, the expulsion of "disloyal" party members, and the use of personal invective to counter what he saw as reform tendencies. In the 1890s, his chief targets were the People's party and Samuel Gompers, leader of the American Federation of Labor.[8]

DeLeon's tactics, which safeguarded the party from heresy, also isolated it from the mainstream of the American Left, let alone from the bulk of American society. Although his greatest contempt was reserved for middle-class reformers, whom he saw as weakening the movement for social change, he nevertheless felt the need to cooperate with them from time to time. Early in the life of the Populist movement, for example, he thought he could discern some signs that the Populists were moving in the right direction, although he soon changed his mind and viewed the party as nothing but a middle-class reactionary movement.

It was at that time that Wayland first came to blows with DeLeon: the then-Colorado editor wrote to DeLeon that the Populists were indeed socialists and were more willing at the polls than were the eastern members of the SLP. Wayland was the symbol of what DeLeon was fighting. The "One-Hoss" editor was the person who was trying to smooth over the differences among socialists, not through the use of theory, but through his brand of socialist agitation. DeLeon must have experienced the same kind of repulsion from Wayland's nonscientific socialism that Wayland must have felt for DeLeon's rigidly doctrinaire approach.

Wayland's hesitancy to support the SLP may have come not only from the difference in emphasis on theoretical clarity but also from the regional, religious, and personal differences between the two men and their brands of radicalism. Although Wayland published the SLP's platform next to the Omaha Platform in the *Coming Nation* and although he boomed the *People* along with such Populist papers as the *Non-Conformist*, he saved his praise for the Populists, organized a local for them when he was in Greensburg, Indiana, and called the *Non-Conformist*, not the *People*, the best reform paper in the country.[9]

Smelling success after their strong statewide and national showings during the first half of the decade, the Populists were being drawn to a free-silver platform, which, as Goodwyn has called it, was the manifestation of the shadow, not the basic Populist movement. Gaspar C. Clemens was an early convert to the Populist cause. Clemens was a Kansas radical of long standing who, like Wayland, had been part of an unsuccessful colony experience. Clemens sensed the party's basic problem when he published "An Appeal to True Populists," which Wayland reprinted in the *Appeal* on January 18, 1896. It probably gives a fair estimate of Wayland's own feelings. Clemens claimed that if fusion with the Democrats went through, it would be the death of the Populists. Single-issue politics was wrong; it was conservative. "In a heavenly atmosphere, richly laden with blessed free silver, will federal judges turn labor reformers and issue injunctions no more? . . . Yet to demonstrate this folly [of silver as a panacea] and make a few men rich, we are to give up agitation of our really important principles and lose for that agitation the most precious years of all time." Clemens's opinion did not stop him from supporting the ticket in the fall, although he was moving in a more radical direction. Wayland vacillated on the question of whom to support, one week appearing to come out for the fusion-ticket candidate for president, William Jennings Bryan, and the next week retreating. Wayland's unsettled thinking no doubt helped to weaken the newspaper. Later he was to lay the entire blame for the suspension of the *Appeal* on the effect of the Bryan campaign.[10]

DeLeon noticed Wayland's leanings towards Bryan, which led the Kansas City editor to defend himself in this way: "The one-hoss at no time contemplated supporting anybody whom the democrats would nominate on any kind of platform. . . . It [the *Appeal*] feels that from now forward it can do more good by supporting a purely socialist party than any other course. There were conditions when it could do greater good in supporting the people's party, but since it died the field of socialism is the place to do effective work. . . . A small section of earnest men is of more worth than a large following of a heterogeneous aggregation of uneducated voters."[11] If this sounds more like DeLeon than like Wayland, it may have been the result of a visit by the SLP leader to Kansas City the previous week, at which time Wayland published the SLP platform on the front page.[12]

This change of sentiment was not as sudden as it may have appeared to most readers, but it was still a very difficult position for Wayland to take, and the friendly relationship did not last long. Wayland was looking to convert the mass of voters, and the idea of accepting a tightly knit, rigidly structured, and disciplined party was contrary to his basic assumptions. The personal element was also important. There were almost certainly no two leaders in radical circles who could have been more different in every respect or less likely to have confidence in one another. Although Wayland's deference to DeLeon was short-lived, at least it did last for a while. DeLeon, on the other hand, had nothing but contempt for Wayland the person, the theorist, and the editor. DeLeon was appalled by Wayland's work habits and was shocked by Wayland's relatives and associates. In a letter to party headquarters, DeLeon reported:

This morning I met Wayland. He can't be described in a word, or a couple of sheets either. He seems to attract cranks, some of whom are crookish. Fully 4 of them dropped in during the 2 hours I was in his office, one of them from Pueblo. But he also attracts a better sort. The Kansas freight handler [probably a man named Putnam, whom Mother Jones cited as one of the men who helped launch the paper] surely was a good specimen. . . . [The] incapacity of the man [Wayland] is indescribable. I suspect he is being played for a dupe by his wife's brother. This worthy looks like a peddler of wooden nutmegs. To him I ascribe all the executive ability one is inclined to give Wayland credit for in view of his having set up the "Coming Nation" & now the "Appeal to Reason." Wayland is a Salvation Army sentimentalist; his brother [-in-law] thinks he (W.) is a great writer; compound the two and you have it. The brother [-in-law] made upon me such a bad impression (both he & Wayland look like the geniuses of famine) that I have put myself the questions: "Can it be that their paper's sudden coming over to the S.L.P. ticket is the result of their being in a sinking condition and of their feeling that the S.L.P. is rising?"[13]

Although Wayland's contact with the SLP went back at least to early 1894, when he first published the SLP's platform in the *Coming Nation*,[14] DeLeon was probably correct about Wayland's recent support. The paper was failing, the Bryan movement was sapping the radicalism out of the Populists, and the *Coming Nation* had taken the road of colonization. Wayland needed a cause, but more important, he needed a concrete party to support. It was only in the spring and summer of 1896 that he openly supported the SLP.

Three months before DeLeon's visit, which in spite of his withering remarks did result in a successful founding meeting for a local SLP chapter and good future prospects, Wayland was in contact with the New York office. He emphasized that he was agitating for socialism, not for populism, and that he employed a man to work the streets of Kansas City every night for the cause. Wayland was trying to organize a Kansas City chapter, but he confessed that he was no organizer and suggested that the SLP send one out to do the job. "The pops here give me h— for circulating and talking S.L.P. literature, as they say it will divide the vote. . . . The pops are dropping the *Appeal* and it is not so healthy as I could wish, but will get on. Its policy as an educator will remain the same this year, so far as I can see. After this year, it may be partisan for the S.L.P."[15]

Wayland stopped just short of turning the paper into a propaganda sheet for the SLP. "When organized under the Socialist-Labor party section method, there is no danger of the party fusing, compromising or selling out. All matters are referred to the members of the sections direct. No person not a member of a section in good standing has any vote or any voice in the party. . . . No populist harem-scarem methods about the S.L.P."[16] "Socialism can be advanced not by the election of Bryan but votes for the S.L.P."[17] Here are Wayland's oldest instincts for principle over temporary gain, which he had shown as a young Republican. This was written shortly before the suspension of the paper and shortly before election day. McKinley's victory, aided by a timely infusion of corporate funds gathered as a result of scare tactics, marked a divide, not just for Wayland, but for the entire radical movement.

If Bryan had been elected president in 1896, Eugene Debs, who campaigned for Bryan, might never have become a socialist.[18] Debs never dropped a compromise solution until it showed itself barren, as the Populist-Democratic fusion had. What happened to Debs could probably describe what happened to other reform-minded people in the aftermath of the McKinley victory. Bryan certainly posed no real threat to the status quo, but the Republican party and press described his mild reform policy as revolutionary. It became clear to Debs, Wayland, and many other reformers that the "money power" could control the political system as it controlled the economic system, so it was the system that had to be changed. Only by educating the people to socialism, by putting together a political party that would not be compromised, could things be different. They felt that the ground rules had been revised while they were playing the game. It might not be enough now just to vote, because the corrupting influence of economic power could buy an election. A strong, disciplined, and educated party had to lead a committed electorate. No longer would a party in power be able to institute a massive change, as the reformers thought Lincoln had, unless it accorded with the views of the economic elite. Although Wayland now saw this as clearly as Debs did, and although the editor proclaimed the need for socialist discipline, the basic incompatibility of his temperament with the demands of the SLP necessarily appeared. For in Wayland the desire for a principled socialist party was combined with a need to include, rather than exclude, and to educate, rather than criticize. And Wayland never really assimilated the lesson that the ballot box was not the perfect democratic instrument that he had always believed it to be.[19]

The *Appeal to Reason* resurfaced on February 6, 1897, in the small southeastern Kansas town of Girard, the seat of Crawford County, which lies about 120 miles south of Kansas City, close to the borders of Missouri and Oklahoma and not too far from Arkansas. Girard was Wayland's last stop on his tour of small midwestern and southwestern county seats. He reintroduced himself to his readers: "Well, how do you do? Been some time since I annoyed you with my presence for which some of you rejoiced and others felt otherwise. . . . I concluded to move to a smaller place, buy a home, put in a printing plant [in Kansas City he was contracting for the printing] and settle down permanently . . . Girard, Kansas, the prettiest little town I found in three months hunting for a place to make my home." He complained that his eyes were failing him and that he had needed a rest, his first in five years. He may also have chosen Kansas as a result of its reputation for being "ripe for socialism," in Gronlund's words; and the choice of a small town helped to lower the cost of producing the paper. There is some evidence that Edwin Read Ridgely, an important Populist congressman from Pittsburg, Kansas, a larger town southeast of Girard, helped to lure Wayland's business to the area with promises of support.[20]

Wayland resumed his enthusiasm for the SLP, but he was increasingly in a position that offered little other choice. Eighteen ninety-seven was the year when the *Coming Nation* was reaching its greatest influence as the exponent of socialism through colonization. The Ruskin Colony engaged Debs, who was seen as the leader of the forces of change, to be the national organizer for the newly formed Brotherhood of the Cooperative Commonwealth (BCC). The *Appeal* took the other side, the side of political action, which the *Coming Nation* was relegating to second place. Wayland, who still admired Debs and hoped to lure him to work for the *Appeal* some day, even said a few good words about the BCC, no doubt because of Debs's support. But Wayland's main thrust was towards the original goal of education and towards enjoining his readers to throw in with the SLP.[21]

F. G. R. Gordon, who had joined the SLP in 1895, wrote for the paper, and he missed few chances to impress the readers with the importance of joining up. Gordon, a native of Vermont who was active throughout New England, had been a Greenbacker, an early Knights of Labor member in New Hampshire, an organizer of that state's People's party and a member of the Nationalist Club of Boston. A shoemaker by trade, he was also active in the International Shoe and Boot Workers Union. Relocated to Girard, Gordon produced a pamphlet, "Hard Times: The Cause and Cure," which Wayland published as the second issue in a new quarterly, *One-Hoss Philosophy*, in July, 1897. Eventually topping one hundred thousand copies in print, Gordon's pamphlet argued for socialism as the only way out of the situation in which workers found themselves.[22]

In the pages of the *Appeal*, Gordon wrote a column in which he "talked" to "Samuel Simons, Wage Worker," pointing out to him why it was important to join the party. The problems of reform parties during the past twenty years, Gordon claimed, stemmed from the fact that they had been organized like the major parties. The SLP, however, was small but growing, controlled by the working class, and revolutionary. He advised Samuel Simons to join the SLP, but soon Gordon himself left the party to join the Social Democracy of America (SDA).[23]

Gordon left the SLP because of its internal problems, which were coming to a head at the end of 1897, and because another course was opened to him when Debs started to work with the *Coming Nation*. DeLeon, as usual, was the precipitating cause of the crisis in the party. He had decided that union labor was the most important stronghold for a socialist party to capture, and when he failed to gain control of the Knights of Labor, he chose to go into direct competition with the American Federation of Labor by setting up his own rival labor organization. The AFL, which Gompers had organized to adhere to the cause of "pure and simple" unionism, was a confederation of craft unions that had some socialist membership but that held to the belief that a union would be concerned solely with wages and hours. DeLeon's union, the Socialist

Trade and Labor Alliance (STLA), was meant to compete head on with the AFL locals. This enraged many of the AFL union men inside the SLP who had fought against the party's plan to implement the STLA policy. Whole sections of the party started to rebel. DeLeon and his New York-based National Executive Committee were forced to act within their own party as if they were only a faction of it.

At the same time, the *Coming Nation* organizers of the Brotherhood of the Cooperative Commonwealth held a joint conference with the remnants of Debs's American Railway Union, which had been decimated by the effects of the federal intervention against them during the 1894 Pullman strike. The two bodies decided to merge into one organization, the Social Democracy of America: the result was half political party, half colonizing venture. Unable to field candidates in time for the fall 1897 elections, Debs urged SDA supporters to vote the SLP ticket. A Socialist, James F. Carey, was elected, albeit to a minor post, as a city council member in Haverhill, Massachusetts. As a member of one of the dissident groups within the SLP, Carey advocated reform measures that appalled the DeLeon group. By March, 1898, most of the Haverhill SLP had gone into the SDA. Gordon's own change of heart almost certainly came because of this fight.[24]

Wayland's own SLP man had become an SDA man; but although the new political organization held some strong attractions for Wayland, he had reasons for holding back. Debs and the broad base of support that the SDA aimed for must have looked good to Wayland, who remained committed to a popular party in spite of his recent calls for a disciplined party. But the Ruskin connection and the colonizing idea that developed out of it held him back from supporting the SDA in 1897. The scheme that the SDA envisaged was the logical culmination of the belief that colonies would be the practical entering wedge for American socialism. This had been Wayland's idea when he had hatched Ruskin; and though he had abandoned it, the colonists had not. Ruskin at that time was at the height of its prosperity, and the idea had gained credence. The SDA's program was to attempt to colonize an entire western state, probably Washington, with disciplined but unemployed workers and to take over the state government through the force of voting numbers. The state would then enact socialist legislation. After socialism had succeeded in one state, other states would fall to it like dominoes. Debs even attempted to solicit the aid of John D. Rockefeller for this plan. Within a year, the idea was in shambles: the planning committee had squandered the seed money provided for the operation. At the second convention of the SDA, in June, 1898, the problem came to a head; this led to a split in the group and gave rise to the Social Democratic Party of America (SDP), which comprised the political action elements of the SDA, and left the rump of the convention to carry on in a purely colonizing venture, which met with little success.[25]

Debs went with the new party, the SDP. The SDP had dropped the colonizing scheme, but Wayland still did not fully support it, probably because his old nemesis at the *Coming Nation*, A. S. Edwards, became editor of the official party newspaper, the *Social Democratic Herald*. Although Wayland could not display much enthusiasm for the party at first, his support for the SLP did weaken, even before the formation of the new party. The surest reason for this change was the election in Haverhill. Wayland had been waiting for this kind of success. F. G. R. Gordon, in a major article in the *Appeal*, traced the election directly to the amount of radical literature that had circulated in that Massachusetts town, pointing especially to the *Appeal* and his own pamphlet. Although Wayland still acknowledged privately that the *People* was a superior paper because it treated issues on a more profound basis than he did in the *Appeal*, he started to allow negative comments about the SLP leadership to creep back in, while he still supported the local organizations.[26]

But as the new SDP was forming, in mid 1898, Wayland let loose on his one-time uneasy ally:

The assumption that everybody but those belonging to the New York outfit are labor fakirs is ample proof that there is a nigger in the woodpile somewhere. More socialists do not belong to any party than belong to one. The very spirit exhibited by some who profess socialism show them not to be socialists. Had it not been for that kind of management at the New York end, there would never have been any social democracy, but there are lots of people who are just as well posted in socialism, have made more sacrifices than the $30 a week editors of the New York machine, are not dumb driven cattle, to be deprived of freedom to think or speak. (When I was publishing the *Coming Nation* and supported the people's party the New York people voluntarily carried an advertisement without pay! How wonderful the change since!)

The Appeal has lost some support by reason of the S.L.P. quietly ordering its members not to have anything to do with the paper, that the People would thus get the more. This is their right and the Appeal can stand it, and wished the People, as an educator, had a million readers. It is not the platform of the S.L.P. against which there is a kick, but those who have possessed themselves of the party machinery and entrenched themselves behind rules that give them the power to reelect themselves much as does the president of Mexico. Where there is so much smoke, there must be some fire, and if the S.L.P. members will open their eyes they will see something must be wrong where some of the best socialists are expelled from the party because they have dared to exercise the right to think. It may not be that there is a nigger in the woodpile, but if the action of the New York board toward everyone who bows not to its will is not in the interest of capitalism, the capitalists could not better manage it, for it is preventing and will continue to prevent the masses from associating themselves with the party, even when they are favorable to socialism. I have voted the ticket and contributed to its funds and have a right to kick. If I had to choose between the two parties today I would certainly not take the New York management. It has lied about those who do not bow to its rule, denounced those who have done more than any of its members for socialism without pay, and even flies in the face of its own platform, because that part had advocates among people who are not contributors to the machine. It is such men and management that have caused the split, not the men who were forced to start a new organization in which the czar rule was not present. (If the members of the S.L.P. will examine the vote and the conditions in the Milwaukee election, and then read the People's articles on it, perhaps they will see something.)

The New York machine does not want to favor socialism unless it pours water into their mill race, and the toll has been pretty big.[27]

Here, Wayland clearly stated what was in the minds of many of the reformers who would make up the leadership of the American socialist movement in the twentieth century. Narrow, autocratic rule was not what Wayland envisioned as a feature of the socialist future, although one could argue that he left Ruskin because he could not make his own ideas prevail. He associated socialism with open-mindedness, freedom, and self-sacrifice, and his definition of what socialism was encompassed much beyond the strict Marxist construction that DeLeon offered.[28]

The battle lines were drawn. Wayland and the *Appeal* became the refuge for many renegade sections of the SLP.[29] He first suggested starting sections of the SDP at the end of July, because he saw no need for two socialist parties. The *People* fought back, telling its members not to subscribe to the *Appeal* and expelling sections that refused to obey. The circulation of the *Appeal* did go down, possibly as a result of the action of the *People*, possibly as a reaction to the change in tone of the paper from one of tolerance to one of party infighting. Perhaps this was because of the brief surge in quality of the *Coming Nation* under the joint control of Casson and Commander or because of Wayland's own personal situation. A series of crises marked his life during the last half of 1898. His wife was dying, he was suffering from what he called cancer, his youngest daughter had been severely burned, and his eldest daughter had also been badly injured. The quality of the paper plummeted as Wayland left it in the hands of a previously anonymous assistant, W. F. Phelps, who turned the front page over to a series of guest editors.

The greatest blow to the paper, however, was the surge of jingoism that accompanied the Spanish-American-Philippine War, which held the attention of the country from the sinking of the American warship *Maine* in February, 1898, to the cessation of formal hostilities in August. No reform paper held much interest in the wake of the "splendid little war." As World War I would show conclusively, radical politics could not compete with popular wars for the public interest. The failure of the Bryan campaign seemed to show that big money could sway the voters away from even the mildest reform. The Populist press virtually ceased after McKinley's victory. The socialist press suffered heavily from the 1898 war. All the educating and propagandizing did not change these basic facts of existence.

Wayland's wife, Etta Bevan, died of cancer on October 3, 1898. They had been married for twenty-one years, and there had been five children from the union; but Wayland never mentioned anything about her in the paper or in his various memoirs, as he kept almost all of his personal life out of the public eye. Wayland allegedly cured his own cancer about a month after his wife died, by using a simple herb remedy. He did allow this kind of information in the paper, because he could use it as propaganda against the medical establishment.[30]

At the end of 1898, both the *Appeal* and the *Coming Nation* started to rely increasingly on reprints.[31] Casson was about to leave the *Coming Nation*, and the colony was beginning to collapse. Wayland had ceased printing circulation information and had dropped outside columnists.[32] In early 1899, Wayland was ready to throw in the towel. The paper was losing a lot of money, and the weight of his personal problems was moving him to despair. He claimed in his memoirs that only a small increase in the weekly take, after months of declines in revenue, stopped him from ceasing his activities as a socialist propagandist.[33]

It was Wayland's change of tactics that probably brought about the upward turn in the fortunes of the paper.[34] As usual, circulation was his focus: the main change was the addition of a circulation manager and the institution of high-pressure tactics to increase circulation. E. W. Dodge was a black-listed telegraph operator who had come to Wayland in late 1895, suggesting a partnership to start a paper for telegraphers, similar to the *Appeal to Reason*. Wayland had to turn him away at the time because of lack of funds, and Dodge next turned up at Ruskin, which he joined in late 1897. He wrote articles for the *Coming Nation*, and the colony agreed to publish the *Telegrapher's Advocate*, which, however, soon went under.[35] The *Appeal to Reason*, for the first time under Dodge's direction, started to emphasize the need to build up the circulation, not in the low-keyed confidential manner that Wayland had previously employed, but by using the techniques of modern advertising, which had so recently proven their effectiveness in the circulation wars that accompanied the war of 1898 (see chap. 5). Even as this change was taking place, the final battle with DeLeon and the *People* was being fought, and the Ruskin Colony found itself in receivership.

Without competition from a strong paper, with the circulation of the *Appeal to Reason* now comparable to the finest performance of the *Coming Nation*, and with the SLP in disarray, Wayland went for the jugular. The *People* started the skirmish with an article criticizing Wayland's part in the founding and the first year of Ruskin Colony.[36] Wayland reacted on June 17, and then the two papers traded insults and reprimands. On June 28, Wayland wrote to Theodore Debs, Eugene's brother, who was the national secretary of the Social Democratic party, predicting that the SLP would go to pieces before the end of the year: "We are starting a row in a dozen places over the boycott. They made a mistake and they will find it out."[37] In the *Appeal* of July 22, Wayland exulted: "Kicked Out! DeLeon and his Gang Fired Bodily from the Socialist Labor Party by the New York Section." Wayland claimed a good bit of the credit for the turn of events: "DeLeon and his gang have been the dictators of the SLP for many years. On June 17th the *Appeal* opened up on them and on July 10th they were unanimously removed from every office they held in the party. It took 24 days to turn the trick. . . . The DeLeon gang, noting the rapid growth of the *Appeal* on the coast, rushed their man Brown from New York to California to put boycotts on it. Brown tried to hold a meeting in Los Angeles but it was a frost. And the next day the DeLeon gang were buried in New York."

There was much more to DeLeon's setback than that, and the New Yorker was not quite buried, but the effectiveness of his party had been shattered. The problems of DeLeon's leadership had led Morris Hillquit, a New York lawyer and DeLeon's chief rival, to organize an effective counterweight within the SLP to DeLeon's group, whose strength was centered in Rochester. Hillquit led his faction out of the party, and eventually, after two more years of partisan wrangling, many of the SLP's eight thousand members joined together with the SDP to form the Socialist Party of America (SP). The events in New York were riotous: meetings dissolved into fist fights; offices were barricaded; and the police were called in to settle matters between the rival socialists. The irony was lost on the participants, and the result was the eventual triumph of the idea of a broad-based party, intent on electoral success. Wayland's full role in the split will probably never be known, but what is significant is that his strength and the strength of the *Appeal* were such that he could help to overthrow the DeLeon faction, if only for a while, and to open the way for a more tolerant party which would include diverse elements.

These political exploits by Wayland, who in later years asserted that he had kept the paper out of the factional disputes of the Socialist Party of America, were the height of his direct involvement in party politics.[38] He seems never even to have joined the SLP or the SDP, or at least he never advertised the fact if he did.[39] In the period of the dispute with DeLeon and afterward, Wayland turned his attention more and more to the build-up of the *Appeal*'s circulation as his contribution to the cause. He came to identify the number of readers with the success of the movement; if the voters were educated, as shown by the circulation of the paper, another 1896 fiasco could not occur. Wayland's personal choice—for a broad-based, educational party—had for a short while been dropped in favor of DeLeon's arguments and the collapse of populism. Wayland described DeLeon as a czar; yet in his own way, though Wayland may not have insisted on as much loyalty as DeLeon did and though Wayland's desire to have his way may not have been as obvious, in the long run, he seemed to have gotten both. The feud between DeLeon and Wayland was in many ways the key to the development of socialist strategy in twentieth-century America. They carried out their battles in the press, and it was through this press that the members and sympathizers got their information.

Wayland had the greater impact on the course of radicalism in America. At the age of forty-five in 1899, Wayland found Girard much to his liking. When he had arrived there in early 1897, he was still lugging his gold around with him in tin cans and in boxes marked "books." He chose a house with about a half block of land on the outskirts of town. He kept the land as a small farm, with a pasture, fruit trees, a large front yard, and a berry patch. Like most of the surrounding area at the time, the land was shaded from the street by a stand of catalpa trees. The house (which is still standing) was a large one, built by a retired sea captain with the finest local materials. Wayland kept a small library at home, which, along with books from the office, he lent out to people whom he was trying to convert to the cause. On the library wall hung a framed photograph of his Ruskin cottage. The Girard household included, after the death of his wife, his two sons and three daughters: Jon, Ollie, Julia, Walter, and Edith. Jon started to work at the *Appeal* as cashier in 1899, and Walter also helped out there from time to time.[40]

Wayland had come to Girard at the urging of area Populists, people like Wayland himself who combined radical politics with a local booster spirit. Girard was and still is a small town in a largely rural area of southeastern Kansas; but it is an area that was set apart from much of the rest of the heart of the rural Midwest by its coal and zinc mines and by its population, which included a fair proportion of eastern and southern European immigrants, brought in to work the mines. Pittsburg, a town about ten miles to the southeast, was the largest in the area; it was the base of industrial and mining operations. The Populist boosters there, in addition to attracting Wayland, were helping to start the Pittsburg Normal School (now Pittsburg State University) and trying to make Pittsburg like Pittsburgh, Pennsylvania, a dream not unlike the one that the boosters in Pueblo, Colorado, had dreamed for their town a decade before. Girard, the county seat, and Pittsburg, the county's largest town, were the setting for Wayland's dream for the next decade and one-half.

His reception was well planned, and he was welcomed to the local Girard community because he brought business with him, though at the same time, the local press chided him for his politics. In the midst of the many problems he faced in the fall of 1898, the *Girard Press* summed up local mainstream thinking in this way: "Whatever may be the thought of Mr. J. A. Wayland's political vagaries and isms, he has the heartfelt sympathy of the newspaper fraternity of the county."[41] As fellow businessmen, members of the local establishment were nonplussed by Wayland's attraction to what they saw as a losing proposition: "Wayland has lost $4000 on the Appeal to Reason. His repeated failures ought to appeal to the reason of all those enthusiasts who imagine they can print a reform paper without advertisements and sell it for one-fourth the price it ought to bring."[42]

But Wayland saw socialism as good business: in Colorado, he had claimed that he was the only one who, in his own words, "escaped whole" from the financial disaster of the Panic of 1893. "If that be true, I have been amply paid for my study of socialism, for without that study I should not have seen the inevitable trend of society and arranged my material affairs to avoid the catastrophe."[43] Therefore, socialist theory had provided Wayland with the insight to avoid financial catastrophe. The seamless merging of gain from real-estate speculation and hard-headed business practice with socialist ideals is a key to understanding Wayland's view of society, his politics, his successes as a publicist for socialism, and the ultimate contradiction at the center of the American socialist movement.

J. A. Wayland, printer—who had grown up to be a tough businessman, a Republican editor, a Populist, and a real-estate speculator—had survived 1893 with $80,000 in gold and securities. He had then tried cooperative society at Ruskin, had rebounded from the loss of the *Coming Nation*, had started the *Appeal to Reason* and seen it through tough battles with the Socialist Labor party and with jingoism that attended

The staff of the Appeal to Reason *in Girard, 1902. Courtesy of the Archives of Labor and Urban Affairs, Wayne State University.*

the 1898 war, and had survived personal health struggles, the loss of his childhood sweetheart, and the near-fatal injuries of his daughter. In late 1898, forty-four years old, he was poised on the brink of publishing history and a central role in the fortunes of American socialism.

On a personal level, the winter of 1898 was the most unhappy time of his life, and Mother Jones, who stayed with the family throughout that period, helped to see Wayland through. But even in this darkest year, Wayland could still see bright prospects. He noted in his diary on December 31: "At office all day. Employes worked until noon. Footed up year's business: Total subscriptions received, 38,650. Cash received $9,933.72: Office expenses $7,670.39. Leaving the sum of $2263 for my labor. Prospects for the paper best I could ask. Mother Jones still with us: we sat up until the new year talking of the awful social conditions of the world's workers."[44]

At Ruskin, Wayland had resisted any change beyond the economic arrangements under which the colony had been founded, and even those did not differ much from business practice. At Girard, he was gathering about him the trappings of a country squire. He was becoming the oracle of the movement. Working anonymously behind the scenes, he would make Girard into a socialist mecca. The local gentry would accept him after a while as a successful fellow businessman, even though his bus-

Employees of the Appeal to Reason's *mailing room, 1898. Courtesy of the*
J. A. Wayland Collection, Pittsburg State University.

iness, if really successful, would have put them all out of business.
Wayland stood at the juncture of publishing success and political success. The way was paved through the use of American selling techniques
that had helped to create the modern newspaper. Among his radical
contemporaries, Wayland was the first to sense what was needed in order
to make a successful movement newspaper. That the same techniques
might work against the ultimate goals of the movement was the danger
he ran.

5
Advertising the Socialist Dream: Radical Publishing at the Turn of the Century

> The day has gone by for small mediums to tackle great undertakings and we must prepare to propagate Socialism in just the proportions that Capitalism operates.
>
> —J. A. Wayland, Appeal to Reason, *1903*

> H.G. Wiltshire [*sic*] is setting up a bill posting trust. Nelson of St. Louis is setting up a plumbing goods trust. . . . The fact is that any one who is doing business today must adopt the methods prevailing or go out of business.
>
> —J. A. Wayland, Appeal to Reason, *1899*

For socialism to catch the attention of the American public at the turn of the century, several avenues seemed to be available; but only one promised the mass audience that Wayland and most of his contemporaries craved. The chief obstacle was publicity. How to bring the program and promise of American socialism before the citizenry was the problem to which Wayland had devoted his efforts during the 1890s. Organizing local chapters of a socialist party would attract recruits, especially if the party was broad-based, rather than an exclusive organization like the Socialist Labor party. Lectures on the various circuits that were popular in the period helped and publicity in the mass press about strikes and local political successes added to the growing awareness of socialism in the United States. But none of these promised as much as a national organ that served both to educate the public and to provide a sense of reality to an aspiring movement that stretched across the vast continent.

Wayland aspired to develop the great nationwide socialist newspaper. Small-scale newspapers—with one man serving as writer, publisher, printer, chief reporter, and editorial writer—were the rule all across America when Wayland began his career. A few large daily urban papers that were driven by the personality of individual editors existed; but their heyday was yet to come. Throughout the 1870s and 1880s, American journalism was personal journalism. Indeed, much of the nation's business fit this pattern. As the pace of industrialization quickened, as populations grew and concentrated in cities, and as technology progressed, fewer and fewer men governed larger and larger enterprises. This was the birth of the age of Rockefeller and Carnegie, of industrial-capital formation in the United States. During this period of transition the modern newspaper emerged, and with it the need for radical papers to adapt.

How else could an American socialism get the nation's attention? American consumer culture came of age in this period, honed by selling techniques that had developed for a century. Billboards, placards, and fence painting raged through the land, extolling the virtues of such items as patent medicines—for example, the Mormon Elders Damiana Wafers or the popular elixir Buchu. The period after the Civil War was called not only the Gilded Age but also the Age of Disfigurement, because of the exuberant excesses of advertising. While advertising won its spurs by extolling patent medicines, thus capping a century of development that stretched back before the Revolution, it was a ready tool for whetting the appetite for newer mass products that started to flow more abundantly during the 1890s. The newspaper industry and the advertising industry fitted each other's needs.[1]

Newspapers were indeed becoming an industry. As the 1890s wore on, they came to resemble factories in other industries. The process began when Joseph Pulitzer bought the *New York World* in 1883 and laid the groundwork for the mass-circulation daily. The new demand on reporters was to fill the paper every day with exciting copy. To this end, reporters were usually paid by the amount they delivered—column inches of published material per week. Thus they tended to write for length and to pepper their stories with unsubstantiated details. Reporters on the smaller dailies, who were burdened with impossible duties, resorted to pooling information; and their articles became even more inaccurate as they wrote copy for events they had not witnessed.[2] When Wayland complained about the inaccuracy of the daily press, he was right.

Wayland had also warned about the danger posed by news monopolies. Since its inception after the Mexican War of 1848, the Associated Press (AP) had repeatedly attempted to control the flow of news. The AP's first success came in 1855, when it secured favorable rates with the Western Union Telegraph Company; the AP drove competition from the field and gained a monopoly of wire news to newspapers. Its continuing policy was to keep the ground to itself, punishing newspapers that strayed to new services by cutting them off from the AP. Western Union helped by raising rates for the wire reports of rival newspapers. It was not until the 1880s that strong competition could develop, although the new group learned that there were benefits in cooperating with the AP. Torn by a factional dispute, the most powerful papers remained in the AP and a handful in the United Press (UP; not to be confused with the modern UPI); these two groups owned a virtual monopoly on cable news. The desire for more timely reporting, which was brought on by a host of factors, including the circulation wars between the big papers of many cities, led to a huge increase in the use of cable reports by the press.[3]

Wayland criticized the Associated Press for the superficial way that it treated stories and for its lack of radical news.[4] He also criticized the American News Company for its monopolistic control of the distribution of periodicals. The American News Company, a distribution organization, had had its own way in the field since the late 1860s. It secured a monopoly in 1872, when its subsidiary, the Railroad News Company, bought into the Union News Company, the leading owner of newsstands. By the 1890s, it was doing an annual business of more than $17 million and had virtually absolute control over displays on the newsstands.[5] The only successful challenge came from *Munsey's Magazine*, which began in 1893 and which had to build an entirely new rival organization to secure what it felt was a fair return. The influence of the wire-service monopolies led to facile, sensational short newspaper reports, which seldom if ever questioned basic social assumptions. The American News Company could and did restrict the public circulation of uncooperative and radical journals.

Aside from the growth of large population centers and the accumulation of capital, several developments contributed to the expansion of the newspaper industry. Probably most important was an increase in the amount of available paper and a dramatic reduction in its cost. When Wayland began his career in the early 1870s, the price of newsprint to major consumers was twelve cents a pound. The price fell steadily, dropping to four cents by 1893 and below two cents by 1897. A further breakthrough came when wood pulp replaced rags in paper manufacture and when papermaking machines were developed that were capable of meeting the growing need. New steam-powered rotary presses, which were fed by a roll of newsprint and which printed on both sides at once, dramatically increased the speed and cut the cost of production. Speed was further increased when presses operated on power—first steam, then gasoline, and later (by 1896, in the biggest plants), electricity. Also, newspapers improved their appearance considerably after the inventions of halftone printing and photoengraving. Two changes by the Post Office Department led to an increase in subscriptions: a new second-class postal rate of one cent per pound, which went into effect in 1885, lowered the cost of mailing weeklies and magazines; and Rural Free Delivery (RFD), which was instituted in 1897, made the wider distribution of them possible.

Newspapers of all kinds had relied on circulation as the chief measure of success, as they had always relied on advertising for some revenue; but the causal connection between circulation and advertising was not recognized until the 1880s. Before Pulitzer, the relationship between newspapers and their advertisers was hostile; the latter were restricted in space and were confined to the smallest available type—partly to encourage the smaller advertisers on whom the papers relied for steady income. Pulitzer changed this relationship. He linked the circulation of the paper with the price of ads; he allowed column rules to be broken and illustrations to be used without penalty to the advertiser.

The reasons for Pulitzer's move, which was soon followed by his competitors, were not hard to find. The key was the development of the huge department store and of name-brand merchandise that was sold nationally. These two were natural outcomes of the industrialization of the country and of the communications industry. The amount of advertising matter rose dramatically; before 1880 the ratio was approximately 70 percent editorial content to 30 percent advertising; but in the 1880s, it drew even or, in some cases, shifted to more ads than editorial matter. The revenue from advertising rose in importance, from 40 percent of total income in 1880 to 55 percent in 1900. Information about circulation started to be a public matter, with two agencies, George P. Rowell's and N. W. Ayer's, coming into existence to verify the newspapers' own reports. The relationship between the advertisers and the newspapers was cemented in 1887 by the creation of the American Newspaper Publishers Association, which became the mediator between the papers and their advertisers.[6]

Circulation building and advertising came to be requirements that all publications had to meet. When Wayland decided to attract a national audience for his views in 1893, he first thought only ten thousand subscribers would guarantee success. Soon, he was talking about one hundred thousand—without advertising. In the entire country in 1885, only twenty-one out of thirty-three hundred periodicals had more than one hundred thousand subscribers; by 1893, there were only about fifty such out of almost five thousand publications. The most widely read was *Comfort*, a fifty-cent-per-year journal that was nearing the million mark, using a combination of juvenile games, puzzles, women's home advice, gardening tips, and serialized fiction to carry its lucrative mail-order advertising. Its closest rivals were the *Youth's Companion* and the *Ladies Home Journal*, with more than a half million monthly readers at ten cents an issue. The move down to ten- and fifteen-cent issues from the prices of thirty to thirty-five cents, which had prevailed a decade before, was made possible in large part by technological improvements and increased revenue from advertising.

Though *Comfort, Ladies Home Journal,* and *Youth's Companion* existed almost solely for their advertising matter, other general magazines satisfied a new demand for popular education and information. The newspapers responded with Sunday supplements, which popularized science and history; and the Chautauqua movement and its imitators throughout the country drew thousands to their lectures. These popular educators spread the message about "getting ahead." The most spectacular Chautauqua address was "Acres of Diamonds," which the Baptist minister Russell H. Conwell delivered six thousand times, preaching the gospel of success. The idea was evident in the advertisements that dotted the magazines and the newspapers, and it turned the novels of Horatio Alger into best sellers. But even in the view of the leading historian of the nation's press, there was no time between 1885 and 1905 "when the cry of protest was not almost as loud as the shout of success."[7]

Protest was the first step towards radicalism, and America had a long history of radical publication. Led by the publication of Thomas Paine's *Common Sense*, there was a respected tradition in radical publishing from at least the time of the Revolution. Radical publications, such as William Lloyd Garrison's *Liberator*, spurred on the abolition movement, and the cause was aided by Horace Greeley's *New York Tribune*. Greeley was a self-acknowledged socialist who frankly espoused Fourier's ideas. Greeley filled his staff with former members of the Brook Farm experiment, and his chief European correspondent in the 1850s was Karl Marx. The weekly *Tribune* circulated throughout New England and the Midwest; this prompted Emerson to remark that Greeley did all of the "thinking and theory" for midwestern farmers "at two dollars a year."[8]

But Greeley was an exception to the rule. From at least the time of the Paris Commune in 1870 and certainly after the Haymarket affair in 1886, socialism began to be suspect, and the word itself became fearsome. If protest was abroad in the nation's journals, it was not Greeley's kind of protest. By the early 1890s, it was a plea for an end to corruption in politics; a fair return for the farmer; or questions of trade and monetary policy, such as protectionism or deflation or free trade and inflation, that characterized the protest in the mainstream of American publishing. Amid advertisements and articles that bespoke unlimited opportunities, people read about flaws in the social fabric.

An undercurrent of radical thought continued to run through American publications, even if it was not available to the mainstream in the doses that Greeley had provided. In the 1870s, 1880s, and 1890s, there were always a number of free-thought, anarchist, feminist, and socialist publications that printed a limited number of copies for small audiences. One exception in terms of circulation, and one that is anomalous in terms of placing it in a radical continuum, was William Cowper Brann's *Iconoclast*, which, from its Texas base, reached ninety thousand readers during the

1890s. The "smasher of shams" tried to cut through the veils of respectability that covered the sordid politics and society of the Gilded Age.[9] Also during Wayland's early years of radical publishing, but at the other end of the circulation scale, Benjamin R. Tucker published *Liberty* from 1881 to 1908, an individual anarchist magazine, for a loyal band of six hundred subscribers.[10] And the *Workman's Advocate*, which became the *People*, spoke to no more than eight thousand readers when Daniel DeLeon, as spokesman of the Socialist Labor party, analyzed current events in a Marxist vein.

But the real mass radical press during Wayland's early years was the Populist press, of which Wayland, at least from 1893 to 1895, could be counted an important part.[11] The Populists created hundreds of periodicals, almost all of them weeklies, which carried their messages of reform. Wayland's *Coming Crisis*, from Pueblo, was among them. They ran on the smallest budgets and usually lasted only a year or two. In 1890 the Alliance (not yet the People's party) created the National Reform Press Association at Ocala, Florida, the site of its national conference, which was to coordinate internal communication for what was soon to be the People's party. Of the many papers across the country, several were outstanding in terms of circulation or influence. When Wayland was publishing the *Coming Nation*, his "clubbin' list" (Wayland's term for cut-rate joint subscription with other periodicals) included the most important of them: *Tom Watson's People's Party Paper*, the *Topeka Advocate*, and the *Non-Conformist*, as well as the SLP's *People* and the Bellamyite *Nation*.[12]

It was not easy to keep these papers afloat, especially when advertising was becoming the most important source of revenue. Most readers could barely afford the low price of subscribing, while major advertisers stayed away. Wayland's position, which was antagonistic to any advertising, was the rule, although local ads were often accepted in smaller papers, which ran in localities in place of or in competition with Republican and Democratic organs. The usual circulation was under one thousand copies. The income from selling "movement" literature, and from constantly dunning supporters and subscribers, was usually not enough to prevent the editor/publisher from having to invest his own capital to keep afloat. When the Democrats swallowed up the Populists in 1896, most of the papers—which had been nourished by the fierce determination and dedication of their editors and the willingness of supporters to scrape up enough to keep them going—died, and with them the National Reform Press Association.[13]

At the height of the Populist movement, the *Topeka Advocate* exceeded Wayland's *Coming Nation* and the *Appeal to Reason* in circulation. The *Advocate*, which had eighty thousand subscriptions in 1894, was the leading paper in Kansas, while *Tom Watson's People's Party Paper*, although it occasionally printed twenty thousand copies, never exceeded five hundred paid subscribers.[14] Many of the smaller Populist papers were sustained by ready-print services, which were common to smaller country weeklies. One such service was run directly by the National Reform Press Association; another was run by Henry Vincent of the *Non-Conformist* to provide so-called patent insides for other populist weeklies. The patent insides were the interior pages of a four-page weekly, which had already been printed with news of national interest and was full of ads for patent medicines, from which they took their name. Albert Sanderson, a breakaway SLP member from St. Louis, was providing the same service to tiny socialist papers throughout the Midwest at approximately the same time. He moved his operation to Ruskin Colony in 1896, but it soon failed. What these services did was to relieve the editor, who was often also the printer and everything else, from having to fill up the entire paper; they also incidentally halved his typesetting costs.[15]

The tendency for the radical press to use techniques that were proving successful in the mainstream of the newspaper industry was apparent from the 1890s, as was the counter ideal to print and publish without resorting to advertising. The tension between these two positions—to succeed as publishing enterprises while developing a radical consciousness—is illustrated by the example of Henry Vincent's *Non-Conformist*.[16] Eight years younger than Wayland, Vincent was born in a small town in Iowa into a large family that had abolitionist sentiments. His father had started the *Non-Conformist* in 1879, essentially as a Greenback paper, which sought by analogy to continue the work of emancipation by endeavoring to free the wage slaves. Henry Vincent took over the paper in 1886 and, with his brother, moved it to Winfield, Kansas. They changed its name to the *American Non-Conformist and Kansas Industrial Liberator* and built the circulation to twenty thousand by 1891. While in Winfield, Vincent was active both in creating the Farmers Alliance movement in Kansas and in the political discussions that were generating the People's party; he was one of the founders of the National Reform Press Association. And he was printing patent insides for about forty newspapers in Kansas, Colorado, Nebraska, and Missouri through the Independent Newspaper Union, a chartered corporation.

While at Winfield, Vincent and his family were connected with the infamous dynamite incident of 1888 in Coffeyville. This was allegedly an attempt—and a successful one at that—by Republican office seekers to discredit Vincent and his supporters by charging them with sabotage, because they were fielding Union Labor candidates in that year's elections. The Vincents fought back through the columns of their paper and through vigorous political organizing. The Populists had a good measure of success in the 1890 elections, so in 1891, Vincent decided to move the plant to Indianapolis, closer to the center of the country, and to make the *Non-Conformist* the national organ for the People's party in the upcoming 1892 presidential election. The decision proved to be a mistake; the Populists did not sweep into office, although their candidate, James B. Weaver, did receive more than one million votes; and Henry Vincent lost the paper in the Panic of 1893. From then on, he lent his efforts to other papers, most notably the *Chicago Searchlight*, which supported the attempt of the Populists to win control of that city's government in 1894. He also worked with Jacob S. Coxey as publicity director of Coxey's Army in its march on Washington. More than a decade later, Vincent moved to Girard to work closely with Wayland (see chap. 9).

The careers of both Vincent and Wayland illuminate the problems of radical publishing and radical politics. Vincent was born to reform, and Wayland was converted to it; but both found that their power in the movements that they supported derived from their positions as editors. Wayland had made money before his radical career, money that sustained him through the slack periods that his newspaper faced. Vincent could rely on two of his brothers for labor, but he had no money to fall back on when the paper was forced to the wall. Both Vincent and Wayland conceived the idea that it was necessary to move to Indiana, to be literally in the center of the country, in order to produce a national organ; and both arrived in Indiana at approximately the same time, looking to win essentially the same audience. Wayland prospered because of the Panic of 1893; at that time, Vincent was forced to sell his paper, and the buyer then tried to sell it to Wayland. Both Vincent and Wayland eschewed the idea of making money from the movement, but Wayland's disdain came from the security afforded by his stock of gold. When Vincent looked back on the years of poverty that he and his family had suffered, he wondered if he had done the right thing: "Everyone had agreed that the state printing should logically go to the Non Con [*Non-Conformist*] boys [after the successful Kansas Populist elections of 1890]. But we had declined to enter the race for any of the spoils whatsoever. Such a self-effacing, altruistic, un-practical, shortseeing lot we were afterwards was vividly brought to mind when the tide of the Populist movement went out."[17]

Vincent stated the problem clearly for those in radical publishing: without funds, one could not publish at all; relying only on subscribers, one could have only a tenuous existence. In turn-of-the-century publishing, advertising was providing more than half the revenue of profitable papers; without advertising revenues or personal wealth, a radical publisher could have only poverty. Also, most radical publishers felt, probably correctly, that they had to keep their prices as low as possible so that their supporters could afford to buy. Advertisements from similar publications were accepted, but these often were on an exchange basis, and those that paid could not generate much revenue. Without a healthy margin of profit, investment in new equipment would be next to impossible. As Wayland himself estimated in 1901, the difference between modern and out-of-date equipment (and one must keep in mind that the technology of printing was changing very quickly then) could mean needing five thousand more subscribers in order to break even.[18]

With the Bryan campaign of 1896 in full swing, the Populist press was itself packing up. Wayland suspended the *Appeal to Reason* for more than three months. Later, the Spanish-American-Philippine War captured the popular imagination and almost ruined the *Appeal to Reason;* without his ample resources, Wayland would have had to suspend again. The Bryan-McKinley campaign of 1900 also had a negative impact on the *Appeal,* which by then was publishing over one hundred thousand copies. Wayland had to invest an additional $3,000 to keep it going.[19] Wayland, as we have seen from the Ruskin experiment, was generous with only some of his money; he was not willing to part with all of it for the cause. Even a captive labor force, under either Wayland or his successors at Ruskin, was not enough to support the *Coming Nation;* it needed substantial outside funds. The radical press could not go to the bank for loans: bankers who had conventional political views were hostile, and publishing in general was not looked on as a safe investment. Lacking an "angel" with unlimited funds, a radical paper—even one with large circulation—needed advertising revenue. Wayland learned that lesson somewhat sooner than did his Populist and socialist colleagues, and because of his business experience, he had less trouble adjusting to economic necessity.

Almost everything in Wayland's background pushed him towards advertising; only the argument against it that John Ruskin had so eloquently made in the *Fors Clavigera* and Wayland's own sense of self held him back. Ruskin had thundered against advertising (see chap. 2), and Wayland had promised his readers that what they read in his paper were his thoughts, unsullied by the possible taint of which the subsidized press could always be suspected. The two sources, Ruskin and Wayland's own individual sensibilities, struck a common chord with the yearning for a pure politics. If one didn't like what Wayland said, one didn't have to read his papers; but when one read the *Appeal to Reason,* one could trust that it was the One Hoss who was speaking, not an apologist for the trusts or the patent medicine peddlers or the get-rich-quick schemers. Socialism had meant, for Wayland, a return to a politics that he believed had held sway before corruption had set in in the Republican party as the spoils of victory in the Civil War. So it was a strong counterargument.

But market forces were strong, and Wayland was the least prepared by his background to stand against them. Here was a man who had made good as a speculator and who knew how to run a successful newspaper before he became a socialist. Here was a man who had thrown himself into the Populist campaign in 1890 in Colorado by reviving a weak party newspaper, in part by buying advertising space for it in the mainstream press, and who had flooded the state of Colorado with standard Populist pamphlets, a typical advertising stratagem. His own sources of funds were not inexhaustible, and he was caught up in the tide of the times, in the siren lure of advertising the socialist dream. Once the first step had been made, the subsequent ones were easier to take.

We know when the self-promotions, subscription bonuses, giveaways, and advertisements crept into the paper, even though we do not know precisely why: but the answer might lead to a more basic understanding of why, in the United States, socialism never took root as it was doing in Europe at the same time. For, as Eric Foner has suggested, America was rushing headlong into a consumer culture at exactly the same time that socialism as a movement and as a political party was growing.[20] Wayland was certainly as much a man of the age as any of his contemporaries were, a man for whom numbers of followers, of subscriptions sold, and of pieces of mail sent out were all important indicators along the road to success. He wanted to prove socialism to be practical at Ruskin by showing that cooperation worked; and though he admitted failure there, the basic impulse remained. Wayland tried again to join in the competing chorus for the attention of the American consumer, for he had something he wanted to sell.

Wayland learned the same lessons from the 1898 war as did the yellow journalists in New York. Circulation was king, and self-promotion to boost it was now the rule. Pulitzer's *World* boasted about its circulation on the front page. Its illustrations helped bring in more subscribers, and its bold headlines attracted attention and readers. Wayland picked up all these gimmicks within a few short years. The first to come was self-advertising, probably at the instigation of a new circulation manager. Changes began in the early months of 1899, and commercial advertising came within the year.

Wayland had hesitantly tried other innovations the year before. In the dark days of the Spanish-American-Philippine War, he lowered the yearly subscription from fifty to twenty-five cents, but this only cost him revenue, so he reinstated the original price.[21] He called for contributions to equip people to sell the *Appeal* from covered wagons and to hire agitators to hawk subscriptions around the country.[22] He also tried to provide regional editions, as well as inside matter for other socialist journals.[23] The circulation fell steadily during this period until he resorted to the kind of advertising that a reform publication could carry without fear of taint: "Ads being accepted at 15¢ a line or $1.50 an inch a week restricted to reform publications, lectures and meetings." Yet he could sell only a couple of inches.[24]

The high pressure began in February, 1899. To increase the circulation, premiums were offered. The first item to be given away was a "first class sewing machine."[25] On May 6, the paper instituted a monthly contest featuring a gift to the most successful subscription hustler—an "art vase, suitably inscribed."[26] This issue glowed with the white heat of aggressive sales tactics; the copy, probably written by circulation manager Dodge, extolled the qualities of the vase in language that was usually reserved for describing the advances of the movement. In the next issue, promotions hit the front page, where Wayland solicited a special fund to send the *Appeal* for a year to editors of all weekly and daily newspapers in the United States and Canada.[27] In another promotion, those who sent in five annual subscriptions were offered "a free 16"×20" crayon portrait that traveling agents charge 4–8 dollars for."

While the vase contest and the editors'-fund solicitation were still running, the *Appeal* sweetened the pot a little more. A ten-acre farm in the heart of the Arkansas fruit belt would be given to the worker who sent in the largest number of yearly subscriptions in a six-week period; the *Appeal* claimed that "growers will have to beat the fruit off the trees to keep them from breaking under the load."[28] The next week saw a letter from Eugene Debs pitching for the editors' fund and mentioning in passing that Wayland himself had contributed $100. When the editors' fund had been subscribed,[29] a new gimmick appeared: instruments to outfit a complete brass band would be given to socialists in the city with the highest circulation when the paper's circulation itself topped 75,000.[30]

At the end of 1899 the circulation stood at 61,000.[31] The promotions no doubt helped to bring it up to this level. What also helped and became a lasting part of the *Appeal*'s existence, was the Appeal Army, an idea of Wayland's that emerged slowly, beginning as an attempt to praise those who sent subscriptions. When Wayland first started the *Coming Nation*, it will be recalled, he printed the names of all of the subscribers until the lists took up too much space. He ran many letters from his readers, which often filled nearly a quarter of the four-page paper. The letters first came under the name of "Shot and Shell of the *Coming Nation* Postal Battery." Later, to describe the exploits of the paper's hustlers, Wayland ran columns named "Roll of Honor" or "Patriots—Men and Women Who Are Stirred by the Sufferings of Humanity." On May 20, 1899, the column was called the "Appeal Army," and was written by circulation manager E. W. Dodge in the same folksy manner as the Ruskin "Village Jottings" in the *Coming Nation*.[32]

The idea of the army was to grow through the next two decades, but at its birth, it was a means of increasing circulation. It was also a rhetorical foil to justify compromises, such as nonmovement advertising, and to address the problem of insufficient revenue. Speaking confidently to his workers at the turn of the century, Wayland said that newsprint, now controlled by a trust, had so increased in price that he was losing money at the club rate of twenty cents, but "25¢ will do it." The Appeal Army made money sometimes. Fifty cents was the going rate for an individual subscription, but by putting together a group of people who received their papers at a single address, the *Appeal* could save postage and work, so it offered a large discount. If the hustler took the difference between fifty cents and the club rate, he could often make a living. One man, in fact, lived on this kind of income for more than a decade, starting first with the *Coming Nation* in 1893 or 1894 and adding the *Appeal* in 1895, as well as other reform journals. By the end of his life he had taken more than one hundred thousand subscriptions and had sold twenty thousand books and pamphlets for Wayland alone. He had, however, been arrested, pelted with rotten eggs, and otherwise intimidated along the way. When Wayland asked for another five cents in the clubbing rate, he was taking a nickel out of the pockets of the army's members.[33]

Wayland used the army to announce that he was "going to take one column of advertising if that is all right with them." He added cryptically that, "Things are changing and have changed."[34] The ads started out harmlessly enough, as they were mostly for socialist publications. Nine months after the experiment began, only two ads were commercial in nature: one from Wayland's son Jon, who was selling lead pencils, and another from a local man, who was offering a shorthand course. The policy was to accept only local ads at first, but eventually to take ads from a little further afield and from other socialists. By January 5, 1901, aside from the ads for *Appeal* books and other socialist publications, readers could buy typewriters c/o the *Appeal*, or rubber stamps from Fort Scott, Kansas, or poultry feed from Parsons, Kansas, or Nature's Remedies, also from Kansas; they could have their fortunes told from Springfield, Missouri, or they could buy a blacksmith's forge a little farther away, from Minnesota, but from "a firm whose every man voted socialist" in the past election. A year later, the ads changed shape again. Although there was still only about half a column of them, the number of non-publication ads increased: for example, "Why Work for Others? When you can become your own boss and become independent at home."[35] This was essentially the same message that Wayland preached when he gave away farms to subscription hustlers, a message that differed dramatically from the editorial intent of the newspaper.

Illustrations came in the ads in 1902, and the column length grew as the price rose from sixty to seventy-five cents a line to reflect the growing circulation.[36] By October 4, 1902, there was considerable spillover, though Wayland was still claiming that only one column of ads would be sold. The next week someone in the office must have noticed the contradiction; the announcement that only one column would be sold was quietly withdrawn, and with it, the last public notice of advertising rates. The paper had just surpassed two hundred thousand in circulation. To celebrate the amassing of four hundred thousand Socialist votes in the 1902 off-year election, the *Appeal* ran a special eight-page edition on November 22, which included one full page of advertising. The ads promised cures for gray hair, epilepsy, consumption, rheumatism, and impotence in men (an electric belt would do the trick), as well as offering bargains in watches and fountain pens.

This edition publicly marked the important change that had been taking place. In a two-column story on the back page, under a cut of the latest Hoe Press that had just been installed, Wayland spoke frankly about the dimensions to which the business had grown. He talked about the moves to five different, successively larger locations in Girard; the new press; the growth of the staff to forty people; and weekly expenses of $1,300 to $1,400, with income approximately the same. He made plans for a regular eight-page edition, with more advertising in order to keep the costs down. Already his weekly had the fourth-largest circulation in the country, but he wanted a million readers. As 1903 opened, he trumpeted his need to buy a color press (he had just bought the Hoe Press but wanted to trade it in), equal to that used by the big dailies: *"The day has gone by for small mediums to tackle great undertakings and we must prepare to propagate Socialism in just the proportions that Capitalism operates."*[37] In the same issue of the *Appeal*, H. Gaylord Wilshire, the publisher of *Wilshire's Magazine*, Wayland's chief competitor, who was also after a million readers,[38] placed an advertisement announcing $3,000 worth of prizes for sending in subscriptions; they included a piano, a billiard table, and a graphophone.

The issue was now, in 1903, fully joined. Under the pressure that had led to the beginnings of advertising, the competitive fires in Wayland were unleashed. The *Appeal to Reason*, the largest circulation political weekly ever to be published in the United States, had decided to fight the enemy with capitalism's own tools and on its own ground. Big capital would be tackled by big socialism. The American consumer could choose between their relative merits. The contradiction was not lost on the people with whom Wayland shared a common background, the county-press editors. Here is one potshot from 1903:

The Appeal to Reason, down in Girard, that great and noisy mouthpiece of Socialism, is selling its space to advertise some of the rankest and most barefaced frauds that we know of. The Appeal pretends to be a consistent lover of truth, justice and equal rights to all mankind, and to allow quack doctors to use its columns for the dollars there are in it smacks very much of the consistent love of monopolists for all mankind, and their great need for gain. If the one-hoss editor, as he styles himself, of the Appeal, has common horse sense he knows such advertisers are frauds and grafters. And he should not rave so about a subsidized press while serving the catchpenny humbugs.[39]

As Wayland pushed the *Appeal* past the one-hundred-thousand and then past the two-hundred-thousand mark, he began to get serious competition for the eye of the socialist reader. The competition (in addition to the profit squeeze he was feeling) may have pressured him to start advertising commercial products. Two serious competitors were Charles H. Kerr and Gaylord Wilshire. In July, 1900, Kerr published the first number of the *International Socialist Review*. For a time, Kerr, who wanted to make his press the intellectual center of the movement, took over the *Appeal's* book business.

Six months later followed a more serious contender for mass circulation, Wilshire's first magazine, the *Challenge*. For the next ten years, Wilshire was the only publisher to challenge Wayland in total circulation; once he briefly surpassed the *Appeal*. Wilshire, according to a recent historian, "stands out as one of the oddest characters in a movement where eccentricity was entirely normal." A contemporary called him the "P. T. Barnum of American socialism."[40] Wilshire shared a few traits with Wayland: they were both real-estate speculators, publishers, and socialists who propagandized the movement. There the similarities ended. Wilshire was born into some wealth; he liked to dress as a dandy and to exploit his superficial resemblance to George Bernard Shaw. He knew the leading literary and radical figures in London and New York. He became a billboard magnate and used his billboards to promote his own Socialist candidacy as well as the *Appeal to Reason*. At one point, Wilshire sold gold stock to promote himself, his magazine, and socialism; he promoted health foods, miracle cures, Maxim Gorky's ill-fated American tour, and recordings of famous socialist orators, some of which he faked himself. Above all, Wilshire promoted Wilshire and *Wilshire's Magazine*.[41]

Born in 1861 the son of a wealthy businessman, Wilshire twice ran on socialist tickets in the early 1890s and then spent four years in England,

$1.00 A YEAR   10 CENTS A COPY

T̲H̲E̲ INTERNATIONAL SOCIALIST REVIEW

A Monthly Journal of
International Socialist Thought

Vol. I   JULY 1, 1900   No. 1

Contents

Published by CHARLES H. KERR & COMPANY
(Incorporated on the Co-operative Plan)
56 FIFTH AVENUE, CHICAGO, U. S. A.

H. Gaylord Wilshire during his campaign for Congress in Los Angeles in 1900. From the Challenge *(New York), October 12, 1901, p. 15.*

where he met the radical elite. Returning to southern California in the late 1890s, he began the publication of the *Challenge* in support of his attempt to secure the SDP nomination for California's Sixth Congressional District, which he won, though he lost the race. Where Wayland used the first person singular to emphasize his ideas, Wilshire used it to glorify himself and his one basic idea, the motto for his publication: "Let the Nation Own the Trusts." It was a powerful slogan, for it was between 1899 and 1901 that the consolidation of American industry took place, the time when great combinations such as U.S. Steel were born. Wilshire used his message—self-promotion in the form of publishing countless letters of praise—and the depth of his pocketbook to reach thirty thousand readers in short order.[42]

From the start, Wilshire accepted advertising in his well-designed eight-page weekly (priced at fifty cents a year). The ads slighted socialist literature, instead concentrating on local and national products. Before 1901, Wilshire was publishing advertisements for such national brands as Lea & Perrins sauces, Pearline soaps, Williams shaving products, Van Houten's cocoa, Libby's soups, Remington typewriters, Bicycle playing cards, and Elgin watches. In spite of a savage obituary on Philip D. Armour, Armour's company bought quarter-page ads for its extract of beef.[43] Wilshire's success in getting these ads probably stemmed from his position as a businessman in Los Angeles, where he was responsible for developing the West Lake district. (Wilshire Boulevard was named for him.)

McKinley's assassination in 1901 caused a wave of antisocialist and antianarchist feelings throughout the country. The press characterized the assassin as a "crazed anarchist." Most national brands no longer advertised in the magazine, except for quack remedies. It is interesting to speculate whether the decision to cancel these ads was made by individual corporate owners, their advertising agents, or Washington politicians.[44]

The period after the assassination proved to be difficult for all radicals, and it coincided with Wilshire's attempt to broaden his influence by moving to New York City. He hoped that the paper, which had grown to sixteen pages, could take advantage of more modern equipment and that he could be more in the center of activity. He was stopped on reapplying for his second-class mailing permit, possibly on orders from President Theodore Roosevelt. Denial of the permit would mean a tenfold increase in the amount of postage the magazine would have to pay. Instead of New York, therefore, he went to Canada, where he continued to publish and where he could take advantage of the reciprocal postal agreement between the two countries. He returned to New York City in 1904, and a local politician, convinced that a constituent was being deprived of Wilshire's sizable printing bill, eased the process for getting the new second-class permit. Wilshire spared no effort to gain circulation. He used every kind of premium, and he cut his subscription price to ten cents for a handsome monthly, whose size, frequency, price, and design fluctuated often, in the hope that with four hundred thousand readers, he could charge advertising rates that would make the paper a success.[45]

Wilshire was always pushing for circulation, but Charles Kerr, with his *International Socialist Review,* never seemed to hope for a large audience. He was more interested in Marxist theory than were either of his fellow publishers, and he attempted to circulate the classics of the movement. But ultimately, Kerr had to turn to the same kind of advertising as his rivals, emphasizing patent medicines and get-rich-quick schemes.[46]

After getting a college education (his father was a professor of Greek at the University of Wisconsin) and reading Bellamy's *Looking Backward,*

Kerr dabbled in populism, because he never cared much for "DeLeon's extremely unattractive version of Engels."[47] When Kerr founded his own press in 1893, having learned the business from Unitarians, he first published a number of Populist books. Then with two other reformers, he published a periodical, *New Time*, which reached a circulation of thirty thousand before it collapsed in the general demise of reform journals during the Spanish-American-Philippine War.

The next year, Kerr returned full time to the book publishing business. He published works of more weight than had previously been available to the American socialist movement. DeLeon was the only other Marxist providing what Kerr called "a half dozen excellent but badly translated pamphlets from the German." Kerr observed that the "really popular and widely circulated books in 1899 were of a sentimental, semi-populistic character, and were of doubtful value to the building up of a coherent socialist movement."[48] Those were the books and pamphlets that Wayland sold in the tens of thousands of copies, and they preached the kind of socialism that Wayland propagated. Kerr now published English translations of works by such Europeans as Karl Kautsky, Emile Vandervelde, Paul Lafargue, Antonio Labriola, Karl Marx, and Friedrich Engels, as well as works by such emerging American Marxists as Algie Martin Simons and his wife, May Wood Simons.

The Charles H. Kerr & Co. publishing house was run differently from Wayland's or Wilshire's operation. It had originally been set up as a corporation in 1893, but little of the stock was sold, and it remained in Kerr's hands. Kerr later turned it into a cooperative; he had sold between eight hundred and one thousand ten-dollar shares by 1905, but he continued to control the company personally. In July, 1900, he began the *International Socialist Review* (*ISR*) with University of Wisconsin alumnus A. M. Simons as editor; it offered fairly rigorous "scientific" socialist articles, without the didactic overlay of DeLeon's work. Unlike Wilshire (who told Kerr he had invested $70,000 of his own money in his magazine during its first five years),[49] or Wayland, Kerr had no money to launch the *ISR*. As the shares of cooperative stock were bought and as the initial subscriptions were taken, the first issues went out, and the bills were slowly paid. During its first four years of operation, the *ISR* never had more than a $500 balance in the bank, making advertising revenues necessary to ensure the life of the publication.

The *Appeal*, *Wilshire's*, and to a lesser extent, Kerr's *International Socialist Review* performed a vital function for the young socialist movement, as they were its major means of communication. Like other institutions, they began to take on lives of their own, separate from and independent of the party. Their struggles to exist made them compromise their ideals by accepting advertising. Staying in business became their first priority.

There was, of course, another avenue that they could have traveled, the one that seemed to make the most sense for a socialist movement: a party-owned and -directed press. The example of DeLeon's SLP, with its controlled press, was a powerful deterrent which no one else wanted to repeat. The question did agitate the leaders of American socialism so much that they debated it furiously in 1900 and especially in 1904, as we will see in the next chapter.

Wayland's entrepreneurial sense, Wilshire's capital, and Kerr's cooperative-stock publishing house afforded three answers. Kerr knew that the socialists could not rely on commercial houses to supply socialist books and pamphlets, even though there was obviously a demand for them and some profit to be made. To sell books cheaply enough for large audiences, publishers would have to make them popular in style, watering down their radical contents. More serious works, Kerr felt, were out of the reach of workingmen.[50] Wayland long ago had argued that the capitalist press could not sustain radical news coverage, although he seemed to forget his own argument when he urged the editors of the nation's press to include more radical and socialist news.

Wayland's *Appeal to Reason* was, first and foremost, a business enterprise. He was attacked by a subscriber for having bought a new linotype machine which displaced a number of typesetters: "The great trouble with a large number of our 'journalistic emancipators' today is that while advocating the 'rights of labor,' they allow their own selfishness to manifest itself on every 'profitable' occasion."[51] Wayland replied that he was operating in a competitive system, that socialism had not come yet, and that he had to pay for the extortions of five hundred trusts. Once, in a lead article, Wayland remarked that the socialists themselves were setting up trusts. "H. G. Wiltshire [*sic*] is setting up a bill posting trust. Nelson of St. Louis is setting up a plumbing goods trust. . . . The fact is that any one who is doing business today must adopt the methods prevailing or go out of business."[52] Wilshire made the same argument, but characteristically he made it flamboyantly and paradoxically. He received numerous complaints about the capitalist advertising that appeared in his magazine, especially about the ads from C. W. Post (who was notorious for his outspoken antiunionism) for Grape Nuts and Postum, a cereal coffee. Wilshire argued that his other advertisers were probably just as adamant against organized workingmen, but he would continue to take their and Post's money. The readers were free, if they liked, not to buy those products. Almost everything in America was made by capitalists, he said, but consumers could choose not to purchase. Without advertising money, *Wilshire's* would not be able to publish: "We ourselves think it would be foolish to stop the publication of this journal for any such sentimentality."[53]

The staff of the Appeal to Reason *in front of the third building it occupied in Girard, Kansas, May 8, 1900. J. A. Wayland is second from the right in the back row; his brother-in-law C. D. Bevan is in the row in front of Wayland, fourth from the right. Courtesy of Virginia Lashley and the J. A. Wayland Collection, Pittsburg State University.*

Wilshire's was tied more closely to the revenues of capitalist advertising than was Wayland's paper, whose publishing costs were lower and whose subscription price and circulation were usually higher. But Wilshire made a telling point when he remarked that they all depended on the capitalist to help make their way. The note that Wilshire had penned about advertising revenue accompanied an ad from the Girard Cereal Company, promoting its own cereal coffee, Nutrito. (Wilshire happily advocated buying from this advertiser instead of from Post.) That company was allied with the *Appeal*, as the *Appeal* was attempting to make itself less dependent on the outside world. From 1900 on, the *Appeal* was growing and becoming Girard's largest employer. It was also growing beyond Wayland's single-handed control; he had to rely more and more on hired help to run his expanding enterprise.

The people who came to work for him were still inspired by the goals of the movement more than by business necessities. Most of them did not have Wayland's hard-won business sense; none had his wealth. The issues that aroused them after the turn of the century were those that aroused many others in the industrialized parts of the country: labor conditions, monopoly capitalism, women's issues, socialist organizing, and the role of the *Appeal* vis-à-vis the Socialist Party of America. Wayland had confronted these issues, too, and had made his own compromises.

The younger people who were attracted to Girard confronted them again and, in so doing, clashed with Wayland and revealed many of the problems that would continue to stalk the socialist movement as it sought to gain adherents among a majority of Americans in the mass culture of the early twentieth century.

6
Strike

Wayland's original plan of printing a small paper at a nominal subscription rate was long outmoded, and the *Appeal* in 1904 was no more like the *Appeal* of Wayland's dream than hell is like heaven.
—*Fred Warren, "The Little Old Appeal"*

In October, 1903, most of the fifty or so employees at the *Appeal*'s office in Girard, Kansas, organized, set up a union, bargained, went out on strike, settled the strike, and went back to work. The paper did not miss printing an issue, and it would not experience labor troubles again. The strike opened up many issues besides narrow labor-management questions that begged for resolution; but resolution did not come, probably because no answers could be found that would resolve all of the dilemmas facing a radical movement in the consumer society of turn-of-the-century America. The *Appeal* emerged from the struggle as a solid commercial enterprise. Its business was socialist propaganda. Instead of a learning experience, the strike was an extreme embarrassment, from which the socialist movement drew only one lasting lesson: avoid labor problems within socialist institutions. The lessons that it did not learn concern us here.

The obvious causes of the strike were straightforward labor-management problems: wages were low for workers but high for management. Some of the bosses were seedy characters who were solely interested in lining their own pockets. Working conditions were poor. But what brought these conditions about in the first place? How could a socialist publication come to this kind of confrontation? The movement in general had a blind spot, which this strike seems to illustrate well. A series of dualisms lay at the core of problems that the socialist movement in America continued to experience: the relationship between management and worker, between advertising and socialist principles, between independent radical newspapers and official party papers, and between what was considered female and male. These dualisms point

The staff of the Appeal to Reason *in front of its fourth office in 1904. Courtesy of the Historical Society of Crawford County, Girard, Kansas.*

up the ways in which the mass culture of which the *Appeal* was a part helped to shape decisions, regardless of the employer's commitment to socialist principles. In this chapter, we will look at the immediate causes of the strike. In the next chapter, we will focus on two aspects of it, an attempt to turn back the clock by a group of idealistic editors, and the question of women at the *Appeal*.

The most important single factor leading up to the strike was Wayland's belief that the "time had gone by for small mediums to tackle great issues." J. A. Wayland and his competitors accepted the spirit of American enterprise at the same time as they rejected the development of American industrial capitalism. Wilshire had said that he would not stop publishing his paper for the "sentimentality" of not accepting advertising, even advertising from one of the nation's leading union-busting firms.

Wayland's embrace of the basic motivating premises of American mass culture led him to want the biggest and the best newspaper plant that money could buy. Once the basic premise was accepted, two corollary principles followed: keep costs down and keep income up. What followed from the first principle was to locate in a town where labor costs were low and to displace skilled workers with efficient machinery. He had

J. A. Wayland, Editor of the *Appeal to Reason*.
A character study by Ryan Walker.

From the Comrade, *vol. 1, no. 12 (September, 1902), p. 272.*

remarked shortly after arriving in town: "Why right here in Girard men are paid 50 cents a day for labor though of course there is not work for all of them."[1] Although the remark was meant sarcastically in an *Appeal* paragraph, as a goad to push people to change their situations, Wayland wasn't going to help out by paying higher wages. What followed from the second principle was circulation at all costs, abetted by all the gimmicks mentioned in the preceding chapter, low subscription prices, and the Appeal Army. The collision between the pragmatic methods that were being used and the idealistic goals that were envisioned for the future created tensions at the core of the American socialist movement. The strike at the *Appeal* was the clearest manifestation of these contradictions.

The pursuit of a national paper was Wayland's first motive when he moved from Colorado to Indiana in 1893, and it became an end in itself. The cost-cutting factors that landed him in Girard, Kansas, in 1897 made the construction of a great national paper seem even more possible. In a small town that had no big factories, no rival intellectual group, and none of the harsh realities of modern city life, Wayland was isolated and content. He could create the kind of conditions in Girard that would insulate his thinking and allow him to make decisions that would not have been possible in an urban setting. His own personal circumstances became easier as the years wore on. By the turn of the century he managed his household on an increasingly lavish scale; after the death of his wife in 1898, he indulged his daughters and sons, lived in one of the town's grandest homes, with servants to cook, clean, and transport him around town, and continued to travel extensively for the purposes of real-estate speculation.[2] On one trip in the summer of 1899, Wayland made a whirlwind tour of these old haunts: Memphis, Tennessee City, Ruskin, Nashville, Cincinnati, Osgood, Versailles, and St. Louis.[3]

After the death of his wife, Wayland tried to keep up the household with the aid of a succession of housekeepers, cooks, and governesses, who came and went, none of whom he liked very much. He started to become attached, however, to Pearl Hunt, who worked at the printing office and who, for a time, became the housekeeper at the Wayland residence. After three months, she went back to the paper, and in another three months she "gave up her case and started shorthand school at Pittsburg."[4] Wayland courted her throughout 1900, and the two were married in April, 1901. In these times, Wayland not only turned to Miss Hunt for solace but also went to fortune-tellers in Pittsburg, Kansas, whom he took seriously enough to record a prediction. He went to as many entertainments as possible, including Buffalo Bill's Wild West Show in Pittsburg.[5]

In his diary for these years he turns reflective only once. Taking his daughter Ollie and her friends on a camping trip in the summer of 1900, he jotted down these thoughts:

> Monday morning, Aug 13, while the girls and driver were out on a trip, I rowed down to the old mill, once the pride of its owner, now falling to decay. Its massive stone walls are crumbling by the hand of time. And I thought how like it are all the works of men—merely the passing incidents of time like a blade of grass. And somehow it came to me that men who climb up the ladder of fame merely to write their name there for the coming generations to see, are like the mill. The thoughts or deeds of men, when worthy, will be written enduringly only by others in love of the benefits of the action.

Wayland was looking backwards as much as he was looking ahead. His marriage to Pearl Hunt had many of the appearances of an attempt to re-create the first half of his life. Most telling, perhaps, was the honeymoon that he planned, which included many of the same stops as twenty-four years before, when he and Etta had gone on their honeymoon. The newlyweds went back to Mammoth Cave; they even stayed at the same hotel. This time, however, Wayland and his new bride took in a play every night they were in Chicago and St. Louis and stayed at the finest hotels. But just as in years past, Wayland accounted for every penny. The three-week trip cost $572.70. Counting the team of sorrels that he bought for $260 and the carriage for $200 and harness for $40 and the $1,000 that he gave to Jon on his wedding day, J. A. Wayland in 1901 was living the life of a rich householder in a prosperous small town. It wasn't just real-estate speculation that was allowing this luxury, for the "office did big business while I was gone"; in three weeks, $8,000 had been taken in by the *Appeal to Reason*.[6]

The success that the paper was having as a business enterprise helped to fuel criticism of the One-Hoss editor. Wayland was not without his critics. Most socialist opinion makers were not so isolated, and not all socialist leaders and publishers felt that a strong national paper was essential in order for the movement to gain power. Many felt the need for strong socialist local organizations and strong regional newspapers to give the movement a solid foundation and a strong sense of community identity. The competition that the *Appeal* created for the local readership drew strong criticism. Two of the most prominent critics who clashed with Wayland on this issue were Herman Titus of Seattle and Victor Berger of Milwaukee.

Both men were roughly contemporary with Wayland but had had radically different upbringings. Titus was born in Massachusetts in 1852, attended several colleges, and graduated in 1890 from Harvard University Medical School. Shortly afterwards he moved to Seattle to practice medicine and to rise to the leadership of the local party and the editorship of the *Socialist*. Berger was born in 1860 in Austria, to a substantial innkeeper family, and attended the University of Vienna and the University of Budapest; however, he emigrated with his family to the United States before completing a degree. Victor Berger ended up in Milwaukee, a city dominated by ethnic Germans. He taught German in the public schools and soon became the leader of the Milwaukee socialists.[7] The two men were active in cities where factories and poverty were much more evident than in sleepy Girard.

Titus attacked Wayland from the left; Berger, from a reformist position. Titus criticized the One-Hoss Philosophy for not acknowledging the existence of class struggle. During 1902, while Titus and Wayland were trading barbs, a letter to the *Socialist*, attacking the *Appeal*, had it this way:

> The comrades—some of them well meaning, no doubt—who would have us disregard the principles of the class-struggle in our fight for

Drawn by Ryan Walker, in the Comrade, *vol. 3, no. 8 (May, 1903), p. 194.*

Herman F. Titus
—Appeal to Reason

political supremacy, are like a man who would enter into a fight with another man upon unequal terms; the one having a sword and the other throwing bouquets or epigrams at his adversary in answer to his sword thrusts. So also are our well meaning but misguided sentimental comrades. In answer to the thrusts of the capitalist class, i.e., strikes, lockouts, shooting down of workers by the militia, bull penning, merciless exploitation of men, women and even children, they would answer those thrusts with sweet sentiment and advocacy of petty reform.[8]

That was treating Wayland too harshly. He surely advocated more than petty reform, but in his desire to make socialism palatable to the largest possible audience, he certainly fell short of a revolutionary spirit. Titus adduced another "proof" of Wayland's scattershot approach to socialism by pointing out that the *Appeal* kept selling "old theological literature [i.e., Populist pamphlets] it had kept on its shelves for years and calling it Socialist propaganda."⁹ But it was on another issue, related to the ideological one, that Titus was joined by Berger.

In Berger's *Social Democratic Herald*, the Milwaukee socialist laid out the problem clearly. He noted in 1904, a half-year after the strike at the *Appeal*, that the latest edition of Titus's paper carried the banner headline "Shall *The Socialist* Live or Die?" and Berger bemoaned the fact of the "sign of distress from a paper that has come to be a pillar of strength to the western movement." In spite of such favorable publishing conditions as not paying for rent, heat, and light and of receiving a lot of volunteer help, the paper was about to go out of business. The cause? "The *Appeal to Reason* is up to its old tricks again," trying to increase its own circulation at the expense of other socialist papers. "And in order to do this has been exploiting its workers in the most miserable manner and using the profits it bleeds from their veins to reduce the price of its paper for various localities where it has a competitor to run into the ground." The *Appeal* was, in a period that produced the greatest capital concentrations in American history, threatening local socialist publications with extinction.

Berger pointed out that much of the early success of the Populist movement had been the result of a strong local press, responding to local issues. But that success was not being repeated by the socialists. Instead, the local socialist papers were folding: "Their local movement gets a setback and their locality fills up with the sorts of converts who have come to be called 'Appeal to Reason Socialists,' that is Appeal Army Socialists, who care more for a chance to win some trumpery prize than they do to win the cooperative commonwealth."¹⁰

The *Social Democratic Herald*, on the other hand, didn't suffer from *Appeal* competition because Berger claimed strong local support, some of which is clearly evidenced by the nature of the advertising in his paper. There was also some in Titus's paper. Local merchants, factories, and businesses of all kinds, in trying to attract the considerable number of workers who read the papers to buy their goods and services, bought much advertising, in contrast to the patent medicine and get-rich-quick schemes that were the bread and butter of most national publications, regardless of political bent.

The Populist papers lived till the movement itself had died. With us, it will not be the movement that will eventually kill its papers but its papers may fall away and nearly kill the movement. Look at the list of recent suspensions: The Coming Nation (swallowed up by Wayland when it was in distress), the New Nation, California Socialist, Utah Socialist, Erie People, Socialist Standard, Socialist Spirit, Colorado Socialist, Wage Worker, Humanity, etc., etc.[11]

Without admitting that all of the distress that Berger and Titus pinpointed had been caused by the *Appeal to Reason*, the point that the *Appeal* itself would grant was the irresistible pressure it felt to "expand or bust," as Fred Warren, the editor who took over the reins shortly after the strike, would characterize it. The opposing pressures that were bubbling forth flowed irresistibly from Wayland's desire to help make the *Appeal* the great paper that it was becoming, the natural conclusion to which anyone who had been steeped in American values would be led. In so doing, he tried to combine the folksy nature of his One-Hoss presence in the context of a publication with a huge circulation. The strains quickly became evident.

The whole notion of personal journalism that Wayland had proclaimed with his One-Hoss Philosophy—namely, that his readers would trust that he alone was at the helm—was fiction from at least the turn of the century, if not earlier. When circulation surpassed one hundred thousand, the *Appeal to Reason* could no longer be managed from Wayland's cluttered desk. It never had been solely Wayland's work; it had involved printers and typesetters and "girls" who wrapped and addressed papers and kept track of subscribers, at least since the hard times after the Spanish-American-Philippine War, when it seemed possible that the paper might fail. But Wayland himself had written the front page of the *Coming Nation* and then the *Appeal* since 1893, except for a short period before his first wife's death; and he had often written the back page, as well as other articles. Only for a brief unhappy period had he admitted an associate editor, A. S. Edwards, to the masthead. He was loath to do it again after the Ruskin debacle, when Edwards helped to engineer the takeover of the paper. There were his two associates, brother-in-law Bevan and business manager Phelps, along with the circulation booster Dodge, to help out; but none of these men ever signed Wayland's articles. All three would be denounced by the rank-and-file workers at the plant. F. G. R. Gordon, who worked his way in succession through the Greenback, Populist, and Socialist parties on his way to the *Appeal*, had been the first to write articles for the paper on a regular basis, probably as a paid member of the staff. But he had moved on.[12]

Wayland needed constant editorial assistance to bring fresh ideas to the front page of the paper, which had continued to make the same points, often in the same words, year after year. As his enterprise grew, he had to bring new talent to Girard. At first, he naturally turned to the group he knew best and felt comfortable with: the country editors. Sharing his concerns as well as having similar backgrounds and working lives, these people understood one another. Most were socialists who had subscribed to the One-Hoss Philosophy and to the *Appeal* before they had come to Girard. As the group grew, it expanded to include labor leaders, Marxists, and three women in prominent roles during the first decade of the twentieth century. Several had attended Ruskin College in Trenton, Missouri, a new labor institution, which sought to make socialists through education.[13] Thus, after 1900, the *Appeal* began to take on a new look.

In 1903 the *Appeal* added a women's feature, due mostly to the pressure that Wayland was feeling from a group of socialist country editors who had taken over the *Coming Nation* in 1902, just as the last commune attempt had died. This group, which we will focus on in chapter 7, was made up of a core of three men who left the *Appeal* in disgust a year and one-half before the strike. They had induced Kate Richards O'Hare to write for them. O'Hare had been one of the group that had been attracted to Girard by the International School of Social Economy, a successor school to Ruskin College. The new school was run by a veteran of reform causes, Walter Thomas Mills, whom the local press in Girard called "a circus clown" because in 1888 he had been for Prohibition, in 1896 for Bryan, and in 1900 for Debs.[14] Kate Richards was married to Frank O'Hare at the Wayland's, but she nevertheless helped out others of the *Appeal* staff who left Girard in 1902 to go to Rich Hill, Missouri, in order to recapture some of the more innocent fire of the 1890s movement. Most, however, elected to stay with the flagship paper.[15]

The women's column of the *Appeal* was under the by-line of Josephine Conger. Born in Centralia, Missouri, she was a niece of J. A. Wayland's and had learned the newspaper business from her brother. She was drawn into the movement through the influence of Ernest Untermann, a translator of Marx, who was also a colleague at the *Appeal*.[16] Untermann came on board as managing editor to succeed Warren. The first rigorous Marxist to join the staff, he was fluent in German and had translated a number of socialist classics. These were published by Charles Kerr and were also sold by the *Appeal*'s book department. Untermann contributed analytical articles on current topics of interest in a column that he wrote for the second page. In the words of a future colleague, "he was scientific to the core and gave his message of solidity that was new to the *Appeal*."[17] In June, 1903, Wayland hired Charles L. Breckon away from the *Chicago Socialist* to write a labor column, which was to place the paper for the first time squarely in support of labor. Breckon was a veteran of the trade-union movement.[18]

By 1903 the *Appeal* was changing its style. Wayland's paragraphs still

*Ernest Untermann. From
the* Comrade, *vol. 2, no. 3
(December, 1902), p. 62.*

dominated the front page, but the inside was filled with more labor news, articles written from a more-or-less-rigorous Marxist perspective by Ernest Untermann, and Josephine Conger's new column, which presented women's concerns. But the expansion that led to the hiring of new staff, ever-increasing circulation, and almost yearly moves to larger quarters around the square in Girard began to expose the weaknesses at the *Appeal* office. After the disaffected group had left for Rich Hill and the *Coming Nation*, there were still at least two people in the office who were upset with the way things were going internally at the paper: labor editor Breckon and Allan W. Ricker.

Ricker was hired as the chief editorial writer in December, 1902.[19] He had studied briefly for the ministry as a youth but had given it up for populism in the early 1890s. He worked as a secretary to a state central committee before he became a socialist and worked two years as a party organizer, active in both Iowa and Nebraska. A farmer, Ricker wrote on agricultural questions for the *Appeal* and tried to respond to the needs of the southwestern and midwestern Populists in an attempt to get them to join the Socialist party. Ricker was well fitted for this task, because he never lost the religious impulse that had led him to the ministry in his early years. The most extended statement of his political philosophy appeared in a piece called "The Political Economy of Jesus." In it, Ricker emphasized the essential moral and ethical goodness of socialism by working out some theological questions that interested him, finding, for example, that although one could not claim that Jesus was a socialist,

A. W. Ricker and George D. Brewer, October 23, 1903. Courtesy of the Archives of Labor and Urban Affairs, Wayne State University.

his attitudes towards entrenched wealth and towards the "working class should be interpreted by the church as a ringing endorsement of the socialist position." The *Appeal* advertised the book, a special edition of *Wayland's Monthly*, as containing these "startling things":

> Trade unions were in existence a thousand years before the time of Jesus. The first missionary work of Jesus and his followers was among the working class who heard him gladly. Jesus was crucified by the ruling classes because He was a labor agitator, arousing discontent among the poor. The early Christians practiced communism and condemned private property until the wily Constantine corrupted the church. The dark ages began soon after Christianity became respectable and deserted the cause of the oppressed working class.[20]

The appeal to popular sentiment in this work no doubt attracted Wayland as much as it would have angered Herman Titus.

It was the coming together of the Chicago union man Breckon and the farmer organizer Ricker, just at the time when the paper was going through its growing pains, that set the stage for the acrimonious strike in the fall of 1903. Ricker defined his role at the *Appeal* as an extension of his previous activities as an organizer for the Socialist party. To this end, the paper started to collect money for an agitation campaign that would fund lectures and meetings for the dual purpose of securing subscriptions to the paper and members for the party. The Socialist party, which was only two years old in 1903, was struggling to do the same things, and the national office was offended by what looked like the *Appeal's* attempt to usurp a primary function of the party. Ricker exchanged many letters with William S. Mailly, national secretary of the party, in an effort to resolve this question. On one occasion, Mailly wrote that the fund being raised by the *Appeal* should be turned over to the National Committee, where it would benefit the entire movement: "If I had $1000 in this office, I would be able to do an amount of work that would astonish your own people," Mailly wrote.[21] Ricker tried to maintain his position against Mailly, asking at one point for some Socialist party financing for Ricker himself to do some organizing among old Populists in Texas, as a joint *Appeal*/party effort. Mailly turned down that proposition and was backed up by a party resolution.[22] Ricker argued that the *Appeal* was interested solely in going to those places where the Socialist party had yet to penetrate and where there were as yet no *Appeal* subscribers and in doing this by financing members of the Appeal Army, who would sell subscriptions and socialism while trying to set up locals. They had done precisely that, he argued, in parts of Kansas.[23]

Their discussion was conducted in a friendly fashion, and some measure of trust developed between Ricker and Mailly, so that Ricker had begun to confide in the national secretary in the fall of 1903. The *Appeal's* editor spoke of many small irritations in the office, some of which had led to Ernest Untermann's departure and had provoked Ricker himself to journey to Washington to procure a union charter.[24] No job was secure at the paper, Ricker pointed out. Many people were paid only $3.00 per week.[25] "The help, from editors on down, have been brought in and let out on the merest whim," making planning impossible.[26] There was, as Ricker saw it, plenty of fuel for a labor dispute. His observations were borne out when Wayland attempted to dismiss two printers who happened to be members of the Socialist party, thus touching off a small explosion which led finally to the organization of a union at the *Appeal*.

Everything was coming to a head. Wayland's ambiguous position towards unionization had been revealed over the five or so years that he had been in Girard as a position that would reflect his own personal circumstances and the extent to which the paper was growing. Shortly after coming to Girard, he noted in an *Appeal* paragraph that he was adding a Linotype, which, under socialism, would have shortened hours instead of replacing men. "Labor, unless it desires to starve, will have to learn the lesson of public ownership."[27] A year later, the printers at the paper, who were making about $5 a day,[28] seemed to be taking Wayland's advice, by organizing and applying to the International Typographical Union: "I have been urging this on my employees for a year. Labor should organize for its protection, no matter how kind and friendly an employer may be."[29]

But at the same time that he was advocating unionization, he was changing the management structure at the paper. His first move in that direction came in early 1900, when he announced that due to the volume of business, the office force would be classified and specialized.[30] "Until recently, the office had no system for the dispatch of business, because I never had any business training. But I have put one of the best trained office men in the country in charge of the office, competent men at the head of every department, and will soon have the office on a basis as accurate as clockwork. . . . At first I was the whole paper, but I feel like I am only a small cog in it now."[31] What that would mean for labor relations was unclear.

Small cog, but one that still was in control of the thirty-one staff members in 1900: "The Appeal office is one of the happiest families of workers in the country," and J. A. saw to it by entertaining them all at his home from time to time.[32] The patriarch who announced in the paper that he was bringing in one of the "best trained office men in the country" did hire Martin Holcomb of Atlanta, Georgia, at $15 a week;[33] but in a few months, Wayland discharged Asa Holcomb, almost certainly Holcomb's son, in favor of hiring Wayland's own son Jon in the mailroom.[34] He wanted to be both an enlightened modern manager and the father of a happy family.

The local press sensed another aspect of the dilemma that lay behind the move to a strike. Although the *Girard Press* constantly reprinted articles attacking socialism, the editor continued to favor J. A. the businessman. However, the *Press* loved to point out such things as the fact that Wayland bragged about his printing plant, which he estimated to be worth about $100,000 in 1903 (almost certainly an overstatement), showing how rich he was; yet he said in his paper that everything should be held in common.[35] Then, like the businessman he was, although he claimed that the plant was so valuable, when it came to taxes, the plant was only worth $5,000, and the stock, $805, yielding a tax bill of $107.68. "How the poor are ground down by this tyrannical government."[36]

In this anomalous milieu, events began to move rapidly in the fall.

Ricker tendered his resignation on October 22, 1903, to take effect in December. He wrote to Mailly that Wayland did not intend to act in good faith: "Internal workings of the *Appeal* are rotten. It has been a sweat shop. It has treated its help like slaves. Its business Manager [Phelps] has made a habit of making insulting approaches to girl employes during periods of semi-intoxication." Ricker felt that there were "abuses in the office that will never be cured as long as Comrade Wayland lives, for they are incidental to his personality. We have enough evidence and could present it in such a way to crush the *Appeal* to atoms but most of these things have existed for years and the *Appeal* has been a mighty educator in spite of them."[37] Here, Ricker got to the nub of the problem. Was not the movement and the good work that the paper was achieving in developing a socialist consciousness more important than the labor abuses at the paper?

The entire story would not be told in the *Appeal* for more than a year. In particular, the paper failed to admit that the dismissal of the printers had led to the organization of the union. Instead, Ricker, who wrote the story, chose to concentrate on another of Wayland's arbitrary acts: his decision to turn over to the party the $1,000 that the *Appeal* had collected for organizing purposes. Wayland might have done this hoping to placate the staff in the office; perhaps he knew of the Ricker/Mailly correspondence and was trying to ingratiate himself with the national office of the party.[38]

Wayland's action managed to make matters worse. It turned out that the staff was incensed by this decision; Ricker claimed in the *Appeal* that the money was really taken out of staff wages. With Wayland away at the time in Texas on a business trip, Ricker described at length in the paper how and why the union was formed, though he did not mention the dismissal of the socialist printers. To be sure, the *Appeal's* work force did already include a handful of union printers, which allowed the paper to carry a union label; and the paper did observe the eight-hour day. But as Ricker had reported to Mailly, wages were low, and other union standards were not observed. Ricker and Breckon spearheaded the move, holding a public meeting on October 10, 1903, in which an AFL federal union was formed. All fifty employees on the staff—of which one-third were women—joined up, with the exception of the business manager and the cashier (Wayland's son).[39]

The *Appeal's* reporting of the labor situation to readers was revealing. Wayland obviously got back to Girard in time to write a short column above Ricker's unionization story, in which he patronized the workers at the *Appeal* and twisted the facts slightly: "The *Appeal* has been preaching unionism and urging the working class to organize for years, and only just now have its own employees taken its advice. The printers would not have organized here but for my urging them to do so, but I waited for the other employes to organize as they saw fit." In fact, he had preached that labor strikes were not the best route for socialists, even if unions might be a step in the right direction.

Ricker, for his part, was seeing unionism up close for the first time. In his published statement, he spoke of the thrill of belonging to a union, and he expressed admiration for the skill of union organizer Breckon. On Wayland's gift to the party, Ricker declared:

> More support has been promised, but there is not a loyal socialist in the land, but that would spurn any further gifts of money, did he know that it was the [result?] of the exploitation of the wrappers, soldiers and humble wage workers at the *Appeal* office. We cannot do right by doing wrong. We must get the help better wages, and give them better treatment and then every dollar that goes out of this office will be as clean as when it came in.[40]

Clearly, the grievances that were piling up against Wayland, and not the boss's urging, had provoked the organization of the union and had precipitated a strike.

Charles Breckon led the walkout on October 23, 1903. He described the situation to a colleague at the *Chicago Socialist:*

> Yesterday at 11:30 the entire force, some 50 employes, walked out of the *Appeal to Reason* Office. The reason was based upon demands made by the editorial staff that certain wrong practices should cease. When J. A. Wayland absolutely refused to concede the justice of our demands, the resignation of the entire staff was at once placed in his hands. Each one immediately called for his time and quit work instanter.
>
> A little over a week ago a Federal Labor Union, No. 11,478, was formed. . . . In brief, our demands have in them a thorough reorganization of the office and that the prevailing sweatshop practices and terrific exploitation of the employes shall cease. . . . The demands cover the principle of making the appeal office a thorough clean and honest place, and what the paper teaches in its columns it shall practice in its office. . . . We have discovered that the use of the union label in the office was but a fiction, and that men and women were made to "walk the plank" at the merest whim of J. A. Wayland, and that the great majority of employes received but $3 per week, and in many cases have been fired if they dared ask for more. . . .
>
> We shall appeal to the local citizens. They are up in arms. Wayland

declares he will suspend the paper which would junk the whole shop and also default on 200,000 subscriptions or $25,000. We declare this to be a deception, and a move to get us out of town, and then commence re-publication with the same old tactics and barefaced deception.[41]

The local establishment viewed Girard's first strike much differently than did Breckon and Ricker. The *Girard Press* made no mention of low wages or poor working conditions, and it saw the personality and character of the foreman at the office as a private matter:

> Several weeks ago, during the absence of J. A. Wayland, the proprietor of the Appeal to Reason, in Texas, the employes organized a branch of the Western Federation of Labor, and upon his return demanded that he discharge from his employ Chas. D. Bevan, his brother-in-law and holder of a few shares of stock in the Appeal to Reason Publishing Co. The employes claim he consented to do so if given two weeks time. When the two weeks had expired they again made the demand, when Mr. Wayland informed them that he would not discharge Mr. Bevan, and had no power to do so, as he was a stockholder. This was no sooner stated than the order was given for a strike, and work stopped almost instantaneously, all the employes walking out except C. D. Bevan, W. F. Phelps, business manager, Mr. Chapman, head pressman, and his assistant, Mr. Bumgardner, and W. T. Nelson, a job printer.
>
> A number of meetings were held by the striking employes, and after going out they demanded that Mr. Phelps, the business manager, be discharged. He held a few shares of stock as well as Mr. Bevan. Mr. Wayland gave them to understand that neither of the two men would be discharged and also gave notice that C. L. Breckon, A. W. Ricker and W. P. Mason, three strike leaders, would not be re-employed, but Friday evening Mr. Phelps handed in his resignation, which was accepted by Mr. Wayland.
>
> Mr. Wayland then said the Appeal to Reason newspaper had suspended and he would never issue another copy, even sending hundreds of letters to the postoffice to be returned to the writers.[42]

In spite of Wayland's threats, the strike was settled in one day. As Breckon's arguments make clear, the workers had Wayland over a barrel. He could not ignore what they had made known without destroying the paper. The following week's paper contained a short lead story, which announced that a strike at the *Appeal* had been settled and that Wayland had acceded to all the union's demands, although he managed to carry out part of his threat against the strike leaders (see below). The article revealed that the employees believed that Wayland's brother-in-law and his business partner had both exploited them. In addition to raising bread-and-butter issues, the union demanded that Wayland sever his relatives' connections to the paper and that the Socialist party be asked to appoint a cashier to replace Jon Wayland. Finally, the union demanded that all profits from the newspaper go to the party.

The pillars of the Girard community, although clearly against the strikers, were gleeful to point out the contradictions from a practical business standpoint:

> J. A. Wayland, by his business capacity, energy, and capital, built up the Appeal to Reason until it has a wonderful circulation. Many thousand dollars of his money are invested in the plant. But along comes a Socialist agitator from Chicago [i.e., Breckon] without a penny's worth of stock in it, and declares that he "will run it or bust it," and succeeds in making Mr. Wayland come to his terms. We suppose this is right from a Socialist standpoint, if Mr. Wayland likes it, but from the standpoint of justice, common sense, and business it appears like an outrage. However, Mr. Wayland has advised and invited just that condition of affairs, and is, perhaps, supremely happy in the knowledge that he is the "slave" he has talked so much about instead of the man to whom he has paid good money for his labor.[43]

Wayland immediately acceded to the wage and working-condition demands, but he demurred on firing his son and dissolving the partnership that tied him, the paper, and his friends and relatives together. At first, in desperation, he tried to get out of the situation by offering to turn the paper over to the National Committee of the Socialist party, but he was rebuffed, because of a provision in the party constitution that forbade an official party paper. Wayland's next thought was to discontinue the paper, but reflecting on the Appeal Army, he thought:

> I saw poor men and poor women . . . and the work for industrial deliverance. They confided in me. I never asked but they responded. What would they think? What would they feel? How many would sink discouraged, hopes blasted, confidence lost? Should a few be permitted to stand between? Shall I sink self, even life if need be, for those who need it? Shall I take up the burden and go on? The wife said, "The Army has been faithful to you!" And I decided.[44]

Although the *Appeal* had trumpeted complete agreement between Wayland and the staff and although Wayland did appear to have acceded to dissolving the partnership and removing his son from the cashiership, he did not turn over any profit to the party. Phelps was, however, removed from the staff; and he moved to St. James, Missouri, where he set up a printing establishment, Phelps and Wayland, which advertised in the *Appeal.*[45] The connection between Jon Wayland and Phelps thus was retained. The demand to turn over the profits to the party did not, however, come to pass; and for this, one can blame, not Wayland, but Socialist party resistance. In spite of his maudlin protestations to the contrary, Wayland got out of the day-to-day business of running the *Appeal*, as we shall see in the next chapter.

A closer connection to the Socialist party was what the staff seemed to want, but the party refused to become involved. The questions of what to do with the profits and of the appointment of a new cashier were tied to previous bitter experiences, remembered vividly by those veterans of the Socialist Labor party who were now members of the Socialist Party of America. Daniel DeLeon had used the *People* as a weapon to keep a tight rein on that party and to whip recalcitrant members into line. Many in the new Socialist party had been involved in the comic-opera battles in New York over the jurisdiction of the *People* and in setting up a rival party organ. So, when the Socialist party was finally formed in 1901, the question of an official party organ was a sensitive topic. The *Appeal* was the number one weekly paper for the movement; it was challenged in circulation only by the monthly *Wilshire's Magazine*. The party, without an organ of its own, had to rely on unofficial party papers, chiefly the *Appeal*, to spread its message. As the idea of socialism became more attractive during the first decade of the twentieth century, so did the *Appeal*. Its circulation and party membership continued to rise.

The party constitution expressly forbade the adoption of an official party organ. The fear of enforced orthodoxy and the distrust of allowing rival factions to seize control overrode the need to inform the public of the party's intentions. When the party met in May, 1904, to nominate its first presidential ticket, the question of an official organ was hotly debated. The *People* and the *Appeal to Reason* were on everybody's minds. One delegate declared: "It is a danger we should avoid, unless we want a repetition of the DeLeonism. . . . I believe that if there is any one thing that has perpetuated this DeLeon in the Socialist movement . . . it is the publication of that paper called *The People*, and it is within the possibilities that if you give that right to a committee, that we would have a repetition of that again."[46] The revised constitution, though a short document, nevertheless contained two express references to the question of an official publication: "The National Committee shall

Delegates to the National Convention of the Socialist Party of the United States of America, Chicago, May, 1904. Charles L. Breckon is in the top row, seventh from the left (no. 7). Wilshire is in the cameo at the bottom (no. 199), and Debs is in the bottom row center (no. 207). From the Comrade, *vol. 3, no. 11 (August, 1904), p. 231.*

neither publish nor designate any official organ" was the second of only two sections on the powers of the National Committee; in the article on a Literature Bureau, the clause read that the bureau should have the right "to publish works on socialism for the purposes of socialist propaganda, but this clause shall not be construed as authorizing the Bureau to publish any periodical."[47]

The convention, coming seven months after the strike at the *Appeal*, thus dismissed the opportunity to take over the paper while conditions were still fluid. But developments at the *Appeal* in the fall of 1903 were still explosive material for the party. The question of Ricker's letters to Mailly, the national secretary, came to the floor several times; but Mailly adroitly managed to foreclose debate on the topic. Charles Breckon, who had been dismissed from the paper shortly after the strike, tried unsuccessfully, as a delegate from Illinois, to get the convention to discuss the allegations in those letters. The power that the *Appeal* had over the movement was recognized by all members of the convention, but the fear of allowing it official status threatened them even more.[48]

Although the decisions to reject the offer of the *Appeal to Reason* and to not have any official paper were understandable, it was a lost opportunity for the party to become perhaps more influential and secure. The

Appeal's circulation would continue to rise for the most part, and that circulation and the party's vote-getting ability would be linked together in the next decade. Where the most members were, the most subscriptions were. It therefore seems safe to say that many of the readers were already party members and confirmed socialists. The *Appeal* would lead in presidential campaign efforts and would generally support the party. So, on the surface at least, there may not have appeared to be much to gain from party control. But the *Appeal*'s vast circulation, which rose to 750,000 in 1912, could have brought in an immense amount of money even without advertising. The party lost any right it might have had to this income. The addition of $25,000 to $50,000 in the years after 1910 might have helped the party's organizational efforts. There would be matters of importance on which the party and the paper would differ in the years ahead, and perhaps a party-led paper might have pursued a path different from the one that was followed; but it might then never have become so large in circulation.

The party balked at running it; other members of the party complained that the *Appeal*'s subscription price was so low that other papers could not survive its competition. The *Appeal* argued that a low price would increase readership, leading to economies of scale. Wayland had claimed that because he had to pay the extortion of all of the trusts, he had to run the paper in a capitalist fashion. So the *Appeal* had its strike, its uneasy relationship with advertising, and calls of unfair competition from its fellow journalists.

The question of party ownership was intimately bound up with the question of union relationships to the institutions of the Socialist party; this continued to be a sensitive issue for years. A letter in the *Cigar Makers' Official Journal* in 1908 described the strategy of a group that had just set up a private corporation to own and run the major New York socialist paper, the *Call*. The letter gave two reasons why it was better for the party to keep out of the day-to-day management of such an enterprise—namely, the questions of maintaining democracy in the work place, and of union-management relations—and warned: "Remember the walkout on the *Appeal to Reason*. Under no circumstances could the Socialist party afford to have a strike of its employes."[49]

The admission by the workers at the *Call* that a paper could not be run democratically certainly helped to alienate a section of the union movement from the party, and it also pointed up starkly the contradictions that those who were working for socialism in a mass society had to face. There were good reasons why the *Appeal to Reason* could not run a good union shop, as capitalist employers could afford to do and sometimes did. In order to do so, it would have to become even more like a capitalist enterprise. Limited in the amount of advertising that it could get, harassed by postal authorities, treated unfairly by the trusts that provided it with ink and paper, deliberately keeping the subscription price low to make the paper as widely available as possible, the *Appeal* was never in a financial position to offer as much in wages and benefits as a capitalist employer could. It is true that the paper could have been managed more fairly, but it is questionable whether it could have developed into such a successful mass-circulation paper had it been managed collectively.

But Wayland's basic ambivalence toward union labor remained. The United Mine Workers, two years after the strike, like the Cigar Workers, still seethed with resentment against Wayland. They reprinted a One-Hoss paragraph, which attacked the Civic Federation that called workers "working mules" for listening to such men as August Belmont, the Rockefellers' business agent. The UMW *Journal* proceeded to describe Belmont as a "fair-minded, liberal employer, who meets committees from labor unions, holds conferences with them, pays union wages and insists upon union conditions." It continued:

That is one picture. Here is another: The editor of the Appeal to Reason is J. A. Wayland. He is the man who calls the men who made the United States great "working mules." Elegant classification. Well, in 1902 [1903], Mr. Wayland's employes asked for an advance in wages. Did he grant it? No; he would not receive a committee of his employes and locked them out and filled their places with scabs. The Appeal to Reason's wage scale showed that the girls got $3 per week. Mr. Wayland nearly ruined himself by his lavish generosity. Now which, August Belmont receiving his employes, listening to their grievances, adjusting them fairly and honorably, paying the highest wages, or J. A. locking out his $3 a week girls? Which more truly represents the spirit of American manhood? Which could a bona fide trades unionist respect the most? No wonder, with his aggregation of scabs, that he terms working people "mules."[50]

Although the picture that this paints is extremely exaggerated, with Belmont beneficent and Wayland greedy, it hits closely at the problem for union labor and socialism and at the problems that Wayland the small capitalist had in paying and treating his workers as fairly as it might appear that a great corporation could. His labor policy did not work in Girard, as it had not worked in Ruskin.

Wayland's own ideas had changed from his days in Ruskin, Tennessee, when he had tried to prove to the American people that socialism was feasible, through the cooperative experiment. His paper continued to

Ads from the July 2, 1904, Appeal to Reason.

run ads for similar communal projects, even while he confidently applied the mores of a consumer society to the claims of a social and political movement. Thus, like others in the party and in the radical press, he successfully placed American socialism squarely in the political arena, competing for the ear of the American voter and promising that socialism could remedy social evils. When he did so, however, he placed himself at a competitive disadvantage, by trying to use capitalist strategies to interest workers in socialism, while he was unable to compete on equal terms.

What does this strike mean, and what possible explanations are there for the road taken after 1903? On the surface, labor-management issues were resolved, but a number of distinctly unsocialist actions were taken: (1) the ringleaders were fired; (2) the Socialist party reaffirmed its position against an official party paper; (3) advertising the capitalist dream continued unabated in the face of contrary revelations at the paper; (4) the lowest paid and least secure workers, "the girls," in spite of an editorial voice of their own, had no discernible role in the strike or its settlement, even though it was their labor power that enabled the *Appeal* to publish at a low cost. What was going on? The answers are found by looking at two aspects of the strike: first, the attempt by a group of editors within the *Appeal* to overturn the direction in which the paper had moved and, second, the role of women at the *Appeal to Reason.*

7

The Second Coming Nation

After all we are as Socialists, as much under the law of economic necessity as the capitalist or wage slave and whether it is best for the movement to have one big paper or a dozen small ones, is a proposition which is beyond our control. The *Appeal*, like Standard Oil, has to expand or bust.

—*Fred Warren, 1905*

We want you to feel like you know the girls who stand behind the mailers all day long and wrap the bundles of papers, the girls who fold our books and pamphlets, the girls who pore over the letters, complaints and changes, the girls who read the proofs and write the new subscribers' names, the girls who keep tab on the mailing list, the girls who "case" the cards and fill your orders.

To the question, "Shall we have cheap books at price of our girls' wages" we have given an emphatic "No."

—*Appeal to Reason, 1903*

When Wayland began to recruit new faces to help out with the growing success of the *Appeal to Reason* at the turn of the century, a small, wiry man from Rich Hill, Missouri, not too many miles away from Girard, stood out. This man, who would run the paper when it reached the height of its influence, was Fred Dwight Warren. Hired in 1900 as a printer, he became managing editor a couple of months after the strike in 1904; with Wayland in the background as publisher, Warren guided the paper for a decade, till 1914.[1] But for twenty months in 1902 and 1903, Warren had led a rebellion, which helps to illuminate the paradoxes that the 1903 strike showed in starkest relief.

Warren's rebellion was clearly over the issues that Wayland himself had struggled with for a decade: cooperation, socialist ideals versus capitalist realities, advertising, and labor conditions. Warren felt revulsion over what was happening at the *Appeal*, so he set out to retrieve what he perceived as the lost innocence of the earlier days of socialist publication. At the same time as Warren was acting, the issue of women's

138

*Fred D. Warren. Courtesy of the Archives of Labor
and Urban Affairs, Wayne State University.*

equality surfaced, revealing further contradictions between capitalist
reality and socialist ideals. Both the issues raised by women at the *Appeal* and the action taken by Warren help to answer some of the questions raised by the strike at the *Appeal to Reason.*

Warren's career seems to have echoed Wayland's, but a generation later.[2]
Born in the village of Arcola, in east-central Illinois, on March 24, 1872,
the eldest of three children, Warren was eighteen years Wayland's junior.[3]
Warren's father had a flour-and-grain business, which was wiped out by
the Panic of 1873; during Warren's youth, the devout Methodist family
was forced to move several times in search of employment. They settled
down for a time at Fort Scott, Kansas, about twenty-five miles north of
Girard, where the ten-year-old Fred worked for a year as a Western Union

messenger boy and then for two years as a printer's devil in the shop of a family friend. The family next moved thirty miles across the Missouri border to Rich Hill, in Bates County, a small town in a coal-and-zinc mining area. The youngster tried all sorts of odd jobs. At first, he was attracted to the life of the coal miner; next he became a delivery boy for a local grocer; he also tried working on a farm but found the labor a bit more than his small body could handle.[4]

For a short time, Warren worked for a local paper, but it failed during the recession of 1887, and both shop and paper were sold to a man who moved them to the county seat at Butler. Warren went along to retain his six-dollar weekly wage. When he was laid off, the fifteen year old decided it was time to try his luck in the big city—Kansas City—where he went in search of printing work. He got one job, but was laid off again, this time because he did not work fast enough to suit his boss. He tried to get some day work at one of the big dailies, the *Journal* or the *Times*, but he was only one of many who were seeking employment, and his youth and small stature were disadvantages.[5]

Warren returned to Rich Hill, where the family fortunes had changed for the better. His father bought a machine shop, and in 1890, Fred, with the help of his younger brother, Ben, started a Republican paper, the *Rich Hill Tribune*, which took the place of a paper that had moved away. In the tradition of the partisan small papers of the era, it was as bitter in its denunciation of the Democratic party as Wayland's *Cass News* had been twelve years earlier.[6]

Warren's paper failed during the depression of 1893, but Ben and Fred continued in the job-printing business. Fred became a pillar of the community, married Hattie Barton in 1895, and served as a Sunday School superintendent. He was a prohibitionist. Like Wayland in his Republican days, he was an important link in the local Republican party structure, although because the Democrats won in 1892, he was not eligible for a patronage job like Wayland's postmastership. He remained a devout Methodist until the end of his life. Active, especially when publishing the paper, in fighting "vice," he continued to take moral positions on such issues as the "white slave trade" after he became a socialist.

Like Wayland's, Warren's conversion to socialism was partly a reaction against corruption in the Republican party and partly a result of his education by a radical worker—in this case, a miner. The accounts of the event are more consistent than the accounts of Wayland's conversion. The one published in 1910, when Warren was embroiled in a court case with the Post Office Department, was used as propaganda for the socialist movement. It began with Warren's getting his first real taste of local Republican politics during the 1892 campaign. Editing the local paper, he was called in on a tactical session to determine how to raise enough money for whiskey and beer to buy the votes of the local miners. Warren, for whom the party meant Lincoln and a complex of moral issues, was outraged. His eyes were opened. He gradually learned about other forms of graft and corruption in his cherished Grand Old Party, until he could no longer associate himself with the Republicans and therefore ceased to publish the paper. But he continued to make his living from other printing work.[7]

The debatable part of this account concerns the cause of the paper's failure. Warren himself said it was the depression, not a conscious decision based on moral revulsion.[8] Warren's accounts agree with the rest of the story, however. The moral revulsion followed a meeting with Pat O'Neil, "a rough and uncouth miner," who came to get some printing done at some time between 1895 and 1898. On finding out that the miner was a socialist, Warren engaged him in verbal combat, which on future occasions turned into reasoned debate. The initial hostility blossomed into friendship, and after a year, Warren was handed the book *Merrie England*, by Robert Blatchford, a socialist tract that Wayland had distributed through his papers. Warren's "careful reading" of Blatchford's words "tore the veil" from his eyes, and it dawned upon him that the book—along with Pat O'Neil and other socialists whom he had so ignorantly and violently hated—had the right answers.[9] Warren secured other socialist works and returned to the newspaper business in 1898 with the *Bates County Critic*, openly preaching socialism to the local community.

Warren's own accounts of his conversion emphasize that it was people's stealing coal from his printing establishment which made him aware of the extent of the depression and poverty.[10] After the Panic of 1893, "Father lost his job; the mines closed down. . . . The *Tribune* had established a book-bindery in connection with their printing department. We hired a book-binder. He proved to be an educated German. He was a follower of Karl Marx. He was an unassuming individual but a persistent distributor of literature. He talked panics and depressions. I laughed at this but as the years rolled on toward the turn of the century, I thought a great deal of what he had said."[11] Warren confirmed the story about the miner Pat O'Neil in this way:

Along in 1898, I met a double-fisted Irishman. He had been a world traveler, a soldier of fortune and a coal miner. He talked about a new world that some day would take the place of the present mixed-up affair we call capitalism. It sounded strange to me then. But, day after day as we talked I caught a glimpse of what the Irishman visioned. It was the Cooperative Commonwealth—it was Socialism in reality come to rescue the world from its heartaches and its hardships. It was the reverse of what I had seen and experienced as a boy and a young man.[12]

Warren was passionate, devout, and repelled by injustice. The miner and the bookbinder set out a world that was far more enticing than the difficult struggle for existence that Warren had known since he was a child. In his mid twenties, he became an American socialist— about a decade younger than Wayland had been. Warren had not known business success, at least not on the scale that the real-estate speculator had. But like Wayland, once Warren was convinced of the truth, he went back into the trade he knew best and started a paper to spread the word to the local community. His targets were the miners of Rich Hill, not, like Wayland's, the citizens of Colorado or the workers of the entire country.

Warren's first socialist piece was called "The Boytown Railroad," a short story depicting the evils of capitalism. A model railroad, big enough to carry a couple of passengers, is built by one of a group of boys, who charges his friends to ride. Soon he has collected all of their goods and money. He expands the road, putting his friends to work and paying them for their labor, then again garnering all of their funds when they have paid for their rides. Finally, the boys awaken when one of their number suggests that they can build a road of their own and furnish free rides for themselves. Cooperation works, the capitalist line goes out of business, and everyone is happy.

This simple romantic notion of the Cooperative Commonwealth, written by the twenty-six-year-old Warren, cannot be dismissed as naive excitement over newly found truth or as just socialist writing for children, because it was not intended solely for children. Warren republished it on a number of occasions, the last time in 1935.[13] The story, written in boyish vernacular, caught the attention of Wayland, who invited Warren to visit him in Girard in late 1899 and discussed the idea of establishing a magazine.[14]

Warren's *Critic* put forward the tenets of socialism in straightforward, didactic tones:

> Every human being to be well housed, clothed and educated.
> The adoption of a social and industrial system that will put an end to profit, interest, rent and all forms of usury.
> The gradual elimination, and finally the abolition of all useless and unproductive toil.
> Every person of suitable age and physical and mental ability must work or starve.
> "He that will not work shall not eat."

No child labor, except in the form of healthful, well-directed manual training.

Everyone to receive the full value of his or her labor.

Land, water, machinery and all of the means of production and distribution and all of the available forces of nature to be owned and operated for the benefit of the whole people.[15]

The paper served as a nucleus for a growing movement for socialism in Missouri that had as its backbone the miners, mostly Democrats, whose votes the Republicans had earlier bought with whiskey. Warren wanted to gather them into the fold through a socialism similar to that of the *Appeal*, but even less sophisticated in its expression.

The *Bates County Critic* lasted for two years, 1898 and 1899. During that time, Warren experienced some of the same hostility from the local communities that Wayland had felt in Greensburg, Indiana. Wayland's paper was taking off by the turn of the century, and he liked the kind of sentimental but strongly felt socialism that was coming from his neighbor in Rich Hill, who by 1899 was printing an additional monthly edition of his weekly paper in a successful effort to draw more readers from beyond Rich Hill. Warren turned down Wayland's first offer to come to work that year, but he agreed to come as a printer the following year. He began to work in Girard in September, 1900, at a salary of $15 a week, an excellent wage in Girard, where Warren and his family paid only $6 a month to rent a six-room house, and especially good at the *Appeal*, where much of the help was getting $3 a week. According to Warren, Wayland had forgotten to fill the copy book one week, and Warren took it upon himself to set the front page "out of his hat, as had been [his] practice in Missouri to save writing [the articles out first] on paper."[16] Wayland apparently liked what he saw, as he had been impressed by the *Critic*, and he promoted Fred to an assistant editor, replacing him at the press with Fred's brother Ben.

Warren was impressed with Wayland from the first. Wayland was different from the average small-town businessman that Warren had expected to meet when he came to Girard. Wayland was, to Warren, much like what he thought Abraham Lincoln must have been like:

I remember that I thought him a dreamer, but the vision he painted of a better world in which men would live, not by exploiting each other, but by cooperating to the good end that poverty would be abolished, has never left me. To this day [1931] I can recall Wayland's deep earnestness. Though I have met and talked with thousands of socialists, I have never met one who seemed so completely possessed with the ambition to convert the world to Socialism.[17]

But this vision of Wayland was neither reflected nor repeated in the staff that Warren worked with or in the practices that were creeping into the paper. The circulation drive that had pumped up the paper had been largely engineered by E. W. Dodge, a blacklisted telegraph operator. His giveaways and premiums had indeed enlarged the paper's influence, but they were pulling in the opposite direction from the message the paper was proclaiming. Perhaps Wayland brought in the naive but earnest Warren to recapture some of the spirit that had moved him in the direction of socialism in the first place. Perhaps Wayland knew that Warren would be upset by the practices that Wayland himself had sanctioned and that Warren would help to rejuvenate the paper with new ideas. Or perhaps Wayland wanted someone around him with whom he could talk socialism. Dodge was clearly not the man. According to Warren, Dodge "had a head two sizes too large for his body"; Dodge was also arrogant and an alcoholic, which no doubt offended the nondrinking Warren. Warren contended that though Dodge could have made a fortune as an ad man, the contests and giveaways left a bad taste for those who lost. Perhaps the most serious charge that Warren could have brought against Dodge was the fact that Dodge called the men and women who responded to the ads "jaspers," clearly holding them in contempt. Although Dodge helped to build the circulation to one hundred thousand he left the *Appeal* with a legacy of contests, some of which were not settled until 1917.[18]

Along with another assistant editor, Eli Norton ("Baldy") Richardson, Warren took over the position of circulation manager. Richardson, who was ten years older than Warren, had been born on a farm in Illinois and before coming to the *Appeal* had worked for twenty years in railroading, mostly as a telegrapher and station agent. The daily routine of these jobs included large stretches of time, which he devoted to writing, and he placed articles in a number of city dailies.[19] Some of the subscription contests were slowly phased out during 1901 and part of 1902, but it was during this period that advertising was slowly coming to play a more and more important role. This was another practice of which Warren strongly disapproved, and he seems to have managed to stave off, until his departure in 1902, the addition of the patent-medicine ads.

Yet another problem was developing for Warren with other members of Wayland's entourage. Although the exact circumstances are not known, Wayland's brother-in-law, Charles Bevan, who owned some stock in the *Appeal*, apparently did not like Warren's younger brother, Ben, and had J. A. Wayland fire him. Both Fred Warren and Richardson then handed in their own resignations in February, 1902; revealingly, the first

E. N. Richardson. Courtesy of the Archives of Labor and Urban Affairs, Wayne State University.

purely commercial ad appeared in the *Appeal* on March 1, 1902. The timing of the resignations may also have had something to do with what had happened to the rump of the Ruskin Colony, which was then engaged in its terminal squabbles in Ware, Georgia. The *Coming Nation*, after Wayland, Edwards, Casson, and a succession of other editors, expired in the summer of 1901. Richardson and the Warren brothers seized the opportunity, acquired the old *Coming Nation* mailing list, and went to work to replace the *Appeal* with a paper that would hark back to the ideals that both it and the *Coming Nation* were supposed to stand for, not just on the editorial page, but in its advertising and personnel policies as well.[20]

The *Coming Nation* resumed publication with issue number 421, on March 22, 1902, back in the Warrens' hometown of Rich Hill, Missouri, and proclaimed that it favored constructive socialism. The masthead stated: "The coming nation will own collectively the means of production and distribution, operated and managed by the people." Warren was the editor; Richardson was the associate editor for an army column, like the one he had been editing for the *Appeal to Reason.* Warren, after some opposition from people who thought he was trying to subvert the *Appeal*, gathered impressive support. Among the people he attracted to write for his paper were a number who were to become prominent in the movement: Kate Richards O'Hare, the political cartoonist Ryan Walker, Charles Lincoln Phifer, and Walter Thomas Mills. Charles Kerr, Herbert Casson, and John Chase, the socialist legislator from Massachusetts, were also occasional contributors. These people had also worked with the *Appeal*, and they were not reluctant to lend support. This incarnation of the *Coming Nation* was a much more attractive paper than the *Appeal*. It was designed and printed carefully, set in larger type; and it carried a number of new features, such as a woman's section and country-store socialism dispensed "At Finnegan's Cigar Store." It carried no advertising.[21]

"Baldy," or "Rich," another of Richardson's nicknames, was the author of the stories that took place "At Finnegan's Cigar Store." Warren's partner wrote in an engaging style about a group of people known only by their occupations: Station Agent, Retired Farmer, Blacksmith, and Bookkeeper. They gathered at the store at the end of the day to discuss anything from the latest news to the state of the economy. Each short piece dramatized some socialist point about the class struggle, the weakness of unions to stand alone against the capitalist class, or why prices kept rising. The Station Agent, the socialist of the group, who was almost certainly an autobiographical touch of Richardson's, always won the arguments. This country-style socialism was in the tradition that F. G. R. Gordon had attempted in 1897 when he spoke to Samuel Simon, wage worker; but it was much less forced and thus probably more popular (see app. 2). Richardson, whose army columns were written in the same kind of engaging patter, was also responsible for circulation at the *Coming Nation.* He came up with the idea—one that was to be followed when he and Warren returned to the *Appeal* in 1904—that horse-drawn vans could be sent out on the road to get subscriptions for the paper, with the driver being sustained by the subscription revenue.[22] Like the army gimmicks that he had suggested in the past, this would enter into the arsenal of socialist organizing tactics.[23]

Both Richardson and Warren shared a belief in the down-home tactics that Wayland had employed before the advent of advertising in the

Ryan Walker. Courtesy of the Archives of Labor and Urban Affairs, Wayne State University.

Appeal, and both wrote for a midwestern, small town, or rural audience, like the chief audience of the *Appeal*. But they differed in a fundamental way from what Wayland had chosen to do with his front page. The way to get readers, if one were to dispense with the gimmicks such as farm contests, was to use the front page to "biff every head that appeared."[24] Gone were the short paragraphs with morals; in their place would come running battles and scare headlines. If Warren disliked advertising, he certainly was not upset about adopting the other techniques of the yellow journalists. In 1903, Warren took on the National Economic League, which was an attempt to bring together small businessmen and anyone else who would be interested in a fight against unionism and socialism. Warren's attacks drew return fire. He mobilized opposition to the league by organizing a counter group, whose main interest would be to support the *Coming Nation*. It worked, or at least it seemed to,

as the circulation climbed and special editions broke the one-hundred-thousand barrier.[25]

The campaign against the National Economic League did not completely dominate the paper. Warren and Richardson had wooed Ryan Walker, destined to be the leading cartoonist of the movement during the first decade of the century, away from the *Appeal*. Walker, who was about the same age as Warren, was making his living from *Life Magazine* in New York and was helping out the cause with political cartoons for the movement, cartoons that he could not use in commercial publications.[26] Charles Lincoln Phifer, another country editor with a background that paralleled those of Wayland and Warren, occasionally contributed stories that were sentimental tales of lives that had been wrecked by capitalism. Phifer, who had moved from Republican leanings to a position as a political satirist in his own paper, *Push*, came to Rich Hill to work with the Warren brothers and Richardson.

The paper did well in the twenty-two months of its operation, developing a subscription list of twenty-seven thousand readers. It seemed to be succeeding in maintaining its no-advertising stance, where Wayland had succumbed. And there is no evidence that there were any complaints about pay and working conditions. It broke some new ground for socialist publications, especially in the column by Kate O'Hare.[27] Unlike previous attempts in the *Appeal* and the *Coming Nation*, as well as in *Wilshire's* and the *International Socialist Review*, O'Hare's columns were a permanent fixture in the paper; O'Hare was able to develop arguments and to gather a readership. She was herself becoming an important figure in the movement, soon to vie with some of the male leaders of the Socialist party for international recognition. In *Wilshire's* or in the earlier *Coming Nation*, the women's columns were written by wives or lovers of the editors. Here, for the first time in a general-circulation socialist periodical, an independent woman controlled her own column. It was first called "For the Fair One: Upon Whose Welfare Depend the Nations of the Future," and it asked women to become socialists by appealing to their finer sensibilities: tenderness, mother love, and patriotism.[28] By June, O'Hare was calling the column "The Women Folks," then "Mrs. O'Hare's Department for Women," and, finally, by the fall of 1902, "Our Women's Column." The arguments were intended for the woman in the traditional role of wife and mother, the role that O'Hare herself was then filling. It would be several years before women would write for other socialist women in a more socially radical way and make demands on the party for a more equal role. O'Hare seemed to be content, at this stage in her career, to interest wives in their husbands' cause, which should also be their own cause.[29]

O'Hare's vision in 1902/3 was reflected in the views of male journalists;

Women socialist lecturers, circa 1905. Clockwise from top: Grace D. Brewer, Mrs. Ernest Untermann, Lena Morrow Lewis, Pearl Busby, and Josephine Conger-Kaneko. Courtesy of the Archives of Labor and Urban Affairs, Wayne State University.

yet only the women journalists of the period around the turn of the century even tried to come to grips with the assumptions of masculine and feminine roles in a conscious fashion. By 1907 or so, women journalists would begin actively to combat the stereotyping of women and their roles as domestic and sentimental. They did this under the leadership of

Josephine Conger, who was the first woman columnist at the *Appeal* and whose column was begun as a response to O'Hare's in the *Coming Nation*. Back in 1898, Lydia Kingsmill Commander, who edited a woman's column in the old *Coming Nation* and for a time took over the editorship of the paper, viewed women in the socialist movement in much the same way that women were generally perceived in Victorian America; this was partially owing, perhaps, to her position as an ordained minister.[30] Although there were exceptions to this view, they were not to be found in the leading circulation papers of the movement.[31] Commander was the first woman to hold down such a column in a general-circulation socialist paper. As such, she had to face the question of the need for a separate column for the women, when the "whole paper should be for women as well as men. Socialism is in the interest of both sexes equally." Her argument followed these lines: it is true that socialism is equally important to men and women, but no natural fellowship exists between the sexes. The socialist movement was founded and forwarded by men, who had sought each other out in the way in which the women who had founded the WCTU (Woman's Christian Temperance Union) and the suffrage movement had sought out their sisters for support. Because, according to Commander, socialism has been almost exclusively male, "an especial effort must be made to show them [i.e., women] that, in its essential principles, it touches their lives even more nearly than men's." After that had been accomplished, then women's columns and women's editions would no longer be needed. An interesting argument, in spite of recent scholarship that shows that women were active in the movement from the start, though they certainly were in the overwhelming minority.[32]

Commander had more to say, however. Besides the lack of comradeship between the sexes, which tended to exclude women, women themselves were not interested in socialism for another reason: "Women are prone to let the progress of the world rush past them while they sit idly by wishing they had a share in it." She elaborated on the argument in a way that recalls some of the language of the One-Hoss Philosophy:

This may sound like hard doctrine when one thinks of all the oppression and repression that women have had to endure; but, after all, if they had been less submissive and had had more energy, they would have had less to put up with. Those who will submit may. The African is naturally submissive, and he has been the slave of the world. The Anglo-Saxon has within him the instinct of freedom and domination, and he is everywhere the conqueror.

Woman has been a slave, and is scarcely anywhere free today, but she has not been without blame. Those who WILL NOT yield to tyranny DO NOT.[33]

These were appropriate thoughts for Wayland's first radical newspaper progeny, the *Coming Nation*, in language that he could endorse, even though he had been gone from the scene for four years by then. But during this period, almost all of the women journalists in the socialist movement would have endorsed some form of the argument that women's role was separate, if not less important. Kate Richards O'Hare, writing in 1902 in the *Coming Nation*, saw woman's role as being a helpmeet to her socialist husband: "If he wants to talk Socialism to you when you want to talk about the new dress you need, just forget about the dress for a little while. Put your whole heart and interest in what he is telling you, do your best to understand it; tell him how much it means to you and the babies." The reward? "The glow of happiness on your husband's face will more than repay you, and unless it is an impossibility, I'll wager the new dress will be forthcoming in a very little while."[34]

This appeal by O'Hare in the *Coming Nation* was clearly directed to the rank and file of the party. In *Wilshire's Magazine*, "Godiva" had a different purpose, perhaps aiming at an emerging middle class, even though she ostensibly was writing to the working class. She, too, admitted that "woman remains hopelessly ignorant of the cause of her misery. . . . Exactly as if she lived in another sphere, life passes by her, without any philosophy to apply to the great problems that confront her, she accepts them all with a dull placidity which, to the discerning, makes her elevation seem so hopeless." Godiva, though, saw that salvation might be possible through leisure: labor-saving devices and modern decoration, such as Japanese grass rugs and Singapore lattice, without intricate ornamentation to dust, would free her time to study socialism. "The time wasted in dusting useless ornaments is sufficient to open a whole world of intellectual delights to a woman's starved mind." There were more benefits to come: "Such furnishing not only costs much less than the dust-gathering, inartistic furnishing which we generally find in the homes of working men, but it in part helps the overworked housewife gain that leisure which is necessary to her salvation."[35]

Josephine Conger came to the *Appeal* about six months before the strike to establish a column called "Hints to the *Appeal's* Wise Women." She, too, described woman's nature in ways similar to those used by Commander, O'Hare, and Godiva: "Too many women never grow beyond the babyhood of soul development. They meet hardships in life, and seek to avoid them by clinging to the strong arm of another, or by closing their moral consciousness in some such manner as the silly ostrich hides its head in the sand, when danger appears, thinking to avoid trouble and responsibility." But she was more optimistic than her comrades, having more confidence that this natural state of women could be overcome, according to Conger, because times had changed—intellect was now becoming valued in women as it always had been in men. There was an important difference, however: "The woman who has been crushed, and who by her own divine faith and will power has risen out of the debris of the evil time, developing new strength and self-sufficiency that enable her to stand alone," would, according to Conger, help by "giving new hope to the weary, courage to the despondent, pity to the wayfaring . . . and inspiration to the worker."[36] So, woman's development would still be viewed by Conger, at this time in her own development, as an adjunct to male activism.

These views of prominent socialist women journalists would change in the next few years, after the 1903 strike at the *Appeal.* The dilemma that they were dealing with was in some ways analogous to the dilemma that the socialist movement in general found itself in. Women who were attempting to develop a feminist socialism were trapped, as Mark Pittenger has shown in a study on the science of evolution and its crucial role for women. "Uniqueness was for feminist socialists a double-edged sword. Where it implied female inferiority and sharp distinctions between 'male' and 'female' spheres of activity, they attacked its privileged status as science; yet they still sought to make a case from woman's particular evolutionary history that her concerns could not be adequately addressed if relegated to the political anonymity of economic determinism."[37] Likewise was the socialist movement trapped in its attempts to become a large popular movement. The economic determinism that lay at the core of socialist doctrine and the centrality of class struggle stood in the way, people like J. A. Wayland thought, of developing a popular socialist movement that would cut across class lines. So, popular overtures, such as those developed by Wayland in his paper, were condemned by more rigorous Marxists such as DeLeon and Titus, even though they did to a large extent help to build party membership.

Woman's nature and her role in the movement were just beginning to be debated by Josephine Conger and Kate O'Hare; while the men, who numbered the clear majority of members of the party and the journalistic ranks, were content to give women a column in the paper but were not eager to read and reflect on the concerns the women expressed. Perhaps it was done solely as an attempt to attract more readers or, more positively, as a realization that there was a social problem that socialism needed to address. Copy, yes; but change in behavior, no. We have seen what Wayland envisioned for women at Ruskin—that socialism would make the traditional role of Victorian women easier—a position not far from the first thoughts of these women journalists. In most cases, though, it was the division of the world into separate spheres that men and women accepted, that informed action.

Look, for example, at the use of the term *sentimental*. Wayland was accused by his competitor Titus of abandoning the class struggle, "throwing bouquets or epigrams at his adversary in order to answer his sword thrusts." Wilshire would not stop accepting advertising from antilabor firms for any "sentimental" reason. Wayland himself, in paragraph after paragraph, derides sentimentalism, choosing to blame the victim for not standing up and fighting for what was his.

Titus, Wilshire, and Wayland are talking about ways of looking at the world that divide it into two spheres: aggressive masculine and sentimental feminine Victorian notions of gender, which underlay political positions, views about advertising, the role of the party, labor, and management. When Wayland gives in to the workers' demands, he cannot admit that he has done so because they are right and he is wrong. Rather, he interprets his action as weakness and turns the responsibility for making the decision over to his wife. "The wife said: 'The Army has been faithful to you!' And I decided." He decided to give in, to be passive, sentimental, to allow himself to listen to the feminine side of the debate, to respond to long-term loyalty and not to short-term union-management adversarial relationships.

From the beginning of his career, Wayland had been firmly rooted as a man of his times. His attraction to socialism did not dislodge him from his conventional views on most basic social issues; rather, his recent successes with advertising and circulation building, not to mention his continuing success at real-estate speculation, continued to cement in his mind the need to go about the business of bringing socialism to pass by using modern American methods. As we have seen in the experiment at Ruskin, in the dalliance with the Socialist Labor party, in the acceptance of advertising, and in the pure-and-simple capitalist methods of running a mostly nonunion shop, Wayland was able to pass over contradictions by keeping his eye on the goal of achieving a socialist electoral victory. At Ruskin, he refused to cooperate in areas in which he had special expertise, such as managing the paper, or on social questions, where he felt that prevailing social norms were quite acceptable, such as living and dining arrangements. With the Socialist Labor party, he denied the need for a disciplined socialist party, feeling, rightly, that such would not attract a majority of Americans; nevertheless, he overlooked a key element in any socialist program—namely, agreement on basic theory and practice. With advertising and labor issues, he accepted prevailing business practices, in spite of the ideological damage that they implied, because he realized that to a great extent, running a socialist newspaper was like running a business enterprise; so the more people he attracted, the quicker the socialist movement would prosper.

The cumulative effect of these compromises, great and small, was, what the strike was about and what Warren's rebellion was about: an attempt to bring theory and practice into line. Advertising was noticed as a problem by some socialists; unfair labor practices were clearly contradictory to socialist goals. But the least noticed at the time, even by women journalists, was the contradiction between a belief in equality for women and their lot under Wayland.

Although Conger was an editor at the paper, she was not heard from publicly during the strike; although women constituted a good part of the underpaid work force, we don't hear how their domestic responsibilities allowed Wayland and others to look at them as less-than-equal workers. These unspoken and unacknowledged assumptions mask other contradictions as well. Advertising is one example. A few months after the strike, the lead article for *Wilshire's Magazine* was called "Women and Socialism"; it was contributed by Nathaniel Hawthorne's well-known son Julian. This prolific commercial writer cast his remarks, in a familiar style for such light pieces, as a discussion between the young earnest man of socialism and the old misogynist skeptic who wondered: "How are you going to manage your women?" The younger man exclaimed: "It is from women that we expect our most unquestioning support. Think of the saving of household labor. . . . They will have leisure." After this exchange, the old man went on at length about shopping and advertisements, which presumably would end after socialism had begun. "What would woman's life be like without bargain-day sales, I'd like to know? What sort of circulation would the newspapers get if there were no advertisements in 'em for the women to read and figure over? Advertisements? Why socialism would wipe 'em out of existence. . . . A woman has a soul; and if you don't keep it fed on shopping, it'll eat up you and Socialism and morality and religion."

This sort of dialect humor, here at the expense of women, is no surprise in 1904. But what is a surprise in a socialist magazine with a quarter of a million readers is that the editor would allow the conclusion to stand. Instead of refuting the old man, the young one muses: "Upon the whole, I think it might be prudent to retain, if not actual shopping as now practised, something sufficiently like it to keep our wives and daughters from repining, until they had time to get interested in nobler things. And it would seem almost a pity to obliterate the noble art of advertising, just at the moment when it is approaching the stage of being an element in art education."[38]

The link here between advertising and women is intriguing, and it starts to suggest how all of this dualistic thinking fits together. It is instructive to note that most of the national advertising in both *Wilshire's* and the *Appeal* was, during this period, directed to men, while the advertising in regional papers, such as the *Socialist* and the *Social Democratic*

Herald, was of the "bargain-day" variety that Hawthorne described here. It is also important to keep in mind that the attractive advertising that had some "art" value was appearing mostly in the slicker magazines, such as *Wilshire's;* whereas the "bargain day" advertisements, which would, according to this argument, appeal to women, have little more in them than information on prices, which, one presumes, has some impact on the family budget. Without trying to push the argument too far, it seems that the women would be stuck with the ads that have some useful content, while the men would enjoy that advertising that has some "art education" value.

The stark contradiction of the advertising of get-rich-quick schemes, which pepper the *Appeal* and *Wilshire's,* within the context of a socialist publication, seems to be most readily explained by the separate-spheres argument. Wayland makes the problem clear when he reverts to real-estate speculation after swearing off for a short time. Why not make the most out of the existing system, even as you work to overthrow it? One's personal economic life, then, can be kept separate from one's political vision. Here, he throws into question the entire socialist program, by removing his own economic life from that of the whole.

The question of an official paper versus unofficial papers shows the effect of the same kind of thinking. Josephine Conger-Kaneko reflected on this dilemma a decade after the strike at the *Appeal* and the debate at the national convention that foreclosed the idea of an official party paper. During that time she had become the central figure in the socialist-feminist press, having published a series of journals, the *Socialist Woman*, the *Progressive Woman*, and, yes again, the *Coming Nation*. All of them were privately owned, though reluctantly aided— mostly in minuscule amounts—from time to time by the Socialist party as its gesture towards the women. This was in spite of constant urgings by a number of women that the papers be taken under the party's wing. They were helped most strongly by funding from Conger's uncle, J. A. Wayland.

By 1914, Conger-Kaneko was fed up with the bickering that characterized the attitude of the Executive Committee of the party toward women's issues and, specifically, toward her publications. In a manifesto that she wrote in the *Coming Nation* in 1914, called "A Party-Owned Press: Being the Story of this Journal and why it is not Party Owned," Conger-Kaneko pointed out some of the failures of the party in regard to its press. It took a full decade from the 1904 National Convention of the Socialist party, which reaffirmed the fears of a party press and turned down a close relationship with the *Appeal to Reason*, for the Executive Committee to decide finally that the party should own its own press by concluding in 1914 that the privately owned socialist press had caused "the party's

Josephine Conger-Kaneko. Courtesy of the Archives of Labor and Urban Affairs, Wayne State University.

intellectual growth" to be "stunted." Too late, for Conger-Kaneko was announcing the end of her efforts to produce such a paper: "Our woman's paper goes out of existence in its eighth year—when the movement for women's emancipation is at its height and is enlisting millions of women." She pointed out how effective the periodical *Gleichheit* (Equality) had been for the women in Germany, and she commented on the refusal to support women's efforts in America: "It is this sort of needless failure which is enough to break the hearts of those who have seen the vision of solidarity, of united, perfect achievement of the working class!" She continued:

> "There is a tide in the affairs of men, which, taken at the flood, leads on to victory!" This applies also to organizations. But some individuals never see the tide: never are able to take it at the flood; and, being blind and unable, stand with desperate determination in the way of those who do see, who ARE able to grasp the opportunities. And the possibilities break: the tide recedes and nothing but a shadow of what might have been remains. The Socialist movement is filled with shadows—pitiful remains of great promises needlessly destroyed.[39]

The fear of enforced orthodoxy that a scientific socialist movement implied had helped to reinforce native tendencies toward unfettered journalistic independence to make the United States the only Western nation with a socialist movement to have no official paper. In the case of women, who had little of the means available to such people as Wayland and Wilshire, it pushed to the periphery vital elements of the party.

The tensions that bubbled to the surface during the strike showed some of the ways in which the movement for socialism was held back by modes of thinking that derived directly from the majority culture. Advertising, labor relations, official publications in a land where a free press was an important symbol, and male and female relationships were some of the issues that needed to be readjusted in the light of the changes that socialism promised. A set of intriguing juxtapositions that filled the center of the *Appeal to Reason* on the week before the strike illuminates the difficulties that American socialists were facing. On page 4 of the October 17 edition, in the extreme right-hand column, was a strip of what had become the usual advertisements: a number of radical publications, quack cures, farm supplies, printing services. And of course, the get-rich-quick schemes: "$32 a week salary," to sell a poultry compound; "Ginseng. $25,000 made from one acre," selling roots and seeds; and "$3 a Day Sure . . . we guarantee a clearance of $3 for every day a week, absolutely sure," from a manufacturing company.

"Our Union Girls": members of the Appeal's *AFL local 11478, dressed for a Labor Day parade. Courtesy of the Archives of Labor and Urban Affairs, Wayne State University.*

On page 5, in the two extreme left-hand columns,—that is, smack up against the ads—was the article "Our Union Girls." This appeared a week before the strike. The author, W. P. Mason, declared that all was well since the union had been organized; everybody was pulling hard. The only cloud on the horizon was the miscalculation that Comrade Wayland had made by handing over the $1,000 agitation fund to the Socialist party, because it made the members of the Appeal Army think that the paper was prospering and therefore made them slacken their efforts. The paper was losing money. "This deficit must be met, and it will take all the usual and unusual receipts to do it. So any benefits to come for our 'Union Girls' must come from a special source." How could the "Union Girls" be used to bring in money?

> Comrade Wayland has said: "If you can make the book department sustain itself and pay union wages to the girls, do so; if not, discontinue it at once." Now, comrades, the case is up to you. Do you wish our "Union Girls" to have respectable wages, or do you wish the department closed down? We have here a "Union Girls" combination, consisting of the following books for $1.
> What to Do and How to Do It, Woodbey 10
> Introduction to Socialism, Richardson 05

There was more. With every set ordered, a cloth-bound copy of *Karl Marx Biographical Memoirs* would be included. This work, by Wilhelm Liebknecht, was translated by Ernest Untermann, who had just quit the paper because of the labor troubles. The book was advertised as one that showed the human side of Marx's personality. "So many of our readers may have thought him cold and materialistic in his personality because he was clear and merciless in his exposition of economics. The truth is, however, that he was as gentle as a child and his life was full of sorrows."

After laying out all of this, Mason promised one more bonus:

> But we have something else. We are going to take a group picture of the girls in the Appeal to Reason plant. From this we shall have a fine half tone made; we shall print their pictures and paste one in each volume of these "Memoirs." We want to have you feel a personal relation with these girls who are putting their lives into the books and papers we are sending out. We want you to feel like you know the girls who stand behind the mailers all day long and wrap the bundles of papers, the girls who fold our books and pamphlets, the girls who pore over the letters, complaints and changes, the girls who read the proofs and write the new subscribers' names, the girls who keep tab on the mailing list, the girls who "case" the cards and fill your orders.
>
> To the question, "Shall we have cheap books at price of our girls' wages" we have given an emphatic "No."

To complete the picture, snug up against "Our Union Girls," was Josephine Conger's weekly column, which she entitled "Where Do You Stand?" and in which she challenged women to be strong in combating the economic forces that were destroying the home.

The mixture of signals that this center spread in the *Appeal* gives is astonishing. The "Our Union Girls" concept, however patronizing it might look to modern readers, was at least an admission that if the women on whom the *Appeal* depended were to be paid real wages, the money had to come from somewhere. The advertising next to the article promised $3.00 a day, while the girls in the next column were making $3.00 for a six-day week; this contradiction would not appear to be a contradiction to Wayland, who was taking advertising in order to keep the costs of running the paper down and was not considering its larger message. The linking of "Our Union Girls" with a premium that promised to show workers the human side of Karl Marx, with the added bonus of a picture of them all lined up in front of the building so that one could "feel a personal relation" with them, seems to imply that in spite of the presence of these women in the union and in spite of their crucial role in producing the newspaper, sentimental considerations, more than any other reason, forced the payment of union wages. Conger's article about having women take some measure of control over their own lives appeared next to "Our Union Girls," probably because the designer felt that all of this material was about women, so why not put it together. In the attempt to put it all together, Wayland, the *Appeal*, and the movement would make astonishing gains in the next few years; but these contradictions and missed connections would eventually determine the course of events.

Practical matters intervened in a way that bailed out both Wayland at the *Appeal* and Warren at the *Coming Nation*. For as Warren endeavored to make the *Coming Nation* into the large-circulation newspaper that might challenge the *Appeal*, he ran into the kind of financial roadblock that could only be overcome by large capital reserves, by advertising, or by close relationship to a political party. Avoiding advertising, there were several other ways of financing a radical paper at that time.[40] Warren had used the classic method of starting on a shoestring budget, keeping the operation small, holding costs down, and relying heavily on urging readers to support the operation with contributions. This formula could even generate a profit, if the circulation did not rise high enough to demand expensive machinery and a large staff. A second formula involved party support. If a paper was allied to one party, membership dues could be used in part for the support of the paper. The best example of this formula was the *People*, edited by Daniel DeLeon for the Socialist Labor party. A third alternative was to set up a cooperative publishing venture in which shares were sold to finance the paper. A fourth solution lay in the hands of a wealthy patron, whose fortune would subsidize the paper.

What had happened to Warren was that in his drive to build circulation, he found himself at the crossroads of success. The Rich Hill group had by now outgrown two sets of printing equipment and was straining to meet the demands that its increasing circulation was placing on the paper and the staff. A financial angel had come up with $1,000, but that was soon exhausted. Warren wrote to Wayland about buying one of the *Appeal's* presses, and instead, Wayland suggested that the two papers be consolidated, with a payment of $5,000 to the *Coming Nation* to secure debts and pay the staff.[41] Wayland's first great paper, the *Coming Nation*, had come home after being out of his control for eight years.

The Warren who came back to the *Appeal* in 1904, along with his brother Ben, Eli Richardson, Ryan Walker, and Charles Phifer, was not the same naive idealist as the man who had left the paper two years before. He consented to allow what he called the "scaly and compromising" advertising to remain in the paper because of contracts he was unwilling to break, although he did move to cut the ads out little by little until 1910. His own attitude towards money and the financing of a newspaper must have changed somewhat as a result of the problems that he had encountered in keeping the *Coming Nation* going. The settlement with the *Appeal* did not go smoothly. At least one contributor, the artist Ryan Walker, complained that Warren never paid him his fair share of the $5,000 buyout.[42] The dilemma of where to get funds to operate a socialist paper in a capitalist world would bedevil Warren, as it did Wayland.

As managing editor, Warren now had to defend practices that he previously had opposed. The existence of the *Appeal to Reason* was at stake, and so were his job and reputation. The letters that A. W. Ricker had sent to the national secretary of the Socialist party, William Mailly, during 1903, which described the conditions at the *Appeal*, were proving to be an embarrassment, because Mailly was asked to produce them at the 1904 Convention. Although Mailly succeeded in squelching that attempt, the problem reared its head again in December, 1904, when copies of the letters were taken out of the Chicago office of the Socialist party and Warren was blackmailed for money in return for destroying the copies and the originals. Warren short-circuited the blackmail attempt by publishing the letters in the *Appeal*.[43] Ricker, who had suffered greatly from the events of the previous year, took to drink. He was soon sent on a leave of absence back to his Iowa farm to recover. Warren was probably also a party to the firing of Breckon and other union stalwarts; Ricker was treated compassionately because he was a farmer and country editor, instead of from the big city.[44]

Warren accepted the idea that the paper had to grow in order to flourish and to serve the movement, but he rejected what the *Appeal* had become: "Wayland's original plan of printing a small paper at a nominal subscription rate was long outmoded, and the *Appeal* in 1904 was no more like the *Appeal* of Wayland's dream than hell is like heaven."[45] Warren felt that the only way to increase circulation was to increase the news value of the paper, and for that, he had to hire reporters. Instead of relying on the capitalist press to provide the news and then dissect it, as Wayland had done successfully for a decade, Warren would launch the paper into the news business. He would biff every head, not with secondhand stories, but with exclusive stories brought in by the *Appeal*'s own staff. The *Appeal* was going to be a modern newspaper under Warren.[46]

The dangers of such an approach to circulation building were evident to Warren, but he still plunged ahead. The biggest problem was to keep the pot boiling. "Once embarked on news features, it was necessary to 'keep something going' all of the time."[47] Keeping those things going might risk creating news or distorting it for the cause. And as a radical publication, the *Appeal*, because of the nature of its mission, would have to be more scrupulous in its activities than an established paper. But in the heady first years under Warren, the news came in without any need to manufacture stories or to distort intentionally.

Warren's change in direction would thrust the *Appeal* into the middle of national politics, of labor struggles, of presidential campaigns; it would uncover stories that would provide ammunition for progressive change in America. He would be responsible for raising the circulation of the paper to half a million readers by 1912. In so doing, he would complete the transformation of the *Appeal* into a big business and a force to be reckoned with in American society. That change was not without its drawbacks, certain of which were apparent to him almost from the beginning. Stealing some time from his hectic schedule, Warren wrote in response to a letter from a colleague:

I will never forget the many encouraging letters I used to receive from you when we were doing our best to keep the dear old *Coming Nation* alive. The friendships I formed and the comradeship letters that came to me were worth all the struggle. Rich [Eli Richardson] and I often talk over those days, and I do not believe that should I live to be a hundred that any period of my life will be fraught with as many pleasant memories as those eighteen months at Rich Hill. No one felt more keenly than we did the necessity of making the change—there seemed nothing else to do. I tried mighty hard to make the *Appeal* want [what] the C.N. [*Coming Nation*] was—but it seems so much like a big machine—there isn't that personal touch that came to us on the C.N. Every letter that reached Rich Hill was eagerly scanned by both of us, and the personality of the writer seemed to come with it. This feeling is largely swallowed up—as all our better and finer feelings are in this mad scramble we call the struggle for existence. . . . Warm comradeship is really the only sentiment which capitalism has left unsullied, and too often that is strained and snapped by the spirit of commercialism which creeps into our lives.

But, Warren concluded:

After all we are as Socialists, as much under the law of economic necessity as the capitalist or wage slave and whether it is best for the movement to have one big paper or a dozen small ones, is a proposition which is beyond our control. The *Appeal*, like Standard Oil, has to expand or bust.[48]

8
Biffin' Every Head:
The Big Stories, 1904–10

You have lost the strike and now what are you going to do about it?
—*Upton Sinclair*, Appeal to Reason, *1904*

What do you think is the reason subscriptions are not doing as well? My own idea is that it may be possible that this Moyer-Haywood business is not so conducive to getting up subscribers as a good many of the socialists seem to think.
—*H. Gaylord Wilshire to J. A. Wayland, 1906*

Warren expanded the *Appeal*, using stories that developed in three ways: feature articles that he commissioned, labor struggles that he sent his own reporters to cover, and stories that he helped to manufacture out of the notoriety of the newspaper itself. All of this writing was calculated to raise the circulation of the newspaper, which he and Wayland equated with increasing the public interest in socialism and the Socialist party. The first story that he commissioned took the form of a serialized novel. The paper's first labor story covered the Colorado mining wars between the Western Federation of Miners and the mine owners. Stories about the newspaper arose out of running battles between the paper and the United States and Canadian postal authorities, the most notorious of which served as proof of the government's perfidy in the murder trial of the leaders of the Western Federation of Miners. The novel—*The Jungle*, by Upton Sinclair—brought international fame; the Colorado mining wars brought a reputation for editorial toughness; and the postal wars escalated the paper's national notoriety. When these stories did not dominate the front page or overflow into special editions, Wayland's paragraphs appeared as before; the subscription contests continued to flourish; the advertising slowly abated until it was revived after 1910. The paper did not completely abandon its old ways; it simply added modern features.

When Warren launched the *Appeal* into the news business in 1904, he was responding to still another change in the direction of American

From the Appeal to Reason, *April 15, 1905. The artist is Ryan Walker.*

journalism, the new vogue for muckraking, as Wayland had responded a decade before to the introduction of popular magazines at low prices. The muckraking magazines, such as *Munsey's, McClure's, Cosmopolitan,* and even, on occasion, the *Ladies' Home Journal,* hit upon a new way to advance circulation with articles that exposed corruption and exploitation throughout the social fabric of the country. Muckraking, or crusading journalism, which had roots as far back as the 1880s, reached its height in 1902, with Lincoln Steffens's series of articles on the shame of the cities for *McClure's*. It was the public manifestation of an undercurrent of reform that had the Socialist party at its radical extreme and the coalition of groups that made up the Progressive movement in its vanguard.[1]

Most historians of the Progressive period would probably agree that populism and socialism were parts of the same impulse toward reform. Historians might also agree on the importance of journalism to the emergence of Progressive reform as a force in American society: "To an extraordinary degree the work of the Progressive movement rested upon its journalism. The fundamental critical achievement of American Progressivism was the business of exposure. The muckraker was the central figure. Before there could be actions, there must be information and exhortation. It was muckraking that brought the diffuse malaise into public focus."[2]

Socialism differed from progressivism when it viewed the malaise that affected American institutions as being caused by the fundamental relationship between capital and labor: the Progressives stopped short of denouncing the structure of society; they wanted to clean up what had gone wrong, to legislate a fair deal between labor and capital, and to replace bad men with good men in positions of authority in government and industry. Progressive muckraking exposed the evils of society and counseled reform; socialist muckraking exposed the same problems but called for radical change.[3]

The *Appeal to Reason* had not been involved in the muckraking business of investigative reporting before Warren took over in 1904. Until that time, Wayland had been content to base his paragraphs on the more than ample proofs of the problems of American society that he found in other newspapers and magazines. Warren turned to a relatively unknown writer for his first attempt to illuminate corporate rapacity and municipal corruption. The great trusts were on everybody's mind. Combinations of great wealth in oil, steel, and transportation were changing the business landscape in America to a greater extent than had the rise of the corporation itself during the previous generation. To the *Appeal*, the enemy was found in the one city that seemed to represent all of the evils of modern corporate life and capitalist exploitation: Chicago. The enemy was the meat-packing industry; the writer, Upton Sinclair; the book, *The Jungle*.

The *Jungle* became one of the most widely read books by a twentieth-century American author, and it is still the only book of Sinclair's to be part of the reading experience of most Americans. In book form by 1906, it achieved immediate success worldwide, drawing comments from

Winston Churchill and George Bernard Shaw in England and Theodore Roosevelt in America.[4] Sinclair could not be classed as a great writer in any sense, except perhaps for his insistent and persistent ability to place economic and moral problems at the core of his output, but *The Jungle* is his finest work. The story was outlined and commissioned by Fred Warren in the fall of 1904 as an "Uncle Tom's Cabin of the wage slaves," a sequel to Sinclair's *Manassas*.[5] Sinclair was paid $500 for the serial rights to the story. He spent seven weeks in Chicago doing research, then made the down payment on a farm in New Jersey, and wrote the novel there in a tar-paper shack heated by a coal stove. *The Jungle* was serialized in the paper throughout 1905 and in installments in *One-Hoss Philosophy*, a quarterly published by the *Appeal*, which usually contained magazine-style stories.

The *Appeal* was now open to writers beyond the small inside group of editors. No longer were the contents of the paper homogeneous, dominated only by the One-Hoss Philosophy. The breach had been made the year before, with the publication of Untermann's Marxist analyses of current events and Breckon's strident prounionism. Sinclair brought a curious mixture of sentimentality and fierce honesty to the paper, along with a repressed antimodernism and an aristocratic southern paternalistic viewpoint of noblesse oblige. He also brought to the *Appeal*, and to American letters in general, the first extended attempt to portray ethnic Americans—Lithuanians in *The Jungle*—without masking or covering up their style of life. He was a naturalist whose fame rests chiefly on this one novel.[6]

Other socialist muckrakers, outraged by the tainted-meat scandals of the Spanish-American-Philippine War, had covered the same ground before.[7] Algie Martin Simons published his pamphlet *Packingtown* in 1899; with Charles Kerr and Charles Edward Russell he wrote about the same problems in a number of articles in 1904. That same year in the *Appeal*, Ernest Untermann attacked living and working conditions in his article "Black Hole of Chicago,"[8] and Sinclair himself had challenged packing-town workers in an article in the September 17 *Appeal*: "You have lost the strike and now what are you going to do about it?" So the ground was well prepared, and the convincing hammering effect of Sinclair's style made *The Jungle* an immediate success.

The novel is about socialism. It relates the degradation of one family and, specifically, its head, Jurgis Rudkus, and his subsequent conversion to socialism. Significantly, Sinclair portrayed Rudkus's move towards radicalism chiefly as the effect of hearing speeches and reading, not of his economic condition, which the novel describes as having turned him into little more than an animal. It is the educational, the exhortative—in short, the propaganda message of the *Appeal* and charismatic speakers— that makes Jurgis into a socialist.

The radical content of the book was short-circuited. What became its most sensational appeal was the depiction of the disgusting conditions characteristic of the meat-packing industry. To clean up these conditions became the direction that reform took. The reform had the effect of strengthening the case of European packers, who called for a ban on American imports; it led to the Pure Food Act of 1907. It earned Sinclair an invitation to the White House and made him temporarily a well-to-do man. It is doubtful whether it helped to give the *Appeal* a larger audience.

The Jungle, though it was enthusiastically promoted by Warren, was not an unblemished success for the paper. Warren complained that the serial was taking up too much space and vowed never to repeat the experiment.[9] He and Sinclair tangled over the publishing rights. The contract that the young author signed with Doubleday conflicted with his obligations to the *Appeal*, which was forced to restrict the distribution of the edition that it had been publishing in the quarterly *One-Hoss Philosophy*. Sinclair, who hoped to receive enough of an advance to carry him through the final writing stages, suffered his first writer's block over the ending of *The Jungle*, which was not completed before he entered into these further publishing plans. What finally became the ending is a poorly realized sermon for socialism, which, when Sinclair read it to Warren for the first time, put the editor to sleep. Sinclair continued to write for the *Appeal* for the next ten years, and he also continued to fight with Warren over money, publication rights, and space in the *Appeal*. They even came close to an open legal battle in 1914, which was averted only through the strenuous intervention of friends, who feared the effect that such a struggle would have on the party's public image.[10]

The serialization of the novel showed how far the *Appeal* was from being a potent force in American publishing, in spite of the extent to which the business was growing. Warren explained the situation to George H. Goebel, who was a national organizer of the Socialist party and a frequent partner with *Appeal* artist Ryan Walker on national lecture tours. Warren thought the problems that he and Sinclair were experiencing were due to the circumstances of doing business in the capitalist publishing market in the United States:

Upon my suggestion, Sinclair wrote "The Jungle," the Appeal paying $500 for the serial rights to the book and it was understood all along that the Appeal should have the right to print this story in quarterly form in unlimited quantity. This arrangement was tacitly agreed to by the Mcmillan people who were to have published the pook [book]. When the Mcmillan people turned the book down because of its devotion to socialism, Sinclair insisted that the Appeal bring out the book. I was In New York at the time and I remember how earnestly we talked over the proposition, discussing it from every point of view. It was Sinclair's desire that the book be controlled by himself or by the Socialist publishers, so that it would always be available for propaganda purposes at the very lowest price.

But when I went into the business end of the deal I soon made up my mind that it was impractible [*sic*] for the Appeal to undertake to do such a gigantic task as putting a book like "The Jungle" on the market. We did not have the facilities nor the connection with book reviewers to get the book properly before the American public, nor had we any way to reach the book trade. It was a disappointment to Sinclair when the Appeal finally decided that it could not under any circumstances bring out the book as he desired it to be published. I knew that we could not seell [*sic*] to our readers more than ten thousand copies, which would barely have paid for the first edition leaving no margin for pushing the book in other channels.

Sinclair, then undertook to publish the book himself. With the assistance of every Socialist newspaper trying to raise enough advance orders to get out the first edition, only succeeded in raising orders for five thousand copies. Discouraged at the lack of interest on the part of the Socialists and his failure to control the book he made one more attempt to secure a capitalist publisher. I urged him repeatedly to go [do] this because I felt that it was the only way possible by which he could get anything out of the book and at the same time get it before the reading public. These capitalist publishers are smooth business man [*sic*] and understand the game fairly well. They tied Sinclair up with a contract which upon investigation made our printing of our quarterly edition an infringement on their copy[right]. We had a contract with Sinclair that would have enabled us to have established our rights to pring [print] "The Jungle" in quarterly form, but as Sinclair had contracted to protect the New York publishers from such infringement they could have held him for any damage which might have arisen—in other words it was a question of pauperizing Sinclair as the Doubleday, Page & Co., controled [*sic*] his royalty and could have tied him up for years to come. After several heated interviews between myself, Sinclair and Doubleday Page & Co., we settled the matter in such a way as to leave the Appeal free to issue a fifty cent paper edition of "The Jungle" next year. Copies we have on hand we can give away as premiums to subscribers. You should bear in mind that no publisher will bring out a cloth bound book edition of a book and at the same time grant permission to another firm to issue a paper edition until after the expiration of one year.[11]

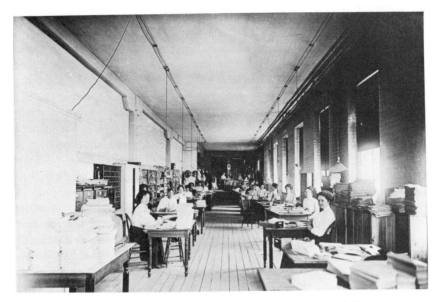

Employees of the mail-order department in 1908. Courtesy of the Haldeman-Julius Collection, Pittsburg State University.

Where Warren and the *Appeal* failed to make money in the marketplace, Doubleday succeeded. The responsible publicity agent for Doubleday claimed to have used the first modern news-promotion campaign, which he spoke of in military terms, to build up the impact of the book on the public, creating a "blockbuster." Emphasizing the pure-food aspects of the book and denying its radical content, Doubleday succeeded in creating a best seller.[12]

While *The Jungle* was running in the *Appeal*, Warren tried to drum up subscriptions for the paper, offering free back issues with earlier parts of the story so that new readers could catch up. Warren was busy peddling subsidiary serial rights to large and small publications throughout the land and, in so doing, attempting to increase the influence and circulation of the *Appeal* by forming a network of friendly publishers. His aim was to develop a daily edition of the paper, a newsstand edition to sell in the big cities. Now equating the success of the movement not only with larger circulation but also with the development of a national daily paper, the *Appeal* had advanced in that direction during the first Socialist Party Presidential Convention in Chicago in 1904, when the paper moved its editorial office to Chicago for a week and published thirty thousand copies every day. That relatively successful foray into daily publication spurred Warren onward.[13]

While the serial was appearing, however, the biggest labor story of the decade was unfolding in the silver, lead, and zinc mining areas of the West. The battle that the Western Federation of Miners was waging with the Mine Owners Association, which was backed by eastern corporations such as Standard Oil, was creating the conditions for the birth of the Industrial Workers of the World (IWW), a large-scale industrial union. The story was made for the *Appeal*: the exploitation of the miners and the ruthless effort to restrict the spread of unionism made a clear distinction between good and evil, between worker and capitalist, between West and East. Immediately upon taking control of the paper, Warren sent the emotionally drained Ricker out to Colorado to report firsthand on the developing situation. Ricker sent back "The Story of the Colorado Bull Pen," which took over the front page in three wide columns and praised the Western Federation of Miners (WFM). The WFM had been organized on the principle of industrial unity, not like the American Federation of Labor, which had been organized along craft lines.[14] The miners' grievances and attempts at unionization went back at least to Wayland's first sojourn in Pueblo in the 1880s. The rough conditions at the frontier and the isolation of the various mining camps gave the unions more of a chance to take root, away from official repression in the eastern states, where police and troops were close at hand.

The mine owners reacted by banding together and hiring private militia men. The election of Davis H. Waite as Populist governor of Colorado in 1892 helped the union in one set of strikes by denying to the side of the owners what official force there was; his reelection bid was turned back, however, by a Democrat/Republican coalition. After that, official as well as unofficial force was used to control the miners, and they responded by taking the law into their own hands. Colorado and Idaho became the scenes of sporadic warfare throughout the 1890s and into the 1900s. The conflict made for lasting hatreds on both sides and brought forth a number of leaders, William Dudley ("Big Bill") Haywood, Charles H. Moyer, and George Pettibone for the miners, and former governor Frank Steunenberg of Idaho, Senator William E. Borah, and Pinkerton agents James McParland and Charles A. Siringo for the owners.

Ricker's reporting was deficient. He wrote in a style of shocked innocence and moral outrage, not with the punch of a skilled muckraking journalist. The strike at the *Appeal* the year before had accentuated his dependence on drink, so he took a leave of absence at his farm in Iowa to recover from alcoholism. Warren turned to George H. Shoaf, a professional reporter from Chicago. It was a fateful choice. Shoaf acquitted himself well in a number of difficult situations, but his zeal for stories made him sometimes manufacture events that had not happened. The eventual decline of the *Appeal* from prominence, and with it the

George H. Shoaf. Courtesy of the Archives of Labor and Urban Affairs, Wayne State University.

popularity of the Socialist party, was to some extent due to his later role in reporting the McNamara case in 1911 (see chap. 10).[15]

Shoaf seemed to be destined for the job of *Appeal* correspondent; yet it is difficult to separate truth from fiction—both about his life and in his news stories. He himself admitted that his reporting was not always accurate. The question is where can one draw the line between veracity and falsehood. Warren trusted Shoaf. Untermann, who had strong personal reasons for his feelings, called Shoaf a spy. Emanuel Haldeman-Julius, who was to take over the *Appeal to Reason* during World War I and who was himself no strong respecter of the truth, said later that Shoaf "had a prejudice against the facts."[16]

Born in 1875 in a small town near Austin, Texas, Shoaf moved with his family to San Antonio when he was nine. There his father, the police chief, made a small fortune running gambling houses. Shoaf met William C. Brann, later of the *Iconoclast*, the hard-hitting independent radical paper published in Texas, and was influenced towards the radical movement by an uncle, who was a Populist member of the state senate. Shoaf himself became a Populist; then he joined the Socialist Labor party after the Bryan campaign of 1896. A visit by Debs to San Antonio influenced Shoaf's change to the Social Democracy and then the Socialist Party of America, and he became the first Socialist candidate for lieutenant governor of Texas. Shoaf had been educated for the ministry, at his mother's wish, but he had resigned from his small pastorate in west Texas a few months after taking it.

It was Brann who suggested a career for Shoaf as a reporter on Brann's *Daily Express*. After Brann's ouster, Shoaf left the newspaper business for a succession of jobs in railroading, where he became active in the Brotherhood of Locomotive Firemen, Davey Crockett Lodge 145. Because of socialist agitation, he was forced out of the Southern Pacific Railway Company and made his way to Ruskin College in Trenton, Missouri, where Ernest Untermann was on the staff and Josephine Conger was a student.[17] There, Shoaf came under the influence of Walter Vrooman, the promoter of the college. Vrooman took Shoaf to Chicago at the turn of the century.

Vrooman, according to Shoaf, had plans for a violent revolution in the United States, using the pretext of the "yellow peril" to recruit and train a private army. Shoaf was the organizer and chief promoter of the scheme, disguising himself on occasions as a Chinese in order to provoke incidents! This farce came to an end when Leon Czolgosz murdered President McKinley in 1901, so Vrooman prudently decided to leave town. Shoaf stayed on in Chicago, sold the weapons they had amassed, and lived on the proceeds until he got a job playing the piano in a brothel. Next, he worked as a conductor for one of the traction companies until he was fired for labor agitation. This time, he publicized his fate in a letter to Hearst's *Chicago American*, which featured it on the front page. This brought Shoaf into contact with the city editor, who happened to be a friend of Shoaf's father from San Antonio. The editor had Shoaf tell his story to Charles Edward Russell, the local-editorial writer for the paper, and soon to be a socialist muckraker and candidate for vice-president. Russell brought Shoaf into the circle of labor leaders in Chicago who were then attempting to organize the streetcar workers, and the young adventurer landed jobs as an organizer for the Amalgamated Association of Street and Electric Railway Employees and as editor of the *Union Leader*, a new paper in 1902. But Shoaf's socialism was too strong both for the union and for the paper, so he moved on to the *Chicago American* as a local reporter.

Chicago's labor violence, replete with Pinkerton antiunion spies, suited Shoaf. His job with the *American* was to write sensational stories. He used all kinds of ruses to get them, such as presenting fake calling cards and taking advantage of young servant women. He developed into a skilled yellow journalist, but he claimed that he never lost his socialist principles. In his own words, he just decided to "sidetrack idealism and pursue the capitalist newspaper game to the reprehensible end."[18] Glib, with a "winning, disarming, charming smile and Texas brogue," Shoaf resembled "a Methodist preacher fresh out of a one-building college. Hayseed seemed to drop from him. He was pure corn. But turn him loose on a story and he'd shake the world."[19] On the Colorado mining wars in 1904, Shoaf used the same tactics he had used at the *American*. Indeed, he retained *American* credentials, writing stories for both papers. He was drawn to the side of the miners by his every instinct, and he immediately idolized the strike's leader, Bill Haywood. Shoaf slanted his articles "to win public sympathy for the striking miners and to arouse hatred against the Mine Owners Association." As a cub reporter in Texas under Brann on the *Iconoclast*, Shoaf had learned how to use invective, while at the *American* he had been taught to stir the emotions of his readers. He wired two sets of stories; one was for the *American*, "but my real story was reserved for the *Appeal to Reason*."[20] He got one story by representing himself falsely, insinuating himself into favor with the commander of the local federal troops. The *Appeal* featured the story, which was smuggled out of the strike area by a sympathetic railroad worker. The *Appeal* warned Shoaf to get out of the area in a hurry, which he did.[21]

The stories that Shoaf sent back to the *Appeal* had a punch that Ricker's lacked. Shoaf injected himself into his reporting, telling the reader about the physical dangers he had to endure in order to get out the truth. The stakes escalated at the end of 1905, when former Governor Frank Steunenberg of Idaho, who had sided with the mine owners a decade earlier after having been elected by the miners, was killed by a bomb that exploded as he opened a gate outside his house. A search turned up Harry Orchard, who at first maintained his innocence but soon confessed to Pinkerton Agent James McParland and implicated the Western Federation of Miners in a tale of violence.[22]

The leaders of the WFM were all in Denver at the time of the killing. James McParland, who was famous for his role in breaking up the Molly McGuires in the Pennsylvania mines more than a generation earlier, engineered the illegal extradition of the union leaders Haywood, Moyer, and Pettibone to Idaho. Securing the cooperation of the governors of the two states, McParland arranged to have the three kidnapped late on a Saturday evening, held incommunicado on the train trip, and then formally charged with murder on their arrival in Idaho.

The *Appeal* went quickly into action. The kidnapping of these union leaders united labor and political organizations, from the American Federation of Labor to the Socialist party, in protest and outrage at the class bias of the judicial procedure. The *Appeal* led the charge and made the extradition of the men from Colorado to Idaho into a cause célèbre. It was obvious that the government took extraordinary measures to implicate the union. The *Appeal*, with editor Warren, Socialist party leader Eugene V. Debs, and Shoaf doing the writing, adopted countermeasures to combat the threat to the labor movement. The *Appeal* announced a "Rescue Edition" of the paper to flood the country with the "facts" of the case. For it, Debs penned the front-page article, "Arouse Ye Slaves," the most radically charged statement of his career, in which he predicted that if Haywood, Moyer, and Pettibone were found guilty, millions of American workingmen would rise up and revolt.[23]

The Haywood trial, the first of three projected trials, which was held more than a year after he was taken from Colorado, was one of the first media events of the new age of reporting. The AP sent out daily reports; the town of Boise was filled with reporters from across the country.[24] It was the third important trial with political overtones since the Civil War (Haymarket, 1886, and Pullman, 1894) and was the first of a number of trials during the first thirty years of the century in which radicals were tried in the national news spotlight. The *Appeal* set the stage. Shoaf, its reporter on the scene, was dubbed the "War" correspondent of the Class War. Debs, who would soon join the *Appeal* staff as its chief editorial writer, replacing Ricker and Wayland, was not wanted at the trial by defense lawyer Clarence S. Darrow. Darrow, who had defended Debs in the Pullman trial of 1894, feared that Debs's vehemence would unfavorably influence the jurors. Debs, along with most people, was convinced of the innocence of the miners' union officials. President Roosevelt, however, with others like Borah and McParland, was sure that they were guilty and that Haywood and Debs were undesirable citizens.

Were they guilty? Orchard confessed the crime, and he also admitted an amazing number of other crimes of labor violence during the previous decade, which he claimed were carried out at the insistence of the inner council of the union. Orchard's testimony was never shaken by the defense; he maintained his position throughout the trial. On the other hand, he admitted having been a police informer and claimed that his confession came only after promises of clemency from Pinkerton agent McParland (promises that were not kept; Orchard died in prison). It was Orchard's word against the word of the union men, for there was no corroborative evidence for his story. The question of conspiracy remains moot after years of debate; probusiness and prolabor scholars have both found what they wanted to find in the facts of the case.[25]

The jury found Haywood not guilty, which was a proper verdict in the absence of corroborating evidence. The labor movement rejoiced: marches and rallies were held throughout the country in major cities and small towns. The *Appeal* took pride in its role, although one hostile observer of Shoaf, Ernest Untermann, wrote several years later "that while he [Shoaf] was writing sensational and overdone articles for the *Appeal*, he was underhandedly acting like a Pinkerton and disrupting the Socialist local in Boise, was even jeopardizing the interests of the prisoners by telling everybody that the boys had confessed to him that they were guilty and that we ought to set the town afire and raise hell, because we oughtn't to let the thing come to trial."[26]

This was the only sour note in the affair, and it was not public knowledge. The *Appeal* had led a movement to get Haywood nominated for governor of Colorado on the Socialist ticket and had helped to raise funds for the defense.[27] Darrow fought the case on the issue of capital versus labor, rather than concentrating on the facts; and his strategy worked. Although it is doubtful that if Haywood had been found guilty, millions of Americans would have taken the law into their own hands, the very winning of such a case set an important precedent for the labor movement. It turned Haywood into a celebrity, to rival Debs for the affection of socialists; and the IWW, which was launched during the period of the trial, was given an initial momentum that sustained it beyond its formative years. The successful verdict helped to cement a united front of labor from about 1907 until the next important political trial, the McNamara Trial in 1911. Most important, labor could organize support for a celebrated trial, and its case could be won. This kind of issue was essentially a defensive one, a tactic in which the legally attacked allowed the government to name the time, the place, and the issue. Using political trials to promote socialism would prove fateful for the course of American radical and labor history. It is significant that Debs's most provocative statement was made during the trial. That statement tacitly admitted that although labor would respond to legal injustice, it would not rebel solely because of economic concerns.

The *Appeal* gained enormously from the successful conclusion of the trial and was convinced that it had played no small part in the outcome. But whatever it may have gained, and the labor movement with it in the short run, the costs of this kind of battle were prohibitive: the WFM's coffers were emptied by the lawyers' demand that no stone be left unturned in their investigations.[28] Not all of the radical papers fared so well. H. Gaylord Wilshire wrote to J. A. at the height of the trial: "What do you think is the reason subscriptions are not doing as well? My own idea is that it may be possible that this Moyer-Haywood business is not so conducive to getting up subscribers as a good many of the socialists seem to think."[29] The *Appeal* now embarked on its own publicity hunt by instigating a lawsuit against itself.

The impetus for the *Appeal* trial, which would become known as the

A postcard captioned "23 Tons of 'Appeal to Reasons.'" Courtesy of the Historical Society of Crawford County, Girard, Kansas.

Warren case, was an attempt to show by analogy the class bias of the court system. The original act in the *Haywood* case that outraged a broad spectrum of the American public was the extraordinary extradition of the three union officials. After the Supreme Court had ruled that the extradition was constitutional, Warren proceeded to offer a reward for a wanted criminal, asking for him to be kidnapped back to the state where he was wanted for murder. The ploy was purposefully transparent: the paper wanted to show that a murderer, in this case former Governor William Taylor of Kentucky, was afforded much more protection under the law than were the three union men. The whole Taylor episode was sordid from beginning to end: Taylor had murdered in cold blood and then had fled the state. The *Appeal* intended to throw mud in the face of corrupt politics, to draw attention to the *Haywood* case, which was then several months before the arguments, and most important, to call attention to the paper itself.[30]

The *Appeal* had had run-ins with the government since the turn of the century, chiefly with the Post Office Department. The laws concerning mass-circulation periodicals were new and dealt with unprecedented publications, such as magazines that were really no more than catalogs, which were circulated virtually free of postal charges. Second-class mailing privileges, which made possible the building of immense circulations, were granted at the discretion of the postmaster. It is difficult to prove whether they were revoked for political reasons, but

the various regulations that went with those rates were changed often during those years and caught the *Appeal* in violation several times.

The *Appeal*'s business came mostly in bundle orders of 25 cents a year, which were sent to central locations whence they were distributed. The ways in which the paper collected names, hawked subscriptions, and mailed its special editions all came under attack. The first attack was in 1901, and the *Appeal* fought back by mobilizing public opinion. Later attacks were dealt with in the same way. Once, after Debs's "Arouse Ye Slaves" article, the paper was banned in Canada for sedition. A socialist letter-writing campaign and the reprinting of the article as a handbill, coupled with a personal appeal from Warren, who paid a visit to the Canadian postmaster, won back the fourteen thousand lost subscribers.[31]

The ability of the nation's Post Office Department to place the paper in jeopardy through simple changes in regulations revealed much of the *Appeal*'s weakness and the vulnerability of the radical movement. The socialists relied on a faith in the essential honesty of governmental operations. They believed that once a majority had voted for socialism, the party would take office and enact its program. This belief hung on, in spite of the exposés of capitalism that the socialist and muckraking press continued to produce. One change in regulation the year prior to the Haywood trial caused the circulation list to drop from three hundred thousand to less than two hundred thousand. Harassment in the form of trials, new regulations, and arrests became major obstacles for the paper to overcome. A word in the ear of local postmasters and letter carriers not to deliver the paper or to send back unclaimed issues was enough to throw the *Appeal* into a crisis. To be sure, all attempts to silence the paper were used in order to increase sales, but this was allowing the opposition to create the issues and the rules of the game. The *Appeal* took no precautions to ensure that it could not become completely undone by the government, such as protecting its mailing list, providing security at the plant, or working out alternative techniques for distribution; rather, it continued to rely on the strength of its readers and the good faith of the courts to justify its stand.

The biggest story to come out of the series of sniping operations was the one that the *Appeal* centered around itself when it offered a reward for the kidnapping of Governor Taylor. On the face of its offer, the paper was merely complying with the recent Supreme Court ruling in favor of the Colorado extradition of Haywood, Moyer, and Pettibone; but the court chose to see it otherwise. Similar reward offers, made through the mail and submitted in defense of the *Appeal*, failed to change the mind of the government. Warren's refusal to plead guilty and accept a small fine set the stage for a new court drama, which was originally scheduled to be held before the Haywood trial. But the federal government used another tactic to bleed radical organizations: it continued to delay the trial, forcing Warren to make repeated trips to Fort Scott and to spend large amounts of time and money on preparation for the case. That the government was gunning for the *Appeal* became clear when it took the extraordinary steps of pardoning former Governor Taylor for the murder that he was charged with, but had never been convicted of, and sending him to Fort Scott for the Warren trial.

It took two years for the case finally to come to argument. Warren was found guilty. He responded with a rousing speech on the class bias of law and its enforcement in the United States, similar to the closing statement that Darrow had made in the Haywood trial. Shoaf, in his usual overblown fashion, reported: "Warren represented in the concrete the agony and woe, the blood and tears of the working class of the world. He typified the issue between the ruling class and those who are fighting the agelong war of human emancipation."[32] Warren did not end the case there; he appealed to the federal appellate court at St. Paul. The first case had cost more than $25,000; the appeal cost $20,000. Although the results were the same, Warren thought that "to put the federal courts on record is worth every cent of this and more!"[33] At the appellate trial, Warren proclaimed: "When the toilers of the mill, factory and mine and farm once understand the true situation, they will realize that there can be no relief from judicial despotism until they use the power latent in themselves to abolish the present iniquitous system based upon the legalized robbery of the nation's toilers and producers in which the courts

From left to right: Fred Warren, George Allan England, Walter Wayland, and Louis Kopelin, circa 1914. Kopelin worked at the Appeal *as an editor after Warren left; England was the official historian of the* Appeal; *and Walter H. Wayland was the publisher of the* Appeal *after the death of his father. Courtesy of the Archives of Labor and Urban Affairs, Wayne State University.*

are mere creatures of capitalist class rule and the instruments of working class subjection."[34]

Warren was sentenced to a $1,500 fine and six months at hard labor, but he refused to surrender himself, using the sentence to whip the *Appeal's* circulation even higher, to reach the 450,000 mark early in 1911. President Taft, refusing to allow Warren to become a martyr, reduced the fine to $100 and canceled the jail term, but Warren refused to pay this fine, on the excuse that the pardon was not printed by union labor. He did offer to pay, however, in the form of *Appeal* subscription blanks. The fine was never collected.[35]

These battles with the government held the main attention of the paper from the Haywood trial until the McNamara trial in 1911. But "War Correspondent" Shoaf sent other stories to the *Appeal* during this period. He went south to report on the burning of American Tobacco Company warehouses in Kentucky by nightriders. Shoaf found that these men, who were labeled as outlaws by the commercial press, were reacting to the monopoly that the company held in purchasing tobacco from small farmers. In Florida, in association with another muckraker from *Appleton's Magazine*, Shoaf went to work in a phosphate mine to get a story on "peonage," the practice of forcing convicts to work under horrendous conditions well beyond the legal end of their jail terms, a practice that involved collusion between law-enforcement and mining-company officials. Shoaf's reporting continued in its grandiose style, but he was uncovering stories of real interest. The inclination towards muckraking was waning in the popular press by 1908 and 1909, but Shoaf continued to hammer away. The biggest story of the next few years was the Mexican Revolution. Shoaf and another reporter covered that story for the paper.

John Kenneth Turner became the *Appeal's* main reporter for Mexico, and he replaced Shoaf in the years after 1911 as the *Appeal's* chief correspondent. Turner's background, like that of almost everyone else at the *Appeal*, was in newspaper work. Born in 1879 in Oregon, the son of a printer, Turner was by 1896, at the age of seventeen, publishing his own reform paper in Stockton, California. Before becoming a reporter for the *Los Angeles Express* in 1906, Turner had been a "hobo, a bronco buster, a day laborer, a 'leverman' at a beet dump, a ranch cook and a teacher," as well as a student of the University of California.[36]

Turner was a socialist who was drawn to the plight of the Mexican Liberal party, most of whose leadership was centered in Los Angeles. Job Harriman, a socialist lawyer, was brought in to represent the leaders of the Mexican party when they were jailed for rebelling against the Mexican government. Turner, alone of the journalists who were reporting for mainstream newspapers, was able to get an interview with them. Shoaf also gained access to the jail in which the men were held, by impressing the reluctant jailer with the power of the *Appeal to Reason*, and he printed an interview in the paper. Convinced of the importance of securing their release and of informing the U.S. public of what was really going on in Porfirio Díaz's Mexico, a country that was known to the people of the United States as a model of enlightened government, Turner secured a contract with the *American Magazine*, one of the few popular periodicals that still engaged in muckraking. The *American Magazine*, formerly *Leslie's*, had been renamed by a group of journalists who had banded together and bought the magazine when *McClure's*, their usual outlet, abandoned investigative journalism.

Turner's series, "Barbarous Mexico," was an immediate success and a national eyeopener. The stories were heralded throughout the popular press, both in the United States and in England. An attempt to enjoin Turner from publishing more articles was instigated by Díaz, friendly congressmen, and other influential Americans. The series, which began in October, 1909, was discontinued in January, 1910; this marked the end of the muckraking movement in the popular press in America. Turner turned to the *Appeal to Reason*, which was delighted to publish the rest of the series, including Turner's version of why it was suppressed, and to hawk the entire collection of articles when it was published in book form at the end of the year by Charles H. Kerr.[37]

Turner was the finest reporter ever to work for the *Appeal;* he was far superior to Shoaf, of whom Turner remarked to Fred Warren: "I think that S. [Shoaf] hurt your paper at various times by covering his ignorance with fake stories."[38] The *New York Times,* in reviewing the book *Barbarous Mexico,* pointed out that "for many of his [Turner's] charges there is too much ground."[39] As John Reed would for both the Mexican Revolution and the Bolshevik Revolution, Turner became an active advocate of the cause he was covering. He helped to raise funds, to smuggle arms, and to write accurate stories for the *Appeal* until the United States entry into World War I.

Muckraking had an impact on the way in which Americans conducted political business. It formed a center around which pressure groups and lobbying organizations made their first real dent in influencing the major parties. But the effect of muckraking was an essentially conservative one, because the excitement that was generated changed only the method through which business corrupted politics, thus serving to end the more blatant forms of abuse but not changing the basic relationship between business and government.[40]

The *Appeal,* which started somewhat late in the muckraking business, continued with it after its Progressive heyday and the enactment of reforms. The *Appeal*'s goal was not to create regulatory commissions but to show the need for a revolutionary socialist party. The *Appeal* used the tactics of popular journalism for radical ends. The *Appeal* was working in other ways to hasten revolution, seeing itself as the biggest and most powerful institution in socialist America and the center of the movement. The paper was the most important part of a growing socialist center in Girard, which included some factories, related industries, a physical plant known as the Temple of the Revolution, and a willing army of volunteer salesmen, who looked to the *Appeal* for the manifestation of socialist culture. As the *Appeal* borrowed muckraking and altered it to fit socialist needs, so did Wayland and Warren and others at the paper borrow from the dominant culture to fashion a little bit of what it was going to be like in the coming nation.

9

The Temple
of the Revolution

> We may not live to see the full fruition of our work, nor does it matter;
> so insidiously can a man feel Socialism, so completely consecrated can he
> be to the Cause of Socialism that he lives within the realization of it even
> now.
>
> —*Eugene V. Debs, 1908*

Not far from the square in the center of Girard, where the courthouse
stood surrounded on four sides by the small businesses of the town, a
group of Socialists sat in a comrade's home around a large table, enjoying ice cream and cake. It was the evening of May 21, 1908, about a week
after the Socialist Presidential Convention in Chicago, and many of the
visitors to the town had a midnight train to make. Thirty-three men and
women had left the children in the care of a young woman and, before
getting back to work, had gathered to share some warm reflections on
the events of the past two weeks and their hopes for the future.[1]

The toastmaster was Eli N. ("Baldy") Richardson, Warren's partner
in the *Coming Nation* days, former editor of the Appeal Army column,
and then of the Hot Cinders column. Richardson set the tone: "It is . . .
good to be living in Girard—good old Girard, where, sometimes, it seems
to me, one can fairly feel the spirit of that world-wide brotherhood which
we call International Socialism. . . . Some time or other the comrades
all come to Girard, and we love to see them and try to make them
welcome! . . . we imbibe inspiration from them and we hope they do
from us." He introduced J. A. Wayland, who praised the Appeal Army
for making the town famous: "Up to the present moment I believe the
Appeal Army has more to its credit than the Socialist Party, but from
now on it will have to take a back seat. . . . It has been a long struggle,
but the Socialist Party is gradually taking its place and the Army will
have to be simply a factor in it."

Henry Vincent, the Populist editor, had come to Girard the year before
to work for Wayland. He noted that since Debs's first campaign speech,

given in the square just a week before, there had been a real change in the way the people in the town responded to socialism. Vincent compared it to the first Populist successes in Kansas almost a generation before. Henry Laurens Call, who had come to town to build an airplane, returned to the theme of Girard: "I had lived in Kansas many years, but more recently had degenerated. I had gone to the effete east and buried myself in New York, Boston. . . . and when I came as far as the line of Kansas the old love of balmy breezes and of its bright skies and all that freedom from that oppressiveness in the east . . . led me to return [to stay]." Lillian Tubbs, a local Socialist who frequently put up visitors in her home, remarked: "As I sat and looked in the faces of the throng of earnest men and women at the national convention in Chicago, I thanked God that I was a Socialist."

A delegate from New Mexico, tired out after a week in the "unmentionable place" (Chicago), found "peace and serenity" in the Girard community. "I have long wanted to make a pilgrimage to this shrine . . . because a shrine is where you go for inspiration, and the *Appeal to Reason* is responsible for my first serious thought in the Socialist movement." Dan Hogan, editor of a socialist paper in Arkansas, emphasized the contrast between Chicago and Girard, which seemed to be on everyone's mind. Could anyone blame him, he asked, for borrowing money in order "to make a trip to the Mecca of Socialism, the center of the revolutionary universe, the place from which emanates the flashes of light and the glory that shall finally illuminate the world!" He could not help but be impressed by the "wonderful accomplishments of the workers and toilers of Chicago," but if the revolution were to triumph, he thought it would be a good idea to push Chicago all into the lake, except that it might mar the only worthwhile thing there.

David C. Coates of Idaho was the next-to-last speaker. He had helped Wayland in 1893 on the *Coming Nation*, and he was certain that the new day would come: "God is to be thanked for J. A. Wayland! If it had not been for his work the movement would not be as great as it is today. He has aroused the comrades from one end of the nation to the other as perhaps no other one man could arouse them, and the evidence of it all is the gathering that surrounds him in this banquet hall tonight." Then, Debs got up to speak. All of those before him had spoken of their affection for the candidate, but Debs responded first by praising Wayland: "When Comrade Wayland first located here . . . he was a resident of a hostile community. . . . He had the misfortune to be in advance of his time. Since then he has grown into the affections of the people. . . . They now understand the man, his principles and his mission." Debs felt that the recently ended Socialist convention was "the greatest and most important convocation of men and women in the history of this nation."

The gathering in Girard that night was a "miniature of the society of the future. . . . We may not live to see the full fruition of our work, nor does it matter; so insidiously can a man feel Socialism, so completely consecrated can he be to the Cause of Socialism that he lives within the realization of it even now."

The One-Hoss Philosophy remained intact. The big city was evil, the small town good. The East was decadent, the West vibrant. The association of good people together was itself as good a reason for socialism as any other. The women took care of the children, and the society of the future was around the corner. It was in Girard that this dream came near to reality in America. In these toasts and this town, the socialist movement found its expression of what life could be like when the Socialist party triumphed. As Debs said, dedication to the cause could almost compensate for the actual realization of the socialist dream. Girard, an isolated island separated from the rest of American society, both gave strength to its socialist inhabitants and weakened their connection to the American mainstream.

From the musings at the table, one might guess that Girard was a sleepy rural hamlet; but this was not the case. The chief sources of income were related to agriculture—milling, dairy works, transportation of farm products—but Girard was also a mining and manufacturing center. Aside from the local machine shops, there were smelting works, which served the zinc- and coal-mining industry. The population of twenty-five hundred was not homogeneously old-stock American, for many of the people had been drawn from Europe in the late nineteenth century to work the mines, although the recent immigrants tended to settle in outlying mining camps and towns. In addition, there was some black presence in the town. But Girard was small, and its smallness led to the assumption that any problems it faced could be handled by the local community. Although there was no socialism in the town, Wayland and others at the *Appeal* fought and often won battles against placing municipal services, such as water and telephone lines, in the hands of private developers. They worked toward and adopted the commission form of government in 1909, managing to elect a socialist mayor, who was one of three men to run the city. It was one of the Progressive remedies sweeping the nation. Wayland was also active in placing under semipublic control an interurban trolley line to Pittsburg, the closest large town, located fourteen miles southeast of Girard. Pittsburg was growing rapidly at the time; it had a fine hotel, a library, and a state normal school.[2]

The *Appeal to Reason* was the biggest employer in Girard, a heavy user of the rails, the mails, and local construction help. In addition to its permanent work force, the paper hired casual labor whenever it published

The Temple of the Revolution and its staff just after the completion of the building in 1908. Courtesy of the J. A. Wayland Collection, Pittsburg State University.

special editions. It occupied five successively larger buildings in Girard; the last, the Temple of the Revolution, which was ready in the summer of 1907, was built expressly for the paper. There, in 1908, approximately one hundred full-time employees, all over the age of eighteen, worked in a union shop forty-seven hours a week, from 7 A.M. to 4 P.M. on weekdays and from 7 A.M. to 3 P.M. on Saturdays. The staff, which had grown from forty during the strike of 1903, worked in a plant that was reputed to be the most advanced in the state in terms of ventilation, lighting, hours, and wages. Child labor was strictly prohibited, safety measures were in effect, and the latest machinery was purchased to print the newspaper and the books. After 1904 the *Appeal* was printing from four to eighteen regional editions, with news columns that described local socialist activity, and was also publishing *Wayland's Monthly, One-Hoss Philosophy,* and *Studies in Socialism.* The *Appeal* advertised more than eight hundred titles in its pages during 1908 alone and was itself publishing dozens of pamphlets and other short publications. It was a modern, efficiently run plant, and it was the most successful industrial endeavor of American socialism.[3]

As the man from New Mexico said, coming to visit Girard was like visiting a shrine. The visitor would be taken on a tour of the plant, like the one outlined for the reader in an issue of *Wayland's Monthly.* He might find Wayland "busy at work on his battered old typewriter," using a desk that "would be instantly thrown out . . . by even a third-rate capitalist," but ready to greet and escort the pilgrim through the Temple of the Revolution. The newcomer would see the sorting room, where

*An original cartoon by Ryan Walker for the
cover of* Wayland's Monthly. *J. A. Wayland is
on the left; E. N. Richardson is on the right.
Courtesy of the Archives of Labor and Urban
Affairs, Wayne State University.*

young staff members divided the daily flow of incoming letters, subscription orders, and complaints, known as "kicks." Wayland's son Walter supervised the operation after the 1903 strike. Each order received a number, was entered on tally sheets, was reduced to a 3-by-5 card, and was forwarded to the proper department for processing. The staff had covered two walls in this large and well-ventilated room with illustrated postcards from around the world.[4]

The visitor would then see the intricate mailing system for keeping

Mr. Chapman, pressman of the Appeal to
Reason. *Courtesy of the Archives of Labor and
Urban Affairs, Wayne State University.*

track of hundreds of thousands of subscriptions. Before the Temple was
built, the tourist would have seen a room in a smaller building, where
a corps of stenographers added and dropped names. After 1907, two men
worked at machines that automatically printed addresses from stencil
cards that had been typewritten by the young women, thus replacing
the cumbersome method of keeping addresses in type.[5]

The visitor would then reach the heart of the plant, the press room,
which was overseen by Comrade Chapman and was dominated by "one
of the largest, three-deck straight-line Goss perfecting presses in the
country. . . , capable of printing 45,000 four-page papers per hour." The
visitor might derive inspiration from the sight, as Fred Warren and other

staff members did. "No revolutionary movement in all the world's history ever possessed so great a printing plant for the propagation of its principles. . . . We are fighting a battle more portentous than ever before waged—but with the printing press."[6]

The visitor would surely have been impressed by this printing press in action, as well as by the substation of the post office located at its end, where *Appeal* workers filled large mailbags and a postal clerk weighed and processed them. The last impression that the visitor would get, one that almost everyone who passed through Girard experienced, was the wait at the railroad station to load the mail. Train schedules were arranged to suit the printing schedule at the plant. Eugene Debs, witnessing the loading of a very large special edition in 1912, noticed with delight the discomfiture that "a fat, rich man . . . with florid features" suffered during the delay in Girard. Debs said that the train "was loaded with light," and he added that "mail cars, express cars, baggage cars, all were packed to the rafters with the deadliest dynamite that ever blew a rotten system into froth and tatters."[7]

The success of their paper spurred Warren and Wayland to look for other potential moneymakers to bring to Girard. The musings at the farewell gathering might have been even more euphoric if one of their visions had come true. The plan had been to fly to the 1908 Socialist Convention. Henry Laurens Call, who spoke at the table about his distaste for the East and his happiness in Girard, may have been pitching his remarks to his little band of investors. Call had come to town at the beginning of 1908, needing $2,500 of further investment to continue work on his own plans for an aircraft that was radically different from the Wright brothers' successful model of 1903. With the backing of the *Appeal*'s senior staff and other prominent local business leaders, he had raised the funds immediately, and the Aerial Navigation Company was born. Call's design was old-fashioned even in 1908, because it relied on the age-old belief that mechanized flight must resemble the flight of birds, and though the project lasted for about five years, through fourteen planes and thousands of dollars, only one actually flew. Warren had wisely insisted that all mention of the plane be avoided in the *Appeal* until it was successful, so the readers never knew about it. Among the many who lost money on the project was Eli Richardson. Years later, the socialists of Girard took some comfort in the claim that they were part of the first airplane company west of the Mississippi.[8]

Another moneymaking venture was more successful. Advertisements started appearing in 1907 for goods made by the Girard Manufacturing Company, which made Nutol, Nutreto, Ceroblend, the Oscilator, and, later in the fall, the Holdfast Champion Clothespin. Nutreto, or Nutrito, as it was known back in 1904 when the paper was boosting it for the

H. L. Call's airship in 1908. Call is on the right. Courtesy of the Haldeman-Julius Collection, Pittsburg State University.

Girard Cereal Company, was a coffee substitute, perhaps made by the same process used in the manufacture of cereal coffee at Ruskin, Tennessee. Wayland had been advertising this local product with free ads ever since C. W. Post had withdrawn his ads for Postum. As president of the National Advertising Association, Post had decided to remove his ads from radical papers. Wayland claimed that the Ruskin pioneers had created the market for cereal coffees and that Nutrito would recapture those profits from the antisocialist Post. The Girard Manufacturing Company endeavored to produce a number of items to wean the public away from capitalist goods.[9]

It appears that Richardson and Wayland were the primary backers. Warren supported the Girard Cereal Company, which relied on a locally produced commodity, wheat; but he balked at the Girard Manufacturing Company, whose primary ingredient was cottonseed oil, which was controlled by a trust. A. W. Lovejoy brought to town the idea of making fine oil from cottonseed, and in order to push Nutol (a vegetable oil for cooking), Nutreola (a salad oil), and Nutreto, Wayland invited Henry Vincent to Girard in 1907. Vincent had retired from editorial work and was living in Pueblo, Colorado, where he was employed at the Bessemer Steel Works. Wayland highly praised him for his ability to sell the products, so Vincent agreed to become sales manager for the plant. Vincent's old enthusiasm for the socialist cause was now directed into sales: "My controlling motive for getting into this work was the possibility I saw for our press in being well backed by a manufacturing concern which could furnish the sinews of war in the form of advertising and job work."[10]

The company paid only $2,000 to the paper over a four-year period. Receipts and disbursements were roughly even, at $90,000. The plant burned down in 1911 and was never rebuilt. The Vincents left shortly thereafter. But during the time that the plant was in operation, 1907–11, many threads of American socialist life had been brought together in and around Girard. The Vincent home was one of a number of homes in which the many socialists who worked in the area or passed through spent considerable time. The colorful Call and his wife, an accomplished pianist, were mainstays in the town. Charles Lincoln Phifer, an *Appeal* columnist and a member of the editorial staff, provided some comic relief as a proponent of automatic writing, providing Shakespeare with the opportunity to write plays that death had prevented him from composing earlier. Not alone in his spiritualist leanings among the *Appeal* staff, Phifer shared a strong friendship with the central figure in the Girard socialist constellation, Eugene V. Debs.[11]

Debs was the central figure of the socialist movement. His popularity with labor was secured by his heroic stand against the Pullman Company in 1894, and he was seen by members of the party as the key to electoral success. A spellbinding orator and a ceaseless labor organizer, Debs was held in affectionate esteem even by those who disagreed with his politics. His combination of personal integrity, Victorian sensibilities, solidarity with the downtrodden, disdain for dirty politics, and personal warmth made for much of the attraction to the socialist cause of those who may not have grasped its underlying principles. Wayland had been a Debs enthusiast from the start. During the Haywood trial, Debs had written his "Arouse Ye Slaves" article, and he had stayed closely connected with the paper thereafter. By 1908, he was a full-fledged member of the staff, an association that would last for five years. During this time, Debs was paid $100 a week for editorials and for speaking engagements sponsored by the paper.[12]

The "Evening in Girard," at which Debs lavishly toasted his socialist admirers, completed one of the most satisfying weeks of his life. On May 16 he had been asked by Fred Warren to take an afternoon stroll a couple of blocks into the center of town. The mayor, a Democrat, joined the pair on their way to the central courthouse, where a large group of local people had gathered. After the speeches had begun, it dawned on Debs, as he reported the next day in a letter to his brother, that "the *people* of Girard, regardless of party, creed or color, had assembled to compliment" him on his nomination for president. After Debs had been pressed to make some remarks, "a large number of little girls in white came forward, each with a huge basket of beautiful flowers." For Debs, the day "drew aside the curtain of the future for a brief moment," allowing him to catch "a glimpse of the fine, sweet, beautiful *human* society—that is to be."[13]

Between speaking engagements that took him on the road much of the time, Debs often stayed in Girard with the Vincent family or sometimes with the Warrens or in a room that he rented on the square. He was adored by the children of the town, not least by Mary Vincent, who was eleven in 1908, and for whom Debs was a constant source of ice cream cones. Mary has described life in Girard between 1907 and 1911.[14] She recalled the socialist center as a cool and tree-shaded place, where the main form of entertainment was the five-cent silent picture, "held in a roofless place with rows of picnic tables to the accompaniment of a piano." The Waylands, she thought, were quite well-to-do, "as they drove around in a lovely carriage drawn by two beautiful black horses." J. A. was unmistakable, "with a bushy brown moustache." Mary remembered a Christian Science Society that had its own building. Her father was a first reader.

The Vincents paid $10 a month rent for a little square house, which had a picket fence, a corn crib, a barn, and a large yard, with fruit trees and a privy. There was an annual Chautauqua held on the courthouse lawn, and there was a Maypole dance. Horses provided the major form of transportation. Ice was brought to town from a farmer's pond. Every Saturday night brought a "bath in the round wash tub on the kitchen floor," filled with water that had been heated on the wood-burning kitchen stove. Between silent pictures, her main entertainment derived from leafing through the Sears Roebuck and the Montgomery Ward catalogs. The Vincent house, probably along with other socialist homes, was known by hoboes to be an easy mark. Mary's mother "fed them, and gave them a dose of socialism at the same time." Her mother also made most of Mary's clothes, in spite of the catalogs.

Several of the Girard socialists made an impression on the youngster. The Calls—Henry Laurens of airplane fame, and Emma Johns, a well-known pianist—insisted on being called by their full names. Herrlee G. Creel, who for a time was an associate editor on the paper and the publisher of a number of pamphlets on the "tricks of the press," made his family chew every bite fifty times before swallowing. Fred Warren and family, Mary recalled, lived in one of the town's biggest houses.

But all was not sweet in Girard. "The Shively family lived down by the tracks. They were beyond the pale, for they were *Catholics!*" Mary's recollection seems to be accurate, for the *Appeal*, Wayland, Warren, and Debs were all openly anti-Catholic. In 1911, W. F. Phelps, Wayland's long-time associate who had been forced off the *Appeal* staff by the 1903 strike, started an anti-Catholic paper, the *Menace*, just across the border in Missouri, helped along by Wayland's financial support and staffed mostly by socialists.[15]

The antipathy towards Catholics that the Vincent family and the *Appeal* editors exhibited was not an isolated phenomenon. Edith Wayland Stephenson, J. A.'s youngest daughter, recalled that her group of acquaintances was limited to Girard townspeople who were not connected with the mining camps that dotted the surrounding landscape. These workers, mostly immigrants from central and southern Europe, were in the main Catholic. She remembers having one miner's child as a friend; but the parents were Welsh, and they lived in Girard.[16]

That Wayland's proclivities were towards northern European immigrants was also made clear in his attempt to help publish a foreign-language paper for the American scene. His choice to do this was Emil Lauritz Mengshoel, whom Wayland invited to Girard in 1903 to publish a Scandinavian-language weekly *Gaa Paa: Folkets Rost* (Onward: Voice of the People). He hired Mengshoel away from the *Republikaneren* in Lake Mills, Iowa. Probably due to the troubles that led to the strike and the restructuring of the *Appeal*, Wayland changed his mind about publishing the paper himself, but he was generous in helping Mengshoel get started. Mengshoel moved the paper to Minneapolis in 1904 to be closer to the Norwegian community.[17]

It is crucial to understanding the isolated nature of Girard, the *Appeal*, and J. A. Wayland, to keep in mind the separation between the town and the paper and the separation of its leading citizen from the surrounding ethnic community. Wayland and his fellow citizens had a real chance to know the immigrant miners, but kept themselves as aloof as their Republican neighbors did. This is in spite of such a frequent visitor to the Wayland home as Mother Jones, who continued to beat a path to his door whenever she was in the vicinity, working to organize those miners, and in spite of the real affection for the *Appeal* that was expressed by such an important figure in the immigrant socialist community as Ivan Molek, the editor of leading Slovenian papers. "In those days [1907] I was very fond of [the] *Appeal to Reason*. . . . This paper was my model, and I wanted *Proletarec* to be a kind of Slovene replica of it. We took the recommendation of the *Chicago Daily Socialist*—then the Chicago Socialists had their own daily—of an artist to design a new masthead. It was produced in italics, such as the one for the *Appeal to Reason*."[18]

There were twenty or so small mining camps located within a fifteen-mile radius of Pittsburg. Welsh miners from Pennsylvania came first in 1877; and for the next two decades, agents recruited immigrants from western, central, and southern Europe right off the docks in New York.

May Wood Simons, who had stayed for awhile in Girard, noted: "At no place west of the Mississippi is there a similar large group of industrial immigrants living in the very midst of a flourishing rural community."[19] In spite of the opportunity, the Girard socialists kept their mecca to themselves.

The Girard, Kansas, that Mary Vincent described, with its local attractions, religious prejudice, and colorful personalities, could have been any early-twentieth-century midwestern town, but with a core of socialism. The airplane fiasco and the Girard Manufacturing Company were monuments to the American booster ideal, extolling the virtues of hard-working small-town America. As in most small towns, Girard had its leading citizen. For Wayland, Girard fulfilled the expectations that had germinated in the Ruskin experiment a decade earlier. With his house, his business, and social connections, Wayland displayed all of the trappings of success that his more politically conventional counterparts enjoyed in other American towns. With them, he shared their fears of the evil city.

The Girard brand of socialism was a model of social convention. In New York, socialist immigrants rubbed shoulders with Greenwich Village intellectuals: anarchism, free love, jazz music, and the ideas of Freud and Margaret Sanger—all dared to question the values of society, to laugh at the hypocrisy of everyday life, while nurturing a literary and artistic excitement. In Girard, the unconventional thinker turned, like Charles Lincoln Phifer, to spiritualism or, like Fred Warren, to vegetarianism. Mary Vincent read the *Wizard of Oz*; her parents delighted in Edwin Arnold Brenholtz's *The Recording Angel*, a socialist romance of the future. Eugene Debs would recite "Annie Laurie" for gathered guests on a summer evening, and Mary would play "Angels Serenade" on the Weber upright piano. Visitors were proudly shown the town's major attractions, a large greenhouse and the *Appeal* plant. Not for Girard was the artistic avant-garde, which was just breaking through the surface in the cities. For socialists in New York City, Girard was the Temple, a place for pilgrimages perhaps, but not for residence. As Ryan Walker, the *Appeal*'s popular cartoonist, said when he was asked to move there from New York, "[In New York] I have all of the phases of life to draw on, and staying long in a small town would dry up my faculties."[20]

In Girard, mainstream American values were upheld. Debs's personal life was felt to be of absolute importance to the success of the movement; no breath of scandal must attach to him, or the widely held fear that socialism would bring destruction of family life might start to bear credence. This sense of morality was kept up as a matter of course. His drinking habits were hushed up, while an extramarital affair of his became public knowledge only recently. Drink in general was a problem for all labor leaders. Samuel Gompers, in public and private correspondence, vehemently denied that he ever drank a drop. An allegation in 1903 that a group of *Appeal* people, including J. A. Wayland, drank some beer while on an outing drew pages of denial from an *Appeal* editor in the local paper. A. W. Ricker, who left the *Appeal* in 1904 to recover from a severe case of alcoholism, had gone to his farm without the *Appeal*'s acknowledging the reason. Even though Kansas had been a dry state long before national prohibition, drink was, of course, available. J. A. Wayland often had claret with his dinner. There were several attempts to close Girard's clandestine bars during the first decade of the twentieth century. Mary remembered quite clearly that Mother Jones had ordered Mary's father to get her a beer, and the nondrinking Vincent turned one up in a hurry.[21]

Debs's reputation as a sterling citizen was guarded jealously by the *Appeal* for the consumption of the socialist public. Two members of the staff, George and Grace Brewer, were assigned to assist Debs. Grace, who edited the Appeal Army column after taking it over from Richardson, also booked Debs's extensive speaking engagements and served as his secretary; George accompanied him on long trips, making sure that Debs reached his destinations punctually.[22]

The *Appeal* and Debs were made for each other. They shared a utopian outlook and a sentimental vision of the coming of socialism. Their positions were sufficiently flexible to hide any disagreements for a long spell. For Debs, the relationship meant a secure income and a haven to return to after the long speaking engagements, away from family pressures in Terre Haute and with a congenial group of like-minded adults. For the *Appeal*, the association with Debs assured its remaining the most important paper in the field: the leading socialist wrote its editorials, and its subscription list rose with Debs's popularity and that of the cause. When Debs spoke under the *Appeal*'s auspices, the price of admission was six hundred to one thousand subscriptions, bought by the local organizers, thus ensuring the paper a continuing and growing audience. Grace Brewer's scheduling was no mean feat, and she executed her task well. When the *Appeal* and Debs had a falling out in 1913 and Debs turned over his speaking engagements to the O'Hares at the *National Ripsaw* (a rising Missouri monthly socialist periodical), the result was a dismal nightmare.[23]

Others worked the *Appeal* lecture circuit too. Ryan Walker worked his way across the country from New York to Girard in the fall of 1906, delivering forty lectures that were illustrated with cartoons and receiving $10 a night, from which he had to deduct expenses. George Goebel, a national organizer for the party, suggested to Walker that they team up, charge $25 or $30 a night, add a motion-picture projector, and if successful, bring along a couple of singers. Goebel observed: "I carried a glee club and fine male quartette on the road for over a year in temperance and prohibition work." At these events, such as the Debs subscription lectures, the socialist locals charged admission and guaranteed to sell *Appeal* subscription cards.[24]

Often Debs spoke at the socialist encampments that were popular in the Southwest from 1904 to World War I. Held on a sympathizer's farm, in a town park, or in any other place near a railroad, these drew thousands to hear groups of socialist orators, including Kate Richards O'Hare, Walter Thomas Mills, Dan Hogan, A. W. Ricker, Algie Martin Simons, and Oscar Ameringer. The larger encampment "was the old fashioned Camp-meeting, but with Socialist speakers instead of religious evangelists."[25] The encampments brought together the faithful for food and thought, and they often revived the leaders as well as the followers, while many stayed up nights talking socialism around campfires. The Girard socialists set up an encampment of their own in the summer of 1911 at Fort Scott, north of Girard, which took advantage of the proximity of the workers at the *Appeal*.[26]

At the encampments, *Appeal* subscriptions were hawked so successfully that other papers and socialist party organizations in Missouri, Oklahoma, Arkansas, and Texas were hard-pressed to make ends meet. As early as 1906, the editor of the *Arkansas Socialist*, "the only Socialist paper in Arkansas endorsed by the state convention," advised Fred Warren that he could not get his paper out for less than 50 cents a year and asked the *Appeal*'s editor for help in a joint circulation attempt.[27] In 1910 the Socialist Party of Oklahoma acknowledged that the amount owed to the *Appeal* for subscription cards was beyond the capacity of the state organization to pay: "Your own system for sub [subscription] getting is so perfect that it leaves us little or no opportunity [to sell off the cards purchased in order to book Debs for speeches]. . . . Throughout the encampment season you continuously flooded the state with your own circulars drawing subscriptions direct to the *Appeal* and cutting off the possibility of our selling cards."[28]

Many of the people at those encampments were full-fledged members of the Appeal Army, the "Salesmen-Soldiers" of the socialist revolution, who also helped to draw funds directly to the paper. More than any other single factor, it was the countless members of this group that helped Warren to double the circulation of the paper between 1908 and 1912, when it was reaching about half a million readers. Five hundred of the leading subscription agents of the paper were polled by the paper for a book called *Who's Who in Socialist America*.[29] Two of the biographies read like this: "Stimson, W. R., farmer, Lodi, Cal. Born Maine, Jan. 5, 1871; formerly populist; converted to Socialism by reading Socialist literature; joined

Socialist party at Medford, Ore., 1904; member Local Lodi; distributed hundreds of pieces of literature; secured hundreds of subscriptions for Socialist papers; attended one city and one state convention." "Horing, E. E., track walker, Irondale Ohio. Born, Ohio, June 22, 1862; formerly democrat; converted to Socialist by *Appeal* at the time of the Haywood trial; joined Socialist party, 1906; member local Hammondsville; helped organize locals at Irondale and Hammondsville."

This *Who's Who* has helped to fuel the continuing debate over the nature of membership in the Socialist party, whether it was largely middle-class, as Daniel Bell and David Shannon have held, or largely working-class, as John H. Laslett and James Weinstein have maintained.[30] James R. Green has studied the contents of the *Who's Who* in depth twice, once using the whole sample and again using a selected portion of agitators drawn exclusively from the Southwest. He found that the make-up of the whole group was overwhelmingly male, drawn from every section of the country in roughly proportionate numbers, with the exception of New England, which was little represented, and the Southwest, which was over-represented. Taken in 1914, the poll showed a largely middle-aged and older group, with only 28 percent of the people under forty. Although only a quarter of the group came from large cities, the group from larger towns was three times the size of the rural contingent, and many of those towns were largely industrial in composition. Eighty percent were American born, while the overwhelming percentage of the foreign born came from areas of older immigration. Only eight people out of the five hundred had come from eastern Europe or Russia.

With these findings drawn from what Green calls the middle rank of the Socialist party, the composite picture of the American Socialist emerges as a middle-aged, native-born town dweller, who was converted to socialism by reading socialist literature. This finding conforms to what Algie Martin Simons guessed to be the *Appeal*'s audience in 1913. An important question for Green is the class composition of the Appeal Army. He found that the majority, 57 percent, were from the working class, and a minority of 43 percent were middle-class. The working-class members were overwhelmingly city dwellers, and the middle-class ones were mostly drawn from the countryside. This, according to Green, shows clearly the contrast between the Socialists and the Progressives, who were largely drawn from middle-class city residents.

If one keeps in mind that the sample is about half middle-class and skilled workers, one sees the truth of Wayland's early contention that the backbone of the movement was men of some substance. Green is right to emphasize the large number of skilled workers, artisans, and tradesmen, who were the backbone of the movement, people in the position of losing the most in the sweeping industrialization. Many of the salesmen were drawn from the railroading industry, which Green classes among the skilled working class. In order to find the time to hawk subscriptions, one either had to live exclusively on the difference between the subscription price of 50 cents and the "club" price of 25 cents (which many did) or have the leisure to get to the large number of people necessary for selling such subscriptions. Conductors and trainmen would be in a perfect position to sell subscriptions, but their income and the nature of their duties may put them closer to the middle class. Other skilled workers, such as carpenters and machinists, were perhaps also making an income close to that of lower-middle-class persons. The group, which was not overwhelmingly working class, even using Green's criteria, becomes more and more roughly divided between classes when one uses income as the determinant. In its ethnic make-up, the group also reflects the overwhelming attraction of native-born Americans to the *Appeal's* brand of socialism.[31]

Subscription lectures, socialist encampments, and the Appeal Army were the three chief techniques of socialist education. In 1908, hopes were high for a large Socialist vote; so the *Appeal*, in conjunction with the Socialist party, flexed its muscles in the post-Haywood victory days, directing the biggest publicity coup of the campaign with a new propaganda effort. The Red Special, a train bearing Debs and a suboffice of the Socialist party, crisscrossed the country making whistle-stop tours, with Debs speaking from the rear platform or in a hall in town. Grace Brewer of the *Appeal's* staff handled the arrangements, and the joint cooperation between the party and the paper had Debs making six to ten speeches a day for sixty-five straight days from August 31 to election day. The small train, which had a sleeper, an observation car, and a baggage car for literature, traversed thirty-three states. It was estimated that Debs spoke to more than eight hundred thousand people. However exciting the tactics, the results were disappointing: Debs raised the total Socialist vote only by a few thousand more than the four hundred thousand received in 1904. Fifteen thousand people paid $35,000 to finance the campaign. Contemporary explanations for the failure to double or triple the previous totals were many; most focused on the reform platform that all parties shared. For Debs and the *Appeal*, it meant only that more educational work needed to be done.[32]

That the *Appeal* could not see that education and propaganda could have reached the limits of their effectiveness may have been the result of living in the tightly knit socialist community of Girard. As Debs had said at the evening gathering, socialists who were working for the cause already enjoyed some of the fruits that would come when the movement reached its political goals: namely, life in small socialist subcultures like that at the *Appeal*. So the answer to setbacks within the movement was to work harder along the same lines that had brought these like-minded people together. A kind of tunnel vision affected those who labored in the socialist press at Girard and at other places: supported by similar views of comrades and dazzled by the size of special editions and the growing subscription list, they had a narrowed view of American reality. They saw only their own limited success, and they ignored the changes in the larger community. As America urbanized and became a country with more and more crowded ethnic urban areas, the *Appeal* continued to rely on counting subscriptions and weighing the tonnage of literature that it produced.[33]

By 1908 the *Appeal* was no longer seriously challenged by competitors for the number-one spot in the socialist publishing world. *Wilshire's*, which was often near the *Appeal* in the number of subscribers, started to take a nose dive as the result of the most bizarre of Gaylord Wilshire's schemes. Whereas Wayland and Warren wanted to produce consumer goods that would support the *Appeal* by buying advertising in the paper, Wilshire hit on another remedy. He asked his subscribers to buy into a gold mine that would finance the socialist revolution! The Bishop Creek Mine, touted in his magazine, was supported by none other than Upton Sinclair. Sinclair, after his success with *The Jungle*, turned to an upper-class version of communalism at Helicon Hall in New Jersey. After it burned down, he lent his name to Wilshire's mine scheme. Wilshire got some support from his readers and was attacked in the socialist press; but the mine was a disaster, and it led to the destruction of his paper.[34]

The *International Socialist Review* (*ISR*), the other serious competition to the *Appeal*, took on a new look and style after the Haywood case. Publisher Kerr and editor Algie Martin Simons had a falling-out over the Industrial Workers of the World (IWW). Kerr decided that the previously staid magazine, which published articles on theory and on the socialist scene in Europe, should be turned into a "Fighting Organ of the Working Class," trumpeting industrial unionism as the wave of the future. Simons, a graduate of the University of Wisconsin and the Socialist party's acknowledged expert on agricultural issues, was skeptical about the importance of the Wobblies (members of the IWW). Kerr replaced Simons as editor of the *ISR*, and after a short and unsuccessful stint at the *Chicago Daily Socialist*, Simons joined the burgeoning ranks at Girard, where the *Appeal* planned to launch another periodical. At the *ISR*, Kerr had worked in close cooperation with the *Appeal*, taking over the latter's book business.[35]

The new periodical was the *Coming Nation*. Resurrected for the third time, it was intended to be the quality publication of the *Appeal to Reason*. Large in format, this monthly featured longer articles, more graphics and fine typography; and—what was most important to Warren—it would not lower itself to grub for subscriptions. Simons was the editor, with the assistance of Charles Edward Russell, the Chicago muckraking journalist. Simons fell readily into the way of life at Girard. He added a big-city polish to the community in 1910. Ryan Walker's artwork became a feature of the new monthly.[36] Josephine Conger-Kaneko also renewed her close connections with Girard at about the same time. After the death of her husband, Kiichi Kaneko, in the fall of 1909, she installed her operation in the Temple of the Revolution to print the *Progressive Woman*, the leading American socialist-feminist publication.[37]

By 1910 the Girard socialist community had blossomed. The impetus was the *Appeal* and the One-Hoss Philosophy that it espoused. As far back as 1904, when the Socialist party had met in convention in Chicago and discussed the strike at the *Appeal*, the Girard community of socialists was already a force. After covering the convention with daily bulletins, the Girard contingent had come back to southeastern Kansas, buoyed by the experience, and was instrumental in calling a convention for Crawford County, of which Girard was the county seat, to be convened in Pittsburg, the county's largest town. There, the familiar *Appeal* names set up committees, voted resolutions, and adopted a platform for its potential elected officials that emphasized pragmatic action but stopped short of compromise with major political parties:

The Socialist party of Crawford county, Kansas, in convention assembled, reaffirms its adherence to the principles of International Socialism as enunciated by the Socialist national convention held in Chicago May 4th, 1904, and declares its object to be the organization of the working class, and those in sympathy with it, into a political party for the purpose of securing political power of the county and using it to the utmost interests of the working class until that time when the Socialist party shall have captured the reins of the national government and inaugurated Socialism.

Whereas, Varying conditions prevent the adoption of any definite, elaborate and rigid program for the activity of Socialist officials; therefore be it

Resolved . . .

3. The principal object in capturing any office is to extend the power of the Socialist party with the purpose of ultimately securing control of the national government and accomplishing the complete emancipation of the working class by the inauguration of Socialism.

7. Compromising, political trading, or agreements of any kind with a capitalistic party tends to destroy the distinctive features of

the Socialist party, and shall be condemned at any time and all times, under all circumstances.[38]

The Girard group succeeded in electing local candidates and capturing the mayor's race in Girard in 1911, but the notion of using political office to further socialist goals ran smack up against practical matters. A good example was the poll tax, which Mayor H. P. Houghton, who first supported the measure, finally opposed, in accordance with the party platform. As one of three, running the town with two commissioners—a form of government that the socialists in Girard had helped to enact in response to a national progressive move towards commission governance of cities and towns—Houghton was powerless to enforce his opposition to the tax, due to the fact that one of the commissioners was a Republican and the other a Democrat and that the poll tax was mandated by state law. In carrying out his duties, the mayor almost inevitably came into conflict with laws that he had sworn to uphold. A provision of the Socialist party's bylaws mandated that a signed letter of resignation be placed with the party by each elected official as a check to hold these men in line. While it helped to ensure political purity, it effectively tied the hands of its elected officials.[39] There were real limits to the ushering in of socialism in one town.

By 1910, everything was in place for Warren at the *Appeal*. He was a major force in American socialism. His own court case, which had been launched during the Haywood affair, was coming to a head, he had almost doubled the subscription list, he had started a new periodical, and he had launched regional editions of the paper. Financially, he was secure. He signed a contract with Wayland in mid 1910 to last for five years, at the then-stupendous sum of $25,000 a year.[40] The terms of this contract, which were not made public for obvious reasons, gave Warren a lease on the paper and freed Wayland to devote more time to the real-estate speculation that he had vowed to end a decade before but that he had never given up. The paper had announced in mid 1909 that it was suspending commercial advertising completely in order to make the paper more appealing and less dependent on the enemy. The ads reappeared in September, 1910, without the explanation that they netted $25,000 a year. It seems obvious that they came back to pay Fred Warren's salary.[41] Also in 1910, oil land that he had speculated on in Preston, Oklahoma, started to produce heavily. Warren was becoming a wealthy man.[42]

Active in Texas, Colorado, Oklahoma, and Girard, J. A. Wayland slipped away more and more from association with the paper. According to Henry Vincent, Wayland had not lost his real-estate touch. Wayland noticed on a map of Texas that Amarillo, because of its location, seemed to be a likely spot for rapid development. He bought some downtown

corners, improved them, invited friends to invest, and started to collect high rents.[43] He would visit Amarillo once a week, taking the
train down in the middle of the week and returning after a day or so.
At home in Girard, he was still very much a part of the community, riding
around town in an automobile in 1911, talking to visitors at the plant,
and entertaining leading socialists at his home. He would travel down

J. A. Wayland in 1908. Courtesy of J. A. Wayland Collection, Pittsburg State University.

to New Orleans once a year to have his fill of oysters, and on one trip, he took his daughter Edith on to Florida and for a week in Havana, Cuba, his first and only trip outside the country. He continued to write paragraphs for the paper, usually at night, dashing them off at the typewriter as he interrupted his solitaire games. Generous to strangers and to those in need of food, he also paid for the college education of many in the town, and delivered food to the needy at Christmas. Never one to attend church himself or to celebrate Christmas or Easter at home, he saw these occasions as a time to give to others. His home life was kept distinct from his public life, and he turned to his daughters for affection and to his wife Pearl for friendship and a rich social life.[44]

Warren's development into the leading socialist editor-publisher, although he was adept as a managing editor, was not without its problems. He overstepped his reach on occasion. Blinded perhaps by some of the *Appeal*'s own statements, he thought he could influence public opinion beyond the newspaper's audience. During the 1908 campaign

The J. A. Wayland home in Girard. Courtesy of the J. A. Wayland Collection, Pittsburg State University.

Lincoln Steffens, one of the country's leading muckrakers, who was famous for the series on the "Shame of the Cities," interviewed Debs for the popular *Everybody's Magazine*, at Warren's suggestion.[45] It was a breakthrough in a sense, for although socialism was being discussed more and more in the popular press, this long and generally favorable interview was quite a positive step.

Debs was given a copy of the text just prior to publication, and although he objected to some of the contents, specifically an exchange between himself and Victor Berger, who had been standing in the room and correcting Debs' statements, Debs praised Steffens for the effort. Debs showed it to Warren, however, who was incensed by what he determined were slights to Debs and to the socialist cause. Seeing himself as the protector of the public image of Debs and the party, Warren fired off this telegram to the editor of *Everybody's Magazine:* "*Appeal* and its army of half million will not boost Steffens interview. When I wrote you I had in mind interview with Debs, did not anticipate lot of extraneous matter. Debs represents Socialist party and as candidate for presidency is the man who should speak for it."[46] Steffens replied to Warren indirectly through Debs: "If Warren can't see that [Steffens quoted Berger in the article only to point out contrasting socialist positions], his judgment is worthless as to the presentation of any matter. Indeed, I think his telegram is but one more evidence of the utter hopelessness of trying to give Socialism a square deal. For he, being dissatisfied with something that is none of his business, threatens at once to use force, the force of his paper."[47]

The force of the paper seemed effective in freeing Haywood, so why not use it on a fellow traveler of the party? Unfortunately for Warren and the party, "biffin' every head in sight" was not the answer to all problems. That Warren tried to act in this way may also have been because of the amount of work that he saw to personally. After he took over as managing editor in 1904, he oversaw every bit of the business, from the traditional duties of an editor, such as dealing with dissatisfied writers, to buying gasoline engines for the boat that the paper gave away to the leading subscription agent. He was constantly in contact with editors of other muckraking journals while retaining his contacts with the smaller socialist papers which were not doing very well, partly because of competition with the *Appeal*'s subscription lectures.[48]

Nineteen ten was a big year for American Socialists. The local election results of that year seemed to show that the national campaign of 1908 was not an indication of having reached a plateau. Socialists were elected to hundreds of local offices; they took over the municipal administrations of Milwaukee, Columbus, and Minneapolis. The *Appeal* had brought the Mexican Revolution to the attention of the American public; agitation over Warren's trial had caused a rapid rise in readership; the *Appeal* had conducted a long and thorough investigation into corruption in the federal judiciary; and Shoaf had uncovered the story behind the nightriders in Kentucky. On October 15, 1910, the circulation stood at 471,000, and the paper carried the tragic news of the explosion of the printing plant of the *Los Angeles Times*, which killed twenty-one workers. Debs wrote the front page story, which contained this passage: "I want to express it as MY DELIBERATE OPINION THAT THE TIMES AND ITS CROWD OF UNION-HATERS ARE THEMSELVES THE INSTIGATORS IF NOT THE ACTUAL PERPETRATORS OF THAT CRIME AND THE MURDERERS OF THE TWENTY HUMAN BEINGS WHO PERISHED AS ITS VICTIMS."[49] Harrison Gray Otis, the publisher of the *Los Angeles Times*, was perhaps the most notorious anti-union capitalist in the country. For years he had threatened to destroy unionism in Los Angeles. Debs had had a serious run-in with Otis in 1894, after the Pullman strike, and was sure that this explosion was part of a plot. When, in April, 1911, union members were arrested for the crime and were brought secretly to Los Angeles to stand trial, the *Appeal* sensed that the Haywood trial was about to be repeated and announced itself ready for "The Last Big Fight!"[50] These words proved prophetic.

10
The Last Big Fight

All philosophical persons know that society all through is usually rotten just before a great revolution, or social change, which we seem to be facing; and on that ground would not be affected by any exposure of underhand methods employed by the working class. But the rank and file are too simple to know this, and I frankly believe every such exposure gives the capitalist class a longer lease on life and sets back our actual work.
—*Josephine Conger-Kaneko to Fred Warren, October 3, 1911*

Debs based his accusation of the *Times* for responsibility in the explosion at the paper on six points: (1) class tension was acute in Los Angeles; (2) the tide of organized labor was rising and the socialist campaign for mayor was in full swing; (3) the *Times* was the "most venomous foe of organized labor in the U.S."; (4) Otis had anticipated just such an eventuality and had built a reserve printing plant; (5) articles describing the situation in Los Angeles had been appearing in papers around the country, saying that Otis was ready to wipe out the unions; (6) bombs that were found at Otis' mansion and at the mansion of the head of the Merchants and Manufacturers Association had failed to explode.[1]

Debs described the situation accurately. By the turn of the century, Otis had built a newspaper and real-estate empire that was unsurpassed in the country. He secretly controlled one of his opposition papers, which criticized him on minor issues but supported his position on major ones. He controlled extensive real-estate holdings in the city, was the prime booster for development in Los Angeles, and took pride in claiming that the open-shop atmosphere in the city was second only in importance to the prodigious natural resources of the state. He developed and controlled the Merchants and Manufacturers Association, whose members supported one another during strikes and other labor-management quarrels. His own battles with the Typographical Union had gone on for more than a generation, and he had succeeded in keeping union influence at an absolute minimum. He ran the paper like the military, drilled his

employees, and kept a stock of weapons at the plant. His automobile had a brass cannon mounted in front and an ammunition box on the rear, ready to do battle with the class enemy.[2]

Otis was as implacable a foe as labor had in the country. He always opposed labor rights and was the symbol of the open shop in America. As such, he was an appropriate enemy for the *Appeal*'s last big fight. In many ways, Otis and Wayland had much in common. Both had similar backgrounds, had risen in the newspaper business from obscure backgrounds, and had received political advancement as the result of supporting Rutherford B. Hayes in the 1876 presidential election. Both were boosters in the traditional American sense, real-estate speculators, and unwavering supporters of their completely opposing political beliefs. For an important period during the fight over the trial of the accused, Wayland took charge of his paper once again and fought Otis directly.[3]

The *Appeal* said little about the explosion in Los Angeles until three arrests were made in Indianapolis and Chicago in April, 1911. Two brothers—J. B. and John J. McNamara—and Ortie McManigal were charged with that crime and with the explosion at the Llewellyn Iron Works, an open shop also in Los Angeles. All three were members of the International Association of Bridge and Structural Iron Workers (BSIW), an AFL union with headquarters in Indianapolis. John J. McNamara was secretary of the union. The defendants were rushed to Los Angeles after going through the bare minimum of legal form. The April 29 *Appeal to Reason*, under the headline "The Last Big Fight!" declared: "I am sure every member of the Appeal Army will endorse our decision to throw this paper and all its resources into the fight for the Iron Workers arrested on the palpably trumped up charges of dynamiting the Los Angeles Times Building." The *Appeal* placed the blame this time, not directly on Otis, but on U.S. Steel, which the *Appeal* claimed was behind the attempt to destroy the BSIW, the only steel or iron workers union that had so far been able to withstand the powerful corporation. Debs, in the lead article, made the obvious analogy to the Haywood case.

The *Los Angeles Times* called the dynamiting "The Crime of the Century" and was just as sure of the guilt of the union workers as the *Appeal* was sure of their innocence. Otis injected himself into the investigation and had the Merchants and Manufacturers Association pay for the services of an investigator. The mayor of Los Angeles brought in William J. Burns of the Burns Detective Agency. The business community in Los Angeles was worried. Debs had correctly diagnosed the situation in the city. The Socialists were indeed moving towards victory in the December, 1911, election for mayor behind their candidate Job Harriman, one of the lawyers who had been retained to defend the McNamaras and a former running mate of Debs. Organized labor, with the help of fellow unionists in San Francisco, was setting up locals and signing up workers at an impressive rate. The explosion at the paper had no dampening effect on the progress that labor was making.[4]

Shoaf went to Los Angeles to duplicate his efforts on behalf of Haywood. His was one of many voices supporting the McNamaras. The AFL, at the direction of its president, Samuel Gompers, raised the funds necessary to support the lawyers and detectives who were brought into the case under the direction of Clarence Darrow. The public seemed more than willing to consider the brothers innocent. The *Appeal* led the offensive, sure that it could reproduce the success it had had four years before in Idaho. It bragged about its sources of information, noting that it had predicted that Haywood would be found not guilty more than a month before the actual verdict had come in.[5] Shoaf advanced the theory on which the defense pinned its hopes—namely, that a gas explosion had caused the accident—he was certain that the defendants were "as innocent as newborn babes."[6] Algie Martin Simons, in the *Appeal*'s quality monthly publication, the *Coming Nation*, questioned whether the working class could free the McNamaras, since detectives were known to be capable of frame-ups.[7] Debs acknowledged that the working class would be drained for the defense of the brothers, and he even hinted that although the brothers might be guilty, they must be supported, if only because of the way they had been extradited to Los Angeles.[8]

Shoaf, though, had no doubts as late as July, when he wrote about himself: "With the assistance of several defense detectives, the *Appeal*'s correspondent is continuing his work, closing in on the men whom Otis hired to destroy the *Times* building." Both Warren and Shoaf agreed that though the McNamaras were innocent, they would be convicted because: (1)Burns was more astute than McParland, the detective in the Haywood trial; (2) Otis's Merchants and Manufacturing Association was better organized than the Mine Owners Association had been; and (3) the public was more complacent this time, not as aroused as it had been for Haywood.[9] Then, the August 26 *Appeal* carried this alarming headline: "Shoaf is Slugged! Disappears, circumstances point to kidnapping or worse." The *Appeal* reported that Shoaf had finally obtained the evidence to free the McNamaras but was now missing. Only a battered hat and an ominous piece of garden hose, filled with lead, were found in his Los Angeles apartment. The paper was full of apprehension over the fate of its ace reporter, and it printed a eulogy for his contribution to the movement. The next week the paper admitted that they had sent Shoaf to Los Angeles, not to report the news, but rather to support a theory that Warren and Debs had concerning the explosion, namely that Otis had set the explosion at the plant by using leaking gas.[10]

For a month the *Appeal* stood by the gas theory and behind its reward for information concerning the disappearance of Shoaf. Then it started to pull back from its position on Shoaf and the case. In the September 30 edition, it noted that the capitalist press, on the initiative of detective Burns, was claiming that Shoaf's disappearance was a frame-up, which placed the *Appeal* "in the most singular position in which it had ever found itself, and the capitalist press is taking advantage of this situation in order if possible to run it [the paper] to earth." The paper asked its readers to put themselves in the *Appeal*'s place: knowing that Shoaf had done such excellent investigative reporting for the last eight years, and knowing, as in the Haywood case, that a frame-up does not work, "Would the *Appeal* engineer such a move, knowing that by doing so it would forfeit the support of the Socialists of the country, and in doing so, that it would destroy itself?"

What had happened? In many ways, Shoaf and Warren's prediction that the brothers would be found guilty because of Burns and Otis was correct. Burns was not only more thorough than his older predecessor, McParland, of the Haywood case, but he also had a much more reliable witness in Ortie McManigal, whose confession implicated both brothers in the explosion. Shoaf, it appears, was either told by Clarence Darrow that the brothers were guilty and could not be saved, or he had figured it out for himself. In a failure of nerve, he refused to write retractions of what he had said, and he went underground, making it look as if he had been silenced by the prosecution.[11]

For the first month, Warren knew nothing of the reasons behind Shoaf's disappearance, and even after he had found out that Shoaf had not been kidnapped or murdered, he was unaware, as was the rest of the American public, that the McNamaras were indeed guilty as charged. The brothers maintained their public stance of innocence until the last moment. What Warren did learn about Shoaf was shocking enough, and when the shock of the McNamaras' confession came in early December, he would come to realize the accuracy of his earlier prediction that the *Appeal* might have destroyed itself.

Warren came back to Girard from a speaking trip in Colorado as soon as he had received word of Shoaf's apparent demise. He sent Shoaf's father, the former police chief of San Antonio, out in search of his son, and he spent more than $1,000 in fees for other detectives. Warren printed a story in the paper, from two socialists who normally were hostile to the *Appeal*, claiming that Shoaf was being held in a ship off the coast of California. Then, in late August, a bizarre turn of events, which involved many of the leaders of the movement and old staff members of the *Appeal*, led to the unraveling of the Shoaf mystery and, indirectly, to a real drop in the popularity and influence of both the *Appeal* and the Socialist party.[12]

Within a week of Shoaf's disappearance his father quickly came to the conclusion that his son had dropped out of sight for his own reasons, having "fooled the detectives" in Los Angeles.[13] Other voices, however, were still telling Warren that Shoaf's disappearance was genuine.[14] But Shoaf's father was right; Shoaf had ducked out, as was clear when a letter to his mistress was intercepted by Piet Vlag, editor of the new New York City radical publication the *Masses*. The letter, dated September 13, told "Dolly" what kind of arrangements she should make to keep her own whereabouts—and Shoaf's—secret.[15]

To all outward appearances, Shoaf was a good family man. His wife and children stayed in Girard when he was out on a story, because the family fit comfortably into the small-town socialist mecca. What was revealed to the editors of the *Appeal* and to most of the members of the Socialist party's Executive Committee, was that Shoaf regularly lived with other women on all of his assignments for the *Appeal*.[16] This time, he chose Elsa Untermann, the teenage daughter of former *Appeal* staffer Ernest Untermann, as his "Dolly."[17]

It is difficult to tell whether Shoaf's immorality or his action in deserting the *Appeal* was more shocking. Piet Vlag seemed to share the sense of outrage at Shoaf's actions; he claimed that he wanted to protect the girl at all costs, so he decided to send her abroad. J. A. Wayland went to New York City to check up on the affair but was unwilling to try to locate Elsa before Vlag had sent her away. *Appeal* artist Ryan Walker, a resident of New York City, the only connection between Girard and the New York socialists, became the go-between. He warned Fred Warren that the New Yorkers wanted to be reimbursed for the $65 they had spent to send the girl to Holland, for they thought the *Appeal* shared some of the blame.[18]

On September 30, Ben Warren, Fred's brother, went to New York to check out Vlag's story. He made copies of Shoaf's letter and of another by Josephine Conger-Kaneko, who had just moved her paper, the *Progressive Woman*, from Girard to Chicago. Conger-Kaneko had sheltered Elsa in Chicago and had known about Shoaf and his proclivities, because Conger-Kaneko, Shoaf, and the Untermanns had all been together at Ruskin College in Missouri at the turn of the century. Vlag made clear what he wanted in return for his silence: "For a reward I will call upon you later in the form of cooperation in the circulation department between the *Masses* and the *Coming Nation.*[19]

The *Appeal* called it blackmail. In return for keeping quiet about the affair, the *Masses* wanted to share the success of the *Appeal*'s glossy monthly magazine. Vlag saw it as payment in lieu of the $500 reward that the *Appeal* had been offering. Ben Warren wanted to go public with the truth at once, no doubt feeling that the *Appeal* would suffer less the sooner it acknowledged the truth. Josephine Conger-Kaneko thought otherwise. She pointed out that at just that moment the party was suffering from a similar sexual scandal involving J. Mahlon Barnes, the national secretary: "It does seem as if the whole labor and socialist movement is honeycombed with rottenness, and to show this up at this time . . . would be bad for the workingclass movement." She thought that more reflective people would realize that all movements include characters like Shoaf, but "stopping to clean our stables now, when we should be fighting for the control of the bread supply only gives the other fellow that much more time for preparation. . . . If the capitalist press will give their columns to S. [Shoaf] to tell the truth about the Western Federation [of Miners] men, the McNamara bros . . . it seems to me it would disgust hundreds of thousands of people with this movement." Kaneko felt that Shoaf thought his dramatic disappearance was the only way to save the McNamaras, that Shoaf had "long argued for such tactics in such an emergency."[20]

Warren was caught in the middle. He reported his version of events to W. J. Ghent, who had written for the paper before going to Washington to serve the newly elected Victor Berger, the first Socialist congressman. Warren hoped to justify his role to the leadership of the Socialist party.[21] He printed in the paper a limited description of what had happened, leaving out Elsa Untermann's name and saying that Shoaf's disappearance was a personal matter.[22] The most amazing response to this limited revelation was a series of letters that Warren received from Cornelius

C. Corker, no doubt Shoaf himself, who was writing from Los Angeles, justifying his actions, and hinting to Warren that the McNamaras needed as much support as the paper could give them.[23]

The affair took its ugliest turn when Ernest Untermann interjected himself as the aggrieved parent, wronged by the *Appeal*, by Shoaf, and by the party. Untermann had been upset with the *Appeal* since his columns on orthodox Marxism had been cut back by Warren five years earlier. He charged that Shoaf was an agent, whom Warren should have taken steps to control. Untermann threatened to widen the circle of those who knew the truth behind the affair by bringing the matter to the attention of the National Executive Committee of the Socialist party. A. W. Ricker, who had recently returned to the *Appeal*, and Debs, were enlisted to calm Untermann down by letter; but Untermann carried through on his threat, broadcasting the problems of his family to the leaders of the party. Untermann's action led Piet Vlag to send an open letter to the socialist press in order to clear his own name. The donnybrook caused Warren to collect all of the letters and send them off to a friend in the party to support his case, along with this note: "I have been beset on both sides by Shoaf's friends who think I have gone too far and by Shoaf's enemies who think I have not gone far enough." Pleading that he could not know of Shoaf's shortcomings, Warren wrote: "The *Appeal* is an employer of labor. Like any other institution it goes into the market and buys the services of those who have the skills and ability to do what we want done. If this service is performed our relationship to the employee ceases."[24]

Shoaf's actions made the relationship between him and the *Appeal* much more than that of employee and employer. He was opening the movement to the kind of criticism that it could little stand. None of Shoaf's problems, however, prepared the *Appeal* or anyone else in the movement for the announcement, just a week after Warren's letter and just before the Los Angeles mayoral election, that the McNamara brothers had confessed. Shoaf receded as a problem; the credibility of the movement was at stake. The AFL was at peril, and the socialist movement in Los Angeles and throughout the country stood disgraced. Gompers withdrew support from Clarence Darrow and the case. More than any one factor, the McNamara case marked the turning point for the AFL, which rejected confrontation and sought to make unions an accepted pillar of society. Would-be socialist voters in Los Angeles tossed their Harriman and McNamara buttons into the streets, and Harriman was soundly defeated at the polls.[25]

The *Appeal* tried to put the best possible face on the debacle, by pointing out who gained the most from the confession. The paper did not excuse the murders, but it did try to make an issue of other murders committed in the name of capitalism. Debs stood up for the McNamaras, claiming that he was right to presume them innocent until proven guilty. The *Appeal* also went out of its way to play up the number of votes that Harriman actually did receive, and it asked questions concerning the timing of that confession.[26]

The timing of the confession was propitious for Otis and others of the Los Angeles establishment, who regained their hegemonic position in city affairs. The compromise was supposed to have dealt leniently with John J. McNamara, the union official, but the agreement that had been engineered by Darrow and Lincoln Steffens with the Los Angeles business leaders fell apart in the courtroom. Years later, John B. McNamara claimed that had the brothers known that public opinion was on their side and had they been able to consult with one another, they never would have confessed; they would have turned the murder trial into a political forum on U.S. capitalism. Two recent studies have speculated on the nature of the brothers' crime; although they were surely guilty, the action of the Burns detectives and others strongly suggested that antiunion spies were working within the BSIW to provoke these dynamitings and thereby discredit the union-labor movement.[27]

The Shoaf/McNamara debacle ushered in the climactic year for the *Appeal to Reason* and the Socialist party. An election year, it was a time to make up the lost ground of four years previously, when the party had just equaled earlier showings at the polls. The first shock to hit the paper was yet another criminal suit, this time thrust upon the paper by federal authorities in Kansas, who cited Warren, Debs, and Phifer for sending obscene matter through the mails. The suit referred to an ongoing investigation that the paper had conducted into conditions in the federal penitentiary at Fort Leavenworth, an investigation that had uncovered wrongdoing by prison officials. This charge was soon enlarged to include J. A. Wayland, although Warren claimed that he alone was responsible for the content of the paper and had been since 1904.[28] As a result of this case's being brought against the paper and perhaps as an indication of the seriousness with which the government viewed the paper and the threat of the socialist movement, the town of Girard seemed to many to be filled with government investigators probing into the *Appeal*.

The town *was* filled with investigators. The *Appeal* had been subject to government scrutiny on and off since Debs wrote defiantly on the subject of the Haywood trial in 1906 and President Roosevelt responded to the attorney general: "This is an infamous article. Is it possible to proceed against Debs and the proprietor of the paper criminally?" The Post Office Department reluctantly concluded that it was not possible to bar the *Appeal* from the mails. The series of trials against Warren, which were now widened to include other members of the editorial staff, were largely conducted by Harry J. Bone, the United States attorney in Topeka, Kansas, who hired at least three local citizens to spy on the *Appeal* and uncover whatever could be used in court against them.

This harassment seemed to have a local bias, although Warren and many others felt it was directed from Washington. Indeed, there were suits brought as a result of inquiries to the Justice Department in Washington, but the most intense series of suits was doggedly pursued by Bone in Kansas, often in spite of advice from Washington that there would be little success in pursuing them. In fact, after the change of administrations, from Taft to Wilson in March, 1913, Bone was discouraged from continuing his attacks on the *Appeal*. But the effect was the same, because support for the court cases was forthcoming from Washington in the form of pay for investigators and attempts to draft new laws that would make it easier to bar radical publications from the mails. The one real court victory that Bone did chalk up, the successful prosecution of Warren for the kidnapping circular, was applauded by the attorney general, who hoped that "the judge will sentence the prisoner to the limit of the law."[29]

The second shock of the year came after the nomination of Debs as the Socialist party's standard bearer. More conservative members of the party chose as his campaign manager J. Mahlon Barnes, who would presumably serve as a check on Debs. Barnes had been in the center of a scandal of his own while he was still serving as national secretary in 1911, and Debs refused to accept him. The *Appeal*, which prided itself on staying out of internal party matters, published Debs's side of the matter but refused space to Morris Hillquit, the leader of the faction that supported Barnes.[30]

The inclusion of Wayland in the indictment against the paper was an ominous sign that the government might be out to get him. The year before had begun for him in tragedy, as his second wife was killed when she was thrown from their motorcar while rounding the corner to their home. Despondent after her death, he had placed his energies into the upcoming presidential election campaign, attending the convention and taking up the lecture circuit for the first time since he had spoken on street corners more than twenty years before in Pueblo, Colorado.[31] Not only did the government include him in the charge against the paper, but Warren learned that Wayland was to be indicted under the Mann Act, which made it a felony to transport minors across state lines for immoral purposes. One of Wayland's former partners in the Girard Manufacturing Company, its president, A. W. Lovejoy, had become angry with the One Hoss over the wind up of company affairs and had made his anger known. Federal officials contacted Lovejoy, along with a disgruntled female employee, and among them, they developed a story that Wayland had seduced a young woman at the plant and had taken her to Missouri, where they had had an affair.[32] Another case against a friend of Wayland's, his former business partner W. F. Phelps, was also rumored, alleging Wayland's complicity in an unsolved murder case involving a fourteen-year-old girl in 1899.[33] Both of these indictments were to be brought immediately after the presidential election.

The 1912 election provided three choices of reform against one of reaction. Reform triumphed. The incumbent Republican, William Howard Taft, was far outdistanced by the progressive Democrat Woodrow Wilson and the Bull Mooser Theodore Roosevelt. Debs finished a distant fourth, amassing about one million votes, the largest total yet for the Socialist party and more than twice the showing in 1908. Yet it was a smaller total than the Populist Weaver had collected in the 1892 presidential election and smaller even than the total for Greenback party candidates in the congressional elections of 1878, both of which had occurred with a substantially smaller electorate.[34] Although most historians of the Socialist party point to this election as a high-water mark for the movement, it was in fact a dismal disappointment, showing conclusively that the Socialist party would neither replace the Democrats nor become a third party of strength. This had been the hope of Wayland and many others, as well as the driving spirit behind the *Appeal to Reason* and the Socialist party. Now, a dozen years after its birth, the Socialist party was well behind schedule. Although it would carry on as if nothing had changed, the chance for a mass socialist movement had passed. Middle-class reform had triumphed.

On November 10, after passing a pleasant Sunday evening following the election, J. A. Wayland went up to his room, took out a loaded gun, wrapped it in a sheet to muffle the sound, and discharged a bullet into his mouth. He lost consciousness immediately and died at 12:15 A.M. No one will ever really know why he did it. Some laid the blame on his despondency over his wife's death.[35] Warren thought that Wayland had wanted to save the paper and the party from having to go through another scandal, even though he was certain that the expected federal indictment was a frame-up.[36] Others felt that he was dying from cancer and wanted to end the pain.[37] But though his personal tragedy was no doubt a motivating factor, and though he may have flinched at going through the public shame of a court battle to save his integrity, the pivotal factor was probably the disappointing showing at the polls. At best, one could argue that it would take years of patient work to build a mass socialist movement. At worst, and to someone in Wayland's frame of mind, it seemed as if half a lifetime's work had been fruitless.

A man of words, who loved his books above all, he left this epitaph, tucked into a book on his bedside table: "The struggle under the competitive system is not worth the effort; let it pass."[38] This seems to confirm the assumption that he had finished fighting for socialism. That the federal authorities were after him and him alone seemed clear when they shortly dropped the suit against Debs, Warren, and Phifer.[39] Sympathy letters from all across the continent poured in, offering words of solace and encouragement to Warren, whom all saw as needing to take up the burden where Wayland had dropped it.[40] A number of friends wrote memorials; Henry Vincent and George Brewer published pamphlet-length eulogies about their fallen comrade.[41] Others were not so charitable. Even after fifteen years, Daniel DeLeon of the Socialist Labor party could not bring himself to say one kind word about Wayland; instead, he labeled Wayland a sentimentalist whose life work was ineffective against the class enemy.[42] Several right-wing newspapers reprinted an article by Andrew Allen Veatch, a congressman from Oklahoma, whose own publication, the *Remonstrator*, was dedicated to publishing antisocialist matter. In it, Veatch accused Wayland and his family for several generations of various sordid acts. A suit by Wayland's children for libel resulted in a $5,000 award against Veatch and a flurry of retractions by kindred publications. R. Don Laws, the editor of one of those publications, the *Yellowjacket* of North Carolina, went so far in his contrition as to investigate the validity of socialism. Even in death, Wayland may have made one last convert.[43]

Debs rallied to Warren's side; circulation built up out of sympathy for Wayland; and new battles appeared on the horizon. In West Virginia, members of the United Mine Workers of America began a ferocious strike in the coal fields, which was kept before the readers by John Kenneth Turner. But the fissures opened by the events of 1911 and 1912 threatened to tear the Socialist party apart. The right wing of the party managed to kick out the working-class hero William Haywood, using against him his own words condoning the use of direct action in strikes.[44] The AFL had moved further away from radical measures. Cut loose from the IWW and the AFL, the Socialist party saw an influx in New York City and other urban areas of members from eastern and southern Europe, while its older bases of support began to erode. Debs, who was usually unwavering in his support of the underdog, went to West Virginia, along with two other prominent members of the party, to investigate the mine strike. Instead of advocating the local socialist position that the strike be supported, Debs concluded that the strike was misguided—inspired by the IWW—and that the governor of the state had acted wisely in using force to overthrow the strikers. This action enraged the local miners, socialists, and the United Mine Workers, estranged Mother Jones from the Socialist party, and added to the burden that the Socialist party had to carry.[45]

*Fred D. Warren. Courtesy of the Archives of
Labor and Urban Affairs, Wayne State
University.*

Trouble piled up. Warren and Debs also became estranged in 1913, and
Debs left the *Appeal* to work for another midwestern paper, the monthly
National Ripsaw, edited by Kate Richards O'Hare and Frank O'Hare, who
set up lecture tours for Debs and the paper. Warren sought to cut the
losses that the publishing company was sustaining and therefore ended
the life of the *Coming Nation*, edited by Algie Martin Simons in Chicago.
Simons, by now clearly aligned with the Hillquit-Berger right wing of
the party, accused Warren of trying to silence him and of misappropriat-
ing funds.[46] Warren again had to defend himself against accusations
within the party hierarchy. Warren also drew flak from Upton Sinclair,
who had been stewing as usual over money that he thought was owed
to him for work for the paper. Ryan Walker complained about his meager
salary, pointing out to Warren that now that Debs and Wayland were
no longer drawing $100 a week each, there should be enough to cover
a salary increase for him.[47] A socialist college, the People's College, in
Fort Scott, Kansas, which was supported partially by funds from the *Appeal*, became embroiled in dissension between socialist and "anarchist"
faculty members.[48] The peace of the Girard socialist mecca had crumbled.

Warren was not about to give up, however. He brought in new editorial talent from the *New York Call*, added several new lines of pamphlet publications, and commissioned the *Who's Who in Socialist America* and a full-length history of the *Appeal to Reason*.[49] He made plans to implement a newsstand edition in New York City, and he worked hard as a consultant to the *New York Call*, in an unsuccessful attempt to make it into a mass-circulation socialist periodical.

However, Wayland's children, particularly Walter, who became publisher of the paper on his father's death, wanted to take over the lucrative position that Warren, by 1914, had held for a decade. Instead of being forced out, Warren submitted his resignation in the summer of 1914, turning the paper over to Wayland's son, who utilized the talents of Louis Kopelin, an editor whom Warren had brought from the *New York Call*. Several days after Warren had stepped down, World War I erupted in Europe. It was the end of an era.

After Warren's departure, the paper continued to publish in a similar manner for eight more years. But it was never quite the same. Circulation dropped each year. Emanuel Julius, who was added to the staff by Kopelin, came to Girard from the *New York Call* in 1915 to share editorial duties. Julius soon married a local heiress, Marcet Haldeman, the niece of Jane Addams, and took her name; and in 1918, Kopelin and Haldeman-Julius purchased the paper for $55,000.[50] At first they supported the Socialist party's antiwar position; but then, when the United States entered the war, they switched sides and supported the Wilson administration. This change forced the circulation even lower, as thousands of loyal socialists dropped their subscriptions in disgust. Nevertheless, the change in editorial policy may have saved the paper from being barred from the use of the mails, as many radical papers had been by 1918. Kopelin and Haldeman-Julius concurrently changed the name of the paper to reflect the new editorial policy. It was then known as the *New Appeal*.

After the war was over, Kopelin and Haldeman-Julius began a crusade to get Debs released from jail. Debs, who had vehemently denounced the paper during the war for deserting the cause and who went on attacking the government's policy until he was arrested for sedition in Canton, Ohio, in 1918, reluctantly acquiesced in the crusade.[51] The paper was effectively reduced, as it had been since the McNamara fiasco, to a defense organ for oppressed socialists; it was a shell of the paper that used to be the main organizing tool of the Socialist party. Kopelin and Haldeman-Julius tried at one point to sell the paper to Upton Sinclair, gleefully planning to keep control of the book business, which was still profitable, and to unload the now-less-profitable paper on the unsuspecting novelist. This fell through; and after Debs's release from prison, they let the paper die, having first resuscitated the name *Appeal to Reason* and then turned it into the *Haldeman-Julius Weekly*. Haldeman-Julius, who was alive to the possibilities of selling books and pamphlets on a mass scale throughout the country, began to hawk Little Blue Books through the pages of the paper. Eventually he turned the Appeal Publishing Company into a large-scale book publisher.[52]

The *Appeal to Reason* was the only mass-circulation radical publication in the history of the United States. After 1912 it ceased to be a radical publication in the sense that it no longer was a rallying point for a movement; rather, it was an outlet for publishing stories that were not politically appropriate for mainstream papers. After 1912 it became an alternative paper, one that pointed out the problems facing the nation but that no longer offered an effective alternative political solution for them. It shared its demise with that of the Socialist party.

The *Appeal to Reason* had continued and deepened the sense that there was still a "democratic promise" in America, to use Lawrence Goodwyn's phrase, a sense that the nation could be returned to its democratic past, before corporate America changed the basic nature of social and political life. The *Appeal* had founded its policy on a naive belief in the effectiveness of "speaking truth to power" and of education. Even in the face of overwhelming evidence that taking power would not be as simple a proposition as gaining a majority of votes in elections, Wayland, Warren, and their successors still believed that simple justice must prevail. That they would not be allowed even to approach that goal should have been clear in view of the harassment that the paper sustained throughout its life. No measures were taken to secure the building, the staff, and the distribution channels against attacks by the authorities. As late as 1913 a correspondent had to insist that Warren take some small security measures.[53] Nor were preparations made for alternatives to the postal system, which could be closed to the socialist press at any time. Even after the suppression of radical papers during World War I and the subsequent Palmer raids, the *Appeal to Reason* was still preaching the same policy of getting more readers, more subscriptions, and more education to people.[54]

The alternative to working openly and trusting in the basic honesty of American institutions was obviously distasteful and ran counter to everything that Wayland and Warren held dear. They were simply incapable of the kind of regimented discipline that the Socialist Labor party and DeLeon advocated: that kind of active revolutionary behavior was not part of their make-up. As could be seen from the atmosphere of the mecca in Girard, these men and women wanted nothing more than to preserve existing ways of life within the context of a more justly run society. As Wayland had shown in Ruskin, he wanted little truck with new patterns of social behavior; rather, he wanted to ensure the possibility that all could lead a conventional life without fear of want and hunger. The commitment to the kind of change that might lead to violence was foreign to the socialists in Girard and, by extension, probably to the bulk of the Socialist party. Although they preached change, they wanted it to happen with a minimum of disruption.

There are many explanations for why their vision did not become the vision of the mass of American society. One recent study points to the arrogance of the Socialist party in its attempt to tell workers from a myriad of ethnic and religious backgrounds what they should be thinking and doing.[55] Although there is no doubt much truth in this theory, there are other, more obvious reasons. Two that are apparent now, more than they were then, are the hostility of the *Appeal* and the Socialist party to blacks, Catholics, and the urban working class, and the nature of the future society that the socialists envisioned. The casual racism to which the paper and the party subscribed, the support that Wayland gave to the *Menace* (the anti-Catholic paper published in Aurora, Missouri, which eventually surpassed the *Appeal to Reason* in circulation in the 1910s and included a number of prominent socialists on its staff), the openly vicious attacks that Debs made on the Catholic Church (which, incidentally, were not supported by Warren, and a possible cause of their mutual estrangement), and the abiding fear of the big city and support for anti-immigration laws, were policies that would doom any party seeking support from the working class in America. That the Democratic party would court these constituencies before the Socialist party did is reason enough to explain the failure of socialism to excite the electorate.

The vision that the socialists and the *Appeal to Reason* held out for the future was also not calculated to inspire everyone. Traced to Bellamy and Ruskin and the One-Hoss Philosophy is a clear strain of regimentation and coercion in the future socialist state. That there was a mechanistic and rationalistic basis to what the radicals were saying should not be surprising, but it should also not come as a surprise that this vision was not shared by the bulk of the electorate. Evidence that the Socialist party was sympathetic to modern corporate management theory is the number of people who eventually left the party to work for the National Association of Manufacturers or to become corporate officers.[56]

Staying in business had created even more problems. Warren had to relearn truths about publishing a radical paper in the capitalist world, which Wayland had never really assimilated through Ruskin, the strike in 1903, and the decision about whether or not to advertise. Warren's need to keep the front page alive had plunged the paper into disputes that demanded additional revenue to sustain. His own desire for wealth pushed him into reviving advertising whose content contradicted the message that the paper was proclaiming in its news stories. When the reporter whom Warren had hired to keep the pot boiling betrayed the paper, the fierce sense of honesty that had maintained the tenuous balance between radical organizing, sensationalism, and circulation building was lost. Subsequent editors traded heavily on the *Appeal's* former glory, but readers never supported it as much thereafter.

In spite of these flaws, the *Appeal to Reason* and the Socialist party did present the possibilities for radical change in the United States. It is almost a truism by now to state that pressure from the socialists forced the pace of most Progressive reforms in the first two decades of the twentieth century. By "talkin' socialism" the *Appeal* was able, as in the case of *The Jungle*, to embarrass the government and corporations into making salutary changes. Revelations about corruption in the federal judiciary, conditions in prisons, the state of the Mexican Revolution, the oppression of various components of the American working class—all had a powerful effect on the ruling establishment in America, forcing it to come to grips with the most obvious iniquities in American society. The measures that the government took to control and harass the party and the *Appeal* were also indicative of the amount of fear that the establishment felt. Whether or not that fear was justified, it helped to produce progressive change.

The course of the lives of the generation that produced the *Appeal* is instructive. It shows in microcosm what alternatives there were for radical journalists and what choices they made from the alternatives open to them. Charles Lincoln Phifer stayed with the *Appeal* as long as Haldeman-Julius would have him; then Phifer drifted around to weekly newspapers in the Midwest, keeping up his friendship with Debs until the latter's death in 1926.[57] A. W. Ricker got a backhanded reference from Warren so that he could work for the circulation department of a New York–based progressive magazine; but Ricker became involved in a messy situation and was forced to resign.[58] Ernest Untermann left publishing altogether; he became interested in dinosaur remains in the Southwest and subsequently spent a long and fruitful career as the curator of a museum and a painter of prehistoric murals.[59] George and Grace Brewer went to California and started their own investment company.[60] Josephine Conger-Kaneko turned the *Progressive Woman* into the fourth *Coming Nation* and became more active in feminist, rather than socialist, organizing, until she retired from political work sometime in the 1920s.[61] John Kenneth Turner continued to write and ultimately became an opponent of socialism during the 1930s.[62] Charles Edward

Russell, a coeditor of the *Coming Nation* with Algie Martin Simons in its Chicago days, managed to write an entertaining and widely read autobiography that contained scarcely a reference to his socialist days.[63]

Of the people who had been intimately concerned with the *Appeal*, Ryan Walker and George Shoaf were the ones who moved further to the left. Walker continued to draw for radical publications, and he died in the early 1930s on one of his trips to the Soviet Union.[64] Shoaf started a new life after his disappearance from the scene in Los Angeles in 1911. He went to the Los Angeles College of Optometry and Ophthalmology, completed an eighteen-month course, and practiced for twenty years in Los Angeles. During that period he wrote extensively for radical publications and, into the 1950s when he wrote his entertaining autobiography, defended the position of the American Communist party.[65]

Upton Sinclair continued to write for the *Appeal to Reason*, the *New Appeal*, and the *Haldeman-Julius Weekly*. For a time during World War I, a periodical of his own, *Upton Sinclair's*, was published in the pages of the *New Appeal*. Sinclair scored a huge success in 1920 with a privately printed book, *The Brass Check*, which attacked the publishing industry in the United States for being antiradical and supinely inclined towards backers and advertisers.[66] In the 1930s he was almost successful in gaining the governorship in California under the End Poverty in California (EPIC) banner, for which he wrote the popular pamphlet *How I Ended Poverty in California*. Unlike Shoaf, however, Sinclair ended his life as a staunch anti-Communist.

It is the life of Fred Dwight Warren, however, that is perhaps the most instructive. In many ways, he had the experiences of Wayland in reverse: he held onto his optimism and naiveté to the end. After retiring from the *Appeal* in 1914, he took a European vacation and then was soon back in the fray. He was invited to take over the *New York Call*, where he worked for a while and then left. He resumed communication with Debs in 1915 and complained that the two of them were the only ones who really could help the party revive, but he did not know how. Clearly a wealthy man by this time, he talked about investing $100,000 of his own money in the *Call*, but thought it would be fruitless. He was wooed to accept the Socialist presidential nomination in 1916, a year when Debs declined to be a candidate. Warren also declined. (The nomination went to Allan Benson, a New York journalist.) Almost a quarter-century after Wayland's bitter experience with colonies, Warren became the publicist for one in Nevada, but he decided against moving there. Instead, he moved to Chicago after World War I, to be near two of his sons who were in college. There he became a stockbroker until he lost his fortune in the 1929 crash.[67]

Warren came back to Girard in 1930. At that time the Haldeman-Julius

Publishing Company was thriving because of sales of five-cent books—over a thousand titles were then in print. The company had steered the weekly, now called the *American Freeman*, towards a libertarian perspective. The Girard publisher was in many ways the American champion of free thought; he provided an outlet for such publications among the self-help books, literary classics, and sex manuals that he was publishing in the old Temple of the Revolution. When Warren came back, the two of them launched the idea of making the *American Freeman* over, back into the old *Appeal to Reason*! Not only would the paper become the mass periodical it once had been, along with taking its old name back when it reached a mass audience, but it would do it in the same way—namely, by resurrecting the old Appeal Army. Warren sent out letters to old friends, using the old mailing lists; he took over the back page of the *American Freeman*; and he reminisced about old times. He even reused articles from a generation before. The same ideas that were current in 1910 were on Warren's mind in 1930 and 1931. Education was what was needed; a mass organ would arouse the working class and lead it to victory at the polls. Even George Shoaf, twenty years after his infamous disappearance, was brought back to do articles for the paper.[68]

The plan, of course, collapsed. Warren and Haldeman-Julius had a falling out over Warren's salary, and Fred filed suit against the publisher for his wages. Warren did not leave Girard in disgrace, however. He stayed on and became once again a pillar of the local community, if not on the scale that Wayland had; he at least moved to the position of president of the Chamber of Commerce in the late 1930s. He attempted to lure industry to Girard: one of his schemes was to invite Charles A. Lindbergh to endorse the idea that Girard would be the ideal location for a massive airplane factory, since it had been the site of the first one west of the Mississippi in 1908![69]

After World War II, Warren moved increasingly to the right. He maintained a large correspondence, exchanging ideas with such people as Max Eastman at the *Reader's Digest* and William Allen White at the *Emporia* (Kans.) *Gazette*. Warren made an attempt to write a history of the *Appeal to Reason*, with the help of Upton Sinclair and Warren's own son Glenn, an executive with a major corporation. In it, and in his various writings about Wayland, Warren emphasized progressive reforms that they had helped to enact, such as postal savings banks and pure-food laws, but downplayed the radical nature of what they were all doing then. Taking stock of his life in 1952, Warren wrote:

Eighty years old and meditating on my past life. Many ups and downs (more of the latter) but withal a very satisfactory experience. I supported Eisenhower for President, because he had promised the

USA peace and prosperity—the latter by using all the resources of the nation to provide jobs for the multitude. I have seen most of the political principles advocated by the *Appeal* enacted into federal laws, endorsed by both republicans and democrats. I am now confronted with the threatened collapse of the western world from Communism![70]

Fred Warren, the "fighting editor," believed that the program of the *Appeal* had been enacted, and he saw communism as a threat to everything he held dear. He died in 1959, at the age of eighty-seven, in Fort Scott, Kansas, the site of his famous trial. At the time of his death he was a pillar of the Methodist Church in Girard, and he held memberships in the Girard Chamber of Commerce, Lions Club, Knights of Pythias, and Modern Woodmen.[71]

There have been thousands of alternative publications since the demise of the *Appeal to Reason*, which have supported all manner of political and social causes. Yet none of them has ever reached the sheer number that the *Appeal* reached, at a time when the population of the country was half what it is now. The *Appeal* stood at an important crossroads in American history. It was the last American radical publication to be published with the most up-to-date technology available to the communications industry. After 1920 and the birth of electronic communications, no radical group has had control of modern facilities. Radio and television and satellite communication are unavailable; print remains the medium for American radicals.

With citizens gaining more and more of their information from non-print sources, the American Left is more isolated than it was before World War I. What it does publish often is not available through such commercial distributors as newsstand agencies—a situation that has changed little since Wayland complained about it during the 1890s. The wire services are as closed to radical reportage as they were a century ago. Yet American radical publishers continue to dream the dream that Wayland and Warren dreamed—namely, of convincing the mass of people to remake American society through the truth of the printed word. One alternative publication has even suggested that it set up a modern Appeal Army in the 1980s.[72] That these dreams are still dreamed shows the indomitable spirit of social conscience, but the means for spreading the word are primitive compared to what was available when Wayland and Warren were talkin' socialism.

APPENDIX 1

A Cooperative Village: He Lives in Vain Who Lives Not for the Good of All

Starting without a reputation, without subscribers and refusing all advertising, in May 1893, the first copy of the *Coming Nation*, was issued. In six months the paper had received 14,000 paid subscriptions and an average weekly sale of 3,000 in addition, and had placed itself on a "paying basis." Having enough to live on, I do not desire to add to it while millions of my brothers and sisters are living in "poverty, hunger, and dirt," and ignorant of the causes that produce their miserable conditions. As a careful and successful businessman, I see plainly that the future of the paper will return many thousand a year profit. I am not only willing to give all that, and more, to founding a village on economic equality that I may live and labor on an equality with my neighbors, but would love to do so. For this I ask neither favor nor honors—the love and respect of my fellows will be all the reward I desire, and if I live right and truly, that they cannot fail to give me. I do not like charity (alms giving) and do not propose to give anything, but to help, by proper organization, others to create for themselves good homes, scientifically constructed, supplied with every convenience that the rich enjoy, permanent employment at wages higher than ever dreamed of by laborers, with all the advantages of good schools, free libraries, natatoriums, gymnasiums, lecture halls and pleasure grounds. If these things were given, they would not be appreciated, and I am not able to give a tithe of one building. When you create these things by your own labor, and know they will be yours so long as you desire them and know your children each will have as much or more than you have, you will appreciate the labor, will love it and its result.

Just think of this: Men make brick, quarry stone, saw lumber, build dwellings, business houses, factories, make streets, sidewalks, raise food and make clothing and other products. Not money does this—but labor. But while they do this a capitalist appropriates all the good except a dog's living. Why not create these things for yourselves? All you need is an organizer like these capitalists and keep the profits yourselves.

Now, for my plan—and I am going to carry it out if not on a larger then on a smaller scale. If you will increase the circulation of *The Coming Nation* to 100,000 (which will come in time anyway) it will leave a surplus of about $23,000 a year. This money will buy 3,000 to 4,000 acres of land and pay for it. Those who send in 200 subscribers or more or contribute as much, will be the charter members, who will proceed to organize the colony on such a basis of equality as in their judgment will produce justice. Each man and each woman shall have an equal voice no matter how much or how little they have contributed. This land will be selected by this committee and title vested in *all*. The land should have at least railroad facilities convenient, good water, soil, stone, wood or coal. When workmen have erected homes for themselves and a place for the *Coming Nation* office, the paper, plant and workmen will be removed there, and will form the nucleus for the employment of the colony. All receipts of the paper will go to the common fund, and all the employees will draw their pay from the common fund. The store will be owned by the whole people and goods sold at wholesale prices, plus the cost of the store keeper's salary. I can also influence several other factories to come on exactly the same terms. Where is all the money to come from to do all this? You watch these columns until you begin to understand the problem of cooperation and you will rest easy on that score. There are many things that can be accomplished by the working people if they would study politics more and politicians less. What will come of those who do not get 200 subscribers? They will have due consideration in time. None but persons of good moral character will be admitted into the association, no matter how many subscribers they send in.

When the colony shall have provided proper quarters for this paper, it will engage in publishing and printing besides the paper, and in a few years it will employ a hundred or more workmen. By having no rents, water and lights to pay for, and having all their food and clothing at wholesale prices, $3 a day in the colony would equal $7 to $8 in places outside. This will give some idea of the advantages.

No one will have to work for the community. Every one must be free to do as he or she wills, so long as in so doing the equal rights of others are not infringed.

Now go to work for subscribers, and show by your zeal that you are worthy of a fellowship in such a community. In doing this you are working not for me, but for yourself, and building up a printing plant that will be worth many tens of thousands of dollars to you and to your children after you. If you can't get a 50 cent subscriber (which alone will be placed to your credit as a charter member) get some for shorter time, and help carry on the education of reform that will wrest this country from the hands of the despoilers.

In sending in your first list for a membership, state your name, age, nativity and occupation, whether single or married, and if married how many children. Wishing you speed in the good work, I am sincerely your friend,

J. A. Wayland

APPENDIX 2

At Finnegan's Cigar Store

"Mr. Finnegan," said the assistant bookkeeper, " 'Company A' is going to give a smoker, and we want you to donate the cigars. A number of the boys are invited and we expect most of them to enlist." Finnegan reached for a box of '610's' when the grocery clerk said, "That's more than you would do for the Retail Clerks when they organized last week." "Well, Jim, you know I wanted to help them but times are hard. Besides the militia is like the police relief fund, and we've got to encourage it."

"That's right," said the bookkeeper. "Besides it would be better if there was a law against unions. Those infernal agitators come around and order a strike and interfere with a man's business. They make unreasonable demands, and prevent men who need work from taking it." The grocery clerk got a little riled and was about to reply when the station agent casually remarked; "Jones, you don't seem to be in sympathy with organized labor."

"Not by a darn sight," replied the b.k. "We are always having trouble with 'our hands.' In the busy season they insist on quitting exactly at six, and no matter how well you treat 'em they are never satisfied. They interfere with business interests entirely too much."

"So, so. By the way, are you a working man?"

"Well,—'er, in a way, yes sir."

"Your interests are identical with your employer's?"

"Yes sir-ee," emphatically replied Jones.

"In what way?" queried the station agent in his quiet manner.

"Well, when business is brisk we are all benefitted."

"More work, eh?"

"Yes," laughingly answered the bookkeeper. "Too much sometimes. The office force worked three nights last week and expect to keep it up for a couple of months. Between that and drilling we don't get much time to see our best girls."

"Firm makes lots of money, eh?"

"You bet, we'll clear over ten thousand dollars this month," answered the bookkeeper proudly.

"You will make a fat little pot by your overtime, I guess?"

"Well—no. We just get supper money, you know."

The station agent lighted another cheroot. "Saw one of the boys from your place at the station today. Left town. How did he come to quit his job?"

"Why, 'we' made some changes. Put in a lot of new adding machines and some girls, and let out a few men. Guess a number of the boys are looking for places. A couple came in to see the old man today," he continued, "but 'we' didn't need 'em."

"Well, you are a bright one," said the station agent as he walked out.

"What does the lobster* mean?" asked the bookkeeper as he turned to [the] group around the stove.

Lobster is a mildly derisive term that here refers to the station agent.

The blacksmith took a fresh chew and looked nervous. "I guess," he said, "that he was struck by the remarkable intelligence displayed by a certain class of white chokered dudes, who organize to use bayonets on the fellows who have sense enough to organize to get extra pay for extra work, and who object to girls doing men's work for $3 per week and who want to see a safe and secure job for every man."

—*Coming Nation* (Rich Hill, Mo.), 29 March 1902

Notes

ACRONYMS USED IN THE NOTES

AtR   The *Appeal to Reason*

CN   The *Coming Nation*. The notes are all abbreviated in the same way, even though this paper was published in several places by different people at different times. From 1893 to mid 1895 it was published by J. A. Wayland, first in Greensburg, Indiana, and then in Ruskin, Tennessee. From 1895 to 1902 it was published by the Ruskin Cooperative Association, first in Tennessee and then in Georgia. From March 1902 to December 1903 it was published by Fred Warren in Rich Hill, Missouri. In 1904 it was merged into the *Appeal to Reason* in Girard, Kansas. In 1910 it was restarted as a monthly large-format publication, edited by A. M. Simons, first in Girard and then in Chicago. After being suspended in 1913, it was taken over by Josephine Conger-Kaneko, whose earlier publications had been known as *Socialist Woman* (1907-9) and *Progressive Woman* (1909-13).

H-JC Haldeman-Julius Collection, Leonard Axe Library, Pittsburg State University, Pittsburg, Kans.

ISU   Indiana State University, Terre Haute

JAMC Jane Addams Memorial Collection, University of Illinois Library, Chicago Circle

JAW   Julius Augustus Wayland

JAWC J. A. Wayland Collection, Leonard Axe Library, Pittsburg State University, Pittsburg, Kans.

KC   Kansas Collection, Pittsburg State University

LL   Lilly Library, Indiana University, Bloomington

NEC   National Executive Committee of the Socialist Labor party

PSU   Pittsburg State University, Pittsburg, Kans.

RCA   Ruskin Cooperative Association

SHSW State Historical Society of Wisconsin, Madison

SLP   Socialist Labor party

SPAP Socialist Party of America Papers, Duke University, Durham, N.C.

INTRODUCTION

1. Nick Salvatore, *Eugene V. Debs: Citizen and Socialist* (Urbana: University of Illinois Press, 1982).

2. James R. Green, *Grass-roots Socialism: Radical Movements in the Southwest, 1895-1943* (Baton Rouge: Louisiana State University Press, 1978); Mari Jo Buhle, *Women and American Socialism, 1870-1920* (Urbana: University of Illinois Press, 1981).

231

3. James Oliver Robertson, *America's Business* (New York: Hill & Wang, 1985), p. 155.

4. Lawrence Goodwyn, *Democratic Promise: The Populist Movement in America* (New York: Oxford University Press, 1976).

5. George Allan England, "The Story of the Appeal to Reason," *AtR*, 30 Aug. 1913 and subsequent issues.

CHAPTER I. J. A. WAYLAND

1. Wilson Cory to *AtR*, 24 Nov. 1912, J. A. Wayland Collection, Leonard Axe Library, Pittsburg State University, Pittsburg, Kans. This library holds the most important collection for the study of the *AtR*; it contains much of the business correspondence, the library and equipment from the *AtR*, photocopies of the diaries, and other personal manuscripts of the Wayland family. The various collections at the library include the J. A. Wayland Collection (cited as JAWC), the Kansas Collection (cited as KC), and the Haldeman-Julius Collection (cited as H-JC).

2. Stewart H. Holbrook, *Lost Men of American History* (New York: Macmillan, 1946), pp. 291–313; Paul M. Buhle, "The *Appeal to Reason*," in *The American Radical Press, 1880–1960*, vol. 1 ed. Joseph R. Conlin (Westport, Conn.: Greenwood Press, 1974), p. 50.

3. Important sources for Wayland's early life are two short works by him: *Leaves of Life: A Story of Twenty Years of Socialist Agitation* (Girard, Kans.: Appeal to Reason, 1912; reprint, 1975, Westport, Conn.: Hyperion Press) and *The Story of "The Appeal to Reason" and "The Coming Nation"* (Girard, Kans.: Appeal to Reason, 1904). The first is actually a conglomeration of Wayland's reminiscences, interpolations by his friend and former colleague Allan W. Ricker, and reprints from his various publications. The second is a collection of pieces about running the newspaper, which includes a short memoir by the author. Another work by Wayland is "A Personal Allusion," *AtR*, 6 Feb. 1897, also reprinted as a pamphlet. Various other memoirs, reminiscences, and appreciations exist: England, "Story of the Appeal to Reason," and, in book form, *The Story of the Appeal* (Fort Scott, Kans.: n.p., 1915); George D. Brewer, *The Wayland I Knew* (n.p., n.d.); Henry Vincent, *Wayland: The Editor with a Punch: An Appreciation* (Massilon, Ohio: the Author, 1912); JAW, *Wayland's Undelivered Address and Ben Wilson's Funeral Oration* (Girard, Kans.: Appeal to Reason, 1913); Algie Martin Simons, "J. A. Wayland, Propagandist," *Metropolitan Magazine* 32 (Jan. 1913): 25–26, 62; Charles Lincoln Phifer, "Appeal's 15th Anniversary," *AtR*, 27 Aug. 1910; J. H. Tyson to Walter H. Wayland, *AtR*, 26 April, 1913; Wayfarer (probably Fredric Heath), "A Trip to Girard," *Social Democracy Red Book* (Terre Haute, Ind.: Debs Publishing Co., 1900), pp. 87–94. This last publication forms the whole of *Progressive Thought* 10 (Jan. 1900). The following account is based on these somewhat contradictory sources and differs slightly from the account in Howard H. Quint, *The Forging of American Socialism: Origins of the Modern Movement* (New York: Bobbs-Merrill, 1964), pp. 175–209, particularly in discussing Wayland's motives for leaving Colorado. It also relies to a great extent on manuscript diaries and family reminiscences that have recently become available at PSU.

4. JAW, "Brookey's dairy from November, 1871 until the 7th day of July, 1872 by Brookey," photocopy in KC, 1872, pp. 5–10 (the original diaries and expense book are in the possession of Wayland's descendants); Ross Wayland Stephenson,

"Julius Augustus Wayland," photocopy of typescript paper at the Girard, Kans., Public Library, using in part manuscript material and personal reminiscences of members of the family. Stephenson is the grandson of Wayland's daughter Edith Wayland Stephenson.

5. George Ernest Barnett, "The Printers: A Study in American Trade Unionism," *American Economic Association Quarterly* 10 (Oct. 1909): 39, cited in Seymour Martin Lipset, Martin A. Trow, and James S. Coleman, *Union Democracy: The Internal Politics of the International Typographical Union* (Glencoe, Ill.: Free Press, 1956), p. 18; Daniel Walden, "W. J. Ghent: The Growth of an Intellectual Radical, 1892-1917" (Ph.D. diss., New York University, 1964): pp. 15-30.

6. JAW, "The Diary of 'Brookey' Wayland from July 8, 1872 until October 26th, 1872 Book #2," KC, 1872, pp. 7-8.

7. JAW, "Brookey's Dairy from October 27, 1872 until. . . ," KC, 1872, pp. 10-27, entry for 9 Nov. 1872.

8. JAW, "Brookey's Book of his Expenses and Wages: Also, A Complete Ledger of his Financial Business generally 1872-1873," photocopy in KC, 1872, pp. 5-10; Stephenson, "Julius Augustus Wayland."

9. *Bugle* (Osgood, Ind.), vol. 1, no. 3 (20 June 1873). The lone issue is at the PSU Library.

10. Phifer, *AtR*, 27 Aug. 1910; Stephenson, "Julius Augustus Wayland."

11. JAW, "Diary of 1877."

12. JAW, *Leaves*, p. 19. A decade later, Henry Vincent, son of the first publisher of the *American Non-Conformist and Kansas Industrial Liberator*, which in some ways was a precursor of the *Appeal to Reason*, added Kansas to the title of his "ultra-reform" journal when he, too, decided that the action was further west than Iowa and used almost the same wording from Horace Greeley (*Non-Conformist*, 7 Oct. 1886, vol. 7, no. 20, from Winfield, Kans.)

13. JAW, "Diary of 1877."

14. Tyson somewhat later became quite wealthy as an owner of the Walgreen Drug Stores, according to Edith Stephenson Wayland, in an unsigned, undated, untitled typed ms. of reminiscences (photocopy in the JAWC); J. H. Tyson, *AtR*, 26 Apr. 1913.

15. *Cass County Courier* (Harrisonville, Mo.), 23 Nov. and 7 Dec. 1877, 18 Jan. 1878.

16. *Cass County Courier*, 4 Jan. 1878.

17. Edwin Emery and Michael Emery, *The Press and America: An Interpretative History of the Mass Media* (Englewood Cliffs, N.J.: Prentice-Hall, 1978), pp. 234-36; Merritt Haynes, "Apprenticeship in the Printing Industry," *Inland Printer* 72 (Oct. 1923): 92, cited from Walden, "Ghent," p. 21; Clifton J. Phillips, *Indiana in Transition: The Emergence of an Industrial Commonwealth, 1880-1920*; vol. 4 of *The History of Indiana* (Indianapolis: Indiana Historical Bureau and Indiana Historical Society, 1968,) p. 526.

18. Walter Williams and Floyd Calvin Shoemaker, *Missouri: Mother of the West*, vol. 2 (Chicago: American Historical Society, 1930), pp. 572-75; see also Minnie Organ, "History of the County Press of Missouri," *Missouri Historical Review* 4 (1910): [111]-33, [149]-66, [252]-308.

19. *Cass County Courier*, 14 Dec. 1877, 25 Jan. and 8 Feb. 1878. Henry Vincent, in his *American Non-Conformist*, boosts the town of Winfield in his first issue, 7 Oct. 1886.

20. *Cass County News*, 28 Sept. 1878.

21. Sidney I. Pomerantz, "Election of 1876," in *History of American Presidential Elections, 1789–1968*, ed. Arthur M. Schlesinger and Fred L. Israel, vol. 2 (New York: Chelsea/McGraw-Hill, 1971), pp. 1380–81.

22. *Cass County News*, 3 Oct. 1878.

23. The charge that Wayland bought his job with the post office he quoted and denied in the 1 Aug. 1879 issue of the *News*. Given the standard political practices in American life and the source of the allegation, the charge is probably true.

24. *Cass County News*, 3 Oct. and 21 Nov. 1878, 1 Mar. and 5 Apr. 1879.

25. Brewer, *The Wayland I Knew*, p. 8; England, *AtR*, 6 Sept. 1913.

26. *Historical and Descriptive Review of Colorado's Enterprising Cities, Their Leading Business Houses and Progressive Men* (Denver: Jno. Lethem, [1893]), p. 193; see also Andrew Morrison, ed., *The City of Pueblo and the State of Colorado* (St. Louis, Mo.: G. W. Engelhardt, 1890).

27. Melvyn Dubofsky, "The Origins of Western Working Class Radicalism, 1890–1905," *Labor History* 7, 2 (Spring 1966): 135.

28. Ray Allen Billington, *Westward Expansion: A History of the American Frontier*, 3d ed. (New York: Macmillan, 1967), pp. 621–25, 648–49; William S. Greaver, *The Bonanza West: The Story of the Western Mining Rushes, 1848–1900* (Norman: University of Oklahoma Press, 1963), p. 202.

29. Milo Lee Whitaker, *Pathbreakers and Pioneers of the Pueblo Region* (n.p.: Franklin Press, 1917), pp. 122–27.

30. JAW, *Leaves*, pp. 21–22, 34, and *Story of "The Appeal to Reason,"* p. 13.

31. JAW, *Leaves*, p. 22. Evidence from the *Directory of the City of Pueblo, for 1886*, vol. 2 (Denver: James R. Ives & Co., 1886), and *City of Pueblo Annual Directory for the Year 1892*, vol. 7 (Pueblo: Rood, 1892), shows that Wayland saw himself as a printer in mid decade but not in 1892. The 1886 volume lists him under "Printers, Book and Job" as One Hoss Print Shop (p. 282). Under "Newspapers," addresses for the *Double Header* and the *Evening Star* may in fact be the same as the One Hoss Print Shop (p. 279), but there is no listing for him under "Real Estate." In 1892, the reverse is true: he is listed under "Real Estate and Loans" (p. 477) but not under "Printers." No issues of the *Double Header*, a semiweekly printed in 1886 and 1887, and no issues of the *Evening Star* for 1886 have been reported in libraries (see Donald E. Oehlerts, comp., *Guide to Colorado Newspapers, 1859–1863* [Denver: Bibliographical Center for Research, Rocky Mountain Region, Inc., 1964]).

32. Wayfarer, "Trip to Girard," p. 89.

33. Most likely, either the Thum brothers or H. W. Young of Independence, Kans., or both. "These gentlemen are natives of Indiana and have been in the printing business about seven years. They came west in 1886 and acted as foremen for the principal printing houses here" (*Historical and Descriptive Review of Colorado's Enterprising Cities*, p. 226). In 1898, Gus Thum's *Pueblo Courier* became the official organ of the Western Trades Union and preached the kind of socialism that Wayland developed (*AtR*, 18 June 1898). Wayland's great-grandson wrote in his unpublished paper: "He gradually sold off the business to H. W. Young arranging to have Young manage it at forty dollars a week until Young acquired it" (Stephenson, "Wayland").

34. The phrase is Parrington's.

35. John D. Hicks, *The Populist Revolt: A History of the Farmer's Alliance and the People's Party* (Minneapolis: University of Minnesota Press, 1931), pp. 4–32.

36. *CN*, 14 Apr. 1894.

37. George H. Mayer, *The Republican Party: 1854-1966*, 2d ed. (New York: Oxford, 1976), p. 172.

38. Goodwyn, *Democratic Promise*, p. xi.

39. Examples of the testaments of faith can be found in the series "How I Became a Socialist," which ran in *The Comrade* magazine in 1902 and 1903 and in *Who's Who in Socialist America for* 1914 (Girard, Kans.: Appeal to Reason, 1914).

40. JAW, *Leaves* and *The Story of "The Appeal to Reason"*; A. M. Simons, "J. A. Wayland, Propagandist"; and Wayfarer, "Trip to Girard."

41. Simons, "J. A. Wayland, Propagandist," p. 25.

42. JAW, "Personal Allusion."

43. Probably something by John Ruskin; see Wayfarer, "Trip to Girard," p. 89.

44. Laurence Gronlund, *The Cooperative Commonwealth in Its Outlines: An Exposition of Modern Socialism* (Boston: Lee & Shepard, [1884]).

45. Simons, "J. A. Wayland, Propagandist," p. 26. I am following Simons's account most closely because, in most instances, he seems to have rendered more obvious things more accurately. Quint also relied on Simons. However, it must be kept in mind that Wayland's own account in his *Story of "The Appeal to Reason"* is much less exuberant.

46. JAW, *Leaves*, p. 27.

47. Edward Bellamy, *Looking Backward, 2000-1887* (Boston: Tickner, 1888); and JAW, *Story of "The Appeal to Reason,"* p. 6.

48. Dubofsky, "Origins," p. 133.

49. *Denver News*, 6 Nov. 1891, as quoted by Leon W. Fuller in "Colorado's Revolt against Capitalism," *Mississippi Valley Historical Review* 21, 3 (Dec. 1934): 345.

50. Fuller, "Colorado's Revolt," p. 348.

51. Bill Haywood, a leader of the Western Federation of Miners and later of the Industrial Workers of the World, admitted "that in Colorado's Cripple Creek district, prior to the 1903-4 civil war, miners and businessmen associated with each other, belonged to the same fraternal societies and were bound together by ethnic ties" (see, especially, *Bill Haywood's Book: The Autobiography of William D. Haywood* [New York: International Publishers, 1929], pp. 117-28); quote and citation from Dubofsky, "Origins," p. 137.

52. JAW, *Story of "The Appeal to Reason,"* p. 7.

53. Fuller, "Colorado's Revolt," p. 345; Dubofsky, "Origins," p. 133. Lawrence Goodwyn's *Democratic Promise: The Populist Movement in America* is the most comprehensive revision of the history of populism. Unfortunately, Goodwyn dismisses the events in Colorado lightly as part of what he calls the "shadow movement," which was solely interested in the money issue and was not part of the "movement culture" that he says was the essence of populism. I think that he is mistaken, although there is no doubt that electoral success there was only achieved through the agitation of the silverites. However, there was a large undercurrent of unrest in which radicals tried to carry the issue far beyond the question of silver versus gold. Goodwyn's major premise, according to C. Vann Woodward, is that the real Populist movement was "the culture of political revolt that grew out of the years of Alliance cooperatives and the elaborate program of structural economic and political reforms that was forged in that struggle, beginning in the 1880s" (from his review in the *New York Review of Books*, 28 Oct. 1977, p. 29). Wayland, as we shall see, adopted the form and content of Populist ideas and culture on his way to socialism, as did hundreds of his contemporaries. For refutation of the dismissal of Colorado populism as being solely concerned with the silver issue see James Edward Wright, *The Politics of*

Populism: Dissent in Colorado (New Haven, Conn.: Yale University Press, 1974), esp. pp. 4–5, 252ff.

54. This discussion of the *Cooperative Commonwealth* is based on Quint, *Forging of American Socialism*, pp. 28–30.

55. Fuller, "Colorado's Revolt," p. 359.

56. England, *AtR*, 6 Sept. 1913.

57. JAW, "A Calamity Howler," *Pueblo Evening Star*, 28 Sept. 1892. The *Star* announced its switch with the October 6 issue. Neither the *Colorado Workman* nor the *Coming Crisis* has been found in any library collection, but the University of Colorado Library at Boulder holds six months of the *Pueblo Evening Star* of 1892, which includes large bits of the *Coming Crisis* in which Wayland quotes liberally from the daily *Colorado Chieftain*, which is available only in a weekly edition for that period. One can follow all sides of the Populist campaign in Pueblo and the earliest radical writing of JAW from the *Pueblo Evening Star*.

58. *Pueblo Evening Star*, 14 Oct. 1892.

59. Ibid., 15 Oct. 1892.

60. *Colorado Chieftain* 4 Aug. 1892. A cut of Wayland's appears perhaps for the first time in print in this issue of the weekly Republican paper, along with ones by Weaver and Lease. The building in which the meeting was held, the Mineral Palace, had been built two years previously as an attempt to boost Pueblo to the rest of the country. Grandiose in design and scale, "it was intended to focus the eyes of the entire world on Colorado's greatness as a mining state." W. H. ("Coin") Harvey was one of its sponsors and, like Wayland, a Populist (see n. 61) and a real-estate speculator (see "Writers Program: Colorado, 'Pueblo City Guide,'" [typescript, State Historical Society of Colorado, Denver], pp. 6–7).

61. Seymour F. Norton, *Ten Men of Money Island: or, The Primer of Finance* (Chicago: Chicago Sentinel, [1891]); Sarah E. V. Emery, *Seven Financial Conspiracies Which Have Enslaved the American People* (Lansing, Mich.: L. Thompson, 1888; Westport, Conn.: Hyperion Press, 1975).

62. *Executive Record of Colorado*, vol. 9, pp. 118–19, as quoted in Fuller, "Colorado's Revolt," p. 350.

63. At this point, the details of Wayland's two memoirs and of the Simons and Wayfarer accounts become confused, probably for good reason, since the exact time when Wayland decided to sell out is crucial to know in order to judge whether his actions in the Populist campaign were somewhat motivated by cynical business judgments. It seems that the winter before Waite's election, rather than the one after, is when Wayland began to sell his real estate. This is a different reading than Quint's (see Wayfarer, "Trip to Girard," pp. 90–91; Simons, "J. A. Wayland, Propagandist," p. 27; Quint, *Forging of American Socialism*, p. 181; JAW, *Leaves*, pp. 25–27, and *Story of "The Appeal to Reason,"* p. 7). I chose the earlier period primarily because of the evidence of his real-estate ledger and an offhand remark by Wayland in *AtR*, 30 Oct. 1897.

64. JAW, "Real estate Holdings, January 8, 1889," uncataloged ms., JAWC. This summary of his real-estate holdings shows the dates of purchase and sale, with prices; it lists at least thirty-four separate properties, rents received, second mortgages, transfers to relatives, and lists of repairs. But he may have kept some connection to his printing business, at least until 1895 (see *Pueblo City Directory,* 1895, which lists "Wayland, J. A. steam job and commercial printer").

65. Bets listed in JAW, "Accounts and Booklist, 1891." Next to the bets, one reads "Otto Kinkle has 'Looking Backward.'"

66. JAW, *Leaves*, p. 28.

67. This description of Wayland is based on a number of sources, especially one written in 1899, about six years after the time we are describing, but most probably accurate in all of its essentials for this time as well. It is the fullest contemporary published description of Wayland, left by Frederic Heath, a Milwaukee socialist, who said that his own ancestors on both sides of his family came to America on the Mayflower (*Social Democracy Red Book*; Wayfarer, "Trip to Girard," pp. 87-94). I have also used a number of other sources, including Fred Warren, "A Suggestion," ms., Warren Papers, Schenectady, N.Y.; Fred Warren, *American Freeman*, 3 Oct. 1931; *Wayland's Undelivered Address and Ben Wilson's Funeral Oration*; Fred Warren, "Julius A. Wayland, One Hoss Editor," typescript, LL; Henry Vincent, *Editor with a Punch*, 2d ed. [Massilon, Ohio: the Author, 1913]).

68. Brewer, *The Wayland I Knew*, p. 1.

69. Vincent, *Wayland*, p. 25.

70. Allan W. Ricker to Fred Warren, 13 Jan. 1905, H-J correspondence. On the expectation of seeing Wayland see Wayfarer, "Trip to Girard," p. 87; on loyalty see Rousseau Hess to the editor of People, n.d., SLP Records of the Party Press, SHSW. A. S. Edwards, a co-worker with whom Wayland tangled—see chap. 3—and Daniel DeLeon were the principal exceptions to almost unanimous support for Wayland.

71. Mother Jones to Walter Wayland, 15 Nov. 1918, Haldemann mss., vol. 2,LL.

72. On the question of photographs see interview with Walter Wayland, in Trout, p. 38; on anonymous traveling see Vincent, *Wayland*, p. 14.

73. Jessie Bross Lloyd to JAW; JAW to J. B. Lloyd, both 31 May 1904, Lloyd Papers, SHSW; interview with Walter Wayland, in Harold A. Trout, "History of the *Appeal to Reason:* A Study of the Radical Press" (Master's thesis, Kansas State Teachers College, 1934), p. 27; Fred Warren, "Trip through 'The Appeal'," in JAW, *Story of "The Appeal to Reason,"* p. 28. The memo book may have been lent by Walter Wayland to a high school student and never returned (Francelia Butler to Elliott Shore, 20 July 1982). DeLeon noted that Wayland was sloppy in his habits and allowed himself to be interrupted constantly (see DeLeon to Kuhn, 29 Aug. 1896, SLP, Records of the NEC, SHSW). When the *Appeal* operation expanded, any old desk or battered typewriter would serve his purposes.

74. Interview with Edith Wayland Stephenson, 9 May 1987.

75. *CN*, 2 Dec. 1893.

76. *Ibid.*

CHAPTER 2. THE ONE-HOSS PHILOSOPHY

1. Howard H. Quint, in *Forging of American Socialism*, chap. 6, discusses the thought of Wayland in some detail. This discussion differs in emphasis and is intended to complement and supplement but not to replace Quint's analysis; *CN* 23 Apr. 1893; Charles Lincoln Phifer, "Appeal's 15th Anniversary," *AtR*, 27 Aug. 1910.

2. *AtR*, 21 Sept. 1895.

3. *AtR*, 18 May 1901.

4. Henry Jacob Silverman, "American Social Reformers in the Late Nineteenth and Early Twentieth Century" (Ph.D. diss., University of Pennsylvania, 1963), esp. chap. 4. His sample was taken from William Dwight Bliss, *The New Encyclopaedia of American Reform* (New York: Funk and Wagnalls, 1908).

5. Goodwyn, *Democratic Promise*, pp. 88, 541.

6. In a way that was not necessarily conservative in outlook; see, on this question, Samuel Bowles and Herbert Gintis, *Democracy and Capitalism: Property, Community, and the Contradictions of Modern Social Thought* (New York: Basic Books, 1986).

7. *AtR*, 2 Feb. 1901.

8. *AtR*, 7 Sept. 1895.

9. *AtR*, 2 Nov. 1895.

10. Reprints of Ruskin appeared, e.g., in *CN* on 8 and 31 Mar. and 21 July 1894; book advertisement, *CN*, 15 Mar. 1894; *AtR* reprints, 31 Aug. and 7 Sept. 1895.

11. Wayfarer, "Trip to Girard," p. 88. Charles H. Kegel, in "Ruskin's St. George in America," *American Quarterly* 9 (Winter 1957): 415, differs strongly with Wayland's contention that the One-Hoss Philosophy was close to Ruskin, claiming that Wayland was too much of a Marxist determinist. This is a misreading of Marx, Ruskin, and Wayland, which I hope the following discussion will make clear.

12. On Ruskin's political thought, I have relied on James Clark Sherburne, *John Ruskin: or, The Ambiguities of Abundance: A Study in Social and Economic Criticism* (Cambridge: Harvard University Press, 1972); and E. T. Cook and Alexander Wedderburn, eds., *The Works of John Ruskin*, library ed., vol. 27: *Fors Clavigera: Letters to the Workmen and Laborers of Great Britain*, vol. 1, letters 1-36 (London: George Allen, 1907).

13. Quentin Bell, *Ruskin* (Edinburgh: Oliver & Boyd, 1963), pp. 85-86.

14. Cook and Wedderburn, Introduction to *Works*, 27: xviii-xix, xxiv-xxv.

15. Ibid., pp. xlviii-l.

16. Sherburne, *John Ruskin*, p. 10. The Ruskin quote is from *Works*, 17:75.

17. Sherburne, *John Ruskin*, p. 152.

18. On the importance of education to American radicalism see Paul Merlyn Buhle, "Marxism in the U.S.,1900-1940 " (Ph.D. diss., University of Wisconsin, 1975), pp. 1-42.

19. *CN*, 21 Oct. 1893.

20. Eric Foner, *Free Soil, Free Labor, Free Men: The Ideology of the Republican Party before the Civil War* (New York: Oxford University Press, 1970); JAW, *Leaves*, pp. 56-58.

21. As quoted in Arthur P. Dudden, "Edward Bellamy: *Looking Backward, 2000-1887,*" in *Landmarks of American Writing*, ed. Hennig Cohen (New York: Basic Books, 1969), pp. 211-12.

22. Michael Fellman, *The Unbounded Frame: Freedom and Community in Nineteenth Century American Utopianism*, Contributions in American History no. 26 (Westport, Conn.: Greenwood Press, 1973), pp. 115-16.

23. Goodwyn, *Democratic Promise*, p. 541.

24. *CN*, 29 June 1895.

25. William Hope Harvey, *Coin's Financial School* (Chicago: Coin Publishing Co., 1894).

26. Frank Luther Mott, *A History of American Magazines, 1885-1905* (Cambridge: Belknap Press of Harvard University Press, 1957), p. 204, although recent scholarship does not mention that Lease spent much time in Colorado (see Dorothy Rose Blumberg, "Mary Elizabeth Lease, Populist Orator: A Profile," *Kansas History* 1, 1 [Spring 1978]: 3-15). Known as Mary Ellen to her friends and Mary Yellin' to her Republican opponents, she was later famous for her exhortation to Kansas Populists to "raise less corn and more hell." It is known that Wayland

arranged a speaking visit by Lease (see *Colorado Chieftain* [Pueblo], 4 Aug. 1892).

27. Goodwyn, *Democratic Promise*, p. 385.

28. JAW to Davis H. Waite, 26 May 1893, Davis Waite Collection, location #27022, Colorado State Archives, Denver.

29. Goodwyn, *Democratic Promise*, p. xii.

30. As quoted in Cook and Wedderborn, Introduction to *Works*, p. lxxiii.

31. *CN*, 25 Apr. 1893.

32. JAW, *Story of "The Appeal to Reason,"* pp. 9–11.

33. *CN*, 23 Sept. 1893.

34. *CN*, 23 Sept. 1893; 17 Mar. 1894; see Foner, *Free Soil*.

35. Sherburne, *John Ruskin*, pp. 220–21.

36. *AtR*, 26 June 1897.

37. See John Higham, *Strangers in the Land: Patterns of American Nativism, 1860-1925* (New York: Atheneum, 1977), pp. 28–34; and Ida M. Tarbell, *The Nationalizing of Business, 1878-1898*, History of American Life, vol. 9 (New York: Macmillan, 1936), p. 15. On anti-Semitism in the Peoples party, see Norman Pollack, "Handlin on Anti-Semitism: A Critique of American Views of the Jew," *Journal of American History* 51 (Dec. 1964): 391–403; reply with rejoinder, Oscar Handlin, ibid., 51 (Mar. 1965): 807–8.

38. Wayland, *Leaves*, p. 130.

39. See, e.g., the reprint of "The Vagabonds: or, The Bonded Vags: A Tale," from Stephen Maybell, *Civilization Civilized: or, The Process of Socialism* (Denver: R. A. Southwork, [1889]), in *CN*, 23 Sept. 1893.

40. *CN*, 1 June 1895.

41. *CN*, 22 June 1895.

42. *CN*, 19 May 1894 and 16 Mar. 1895.

43. *CN*, 30 Mar. 1895.

44. *CN*, 3 Feb. 1894.

45. *AtR*, 2 Apr. 1898.

46. *CN*, 28 Apr. 1894.

47. *CN*, 24 Feb. 1894.

48. *CN*, 24 Feb. 1894.

49. *CN*, 6 Jan. 1894.

50. *CN*, 17 Mar. 1894.

51. *CN*, 6 Apr. 1895.

52. *CN*, 31 Mar. 1894.

53. *CN*, 30 Mar. 1895.

54. *AtR*, 2 Feb. 1901.

55. *CN*, 27 Apr. 1895.

56. *People*, 4 Dec. 1892, as quoted in Quint, *Forging of American Socialism*, p. 180.

57. *AtR*, 8 Jan. 1898.

58. *CN*, 30 Dec. 1893.

59. *CN*, 23 Sept. 1893.

60. As quoted in Cook and Wedderborn, Introduction to *Works*, pp. xxiv-xxv.

61. *CN*, 23 Sept. 1893.

62. *CN*, 6 Jan. 1894.

63. One in the Printery [A. S. Edwards], "Deception an Essential of Capitalist Editors," *CN*, 24 Feb. 1894.

64. *CN*, 28 Apr. 1894.

CHAPTER 3. THE *COMING NATION*

1. *CN*, 21 Oct. 1893.

2. Ibid.; JAW, *Story of "The Appeal to Reason,"* p. 9.

3. JAW to Davis H. Waite, 26 May 1893, Davis Waite Collection, location #27022, Colorado State Archives, Denver.

4. Simons, "J. A. Wayland, Propagandist," p. 26.

5. JAW, *Story of "The Appeal to Reason,"* p. 9, and *Leaves*, p. 22.

6. *CN*, 30 Dec. 1893.

7. *CN*, 23 Dec. 1893.

8. *CN*, 20 Jan. 1894.

9. *CN*, 24 Feb. 1894.

10. *CN*, 20 Jan. 1894.

11. Fellman, *Unbounded Frame*, p. xv.

12. Robert S. Fogarty, *Dictionary of American Communal and Utopian History* (Westport, Conn.: Greenwood, 1980), p. xxiv. Fogarty estimates that there were about 600 communities of various sorts set up in the U.S. between 1663 and 1970, of which 137 were active between 1878 and 1960 and 142 between 1861 and 1919.

13. Bell, *Ruskin*, pp. 86–87.

14. *CN*, 27 Jan. 1894.

15. *CN*, 30 Dec. 1893 and 28 Apr. 1894.

16. *CN*, 24 Feb. 1894.

17. [JAW], "A Cooperative Town," (n.p., n.d.) filed with Wayland to Kuhn, 25 Apr. 1894, SLP, Records of the NEC, SHSW.

18. *CN*, 17 Mar. and 12 May 1894; Wayfarer, "Trip to Girard," p. 117; JAW to Henry Demarest Lloyd, 23 Nov. 1895, Lloyd Papers, SHSW; *People*, 16 July 1899.

19. Isaac Broome, "History of Ruskin," *CN*, 21 Oct. 1899; JAW to Lloyd, 23 Nov. 1895; A. S. Edwards to Lloyd, 12 Dec. 1894, Lloyd Papers.

20. The most extensive bibliography on the community is found in Vera Wilson Gilmore, "The Ruskin Colony, 1894–1901: Experimental Model for the Socialist Commonwealth" (Master's thesis, University of Tennessee, 1973). Gilmore lists numerous contemporary articles on the activities of the colonists. Histories of the colonies, which led to Gilmore's work, are numerous; the first were written before the experiment was a year old. They include those in the *Coming Nation*, 27 Apr. 1895 and 17 Apr. 1897; a serialized history written by Isaac Broome, beginning with the 21 Oct. 1899 issue; and the last, and perhaps most revealing and reliable, "The Secret History," 6 Apr. 1901. The manuscript of the Broome history, which is the official history of the colony, is in the University of Tennessee Library, Knoxville. Broome later published *The Last Days of the Ruskin Co-operative Association* (Chicago: Charles H. Kerr, 1902), which is a more forthcoming account than the official history, which was written under the scrutiny of fellow members. Recent scholarly accounts include two articles by Francelia Butler, "The Ruskin Commonwealth: A Unique Experiment in Marxian Socialism," *Tennessee Historical Quarterly* 23 (Dec. 1964): 333–43, and "From Fantasy to Reality: Ruskin's King of the Golden River, St. George's Guild and Ruskin, Tennessee," *Children's Literature* 1 (1972): 62–73; John Egerton, *Visions of Utopia: Nashoba, Rugby and the "New Communities" in Tennessee's Past* (Knoxville: University of Tennessee Press in cooperation with the Tennessee Historical Commission, 1977); Kegel, "Ruskin's St. George in America," pp. 412–20. There are a number of extensive entries on Ruskin in Fogarty, *Dictionary of American Communal and Utopian History*. Records of the Ruskin Cooperative

Association are at the Tennessee State Library and the University of Tennessee Library.

21. See JAW, *Story of "The Appeal to Reason,"* p. 18.

22. JAW, *Leaves*, p. 28.

23. *Freeland*, 1 and 11 Aug. 1894, as quoted in Julian Pierce, "Wayland the Socialist,'" *People* (Beekman Street), 16 July 1899.

24. JAW to Lloyd, 23 Nov. 1895, and Edwards to Lloyd, 12 Dec. 1894, Lloyd Papers.

25. *CN*, 6 Apr. 1895.

26. Herbert Casson, *AtR*, 10 Mar. 1900; "The Secret History"; A. S. Edwards, *CN*, 17 Apr. 1897; JAW, *Leaves*; Broome, *Last Days*, and "History of Ruskin"; W. G. Davis, "Failure of the Ruskin Colony," *Gunton's Magazine* 21 (Dec. 1901): 530-37.

27. See also Earl Miller, "Recollections of the Ruskin Cooperative Association," ed. Charles H. Kegel, *Tennessee Historical Quarterly* 17 (Mar. 1958): 45-69; and Miller to Mrs. Reaves, 17 Feb. and 12 July 1961, Tennessee State Library and Archives (see note 20 for a list of sources).

28. Probably at the meeting of 3 Oct. 1894 (see RCA, Minutes of Meetings, p. 121; and *CN*, 15 Sept. 1894; Egerton, *Visions of Utopia*, p. 70).

29. RCA, Minutes, 31 Oct. 1894, p. 137.

30. Ibid., 28 Nov. 1894, p. 153.

31. It is not clear who received the rest of the profit. Wayland later claimed that he himself was only paid wages (*AtR*, 17 June 1899). The minutes of the RCA show that the finances of the RCA and the *Coming Nation* continued to be intimately linked. E.g., Wayland reported at the 30 Jan. 1895 meeting that he was opposed to further expansion at that time because the *Coming Nation* could do no more than carry the payroll and payments on the new perfecting press. See also Gilmore, "Ruskin Colony," p. 52: "Wayland pledged the income of the *Coming Nation* for the support of the colony." Unfortunately, she does not cite the source of this statement. It appears, however, that the only actual benefit for the colony was that the profits were being used for the payments on the press throughout the first half of 1895, a problem that helped to precipitate the crisis.

32. *CN*, 11 May, 22 June, 6 and 27 July, and 3 Aug. 1895.

33. Broome, in "History of Ruskin," *CN*, 11 Nov. 1899, asserts that Wayland was the one who claimed ownership. But Broome was not an eyewitness and the account in Gilmore, "Ruskin Colony," pp. 52-53, which is based on a letter from J. A. Kemp to Earl Miller, cited in Miller's "Recollections," p. 50, seems much more probable.

34. Broome, "History of Ruskin," *CN*, 18 Nov. 1899; *CN*, 17 Apr. 1897.

35. Gilmore, "Ruskin Colony," p. 53.

36. *CN*, 24 Aug. 1895.

37. On this latter point, Wayland was certainly correct, for although the masthead proclaimed cooperative editing, A. S. Edwards was in charge. Edwards's name, however, almost never appeared. When he signed an article, he used the pen name "Sevenoaks."

38. *AtR*, 11 Jan. 1896.

39. *CN*, 25 Jan. 1896.

40. *CN*, 17 Apr. 1897.

41. *CN*, 15 Aug. 1896.

42. *People* (Beekman Street), 16 July 1899.

43. "Liberty Edition," *CN*, 2 Oct. 1897.

44. "Secret History," *CN*, 6 Apr. 1901.

45. See, e.g., *CN*, 2 Oct. 1897.

46. "Secret History," Broome, *Last Days*, pp. 59–60. The number and the make-up of the factions are detailed in these two sources.

47. *CN*, 12 Feb. 1898.

48. *CN*, 17 Sep. 1898.

49. *CN*, 28 Jan. 1899.

50. *CN*, 31 Dec. 1898.

51. *CN*, 14 Jan. 1899.

52. "Secret History."

53. Reply to Casson, in *CN*, 17 Mar. 1900; original charge in *AtR*, 10 Mar. 1900. For a contemporary view of Ruskin as a capitalist enterprise that did best when it was in a fertile valley and was most heavily capitalized see Davis, "Failure of Ruskin Colony."

54. *AtR*, 31 Aug. 1895.

CHAPTER 4. THE *APPEAL TO REASON*

1. Mary Harris Jones, *Autobiography of Mother Jones* (Chicago: Charles Kerr, 1925), pp. 28–29.

2. England, "Story of the Appeal," *AtR*, 30 Aug. 1913; George Milburn, "The Appeal to Reason," *American Mercury* 23 (July 1931): 363; Quint, *Forging of American Socialism*, p. 194. Wayland did use his name in a periodical title five years later, when he published *Wayland's Monthly.*

3. See also Warren, *American Freeman*, 3 Oct. 1931, for a similar description of the founding.

4. Quint, *Forging of American Socialism*, p. 194; *AtR*, 7 Sept. 1895, 5 Oct. and 29 Feb. 1896. On Pomeroy see *AtR*, 10 Sept. 1898. The figure of 25,000 comes from Wayland, *Story of "The Appeal to Reason,"* p. 15.

5. See, e.g., Stephen Maybell, "Vagabonds," *AtR*, 4 Apr. 1896, and *CN*, 23 Sept. 1893.

6. See *AtR*, 24 Oct. 1896.

7. Quint, *Forging of American Socialism*, pp. 142–49; Ira Kipnis, *The American Socialist Movement, 1897–1912* (New York: Columbia University Press, 1952), pp. 11–24; L. Glen Seretan, *Daniel DeLeon: The Odyssey of an American Marxist* (Cambridge: Harvard University Press, 1979), pp. 82–115.

8. Seretan, *DeLeon*, pp. 82–115, esp. 91.

9. Ibid., pp. 116–40, describes DeLeon's halting attempts at accommodation. The party platform appears in *CN*, 8 June 1895; the advertisement for the *People*, in *CN*, 17 Feb. 1894; praise for *Non-Conformist* in *CN*, 28 Apr. 1894; Populist local, in *CN*, 31 Mar. 1984.

10. On G. C. Clemens see Michael J. Brodhead and O. Gene Clanton, in "G. C. Clemens: The Sociable Socialist," *Kansas Historical Quarterly* 43, 4 (Winter 1974): 491, who quote other parts of Clemens's article. On Wayland's support of Bryan see *AtR*, 18 and 25 July, 1 and 15 Aug., and 5 Sept. 1896; Wayland, *Story of "The Appeal to Reason,"* p. 15.

11. *AtR*, 5 Sept. 1896.

12. *AtR*, 29 Aug. 1896.

13. DeLeon to Kuhn, 29 Aug. 1896; SLP, Records of the NEC, SHSW.

14. See JAW to Kuhn, 23 Apr. 1894, ibid.

15. JAW to Kuhn, 30 May 1896, ibid.

16. *AtR*, 10 Oct. 1896.

17. *AtR*, 17 Oct. 1896.

18. Ray Ginger, *Debs* (Toronto: Macmillan, 1962), p. 207.

19. See Goodwyn, *Democratic Promise*, p. 354.

20. *AtR*, 6 Feb. 1897; *San Antonio Labor*, 6 Jan. 1894, as quoted in Quint, *Forging of American Socialism*, p. 195; Brodhead and Clanton, "G. C. Clemens," pp. 492–93; *Girard Press*, 24 Dec. 1896.

21. On Debs see *AtR*, 10 July 1897.

22. On Gordon see Wayfarer, "Trip to Girard," p. 112; *One Hoss Philosophy: Quarterly Publication of Radical and Utopian Literature*, five cents per copy, no. 2 (July 1897), from Girard, Kans. Gordon's pamphlet constitutes the whole of the issue.

23. *AtR*, 14 Aug. 1897; and Wayfarer, "Trip to Girard," p. 112.

24. Wayfarer, "Trip to Girard," pp. 53–58; Kipnis, *American Socialist Movement*, pp. 6–57. Carey was formally expelled because of his vote in favor of an appropriation for the local armory (see Quint, *Forging of American Socialism*, p. 169).

25. Wayfarer, "Trip to Girard," pp. 54–71; Kipnis, *American Socialist Movement*, p. 55. The June 1898 meeting was unique in American history: it brought together the leading socialist and anarchist intellectuals and radical labor leaders.

26. Quint, *Forging of American Socialism*, p. 200; *AtR*, 8 Jan. 1898; JAW to Butterworth, 17 Jan. 1898, SLP, *People* correspondence, SHSW.

27. *AtR*, 18 June 1898.

28. It could be argued that if Wayland himself had been the "boss," then there was no "czarism," i.e., he was perfectly willing to play the part, but he didn't like others—especially city-dwelling immigrants—to play the role. However, here Wayland was arguing for the right to be sloppy in thinking and to allow the greatest diversity to be included under the socialist banner. As long as diversity was helping to bring the cooperative commonwealth closer, diversity should flourish. This question was agitating German socialists at the same time. Eduard Bernstein's advocacy of reformist socialism is exactly contemporary with the position taken by the SDP in America and also the one advocated by Wayland. Wayland's role in this whole area has been overlooked by the historians of the socialist movement in America. Kipnis, among others, describes a battle between only Victor Berger, Morris Hillquit, and DeLeon.

29. See, e.g., *AtR*, 2 and 30 July 1898.

30. Wayland blamed his wife's death as much on surgery as on her illness, and he talked about the impossibility of getting adequate medical attention in a profit-oriented society. He promised to write a favorable article about Christian Science and allopathy, but as far as can be determined, it never appeared (see *AtR*, 17 Nov. 1899).

31. They both reprinted the same article from the *Chicago Times Herald* on Chicago women socialists: see *AtR*, 24 Nov. 1898, and *CN*, 28 Jan. 1899.

32. *AtR*, 24 Dec. 1898 and 7 Jan. 1899.

33. JAW, *Story of "The Appeal to Reason,"* p. 17.

34. Mother Jones, a houseguest during that winter and spring, may have been instrumental in helping Wayland through his depression and in providing encouragement and ideas about circulation building.

35. Warren, *American Freeman*, 3 Oct., 1931; Wayfarer, "Trip to Girard," p. 93; JAW to Lloyd, 27 Nov. 1895, Lloyd Papers; Gilmore, "Ruskin Colony," p. 93.

36. *People*, 28 May 1899.

37. JAW to Theodore Debs, 28 June 1899, Debs Collection, ISU. Theodore Debs to JAW, 6 July 1899, ibid., applauded Wayland for his stand against "the bosses in Gotham."

38. David A. Shannon, *The Socialist Party of America: A History* (New York: Macmillan, 1955), p. 33.

39. Although Wayland did claim to be helping to organize a local of the SLP, there is no record of his membership or of his expulsion. As for the SDA, Theodore Debs, in his letter to Wayland of July 6, reminds Wayland that he is not yet a member.

40. Wayfarer, "Trip to Girard," pp. 87-94. Local tradition, according to Gene DeGruson at the Special Collections Department of the University of Pittsburg Library, Pittsburg, Kans., has it that Wayland left his gold unguarded when he first toured the town of Girard (see *Wayland's Undelivered Address and Ben Wilson's Funeral Oration*, p. 20; JAW, "Diary, 1898-1902," entry for 7 Apr. 1899).

41. *Girard Press*, 29 Sept. 1898.

42. Ibid., 31 Dec. 1896, as reprinted from *Civic Review* (Los Angeles), 19 Dec.

43. AtR, 30 Oct. 1897.

44. JAW, "Diary, 1898-1902," entry for 31 Dec. 1898.

CHAPTER 5. ADVERTISING THE SOCIALIST DREAM:
RADICAL PUBLISHING AT THE TURN OF THE CENTURY

1. The classic work on patent medicines and advertising is James Harvey Young's *The Toadstool Millionaires: A Social History of Patent Medicines in America before Federal Regulation* (Princeton, N.J.: Princeton University Press, 1961).

2. Ted Curtis Smythe, "The Reporter, 1880-1900: Working Conditions and Their Influence on the News," *Journalism History* 7, 1 (Spring 1980): 1-10.

3. Frank L. Mott, *American Journalism, 1690-1960*, 3d ed. (New York: Macmillan, 1962), pp. 491-93.

4. See chap. 2 and also Upton Sinclair, *The Brass Check* (Pasadena: the Author, 1920), pp. 346-61, for contemporary accounts of the suppression of news.

5. Mott, *History of American Magazines*, p. 18.

6. Michael Schudson, *Discovering the News: A Social History of American Newspapers* (New York: Basic Books, 1978), pp. 92-94.

7. Mott, *History of American Magazines*, p. 1.

8. As quoted in Mott, *American Journalism*, pp. 276-77.

9. *Brann the Iconoclast: A Collection of the Writings of W. C. Brann*, with a biography by J. D. Shaw, 2 vols. (Waco, Tex.: Herz, 1898); and John W. Gunn, *Brann, A Smasher of Shams* (Girard: Appeal to Reason, n.d.).

10. Herbert G. Gutman, "Liberty," in *American Radical Press, 1880-1960*, ed. Joseph R. Conlin, vol. 2 (Westport, Conn.: Greenwood, 1974), pp. 373-79.

11. See Goodwyn's characterization of the *Appeal* as being Populist, in *Democratic Promise*, p. 354.

12. Ibid., pp. 230-31, 236-37, 354; CN, 17 Feb. 1894 and 30 Mar. 1895.

13. Goodwyn, *Democratic Promise*, pp. 494, 355. It will be recalled that the *Appeal* almost failed at the same time.

14. Brodhead and Clanton, "G. C. Clemens," p. 490; and Goodwyn, *Democratic Promise*, p. 355.

15. Harold Piehler, "Henry Vincent: Kansas Populist and Radical-Reform Journalist," *Kansas History* 2, 1 (Spring 1979): 22; *CN*, 29 Aug. and 24 Oct. 1896. Sanderson's service was known as the Socialist Newspaper Union. Sanderson had previously been secretary of the Puget Sound Cooperative Association. See also Leon W. Fuller, "A Populist Newspaper of the Nineties," *Colorado Magazine* 9, 3 (May 1932): 81–87. The best source for the Populist press is Seymour Lutzky, "Reform Editors and Their Press" (Ph.D. diss., University of Iowa, 1951).

16. This sketch is based on two works by Harold Richard Piehler, the previously cited article in *Kansas History* and "Henry Vincent: A Case Study in Political Deviancy," Ph.D. diss., University of Kansas, 1975); Goodwyn, *Democratic Promise*, pp. 99–108, 411–21, 560; and Henry Vincent to Mrs. Caro Lloyd Withington, 6 Feb. 1907, Lloyd Papers, SHSW.

17. Vincent's unpublished memoirs, as quoted in Piehler, "Henry Vincent: A Case Study," p. 228.

18. *AtR*, 12 Jan. 1901.

19. Ibid.

20. Eric Foner, "Why Is There No Socialism in the United States?" *History Workshop Journal*, no. 17 (Spring 1984): 57–80.

21. *AtR*, 9 July and 13 Aug. 1898.

22. *AtR*, 7 May 1898.

23. *AtR*, 22 Oct. 1898—but not "patent" insides. On regional editions of the *Appeal to Reason* see Sharon E. Neet, "Variant Editions of the *Appeal to Reason*, 1905–1906" (D.A. diss., University of North Dakota, 1983).

24. *AtR*, 12 Nov. 1898.

25. *AtR*, 25 Feb. 1899.

26. *AtR*, 6 May 1899.

27. On 13 May 1899, Wayland estimated them at 15 000, later revised to 17,800, *AtR*, 10 June 1899.

28. *AtR*, 16 Sept. 1899.

29. *AtR*, 28 Oct. 1899.

30. *AtR*, 25 Nov. 1899. The circulation then stood at 52,126. The band went to Los Angeles with 1,300 subscriptions on 24 Feb. 1900.

31. *AtR*, 30 Dec. 1894.

32. Dodge had been at Ruskin for a year or so (see Gilmore, "Ruskin Colony," p. 93). George Allan England, in *The Wonderful Appeal Army* (n.d., n.p.), separately published chap. 6 of *The Story of "The Appeal to Reason."*

33. England, *Wonderful Appeal Army*, pp. 10–11; *AtR*, 30 June 1900.

34. *AtR*, 30 Dec. 1899.

35. *AtR*, 21 Dec. 1901. The ads were probably bringing in about $100 a week.

36. *AtR*, 8 Mar. and 5 Apr. 1902.

37. *AtR*, 3 Jan. 1903; italics in original.

38. See *Wilshires* 7, 4 (Apr. 1905).

39. From the *Spring Hill New Era*, as reprinted in the *Girard Press*, 15 Oct. 1903.

40. Robert Laurence Moore, *European Socialists and the American Promised Land* (New York: Oxford University Press, 1970), p. 198, as quoted in Robert D. Reynolds, Jr., "The Millionaire Socialists: J. G. Phelps Stokes and His Circle of Friends" (Ph.D. diss., University of South Carolina, 1974), p. 73; R. W. Sutters, "U.S. vs. HGW," *Wilshire's*, no. 44 (Mar. 1902); p. 53, as reprinted from *Clarion* (London), n.d.

41. His magazine was first called *Challenge* because in it he challenged William Jennings Bryan to debate. On Wilshire, see Reynolds, "Millionaire Socialists";

the introduction by Howard Quint in Conlin, *American Radical Press*, 1: 72-91; and Quint, "Gaylord Wilshire and Socialism's First Congressional Campaign," *Pacific Historical Review* 26 (Nov. 1957): 327-40; Ralph Hancock, *Fabulous Boulevard* (New York: Funk & Wagnalls, 1949); and almost every issue of the magazine, but especially no. 44, Mar. 1902, pp. 51-59; see also *The Autobiography of Upton Sinclair* (New York: Harcourt, Brace & World, 1962), pp. 103-4; 149-50.

42. He spent $70,000 of his own money from 1900 to 1904 (see Charles H. Kerr, *A Socialist Publishing House* [Chicago: Kerr, (1905)], p. 12).

43. Algie Martin Simons, "In Memoriam—Philip D. Armour: How He Made His Seventy Millions," *Challenge* 2, 1 (23 Jan. 1901): 13-15, also published as *Packingtown*, by Kerr (Chicago, n.d.); see, for advertisements, 2, 14 (Apr. 24, 1901): 11.

44. See chap. 8.

45. Sinclair, *Autobiography*, pp. 103-4.

46. Little has been written about Kerr. This brief sketch draws on Franco Andreucci, "Socialismo e Marxismo per pochi cents: Charles H. Kerr editore," *Movimento operaio e socialista*, n.s., 3, 2 and 3 (Apr.-Sept. 1980): 269-76; Herbert Gutman, "The International Socialist Review," in Conlin, *American Radical Press*, 1:82-86; and Kerr, *Socialist Publishing House*. Allen Ruff's dissertation on Kerr, currently being at the University of Wisconsin, was not yet available when I wrote this chapter.

47. Kerr., *Socialist Publishing House*, p. 9.

48. Ibid., p. 14.

49. Ibid., p. 12.

50. Ibid., pp. 4-5.

51. James A. Power to the editor, *AtR*, 14 May 1898.

52. *AtR*, 8 Apr. 1899.

53. *Wilshire's* 7 (July, 1905).

CHAPTER 6. STRIKE

1. *AtR*, 8 Jan. 1898.

2. See chap. 9 on Girard, and Wayland's expense books and diaries from the turn of the century.

3. JAW, "Diary and Journal, 1898-1902," entries for 6-16 July 1899.

4. Ibid., entries for 8 June, 30 Sept., and 30 Dec. 1899, 1 Jan. 1900.

5. The entry for May 23 notes the prediction that the youngest child would meet a fatal accident in the near future.

6. Entries for 1 April to 5 May 1901.

7. "Personal Attack on the editor of *The Socialist*," *Socialist* (Seattle), 18 Jan. 1903; on Titus see Carlos A. Schwantes, *Radical Heritage: Labor, Socialism and Reform in Washington and British Columbia, 1885-1917* (Seattle: University of Washington Press, 1979); on Berger, Sally M. Miller, *Victor Berger and the Promise of Constructive Socialism, 1910-1920* (Westport, Conn.: Greenwood Press, 1973), pp. 17-18.

8. Charles Ufert, "Letter to the Editor," *Socialist* (Seattle), 4 May 1902. Ufert was state committeeman of the Socialist party in New Jersey.

9. *Socialist* (Seattle), 18 Jan. 1903.

10. "Gleanings from Busy Socialist Fields," *Social Democratic Herald*, 2 July 1904.

11. "A Menace to the Movement," *Social Democratic Herald*, 13 Aug. 1904. On the "swallowing up" of the *Coming Nation* see chap. 7.

12. F. G. R. Gordon ended his career as a lobbyist for the National Association of Manufacturers! (See Charles Pierce LeWarne, *Utopias on Puget Sound*, 1885–1915 [Seattle: University of Washington Press, 1975], p. 56). Gordon was a shoemaker by trade, Dodge a telegraph operator who apparently had been blacklisted for his radical activities (see Wayfarer, "Trip to Girard," p. 112; and Fred Warren, "Warren's Page," *American Freeman*, 3 Oct. 1931, p. 4).

13 . For a list of those who worked on the *Appeal* in some reporting capacity see *American Freeman*, 3 Oct. 1931. On Ruskin College see Ross E. Paulson, *Radicalism and Reform: The Vrooman Family and American Social Thought, 1837–1937* (Lexington: University of Kentucky Press, 1968), p. 183.

14. *Girard Press*, 10 Oct. 1901.

15. Announcements concerning the O'Hares' marriage and the departure of Fred Warren, Ben Warren, and Eli N. Richardson appear in the *Girard Press*, 9 Jan. and 13 Mar. 1902.

16. Buhle, *Women and American Socialism*, p. 114. Conger would later be known as Conger-Kaneko after her marriage to the Japanese-American socialist, Kiichi Kaneko.

17. C[harles] Lincoln Phifer, "Looking Backward and Ahead," in England, *The Story of the Appeal*, cited on p. 303.

18. Breckon represented Illinois as a delegate to the Socialist party convention of 1904 and later became associated with the *Christian Socialist*, published in Chicago (see Phifer, "Looking Backward and Ahead," p. 304; AtR, 23 Oct. 1903; and National Committee of the Socialist Party, *National Convention of the Socialist Party, Chicago 1904*, stenographic report edited by William S. Mailly [Chicago: Socialist Party, 1904], p. 16; William S. Mailly to Charles L. Breckon, 25 Mar. 1903, SPAP). It is probable that Untermann brought Breckon to the *Appeal*.

19. Information on Ricker is scarce. This sketch is based on the introduction to A. W. Ricker, "The Political Economy of Jesus," *Wayland's Monthly*, no. 45 (Jan. 1904); Ricker to Fred Warren, 13 Jan. 1904, H-J correspondence, PSU; A. W. Ricker, "The Quorum Resolution," *AtR*, 25 July and 19 Sept. 1903.

20. *AtR*, 16 Jan. 1904.

21. Mailly to Ricker, 18 Mar. 1903, SPAP.

22. Mailly to Ricker, 9 July 1903, SPAP; Ricker, "Quorum Resolution."

23. *AtR*, 13 June and 25 July 1903; Mailly to Ricker, 30 Mar., 16 Apr., and 14 July 1903, SPAP. The letters from Ricker from this period are missing, and the correspondence ends abruptly in August, because it was stolen from the office (see chap. 7). The later correspondence is partially reprinted in the *Appeal*, 4 Feb. 1905 (see Socialist Galley 2, Minutes of a Meeting of the Socialist party circa 18 Dec. 1904, filed with a note presumably from W. E. Clark, secretary of the Quorum, H-J correspondence, 1914 [should be 1904]; see also *National Convention of the Socialist Party, Chicago 1904*, p. 62; Ricker to Fred Warren, 31 Jan. 1905, H-J correspondence).

24. Symptomatic of Untermann's problems in Girard was his arrest on 15 June 1903 for using abusive and insulting language on the street in town (see *Girard Press*, 18 June 1903).

25. The charge that the *Appeal* paid these wages was repeated by two of the strike's leaders, Charles Breckon and Allan W. Ricker, and was never denied by the management. It also accorded exactly with J. A. Wayland's assertion that

people in Girard worked for 50 cents a day (see Breckon, in the *Socialist* [Seattle], 8 Nov. 1903; and Ricker to Mailly, 10 Oct. 1903, as printed in the *AtR*, 4 Feb. 1905). By any measure, these wages were minuscule. An average yearly wage in 1903 for all workers in the U.S. was $441, even counting unemployed periods. Postal employees made $931 a year, while school teachers made $358 a year. Working fifty-two weeks, these *Appeal* workers made only $156 (see U.S., Bureau of the Census, *Historical Statistics of the United States*, vol. 1 [Washington, D.C., 1975], pp. 164–68).

26. Ricker to Mailly, 10 Oct. 1903, as printed in *AtR*, 4 Feb. 1905.

27. *AtR*, 2 Apr. 1898.

28. *AtR*, 4 Sept. 1897.

29. *AtR*, 17 June 1899.

30. *AtR*, 3 Feb. 1900.

31. *AtR*, 10 Mar. 1900.

32. *AtR*, 10 Feb. 1900. Another office party is mentioned in Wayland's journal, entry for 22 June 1900.

33. Diary entry, 23 Jan. 1900.

34. Diary entry, 9 June 1900.

35. *Girard Press*, 27 Aug. 1903.

36. Ibid., 10 Sept. 1903.

37. Ricker to Mailly, 22 Oct. 1903, as printed in *AtR*, 4 Feb. 1905.

38. See *AtR*, 24 Oct. 1903. Wayland may have reasoned that the money would quiet the national secretary or that Wayland could be seen as bolstering the party and the image of the paper to the insiders who knew what was going on.

39. *AtR*, 24 Oct. 1903; four of the women were Breckons, presumably Charles Breckon's wife and daughters. Breckon presided over the union local, and Ricker reported the unionization effort on the front page of *AtR*, 24 Oct. 1903.

40. Ibid.

41. *Chicago Socialist*, 24 Oct. 1903, as reprinted in *Socialist* (Seattle), 8 Nov. 1903. The *Socialist* and the *Social Democratic Herald* rejoiced over the labor troubles at the *Appeal* (see *Socialist*, 18 Jan., 1 Mar., and 13 Dec. 1903, 24 Jan. and 15 May 1904; *Social Democratic Herald* (Milwaukee), 7, 14, and 21 Nov. 1903, 2 and 30 Jan., 2 July, 13 and 27 Aug., and 31 Dec. 1904.

42. *Girard Press*, 29 Oct. 1903.

43. Ibid.

44. *AtR*, 7 Nov. 1903.

45. *AtR*, 16 Jan. 1904.

46. Delegate Dan White, Massachusetts, in *National Convention of the Socialist Party, 1904*, pp. 119–20.

47. Constitution, on pp. 310–14 of *National Convention, 1904*.

48. *National Convention, 1904*, pp. 81, 86, 88, 92, 93, 97.

49. David Goldstein, "Letter to the Editor," *Cigar Makers' Official Journal*, 15 Oct. 1908, pp. 5, 35; Mailly to Ricker, 18 Mar. 1903, SPAP.

50. As reprinted in *Girard Press*, 26 Jan. 1905.

CHAPTER 7. THE SECOND *COMING NATION*

1. For a list of those who worked on the *Appeal* in some reporting capacity see *American Freeman*, 3 Oct. 1931.

2. Although less has been written about Warren than about Wayland,

manuscript sources for Warren are much more abundant. George D. Brewer, an associate on the paper, wrote a laudatory account that the *Appeal* published in 1910: *The Fighting Editor: or, Warren and the Appeal*. It was reprinted by Beekman in New York in 1974. England's *History of the Appeal* and Charles Lincoln Phifer's fifteenth-anniversary piece, *AtR*, 27 Aug. 1910, also deal with Warren, as do the two master's theses about the paper. Warren left a trunkful of documents with his eldest son, Glenn, in Schenectady, New York, of which the most important have been made available in photocopies to the University of Connecticut Library and the Lilly Library. These include an incomplete autobiography, "The Little Old Appeal," assisted by Upton Sinclair and corrected by Glenn Warren, which dates from about 1950. Lilly Library has a number of other autobiographical reminiscences, and both libraries hold a number of letters from 1908 to 1915. Pittsburg has the largest collection of Warren's letters, which constitute much of the business correspondence of the paper. Warren lived long enough to write about the *Appeal* in the 1930s and 1950s, and he spoke with Howard Quint in the 1940s, leaving an often contradictory but always fascinating account of what he saw as important about the *Appeal* as his own circumstances changed.

3. Brewer, *Fighting Editor*, p. 19, gives Warren's birthdate as 1873; but Warren himself contradicted this in "Thumbnail Autobiography of Fred D. Warren, Girard, Kansas," ms. in Schenectady and LL, and in "The Little Old Appeal," p. 3.

4. Fred Warren, "Warren's Page," *American Freeman*, 1 Jan. 1933, p. 4.

5. Ibid., 17 Oct. 1931, p. 4.

6. See Brewer, *Fighting Editor*, pp. 19-21, on the *Tribune*.

7. Ibid., pp. 22-24.

8. See "The Little Old Appeal," p. 3.

9. Brewer, *Fighting Editor*, p. 26.

10. "The Little Old Appeal," p. 4.

11. Warren, "Thumbnail Autobiography."

12. *American Freeman*, 1 Jan. 1933.

13. This was published as a short pamphlet, probably through the *American Guardian*, a socialist paper from Oklahoma City, Okla., edited by Oscar Ameringer.

14. JAW, "Diary and Journal," entry for 17 Dec. 1899.

15. As reported in *Social Democratic Herald*, 21 Sept. 1900.

16. "The Little Old Appeal," chap. 3, p. 3.

17. Warren, *American Freeman*, 3 Oct. 1931.

18. See "The Little Old Appeal," chap. 3.

19. James G. Scrugham, ed., *Nevada: A Narrative of the Conquest of a Frontier Land*, vol 3: *Nevada Biographies* (Chicago and New York: American Historical Society, 1935), pp. 130-31.

20. "The Little Old Appeal," chap. 3, pp. 5-7.

21. *Coming Nation* (Rich Hill, Mo.), 22 Mar. 1902 to 26 Dec. 1903. Warren discusses the paper briefly in "The Little Old Appeal," chap. 3, pp. 7-9.

22. *CN*, 29 Aug. 1903.

23. Some of the columns were gathered together and published as *Wayland's Monthly*, no. 46 (Feb. 1904).

24. David Paul Nord, "The *Appeal to Reason* and American Socialism, 1901-1920," *Kansas History* 1, 2 (Summer 1978): 76, as quoted from Milburn in "The Appeal to Reason," p. 370.

25. See *CN*, 31 Jan. 1903, for the beginning of the quarrel, and especially 21 Mar. 1903, an issue that sold more than 100,000 copies.

26. Born on a Kentucky farm, Ryan Walker had been employed as a cattle roper in Texas (see biographical sketch in *CN*, 29 Nov. 1902).

27. On O'Hare see Neil K. Basen, "Kate Richards O'Hare: The First Lady of American Socialism, 1901–1917," *Labor History* 21, 2 (Spring 1980): 165–99. Basen did not examine O'Hare's work for the *Coming Nation*.

28. *CN*, 22 Mar. 1902.

29. *CN*, 14 June and 5 July 1902.

30. Catherine F. Hitchings, "Universalist and Unitarian Women Ministers," *Journal of the Universalist Historical Society* 10 (1975): 47–48.

31. See Mark Pittenger, "Evolution, Woman's Nature and American Feminist Socialism, 1900–1915," *Radical History Review* 36 (Sept. 1986): 47–61, for a thorough look at the question among the most articulate members of the feminist socialist community.

32. See ibid., pp. 49–50; and in general see Buhle, *Women and American Socialism.*

33. Lydia Kingsmill Commander, "Woman's Department," *Coming Nation* (Ruskin, Tenn.), 4 Feb. 1899. Commander here neatly summarizes much of her later thought. She went to New York City in the first decade of the twentieth century, where she wrote her most extended work on women and the family— *The American Idea: Does the National Tendency toward a Small Family Point to Race Suicide or Race Development?* (New York: A. S. Barnes, 1907; reprinted in the series Family in America, New York: Arno Press, 1972). In this work she argues that women are changing, working more, developing themselves, and, as a result, having fewer children or none at all. She concludes that "our problem is to so adapt the world to the woman who works that she may combine motherhood with industry" (p. 268 of reprint edition). Commander was active internationally in women's suffrage and peace groups and in placing in new jobs women who had been thrown out of work in economic downturns; see John William Leonard, ed., *Woman's Who's Who of America, 1914–1915* (New York: American Commonwealth Co., [1915]; reprint, Detroit, Mich.: Gale, 1976), pp. 196–97. By the way, her husband, Herbert Casson, whom Commander married at Ruskin, became a big business booster and wrote countless self-help and motivating treatises to spur on the "man on the make."

34. Kate Richards O'Hare, "The Women Folks," *Coming Nation*, 5 July 1902.

35. Godiva, "Our Woman's Page," *Wilshire's Magazine* 6, 11 (Nov. 1904): 12. It is possible that Godiva was Mary Wilshire, who married H. Gaylord Wilshire in April 1904 and remained his co-worker throughout their life together. At any rate, Mrs. Wilshire began to sign the column shortly after this time. In the 1920s she became one of the first practicing psychiatrists in southern California.

36. Josephine Conger, "Hints to the Appeal's Wise Women," *AtR*, 4 Apr. 1903.

37. Pittenger, "Evolution," pp. 48–49.

38. Julian Hawthorne, "Women and Socialism," *Wilshire's Magazine* 6, 5 (May 1904): 231–33.

39. Josephine Conger-Kaneko, "A Party-Owned Press: Being the Story of This Journal and Why It Is Not Party-owned," *CN* 1, 8 (July 1914): 4–6.

40. This discussion is condensed from Elliott Shore, "Selling Socialism: The *Appeal to Reason* and the Radical Press in Turn-of-the-Century America," *Media, Culture and Society* 7 (1985): 147–68.

41. Warren, "The Little Old Appeal," chap. 3, pp. 8–9.

42. Ryan Walker to Fred Warren, 9 Jan. 1914, H-J correspondence; "The Little Old Appeal," chap. 4.

43. *AtR*, 4 Feb. 1905.
44. See Ricker and Mailly correspondence, passim, galley quoted in note 23 in the preceding chapter.
45. "The Little Old Appeal," chap. 4, p. 2.
46. Ibid., chap. 5.
47. Ibid.
48. Fred Warren to Edwin A. Brenholtz, c. 20 Feb. 1905, H-J correspondence; see also Brenholtz to Warren, 28 Feb. 1905, ibid.

CHAPTER 8. BIFFIN' EVERY HEAD:
THE BIG STORIES 1904-10

1. The classic work on muckraking is still Louis Filler's *Crusaders for American Liberalism* (New York: Harcourt Brace & Co., 1939); rev. ed.: *The Muckrakers* (University Park: Pennsylvania State University Press, 1976). Filler devotes one chapter to the question of who was the first muckraker (see rev. ed., pp. 55-67).
2. Richard Hofstadter, *The Age of Reform* (New York: Vintage, 1955), pp. 166-67.
3. The best attempt by an American author to deal with gradations between journalists is David Mark Chalmers's *The Social and Political Ideas of the Muckrakers* (New York: Citadel, 1964). But Chalmers limits himself to personal vignettes. Klaus-Bert Becker's *Die Muckrakers und der Sozialismus: Eine Untersuchung zum politischen Bewusstsein in der Progressive Era*, Europäische Hochschulschriften, ser. 3, vol. 35 (Bern: Herbert Lang, 1974), is a detailed study of the development of the thought of a number of the leading muckrakers who became socialists and the reactions to socialism of those muckrakers who did not move to the left. Becker finds fault with the standard discussions of progressivism, saying that they miss the consciousness of the period by dealing only with narrow issues (p. 3). He finds that in the first years of muckraking, the journalists still appealed to the people themselves to make needed changes. At the beginning, these proto-socialist muckrakers were unable to produce theoretical explanations for what was happening (pp. 39-41), so they took refuge in sentiment. Becker then describes their gradual radicalization (pp. 71-104) and the different socialisms they chose. But the non-materialist background of these journalists, Becker claims, made it impossible for them to become Marxian socialists or to accept the theory of class struggle (pp. 280-84).
4. William A. Bloodworth, Jr., *Upton Sinclair* (Boston: Twayne, 1977), p. 65.
5. *AtR*, 21 Jan. and 4 Feb. 1905.
6. Bloodworth, *Upton Sinclair*, p. 60; Leon Harris, *Upton Sinclair: American Rebel* (New York: Crowell, 1975), pp. 70-71.
7. Harris, *Upton Sinclair*, p. 69.
8. *AtR*, 16 Jan. 1904.
9. Letter to Ernest Untermann explaining why he could not publish articles by Untermann until *The Jungle* was completed (Fred Warren to Untermann, 8 Oct. 1905, H-J correspondence).
10. In commenting on the negotiations with Doubleday, Warren told his lawyer: "Saw Sinclair, but he is just as irrational as ever. I think this was the first time in his life that he was really and truly scared" (Warren to J. C. Williams, 2 July 1906, H-J correspondence). The negotiations between the *Appeal* and Macmillan Company and then Doubleday can be followed in the above-cited letter and in George Platt Brett, president of Macmillan, to Warren, 19 Sept. 1905; War-

ren to L. J. Smith, 22 June 1906; J. C. Williams to Doubleday, Page & Co., 22 June 1906; Warren to JAW, 23 June 1906; Warren to Williams, 23 June 1906; Bruce Rogers, manager of *Appeal's* book department, to Upton Sinclair, 4 Feb. 1907—all in H-J correspondence).

The quarrel between Warren and Sinclair, which was furthered by another story that Warren had outlined and that Sinclair had refused to flesh out, was carried on in a voluminous correspondence, but see Warren to Eugene Debs, n.d., 1914 Debs Collection, ISU; Sinclair to Warren, 17 Aug. 1914, with copy of Sinclair to Walter H. Wayland, 17 Aug. 1914, H-J correspondence; Warren to Sinclair, 22 Dec. 1914, University of Connecticut; Sinclair to Warren, 28 Dec. 1914, H-J correspondence; Sinclair to Eugene Debs, 16 Nov. 1920, ISU. In a short summary of the achievements of the *Appeal*, probably written in the 1950s, Warren credits *The Jungle* as the crowning accomplishment of the paper: "Not for Publication: A Suggestion," Fred Warren, Schenectady and LL. In perhaps the last correspondence between the aging radicals, Sinclair wrote to Warren on 3 Jan. 1951 about the rights to the manuscript by Fred Warren "The Little Old Appeal," Warren Papers, Schenectady.

11. Warren to George H. Goebel, 25 July 1906, H-J correspondence.

12. Christopher Wilson, "The Making of a Best Seller, 1906," *New York Times Book Review*, 22 Dec. 1985, pp. 1, 25, 27. The publicity agent was Isaac Marcosson. Wilson's interesting account leaves the *Appeal* entirely out of the story.

13. On subsidiary rights to *The Jungle* see the correspondence between Fred Warren and Ellis O. Jones, editor of the Columbus, Ohio, *Press Post* in Jan. and Feb. 1905, H-J correspondence.

14. *AtR*, 30 Jan. 1904.

15. Shoaf's first articles appeared in the *Appeal* on 18 and 25 June, 2 and 9 July 1904. Shoaf wrote a lot about himself, but few have written about him (see Emanuel Haldeman-Julius, *My First Twenty-five Years: Instead of a Footnote, An Autobiography* [Girard, Kans.: Haldeman-Julius, 1949], p. 61). The major source on Shoaf's life is his *Fighting for Freedom* (Kansas City, Mo.: Simplified Economics, [1953]), a detailed recounting of his career, which must be approached with caution. He wrote several articles about the *Appeal*: "The Biggest Little Paper This Country Ever Knew," *Monthly Review* 3, 3 (July 1951): 88-98; "Debs and the *Appeal to Reason*: A personal Memoir," *Progressive World*, Nov./Dec. 1975, pp. 13-17, and Jan./Feb. 1976, pp. 26-31. In addition to his numerous articles, some of which were reprinted as pamphlets, Shoaf wrote a novel: *Love Crucified: A Romance of the Colorado War* (Girard, Kans.: [Appeal Publishing Co.], 1905).

16. Haldeman-Julius, *My First Twenty-five Years*, p. 61.

17. On Ruskin College see Earle A. Collins, "The Multitude Incorporated," *Missouri Historical Review*, 27 (July 1933): 305-307.

18. Shoaf, *Fighting for Freedom*, pp. 54-55. This sketch of Shoaf's career is drawn exclusively from this work, and is therefore open to serious question, but in the absence of evidence to the contrary, much of it is probably accurate.

19. Haldeman-Julius, *My First Twenty-five Years*, p. 61.

20. Shoaf, *Fighting for Freedom*, pp. 63-64.

21. *AtR*, 18 and 25 June, 2 and 9 July 1904.

22. There are a number of accounts of the assassination, but the two I found most useful are David H. Grover, *Debaters and Dynamiters: The Story of the Haywood Trial* (Corvallis: Oregon State University Press, 1964), which generally supports the mine owners' side of the story, and Joseph R. Conlin, *Big Bill*

Haywood and the Radical Union Movement (Syracuse, N.Y.: Syracuse University Press, 1969), which takes the defendants' side. The most recent work is Peter Carlson, *Roughneck: The Life and Times of Big Bill Haywood* (New York: W. W. Norton, 1983).

23. *AtR*, 10 Mar. 1906.

24. Louis Adamic, *Dynamite: The Story of Class Violence in America*, rev. ed. (Gloucester, Mass.: Peter Smith, 1963), p. 143.

25. See Grover, *Debaters and Dynamiters*, p. 282; Conlin, *Big Bill Haywood*, p. 71; Carlson, *Roughneck*, pp. 139–42.

26. Ernest Untermann to Fred Warren, 24 Oct. 1911, Jane Addams Memorial Collection, Chicago.

27. Circular letter, JAW to Dear Brother, n.d., with petition, H-J correspondence, 1906.

28. Kevin Tierney, *Darrow: A Biography* (New York: Thomas Y. Crowell, 1979), pp. 208–9.

29. H. Gaylord Wilshire to JAW, 15 May 1906, H-J correspondence.

30. The fullest treatment of the *Warren* case, as it came to be known, is in George Allan England's *Story of the Appeal*, pp. 56–70. It has also been treated, in its early stages, by Brewer in *Fighting Editor*, and in two student papers, by Daniel E. Speir and John Bowes, held at the PSU Library. The original call for the kidnapping appeared in the *Appeal to Reason* on 12 Jan. 1907. At the PSU Library, in addition to the transcripts of various trials and motions, there is a voluminous correspondence, which includes: Upton Sinclair to Harry J. Bone, 9 Dec. 1910; Fred Warren to L. C. Boyle, 12 Dec. 1910, and John Brisben Walker to Warren, 17 Feb. 1911.

31. England, *Story of the Appeal*, pp. 84–86; Brewer, *Fighting Editor*, pp. 59–60.

32. England, *Story of the Appeal*, p. 62.

33. Ibid., p. 64.

34. Ibid., p. 65.

35. Warren kept getting a good deal of mileage out of this notoriety. He made mention of the pardon in a letter to Senator Robert Taft, 7 Jan. 1950 (incomplete draft), Warren Papers, Schenectady, N.Y.

36. The best source on Turner is in the introduction by Sinclair Snow to the second edition of Turner's *Barbarous Mexico* (Austin: University of Texas Press, 1969). The first edition was published by Charles H. Kerr in 1910. A student paper at the PSU Library—William C. Walker's "John Kenneth Turner: Socialist Writer for the *Appeal to Reason*"—is excellent for Turner's career with the paper, and it collects together in its bibliography all of the stories that he wrote for the paper and most of the correspondence that he had with Warren. The above quote is from this paper, p. 3, as quoted in *AtR*, 30 Jan. 1915. William Woodrow Anderson, in "The Nature of the Mexican Revolution as Viewed from the United States, 1910–1917" (Ph.D. diss., University of Texas, Austin, 1967), shows the importance of Turner and the *Appeal's* contribution to American public opinion.

37. Sinclair Snow, Introduction to Turner's *Barbarous Mexico*, pp. xxi–xxiii. Seven articles were published in the *Appeal*, one in the *International Socialist Review*, and one in the *Pacific Monthly*.

38. John Kenneth Turner to Fred Warren, 10 Apr. 1913, PSU.

39. Snow, Introduction, p. xxiv.

40. Richard L. McCormick, "The Discovery That Business Corrupts Politics: A Reappraisal of the Origins of Progressivism," *American Historical Review* 86 (Apr. 1981): 247–74.

CHAPTER 9. THE TEMPLE OF THE REVOLUTION

1. The reflections were recorded by the *Appeal*'s stenographer and were published in a little pamphlet, *An Evening in Girard: Just an Informal Incident Following the Return of Delegates from the Chicago Socialist Convention* (Girard, Kans.: [Appeal to Reason], 1908).

2. On Girard during this period, see Willis Ernest Lamson, "The Historical Development of Girard, Kansas, and Its Community" (Master's thesis, Kansas State Teachers College, Pittsburg, 1933). A good contemporary overview of the town is "Lively Pace of Girard," *Girard Press*, 25 Feb. 1904, as reprinted from the *Topeka Capital*, 14 Feb. 1904. *Little Balkans Review* 4, 1 (Fall 1983): 44–75, contains five short pieces on the Girard background of the *Appeal*.

3. On the operations of the paper, see "A Trip through the Appeal Office," *Wayland's Monthly* 54 (Oct. 1904), and England, *Story of the Appeal*, pp. 270–77; *AtR*, 31 Aug. 1907. On other *Appeal* publications see Gene DeGruson, "The Appeal Publications and Subsidiaries," *Little Balkans Review* 4, 1 (Fall, 1983): 70–75.

4. "Trip through the Appeal Office," pp. 1–3; England, *Story of the Appeal*, p. 273.

5. England, *Story of the Appeal*, p. 275.

6. "Trip through the Appeal Office," pp. 8–9; and England, *Story of the Appeal*, p. 271.

7. England, *Story of the Appeal*, p. 276.

8. Henry Laurens Call to Stephen Marion Reynolds, 6 June 1908, Stephen Marion Reynolds Papers, Indiana Historical Society, Indianapolis. The *Kansas State College of Pittsburg Library Bulletin* 8, 3/4 (Spring/Summer 1974), is devoted in its entirety to the Call experiment. See also Lamson, "Historical Development of Girard," pp. 44–50. The local press was suspicious of the reasons for financing the plane, musing that it would be used to circumvent postal laws and to kidnap heads of state (see *Girard Press*, 29 Mar. 1908; see also DeGruson, "Appeal Publications," pp. 73–75.

9. *AtR*, 15 Oct. 1904, 8 Apr. 1905, 27 July and 30 Nov. 1907.

10. Henry Vincent to Mrs. Caro Lloyd Withington, 6 Feb. 1907, Lloyd Collection, SHSW, as quoted by Piehler in "Henry Vincent: A Case Study," p. 217; see also Mary Vincent Cummings, *Memories of Girard, Kansas, Eugene Debs and Me* (Glendora, Calif.: Merrily Cummings Ford, 1976).

11. On the group of Girard socialists see Cummings, *Memories*. Phifer's enormous output is described in Haldeman-Julius, *My Second Twenty-five Years: Instead of a Footnote, An Autobiography* (Girard, Kans.: Haldeman-Julius Publications, 1949), p. 62. Haldeman-Julius's essentially negative portrait of Phifer is backed up by the general inaccuracy of Phifer's reporting; a good example is his grossly inaccurate history of the paper on its fifteenth anniversary, *AtR*, 27 Aug. 1910. Phifer's spiritualism is attested to by Haldeman-Julius, and there are hints in Phifer's letters to Debs. Debs's replies show a benevolent understanding, if not outright acceptance, for the position: see, e.g., Debs to Phifer, 18 Jan. 1921 and 16 Feb. 1923, at the Debs Foundation, Terre Haute, Ind., and Phifer to Debs, 19 Oct. 1921, and Debs to Phifer, 13 Aug. 1925, Debs collection, ISU. The place of spiritualism in the socialist movement is important, but it is almost impossible to document. Robert Laurence Moore's *In Search of White Crows: Spiritualism, Parapsychology and American Culture* (New York: Oxford University Press, 1977) shows the connection between spiritualism and reform—most of the abolitionists were somehow connected with the movement—but

argues that by the end of the nineteenth century, spiritualism was dead as a serious reform movement (p. 74). It seems, though, that spiritualism was still very much alive, at least among the Girard group, and was favorably endorsed by Wayland (see chap. 2). See also Rodney O. Davis, "Prudence Crandall, Spiritualism, and Populist-Era Reform in Kansas," *Kansas History* 3, 4 (Winter 1980): 239-54. Janet Oppenheim, in *The Other World: Spiritualism and Psychical Research in England, 1850-1914* (Cambridge: Cambridge University Press, 1986), notes the connection between working-class spiritualism in England and Owenism. There is also some evidence of a large group of Christian Scientists in Girard, some of whom were also socialists. The existence of this kind of religiosity on the part of these socialists supports the argument that these were in many respects a sentimental and "unscientific" group. Phifer wrote *Hamlet in Heaven* (Girard: [the Author?], 1916) and *Old Religions Made New* (n.p., 1918) among many other works.

12. Nick Salvatore's *Eugene V. Debs: Citizen and Socialist* (Urbana: University of Illinois Press, 1982) is the latest biography of Debs; it makes use of numerous manuscript sources that were not available to Ray Ginger when he wrote *Eugene Debs: A Biography* (New Brunswick, N.J.: Rutgers University Press, 1947), which was originally titled *The Bending Cross*.

13. Eugene Debs to Theodore Debs, 17 May 1908, Debs collection, ISU; italics in the original.

14. Cummings, *Memories*.

15. F. A. Warrelman to Fred Warren, 15 Mar. 1913, and Warren to Dear Comrade, 17 Mar. 1913—both in H-J correspondence. The *Menace*'s connection with the *Appeal* was circumstantial but nevertheless real. In 1916, when the *Menace*'s staff was prosecuted in federal court in Joplin, Mo., for sending obscene matter through the mail, it was defended by the *Appeal*'s attorney and general attorney for the Socialist party in Kansas, J. I. Shepard, who had helped to defend Warren in his similar case. B. O. Flower—an early supporter of the Ruskin Cooperative Village, a long-time progressive, and a chronicler of radical movements—set up a defense league to support Wilbur F. Phelps and his colleagues at the *Menace* (see Benjamin Orange Flower, *Story of the Menace Trial* [Aurora, Mo.: United States Publishing Co., 1916]).

In her book *The Radical Persuasion, 1890-1917* (Baton Rouge: Louisiana State University Press, 1981), Aileen S. Kraditor makes much of the fact that radical historians look with wonder at the circulation of the *Appeal* but ignore such publications as the *Menace*, whose circulation surpassed the *Appeal*'s during the mid 1910s. What needs to be explained, it seems to me, is the connection between anti-Catholicism and socialism, and the popularity of both in the heart of the country. On this issue see Robert Westbrook, "Good-bye to All That: Aileen Kraditor and Radical History," *Radical History Review* 28-30 (1984): 69-89.

16. Oral interview, 9 May 1987.

17. Odd-Stein Granhus, "Scandinavian-American Socialist Newspapers with Emphasis on the Norwegian Contribution and E. L. Menghoel's *Gaa Paa: Folkets Rost*," in *Essays on the Scandinavian-North American Radical Press, 1880s-1930s*, ed. by Dirk Hoerder, a publication of the project Bibliography and Archival Preservation of Non-English Language Labor and Radical Newspapers and Periodicals in North America, 1845-1976 (Bremen: University of Bremen, 1984), pp. 78-99; and personal communication, 3 June 1984. Mengshoel continued to publish the paper until 1925 for a steady audience of about 5,000 readers.

18. Ivan Molek, *Slovene Immigrant History, 1900-1950: Autobiographical*

Sketches, ed. Mary Molek (Dover, Del.: the Editor, 1979), p. 154.

19. May Wood-Simons, "Mining Coal and Maiming Men," *Coming Nation* (Girard), 11 Nov. 1911, as quoted by Ann Schofield in "The Women's March: Miners, Family, and Community in Pittsburg, Kansas, 1921–1922," *Kansas History* 7, 2 (Summer 1984): 162.

20. Ryan Walker to Fred Warren, 9 Jan. 1914, H-J correspondence.

21. Debs may, in fact, have had another lover in Mary Vincent's mother (see Cummings, *Memories*, p. 8; Salvatore, *Eugene V. Debs*, p. 185; *Girard Press*, 15 and 29 Oct. 1903; Ginger, *Eugene Debs*, pp. 305–6; Samuel Gompers, *Seventy Years of Life and Labor: An Autobiography*, vol. 1 [New York: E. P. Dutton, 1925], pp. 266–68; Edith Wayland Stephenson, oral interview, 9 May 1987).

22. George D. Brewer, "Memories" and "Memos," typescript sketches in the Brewer collection, Walter Reuther Archives of Labor History, Wayne State University, Detroit, Mich.

23. Eugene Debs to Frank P. O'Hare, 1 July and 31 Dec. 1915, Debs collection, ISU.

24. George H. Goebel to Ryan Walker, 21 June 1906, H-J correspondence.

25. Frank P. O'Hare to [Lucy Henschel?], 13 Sept. 1942, O'Hare Papers, Missouri State Historical Society, Columbia.

26. Green, *Grass-roots Socialism*, pp. 151–62; Oscar Ameringer, *If You Don't Weaken: The Autobiography of Oscar Ameringer* (New York: Henry Holt, 1940), pp. 265–67; *Fort Scott* (Kans.) *Tribune*, 29 Aug. 1911.

27. L. W. Lowry to Fred Warren, 17 July 1906, H-J correspondence.

28. (I. F. Branstetter?) to Warren, 24 Jan. 1910, H-J correspondence.

29. *Who's Who in Socialist America for 1914* (Girard, Kans.: Appeal to Reason, 1914).

30. Daniel Bell, "The Background and Development of Marxian Socialism in the United States," in *Socialism and American Life*, ed. Donald D. Egbert and Stow Persons, vol. 1 (Princeton, N.J.: Princeton University Press, 1952), pp. 213–406; David Shannon, *The Socialist Party of America: A History* (New York: Macmillan, 1955); James Weinstein, *The Decline of Socialism in America, 1912–1925* (New York: Vintage, 1969); and John Laslett, comp., *Failure of a Dream? Essays in the History of American Socialism* (Garden City, N.Y.: Anchor Press, 1974).

31. James R. Green, "The 'Salesmen-Soldiers' of the 'Appeal Army': A Profile of Rank and File Socialist Agitators," in *Socialism and the Cities*, ed. Bruce M. Stave (Port Washington, N.Y.: Kennikat, 1975), pp. 13–40. Green, in *Grass-roots Socialism*, pp. 128–35, concentrates on the southwestern members of the Appeal Army and does not emphasize the working-class nature of the groups so heavily. Simons's findings are in "J. A. Wayland, Propagandist," p. 27. On the Appeal Army see also England, *The Wonderful Appeal Army*.

32. H. Wayne Morgan, " 'Red Special': Eugene V. Debs and the Campaign of 1908," *Indiana Magazine of History* 54, 3 (Sept. 1958): 211–36; Kipnis, *American Socialist Movement*, pp. 212–14.

33. See, e.g., *The Appeal's Arsenal of Facts, 1911* ([Girard, Kans.: Appeal to Reason]), p. 68.

34. Stock certificate for 360 shares and credit receipt, Consolidated Wilshire Mining Co., Sinclair mss, LL; Henry L. Slobodin, "Get-Rich-Quick Schemes," *International Socialist Review* 11, 8 (Feb. 1911): 486–87.

35. Kent Kreuter and Gretchen Kreuter, *An American Dissenter: The Life of Algie Martin Simons, 1870–1950* (Lexington: University of Kentucky Press, 1969), pp. 116–43.

36. Fred Warren to Ryan Walker, 4 Aug. 1912, H-J correspondence.
37. *Girard Press*, 25 Nov. and 9 Dec. 1909.
38. As reprinted in *Girard Press*, 28 July 1904.
39. See *Fort Scott* (Kans.) *Tribune Monitor*, 3, 5, and 10 Aug. 1911.
40. Warren, "Thumbnail Autobiography," Schenectady and LL; "Article #2," INCOMPLETE, LL.
41. See *AtR*, 25 Sept. 1909, 13 Sept. 1910.
42. *Girard Press*, 3 Feb. 1910.
43. Vincent, *Wayland*, pp. 9–10.
44. Oral interview with Edith Wayland Stephenson, 9 May 1987.
45. Lincoln Steffens, "Eugene V. Debs on What the Matter Is in America and What to Do About It," *Everybody's* 19 (Oct. 1908): 455–69.
46. Fred Warren telegram to E. J. Ridgeway, 11 Aug. 1908, Debs collection, ISU.
47. Eugene Debs to Lincoln Steffens, 12 Aug. 1908; Steffens to Debs, 13 Aug. 1908, Debs collection.
48. See the enormous volume of business correspondence in the H-J correspondence, PSU.
49. *AtR*, 15 Oct. 1910; italics in original.
50. *AtR*, 29 Apr. 1911, headline.

CHAPTER 10. THE LAST BIG FIGHT

1. *AtR*, 15 Oct. 1910.
2. Robert Gottlieb and Irene Wolt, *Thinking Big: The Story of the Los Angeles Times, Its Publishers and Their Influence on Southern California* (New York: G. C. Putnam, 1977), pp. 32–81; Graham Adams, *Age of Industrial Violence, 1910–1915: The Activities and Findings of the United States Commission on Industrial Relations* (New York: Columbia University Press, 1966), pp. 2–7; Shoaf, *Fighting for Freedom*, pp. 118–19.
3. Warren left Girard in June 1911 for a speaking tour through Colorado. Wayland's second wife died in an automobile accident on June 8, and it is probable that Wayland wanted to get back to work as a result of this tragedy (see *AtR*, 17 and 24 June 1911).
4. Gottlieb and Wolt, *Thinking Big*, p. 87; Adams, *Age of Industrial Violence*, pp. 3–7; Philip S. Foner, *History of the Labor Movement in the United States*, vol. 5: *The AFL in the Progressive Era, 1910–1915* (New York: International Publishers, 1980), pp. 7–10.
5. *AtR*, 6 May 1911.
6. *AtR*, 13 May 1911.
7. As reported in *AtR*, 20 May 1911.
8. Ibid.
9. *AtR*, 29 July 1911.
10. *AtR*, 2 Sept. 1911.
11. Shoaf, *Fighting for Freedom*.
12. *AtR*, 2, 9, and 16 Sept. 1911; Ben Warren to Fred Warren, 17 Aug. 1911, H-J correspondence; Frank E. Wolfe to F. Warren, 23 Aug. 1911, Haldeman-Julius Papers, JAMC.
13. George C. Shoaf to F. Warren, 27 Aug. 1911, H-J correspondence.
14. Frank E. Wolfe to Lincoln Phifer, 30 Aug. 1911, JAMC.
15. JAMC.

16. His pay, $35 a week, compared unfavorably to Debs's and Wayland's $100-a-week salaries (see Cornelius C. Corker [Shoaf] to F. Warren, II Oct. 1911, JAMC).

17. Josephine Conger-Kaneko to F. Warren, 3 Oct. 1911, JAMC.

18. Ryan Walker to F. Warren, 24 Sept. 1911, JAMC.

19. Piet Vlag to F. Warren, 30 Sept. 1911, JAMC.

20. Conger-Kaneko to F. Warren, 3 Oct. 1911, JAMC.

21. F. Warren to W. J. Ghent, 15 Oct. 1911, Ghent to Warren, 19 Oct. 1911, JAMC.

22. AtR, 14 Oct. 1911.

23. Cornelius C. Corker to F. Warren, 16 and 26 Oct. 1911, JAMC.

24. F. Warren to Dick Maple, 25 Nov. 1911, H-J correspondence.

25. Foner, History of the Labor Movement, p. 25.

26. AtR, 9 and 16 Dec. 1911.

27. Gottlieb and Wolt, Thinking Big, p. 104-5; Foner, History of the Labor Movement, pp. 27-30.

28. F. Warren to Ray Ginger, 8 June 1948, Warren Papers, Schenectady.

29. Debs scrapbook, Labadie Collection, University of Michigan, Ann Arbor, p. 29; Albert F. Ferguson, "Federal Spies Trail Socialists," Omaha (Nebr.) Daily News, 13 Dec. 1912; F. Warren to Robert B. Ringler, 25 Nov. 1912, KC, PSU.

The best sources for the study of federal harassment of the Appeal are the Department of Justice classified subject file no. 77175 and the investigative case files of the Bureau of Investigation, 1908-22, both at the National Archives, Washington, D.C. The Department of Justice files include a number of letters of protest about the treatment of the paper and a much smaller number that included clippings and asked that the paper be barred from the mails. In the letters to the various attorneys' general from Harry Bone, one can read the fascinating story of his attempt to destroy the paper, and the enthusiasm that he had for the task. The Bureau of Investigation files mostly cover the period of the late 1910s and focus on the Peoples' College in Fort Scott, Kansas. See Theodore Roosevelt to the Attorney General, 19 Mar. 1906; Charles H. Robb, Assistant Attorney General to the Attorney General, 22 Mar. 1906; Harry J. Bone, United States Attorney, District of Kansas to the Attorney General, 7 May 1909; Attorney General to Harry J. Bone, 10 May 1909—all in Department of Justice classified subject file no. 77175, National Archives, Washington, D.C.

30. See exchange of letters: J. Mahlon Barnes to Eugene Debs, 23 July 1912; Debs to Barnes, 24 July 1912; Barnes to Debs, 25 July 1912—all from Debs Collection, ISU.

31. Stephen Marion Reynolds, "Comrade Love," Debs scrapbook, Labadie Collection, p. 30; Wayland's Undelivered Address and Ben Wilson's Funeral Oration (Girard, Kans.: Appeal to Reason, 1913), p. 27.

32. F. Warren to Ray Ginger, 8 June 1948, Warren Papers, Schenectady.

33. Andrew Allen Veatch, "Phelps, Another of Wayland's Gang Indicted for Murder," Remonstrator 1, 6 (1 July 1913): 9.

34. Seymour Martin Lipset, Agrarian Socialism: The Cooperative Commonwealth Federation in Saskatchewan: A Study in Political Sociology (Berkeley: University of California Press, 1959), pp. 6, 8-9.

35. Reynolds, "Comrade Love."

36. F. Warren to Ginger, 8 June 1948.

37. Andrew Allen Veatch, "Why Did Wayland Kill Himself?" Remonstrator 1, 4 (1 Mar. 1913): 1.

38. Vincent, Wayland, p. 5.

39. Wayland had been thinking suicidal thoughts on election day, according to his son (see John G. Wayland, Debs scrapbook, p. 30).

40. Collected at PSU Library's Kansas Collection, late Nov. 1912. See, especially, Milton M. Smith to F. Warren, 14 Nov. 1912; Wilson Cory to AtR, 24 Nov. 1912; L.L.H. to AtR, Nov. 1912; and J. W. Gammill to F. Warren, 25 Nov. 1912.

41. Vincent, Wayland; Brewer, The Wayland I Knew; see also, e.g., Wayland's Undelivered Address and Ben Wilson's Funeral Oration.

42. People, 14 Nov. 1912.

43. Remonstrator, 1 Mar. 1913; Romulus Don Laws to Daniel C. Gibson, 5 May 1913, H-J correspondence.

44. Kipnis, American Socialist Movement, pp. 391-420.

45. David A. Corbin, "Betrayal in the West Virginia Coal Fields: Eugene V. Debs and the Socialist Party of America, 1912-1914," Journal of American History 64, 4 (Mar. 1978): 987-1009.

46. A. M. Simons to National Executive Committee, 14 June 1913; Simons to Berger, 14 June 1913, Milwaukee Historical Society. See Warren's reply to the charges, in Warren to Dear Bro, 23 [June?] 1913, KC, PSU.

47. Walker to F. Warren, 9 Jan. 1914, H-J correspondence.

48. On the People's College see Debs to Comrade, 23 July 1914, Socialist Party Collection, Duke University; Fred Warren, The People's College Vest-Pocket Edition of the Report of the Industrial Relations Commission (Fort Scott, Kans.: People's College, 1915); [Kate Richards O'Hare] to Eugene V. Debs, 13 Dec. 1915, Debs Collection, ISU.

49. F. Warren to Ryan Walker, 14 Jan. 1914, H-J correspondence; the Ries and Madden Pamphlet Series; the history was England's Story of the Appeal.

50. Bill of sale, 11 Apr. 1918, JAMC.

51. See the attack on the Appeal in Gustav Stohlberg to AtR, 15 Apr. 1919, Debs Collection, ISU.

52. [Emanuel Haldeman-] Julius to Louis [Kopelin], n.d., JAMC.

53. Robert B. Ringler to F. Warren, 25 Jan. 1913, KC, PSU.

54. See, e.g., AtR, 6 Nov. 1920.

55. Kraditor, Radical Persuasion,

56. Scott Nearing, The Making of a Radical: A Political Autobiography (New York: Harper & Row, 1972), pp. 100, 209.

57. See Phifer's letters to Debs, ISU, and Debs foundation.

58. "Pearson's in Court Again," New York Times, 31 July 1918.

59. "Ernest Untermann, Artist, Naturalist," New York Times, 26 Jan. 1956.

60. George D. Brewer [résumé], Brewer Collection.

61. Buhle, Women and American Socialism, pp. 306-7.

62. Sinclair Snow, Introduction, p. xxviii.

63. Charles Edward Russell, Bare Hands and Stone Walls (New York: Scribner's, 1933).

64. "Ryan Walker, Artist, Is Dead in Moscow," New York Times, 25 June 1932.

65. Shoaf, Fighting for Freedom.

66. Harris, Upton Sinclair, pp. 175-83.

67. F. Warren to Eugene Debs, 4 May 1915, Debs collection; George Goebel to Warren, 6 and 7 Dec. 1915, Schenectady; Warren to Goebel, n.d., Schenectady; Halpern and Passage to Warren, 23 Sept. [1914], Schenectady; Wilbur S. Shepperson, Retreat to Nevada (Reno: University of Nevada Press, 1966), pp. 66ff.

68. Warren's page was published in the American Freeman in 1931 and 1932 (see F. Warren to Adolph Germer, 12 and 16 Nov. 1931; George Shoaf, "Bring

Socialism with American Means in an American Way," *American Freeman*, 12 Dec. 1931).

69. "Girard Publisher is Sued," *Girard Press*, 17 Aug. 1933; "Files Answer to Damage Suit," ibid., 28 Sept. 1933; Girard, Kans., Chamber of Commerce, Minutes of the Chamber, 9 Feb., 2 Mar., and 7 Dec. 1937, 1 Mar. 1938; draft letter, F. Warren to Charles A. Lindbergh, 12 July 1939.

70. See, e.g., William A. White to F. Warren, 12 Sept. 1932; Max Eastman to Warren, 3 Apr. 1952; "The Little Old Appeal"; "Thumbnail Autobiography of Fred D. Warren, Girard Kansas"—all in Schenectady.

71. "Fred D. Warren Died in Fort Scott Saturday," *Girard Press*, 26 Mar. 1959.

72. Bob Nicklas, "A Good First Step in a Long March," *In These Times*, 12-25 Aug. 1981, p. 17.

Bibliographical Note

Histories of publishing in the United States have virtually ignored the role of the *Appeal to Reason*, even though its circulation was comparable to that of all but the two or three most popular magazines.[1] Histories of socialism have concentrated on the Socialist party or on Debs, the acknowledged leader of the party and its perennial presidential candidate. Even when they do mention the *Appeal to Reason*, most historians have relied on a single account of the newspaper, one that breaks off in 1901.[2] One radical historian has commented, however, that the *Appeal to Reason* should be studied in the context of the general publishing world of the time; he claimed that it is the only radical newspaper that belongs equally in the history of the movement and the history of the publishing industry in America.[3]

If general histories of publishing and of the Socialist party have paid scant attention to Wayland and Warren and their publications, they have not been ignored by fellow socialists or, more recently, by historians of radicalism. Unlike most radical papers, the *Appeal* has been written about extensively, the first time by Wayland himself, before the experiment was six months old.[4] Years later, that account was given away, first in pamphlet form and then in book form, as a spur to increase circulation.[5] Both of the chief architects of the *Appeal*'s early years were praised in short books written by the staff.[6] Again, unlike the bulk of radical papers, the *Appeal* got some notice from the established press, which published several major articles about it.[7] Two students from schools near Girard wrote Master's theses about the paper, one in the 1930s and one in the 1950s, relying chiefly on those earlier accounts with some important additional information from interviews.[8] But it was not until after World War II that scholarly attention focused on the *Appeal*. The first, and still useful, account can be found in the work of the late Howard Quint.

Quint's dissertation at Johns Hopkins University, later published as *The Forging of American Socialism*, included a chapter on Wayland, which he published separately.[9] Quint surveyed the intellectual and political content of the currents that led to the formation of the Socialist party in 1901. He saw Wayland as one of the vital factors in the creation of this American movement and credited him with the "planting of grassroots socialism." Quint was the first to attempt an analysis of Wayland's thought, which he called "a generous mixture of utopian socialism, ill-digested scientific socialism and radical Populism." Quint focused in some detail on the way that Wayland reached his public, and Quint brought together the various biographical accounts into a short history, which ended in 1901. Quint's contribution was weak in only two areas. He relied too heavily on those early accounts of the paper and was not able to check their accuracy, as no manuscript collections then existed, and the people he was able to interview were generally laudatory in their comments. The other major flaw in Quint's study of Wayland's thought was that he ignored the influence of John Ruskin on Wayland's intellectual development.

Successive students of the *Appeal* have relied heavily on Quint's pioneering work. Paul Buhle is one of three younger scholars who have looked at the *Appeal* in some depth. In his short piece on the *Coming Nation* and the *Appeal to Reason*, which was written as part of an exhaustive survey of radical publishing in America, he was the first to note that the *Appeal* should be studied in the context of general publishing history.[10] James Green has written two works on the activities of the paper's subscription hawkers, the salesmen-soldiers of the *Appeal's* army; he gives broader support to Quint's assessment of Wayland.[11] Using a small book that contained short biographies of the leading subscription agents of the paper, Green produced an impressive profile of the typical middle-rank member of the Socialist party, a first attempt to get at the culture of American socialism. More recently, David Paul Nord has attempted to describe in detail the subjects treated by the *Appeal* in the period after the formation of the Socialist party.[12] Nord's technique of sampling the contents of the paper has major deficiencies, two of which partially invalidate his findings. He ignored small paragraphs and very short stories, even though for a part of his survey period, they were crucial to the paper's content. More seriously, he used time spans that overlapped changes in editors and in the nature of the movement in general. His work is useful, however, in assessing the emphasis that the paper placed on certain topics. Except for Nord's article, the *Appeal* has been treated as part of a larger study of American socialism, rather than as journalism in general. Most major studies of American socialism have devoted some space to the *Appeal*, relying almost exclusively on Quint's account. Most recently, Sharon Neet has produced a bibliographic study of the regional variations in editions of the *Appeal to Reason* and has contributed to a symposium held in Girard, Kansas, in honor of the paper.[13]

The major fault that one can find with these accounts of the *Appeal* is their reliance on the accuracy of the early house histories, something that these same historians would not have done if they had been looking at such figures as Hearst and Pulitzer. These historians also accepted statements made in the paper without checking other sources, and they have been led to emphasize what the *Appeal* itself thought was important: the size of the circulation, the way in which it grew, romanticized biographical details of its editors' lives, and its own importance. Quint took the contents of the paper quite seriously, but his narrative broke off in 1901, and no one has traced the development of the paper after the formation of the Socialist party. Accepting the *Appeal's* own word and that of its historians that it was the largest, most influential, and most widely read political newsweekly in the country, Quint and Buhle offer samples of the paragraphs that characterized the paper, and Quint describes the positions that the paper took on various political questions of the 1890s. We are told by Daniel Bell that it had a Yankeefying flavor;[14] Nord tells us what topics were covered; Green gives us some information on some of the people who made it successful, but largely confines his study to questions of importance in the Southwest. Green assumes that it was a rural paper and that its circulation was limited to poor tenants in the South. Yet the *Appeal* was a national paper; at one time it even attempted newstand sales in major cities. As Nord tells us, farm and rural topics were not big issues in the paper.

This study addresses a major historiographical question, the question that perennially haunts students of American socialism: Why didn't a mass Socialist party develop in the United States? This question has agitated scholars in the West since the beginning of the century. In its classic formulation, western Europe is posited as the model of success, because its Social Democratic parties have gained power from time to time, while, in the U.S., in contrast, democratic socialism has never acquired formal political standing. With the possible and partial exception of Sweden, however, the success model of democratic socialism is quite doubtful. The transformation in the relations of production that is associated with socialism is very incomplete in western Europe. These are still capitalist countries with some quasi-socialized sectors of the economy, notwithstanding big labor and Socialist parties. The United States economy doesn't look much different, even though it has no mass Socialist party. Even western European Socialist parties are no longer the only voice for democratic change. In light of the recent trend in Europe to address single issues such as the environment or nuclear war outside of the question of a transformation of relations of production, Eric Foner has asked whether this is not the result of the Americanization of Europe, the penetration into Europe of the values of mass, consumer society.[15] If that is the case, then perhaps what is happening in Europe now roughly parallels the conditions under which socialism failed in the United States. In other words, the "failure" of American socialism might be historically located in the context of what was happening to American society during the 1890s and 1900s. Or, as Irving Howe has put it, "the distinctiveness of American culture has played the more decisive part in thwarting socialist fortunes."[16]

Several manuscript collections made this study possible. Most important are the J. A. Wayland Collection, the Haldeman-Julius Collection and the Kansas Collection—all at Pittsburg State University, Pittsburg, Kans. The curator has been gathering the business correspondence of the paper, much of it in very poor condition, and has made much of it accessible for the first time. Here, one can see the day-to-day pressures that operated on Warren as they would have on any publisher of the period, and the relationships among the many writers who worked for the *Appeal*. The Jane Addams Memorial Collection, at the library of Chicago Circle Campus of the University of Illinois, holds most of the documents that reveal the story behind the McNamara case of 1911 and how it was handled by the paper. The *Appeal*'s handling of this case was what led directly to the paper's decline in influence. The Debs Collection at Indiana State University, Terre Haute, and the collection at the Debs Foundation, Terre Haute, as well as the Debs Papers Project, centered there—all contain important material that has only recently become available. Of critical importance are two collections of papers that are still in private hands, one in the possession of the Warren family, some of which have been placed as photocopies at the University of Connecticut at Storrs and at the Lilly Library of Indiana University at Bloomington. These include a hitherto unused Warren autobiography and other unpublished papers of Fred Warren, which reveal much that was left out of the columns of the newspaper. The other, the Wayland family papers, being collected by Wayland's daughter Edith Wayland Stephenson, contain diaries kept by J. A. Wayland and financial documents. The Wayland family papers will someday be at Pittsburg State University, which has kindly allowed me to look at the photocopies that have been made.

NOTES

1. The only short notice of the *AtR* in the literature of journalism history is in Frank Luther Mott, *A History of American Magazines, 1885–1905* (Cambridge: Belknap Press of Harvard University Press, 1957), pp. 204–6.

2. Howard H. Quint, "Julius A. Wayland: Pioneer Socialist Propagandist," *Mississippi Valley Historical Review* 35 (March 1949): 585–606.

3. Paul M. Buhle, "Appeal to Reason," in *The American Radical Press, 1880–1960*, ed. Joseph R. Conlin, vol. 1 (Westport, Conn.: Greenwood, 1974), p. 50.

4. *CN*, 21 Oct. 1893.

5. JAW, *The Story of "The Appeal to Reason" and "The Coming Nation"* (Girard, Kans.: Appeal to Reason, 1904); George Allan England, "The Story of the Appeal to Reason," *AtR*, 30 Aug. 1913 and following issues, and later published as *The Story of the Appeal, "Unbeaten and Unbeatable": Being the Epic of the Life and Work of the Greatest Political Newspaper in the World*, with a foreword by Lincoln Phifer (Fort Scott, Kans.: n.p., 1915).

6. JAW, *Leaves of Life: A Story of Twenty Years of Socialist Agitation* (Girard, Kans.: Appeal to Reason, 1912; Westport, Conn.: Hyperion, 1975); George D. Brewer, *The Fighting Editor: Warren and the Appeal* (Girard, Kans.: the Author, 1910; New York: Beekman, 1974).

7. W. J. Ghent, "The Appeal and its Influence," *Survey* 26 (Apr. 1911): 24–28; Algie Martin Simons, "J. A. Wayland, Propagandist," *Metropolitan Magazine* 32 (Jan. 1913): 25–26, 62; George Milburn, "The Appeal to Reason," *American Mercury* 23 (July 1931): 359–71.

8. Harold A. Trout, "The History of the *Appeal to Reason:* A Study of the Radical Press" (Master's thesis, Kansas State Teacher's College, 1934); Charles L. Scott, "*Appeal to Reason:* A Study of the 'Largest Political Newspaper in the World'" (Master's thesis, University of Kansas, 1957).

9. Howard H. Quint, "The Forging of a Modern American Socialist Movement, 1885–1900" (Ph.D. diss., Johns Hopkins University, 1947), and *The Forging of American Socialism* (Columbia: University of South Carolina Press, 1953).

10. Buhle, "Appeal to Reason," p. 50.

11. James R. Green, "The 'Salesmen-Soldiers' of the *Appeal* Army: A Profile of Rank and File Socialist Agitators," in *Socialism and the Cities*, ed. Bruce Stave (Port Washington, N.Y.: Kennikat, 1975), pp. 13–40; Green, *Grass-roots Socialism: Radical Movements in the Southwest, 1895–1943* (Baton Rouge: Louisiana State University Press, 1978).

12. David Paul Nord, "The *Appeal to Reason* and American Socialism, 1901–1920," *Kansas History* 1, 2 (Summer 1978): 75–89.

13. Sharon E. Neet, "Variant Editions of the *Appeal to Reason*, 1905–1906" (D.A. diss., University of North Dakota, 1983). The symposium is in *The Little Balkans Review: A Southeast Kansas Literary and Graphics Quarterly* 4, 1 (Fall 1983): 42–75.

14. Daniel Bell, "The Background and Development of Marxian Socialism in the United States," in *Socialism and American Life*, ed. Donald D. Egbert and Stow Persons, vol. 1 (Princeton, N.J.: Princeton University Press, 1952), p. 214.

15. Eric Foner, "Why Is There No Socialism in the United States?" *History Workshop Journal* 17 (Spring 1984): 57–80.

16. Irving Howe, *Socialism and America* (New York: Harcourt Brace Jovanovich, 1986), quoted from a review by C. Vann Woodward, "The Lost Cause," *New York Review of Books*, 30 Jan. 1986, p. 28.

Bibliography

MANUSCRIPT COLLECTIONS

Berger, Victor. Papers. Milwaukee Historical Society, Milwaukee, Wis.
Bureau of Investigation. Investigative Case Files. National Archives, Washington, D.C.
Brewer, George and Grace. Collection. Walter Reuther Library and Archives, Wayne State University, Detroit, Mich.
Debs, Eugene Victor. Foundation Library. Terre Haute, Ind.
Debs Collection. Indiana State University Library, Terre Haute
Debs Scrapbooks. Labadie Collection, University of Michigan, Ann Arbor
Ely, Richard T. Papers. State Historical Society of Wisconsin, Madison
Eugene Victor Debs Foundation Library. Terre Haute, Ind.
Germer, Adolph. Papers. State Historical Society of Wisconsin, Madison
Haldeman-Julius, Emanuel. Correspondence. Pittsburg State University Library, Pittsburg, Kans.
Haldeman-Julius, Emanuel. Manuscripts II and III. Lilly Library, Indiana University, Bloomington
Haldeman-Julius, Emanuel. Papers. Jane Addams Memorial Collection. Library of the University of Illinois, Chicago Circle
Hillquit, Morris. Papers. State Historical Society of Wisconsin, Madison
Justice, Department of. Classified Subject Files. National Archives, Washington, D.C.
Kansas Collection. Pittsburg State University Library, Pittsburg, Kans.
Lloyd, Henry Demarest. Papers. State Historical Society of Wisconsin, Madison
O'Hare Papers. State Historical Society of Missouri, Columbia
Post Office Collection. National Archives, Washington, D.C.
Reynolds, Stephen Marion. Papers. Indiana Historical Society Library, Indianapolis
Ruskin Cooperative Association. Records. Tennessee State Library and Archives, Nashville
Ruskin Cooperative Association. Records. University of Tennessee Library, Knoxville
Simons, Algie Martin. Papers. State Historical Society of Wisconsin, Madison
Sinclair, Upton. Manuscripts. Lilly Library, Indiana University, Bloomington
Socialist Labor Party. Papers. State Historical Society of Wisconsin, Madison
Socialist Party. Collection. Duke University Library, Durham, N.C.
Waite, Davis H. Collection. State Historical Society of Colorado, Denver
Warren Manuscripts. University of Connecticut Library, Storrs
Warren Papers. Private collection, Schenectady, N.Y.
Wayland, Julius Augustus. Collection. Pittsburg State University Library, Pittsburg, Kans.
Workingmen's Cooperative Publishing Association. Papers. Taminent Library, New York University, New York City

PERIODICALS

American Freeman. Girard, Kans.
Appeal Socialist Classics. Girard, Kans.
Appeal to Reason. Kansas City, Mo.; Kansas City, Kans.; Girard, Kans.
Bugle, The. Osgood, Ind.
Call, The. New York City
Cass County Courier. Harrisonville, Mo.
Cass News, The. Harrisonville, Mo.
Challenge, The. Los Angeles, Calif.
Colorado Chieftain. Pueblo, Colo.
Coming Nation, The. Greensburg, Ind.; Tennessee City, Tenn.; Ware County, Ga.; Rich Hill, Mo.; Girard, Kans.; Chicago, Ill.
Comrade, The. New York City
Fors Clavigera. Kent, England
Freeland. Greensburg, Ind.
Girard News. Girard, Kans.
Haldeman-Julius Weekly. Girard, Kans.
Independent News, The. Girard, Kans.
International Socialist Review. Chicago, Ill.
Menace, The. Aurora, Mo.
National Rip-Saw, The. St. Louis, Mo.
New Appeal, The. Girard, Kans.
Non-Conformist. Winfield, Kans.
One-Hoss Philosophy. Girard, Kans.
Party Builder, The. Chicago, Ill.
People, The. New York City
Pittsburg Plain Dealer. Pittsburg, Kans.
Progressive Woman. Chicago, Ill.
Pueblo Courier. Pueblo, Colo.
Pueblo Evening Star. Pueblo, Colo.
Rich Hill Tribune. Rich Hill, Mo.
Social Democratic Herald. Milwaukee, Wis.
Socialist. Seattle, Wash.
Social Thought. Rich Hill, Mo.
Studies in Socialism. Girard, Kans.
Wayland's Monthly. Girard, Kans.
Wilshire's. Los Angeles, Calif.; Toronto, Canada: New York City; London, England

SELECTED PUBLISHED AND UNPUBLISHED SOURCES

Adams, Frederick Upham. *A Crime without a Name: Remarkable Story of the Trial and Conviction of Fred D. Warren, Editor of the Appeal to Reason.* N.p., 1911.
Adams, Graham. *Age of Industrial Violence: 1900–1915: The Activities and Findings of the United States Commission on Industrial Relations.* New York: Columbia University Press, 1966.
Ameringer, Oscar. *If You Don't Weaken: The Autobiography of Oscar Ameringer.* New York: Henry Holt, 1940.
Anderson, William Woodrow. "The Nature of the Mexican Revolution as Viewed from the United States, 1900–1917." Ph.D. diss., University of Texas, 1967.
Andreucci, Franco. "Socialismo e Marxismo per pochi cents: Charles H. Kerr editore."

Movimento Operaio e Socialista. N.s., 3, 2 and 3 (Apr.-Sept. 1980): 269-76.

Barnett, George Ernest. "The Printers: A Study in American Trade Unionism." *American Economic Association Quarterly* 10 (Oct. 1909): 433-820.

Basen, Neil K. "Kate Richards O'Hare: The First Lady of American Socialism, 1901-1917." *Labor History* 21, 2 (Spring 1980): 165-99.

Becker, Klaus-Bert. *Die Muckrakers und der Sozialismus: Eine Untersuchung zum politischen Bewusstsein in der Progressive Era.* Bern: Herbert Lang, 1974.

Bell, Daniel. "The Background and Development of Marxian Socialism in the United States." In *Socialism and American Life,* edited by Donald Drew Egbert and Stow Persons, vol. 1, pp. 213-406. Princeton, N.J.: Princeton University Press, 1952.

Bellamy, Edward. *Looking Backward, 2000-1887.* Boston: Tickner, 1888.

Billington, Ray Allen. *Westward Expansion: A History of the American Frontier.* 3d ed. New York: Macmillan, 1967.

Bliss, William Dwight. *The New Encyclopaedia of American Reform.* New York: Funk & Wagnalls, 1908.

Blumberg, Dorothy Rose. "Mary Elizabeth Lease, Populist Orator: A Profile." *Kansas History* 1, 1 (Spring 1978): 3-15.

Bowles, Samuel, and Herbert Gintis. *Democracy and Capitalism: Property, Community, and the Contradictions of Modern Social Thought.* New York: Basic Books, 1986.

Brann, W.C. *Brann the Iconoclast: A Collection of the Writings of W. C. Brann,* with a biography by J. D. Shaw. 2 vols. Waco, Texas: Herz Brothers, 1898.

Brewer, George D. *The Fighting Editor: or, Warren and the Appeal.* Girard, Kans.: the Author, 1910.

———. *The Rights of the Masses.* Chicago: Kerr, n.d.

———. *The Wayland I Knew.* N.p., n.d.

Brodhead, Michael J., and O. Gene Clanton. "G. C. Clemens: The Sociable Socialist." *Kansas Historical Quarterly* 43, 4 (Winter 1974): 475-502.

Broome, Isaac. *The Last Days of the Ruskin Co-operative Association.* Chicago: Charles H. Kerr, 1902.

Buhle, Mari Jo. *Women and American Socialism, 1870-1920.* Urbana: University of Illinois Press, 1981.

Buhle, Paul Merlyn. "Marxism in the United States, 1900-1940." Ph.D. diss., University of Wisconsin, 1975.

Burbank, Garin. *When Farmers Voted Red: The Gospel of Socialism in the Oklahoma countryside, 1910-1924.* Westport, Conn.: Greenwood, 1976.

Butler, Francelia. "The Ruskin Commonwealth: A Unique Experiment in Marxian Socialism." *Tennessee Historical Quarterly* 23 (Dec. 1964): 333-43.

Chalmers, David Mark. *The Social and Political Ideas of the Muckrakers.* New York: Citadel, 1964.

Clanton, O. Gene. *Kansas Populism: Ideas and Men.* Lawrence: University Press of Kansas, 1969.

Conlin, Joseph R. *Big Bill Haywood and the Radical Union Movement.* Syracuse, N.Y.: Syracuse University Press, 1969.

———, ed. *The American Radical Press, 1880-1960.* Vol. 1. Westport, Conn.: Greenwood, 1974.

Corbin, David A. "Betrayal in the West Virginia Coal Fields: Eugene V. Debs and the Socialist Party of America, 1912-1914." *Journal of American History* 64, 4 (Mar. 1978): 987-1009.

Cummings, Mary Vincent. *Memories of Girard, Kansas, Eugene V. Debs and Me.* Glendora, Calif.: Merrily Cummings Ford, 1976.

Debs, Eugene Victor. *Fourteenth Anniversary of the Birth of the Coming Nation at Greensburg, Decatur County, Indiana, April, 1893.* [Girard, Kans.: Appeal to Reason, 1907].

Destler, Chester M. *American Radicalism, 1865-1901.* Chicago: Quadrangle, 1966.

Dubofsky, Melvyn. "The Origins of Western Working Class Radicalism, 1890-1905." *Labor History* 7, 2 (Spring 1966): 131-54.

Egerton, John. *Visions of Utopia: Nashoba, Rugby and the "New Communities" in Tennessee's Past.* Knoxville: University of Tennessee Press, in cooperation with the Tennessee Historical Commission, 1977.

Emery, Edwin, and Michael Emery. *The Press and America: An Interpretative History of the Mass Media.* Englewood Cliffs, N.J.: Prentice-Hall, 1978.

England, George Allen. *The Story of the Appeal, "Unbeaten and Unbeatable": Being the Epic of the Life and Work of the Greatest Political Newspaper in the World.* With a foreword by Lincoln Phifer. Fort Scott, Kans.: n.p., 1915.

An Evening in Girard; Just an Informal Incident Following the Return of Delegates from the Chicago Socialist Convention. Girard, Kans.: [Appeal to Reason], 1908.

Featherling, Dale. *Mother Jones: The Miners' Angel.* Carbondale: Southern Illinois University Press, 1974.

Fellman, Michael. *The Unbounded Frame: Freedom and Community in Nineteenth Century American Utopianism.* Contributions in American History no. 26. Westport, Conn.: Greenwood, 1973.

Filene, Peter G. "Obituary for 'The Progressive Movement.'" *American Quarterly* 22, 1 (Spring 1970): 20-34.

Filler, Louis. *The Muckrakers.* University Park: Pennsylvania State University Press, 1976.

Flower, Benjamin Orange. *Story of the Menace Trial.* [Aurora, Mo.: United States Publishing Co., 1916].

Foner, Eric. *Free Soil, Free Labor, Free Men: The Ideology of the Republican Party before the Civil War.* New York: Oxford University Press, 1970.

———. "Why Is There No Socialism in the United States?" *History Workshop Journal*, no. 17 (Spring 1984): 57-80.

Foner, Philip S. *History of the Labor Movement in the United States.* 7 vols. New York: International, 1947-.

Fox, Richard W. "The Paradox of 'Progressive' Socialism: The Case of Morris Hillquit, 1901-1914." *American Quarterly* 26, 2 (May 1974): 127-40.

Fuller, Leon W. "Colorado's Revolt against Capitalism." *Mississippi Valley Historical Review* 21, 3 (Dec. 1934): 343-60.

Ghent, W. J., comp. *The Appeal Almanac and Arsenal of Facts for 1915.* The first edition of the Almanac and seventeenth edition of the Arsenal of Facts. Girard, Kans.: Appeal, 1915.

———. "The Appeal and Its Influence," *Survey* 26 (Apr. 1911): 24-28.

Gilmore, Vera Wilson. "The Ruskin Colony, 1894-1901: Experimental Model for the Socialist Commonwealth." Master's thesis, University of Tennessee, 1973.

Ginger, Ray. *Eugene Debs: A Biography.* New Brunswick, N.J.: Rutgers University Press, 1947.

Gompers, Samuel. *Seventy Years of Life and Labor: An Autobiography.* 2 vols. in 1. New York: E. P. Dutton, 1943.

Goodwyn, Lawrence. *Democratic Promise: The Populist Movement in America.* New York: Oxford University Press, 1976.

Gordon, F. G. R. *Panics: Cause and Cure.* Girard, Kans.: J. A. Wayland, 1901.

Gottlieb, Robert, and Irene Wolt. *Thinking Big: The Story of the Los Angeles*

Times, Its Publishers and Their Influence on Southern California. New York: G. C. Putnam, 1977.

Green, James R. *Grass-roots Socialism: Radical Movements in the Southwest 1895-1943.* Baton Rouge: Lousiana State University Press, 1978.

_____. "The 'Salesmen-Soldiers' of the 'Appeal Army': A Profile of Rank and File Socialist Agitators." In *Socialism and the Cities,* edited by Bruce M. Stave. Port Washington, N.Y.: Kennikat, 1975.

Grenier, Judson. "Upton Sinclair and the Press: *The Brass Check* Reconsidered." *Journalism Quarterly,* Autumn 1976, pp. 427-36.

Gronlund, Laurence. *The Cooperative Commonwealth in Its Outlines: An Exposition of Modern Socialism.* Boston: Lee & Shepard, [1884].

Grover, David H. *Debaters and Dynamiters: The Story of the Haywood Trial.* Corvallis: Oregon State University Press, 1964.

Haldeman-Julius, Emanuel. *My First Twenty Five Years: Instead of a Footnote, An Autobiography.* Girard, Kans.: Haldeman-Julius, 1949.

_____. *My Second Twenty Five Years: Instead of a Footnote, An Autobiography.* Girard, Kans.: Haldeman-Julius, 1949.

Harris, Leon. *Upton Sinclair: American Rebel.* New York: Crowell, 1975.

Hays, Samuel P. *The Response to Industrialism: 1885-1914.* Chicago: University of Chicago Press, 1957.

Haywood, William D. *Bill Haywood's Book: The Autobiography of William D. Haywood.* New York: International, 1929.

Hicks, John D. *The Populist Revolt: A History of the Farmer's Alliance and the People's Party.* Minneapolis: University of Minnesota Press, 1931.

Higham, John. *Strangers in the Land: Patterns of American Nativism, 1860-1925.* New York: Atheneum, 1977.

Hillquit, Morris. *History of Socialism in the United States.* New York: Funk & Wagnalls, 1903.

_____. *Loose Leaves from a Busy Life.* New York: Macmillan, 1934.

Hinds, William Alfred. *American Communities and Cooperative Colonies.* Chicago: Kerr, 1908.

Historical and Descriptive Review of Colorado's Enterprising Cities, Their Leading Business Houses and Progressive Men. Denver: Jno. Lethem, [1893].

Hoerder, Dirk, ed. *Essays on the Scandinavian-North American Radical Press, 1880s-1930s.* Bremen: University of Bremen, 1984.

Holbrook, Stewart H. *Lost Men of American History.* New York: Macmillan, 1946.

Husten, Robert Stuart. "A.M. Simons and the American Socialist Movement." Ph.D. diss., University of Wisconsin, 1965.

Jones, Clifton. "The Socialist Party of the United States, 1901-1920: A Bibliography of Secondary Sources, 1945-1974." *Labor History* 19, 2 (Spring 1978): 253-79.

Jones, Mary Harris. *Autobiography of Mother Jones.* Chicago: Charles Kerr, 1925.

Kegel, Charles H. "Ruskin's St. George in America." *American Quarterly* 9 (Winter 1957): 412-20.

Kent, Alexander. "Cooperative Communities in the United States." *Bulletin of the Department of Labor* 6, 35 (July 1901): 563-646.

Kerr, Charles H. *A Socialist Publishing House.* Chicago: Kerr, [1904?].

_____. *What to Read on Socialism.* Chicago: Kerr, [1906].

Kipnis, Ira. *The American Socialist Movement, 1897-1912.* New York: Columbia University Press, 1952.

Kraditor, Aileen S. *The Radical Persuasion, 1890-1917.* Baton Rouge: Louisiana State University Press, 1981.

Kreuter, Kent, and Gretchen Kreuter. *An American Dissenter: The Life of Algie Martin Simons, 1870-1950.* Lexington: University of Kentucky Press, 1969.

Lamson, Willis Ernest. "The Historical Development of Girard, Kansas, and Its Community." Master's thesis, Kansas State Teachers College, Pittsburg, 1933.

Laslett, John, comp. *Failure of A Dream? Essays in the History of American Socialism.* Garden City, N.Y.: Anchor Press, 1974.

LeWarne, Charles Pierce. *Utopias on Puget Sound, 1885-1915.* Seattle: University of Washington Press, 1975.

Lipset, Seymour Martin. *Agrarian Socialism: The Cooperative Commonwealth Federation in Saskatchewan: A Study in Political Sociology.* Berkeley: University of California Press, 1959.

Lipset, Seymour Martin; Martin A. Trow; and James S. Coleman. *Union Democracy: The Internal Politics of the International Typographical Union.* Glencoe, Ill.: Free Press, 1956.

Long, Priscilla. *Mother Jones, Woman Organizer: And Her Relations with Miners' Wives, Working Women, and the Suffrage Movement.* Cambridge, Mass.: Red Sun, 1976.

McCormick, Richard L. "The Discovery That Business Corrupts Politics: A Reappraisal of the Origins of Progressivism." *American Historical Review* 86 (Apr. 1981): 247-74.

McKerns, Joseph Patrick. "The History of American Journalism: A Bibliographical Essay," *American Studies International* 15, 1 (Fall 1976): 17-34.

Milburn, George. "The Appeal to Reason," *American Mercury* 23 (July 1931): 359-71.

Miller, Earl. "Recollections of the Ruskin Cooperative Association," ed. Charles H. Kegel. *Tennessee Historical Quarterly* 17 (Mar. 1958): 45-69.

Miller, Sally M. *Victor Berger and the Promise of Constructive Socialism, 1910-1920.* Westport, Conn.: Greenwood, 1973.

Mills, Walter Thomas. *The Struggle for Existence.* Chicago: International School of Social Economy, 1904.

Molek, Ivan. *Slovene Immigrant History, 1900-1950: Autobiographical Sketches,* ed. Mary Molek. Dover, Del.: the Editor, 1979.

Moore, Robert Laurence. *European Socialists and the American Promised Land.* New York: Oxford University Press, 1970.

———. *In Search of White Crows: Spiritualism, Parapsychology and American Culture.* New York: Oxford University Press, 1977.

Morgan, H. Wayne. " 'Red Special': Eugene V. Debs and the Campaign of 1908." *Indiana Magazine of History* 54, 3 (Sept. 1958): 211-36.

Mott, Frank Luther. *American Journalism, 1690-1960.* 3d ed. New York: Macmillan, 1962.

———. *A History of American Magazines: 1885-1905.* Cambridge: Bellknap Press of Harvard University Press, 1957.

Muller, William H. *Socialism in a Nutshell.* Ruskin, Tenn.: n.p., 1898.

National Committee of the Socialist Party. *National Convention of the Socialist Party, Chicago, 1904.* Stenographic report, edited by William S. Mailly. Chicago: Socialist Party, 1904.

Nearing, Scott. *The Making of a Radical: A Political Autobiography.* New York: Harper & Row, 1972.

Neet, Sharon E. "Variant Editions of the *Appeal to Reason,* 1905-1906." D.A. diss., University of North Dakota, 1983.

Nord, David Paul. "The *Appeal to Reason* and American Socialism, 1901-1920." *Kansas History* 1, 2 (Summer 1978): 75-89.

O'Hare, Kate Richards. *Wimmin Ain't Got No Kick.* Chicago: Women's National Committee of the Socialist Party, n.d.

Oppenheim, Janet. *The Other World: Spiritualism and Psychical Research in England, 1850-1914.* Cambridge: Cambridge University Press, 1986.

Paulson, Ross E. *Radicalism and Reform: The Vrooman Family and American Social Thought, 1837-1937.* Lexington: University of Kentucky Press, 1968.

Perlman, Selig, and Phillip Taft. *History of Labor in the United States, 1896-1932.* New York: Macmillan, 1935.

Phifer, Charles Lincoln. *Hamlet in Heaven; a five act play, purporting to have been written by William Shakespeare by automatic writing through the hand of Lincoln Phifer.* Girard, Kans.: L. Phifer, 1916.

_____. *Old Religions Made New: In Natural Processes by Divine Intent.* N.p., 1918.

_____. *Quiz & 'Tis.* Toledo, Ohio: O. W. F. Ries, [191-].

_____. *The Road to Socialism: What Has Been Gained and What is Yet to Win.* Girard, Kans.: Appeal to Reason, 1913.

Phillips, Clifton J. *Indiana in Transition: The Emergence of an Industrial Commonwealth, 1880-1920.* Vol. 4 of *The History of Indiana.* Indianapolis: Indiana Historical Bureau and Indiana Historical Society, 1968.

Piehler, Harold Richard. "Henry Vincent: A Case Study in Political Deviancy," Ph.D. diss., University of Kansas, 1975.

_____. "Henry Vincent: Kansas Populist and Radical-Reform Journalist." *Kansas History* 2, 1 (Spring 1979): 14-25.

Pittenger, Mark. "Evolution, Woman's Nature and American Feminist Socialism, 1900-1915." *Radical History Review* 36 (Sept. 1986): 47-61.

Pomeroy, Eltweed. "A Sketch of the Socialist Colony in Tennessee." *American Fabian* 3 (Apr. 1897): 2.

Preston, William. "Shall This Be All? United States Historians versus William D. Haywood et al." *Labor History* 11, 3 (Summer 1971): 435-53.

Quint, Howard H. *The Forging of American Socialism: Origins of the Modern Movement.* Columbia: University of South Carolina Press, 1953; New York: Bobbs-Merrill, 1964.

_____. "The Forging of a Modern American Socialist Movement, 1888-1901," Ph.D. diss., Johns Hopkins University, 1947.

_____. "Julius A. Wayland, Pioneer Socialist Propagandist." *Mississippi Valley Historical Review* 35, 4 (Mar. 1949): 585-606.

Reynolds, Robert D., Jr. "The Millionaire Socialists: J. G. Phelps Stokes and His Circle of Friends." Ph.D. diss., University of South Carolina, 1974.

Ricker, A. W. *What Socialism Is: Socialist Economics in Paragraphs.* Girard, Kans.: Appeal to Reason, 1903.

Robertson, James Oliver. *America's Business.* New York: Hill & Wang, 1985.

Russell, Charles Edward. *Bare Hands and Stone Walls: Some Recollections of a Side-Line Reformer.* New York: Scribner's, 1933.

Salvatore, Nick. *Eugene V. Debs: Citizen and Socialist.* Urbana: University of Illinois Press, 1982.

_____. "A Generation of Transition: Eugene V. Debs and the Emergence of Modern Corporate America." Ph.D. diss., University of California, 1977.

Saville, John. "The Radical Left Expects the Past to Do Its Duty." *Labor History* 18, 2 (Spring, 1977): 267-74.

Schofield, Ann. "The Women's March: Miners, Family and Community in Pittsburg, Kansas, 1921-1922." *Kansas History* 7, 2 (Summer 1984): 159-68.

Schudson, Michael. *Discovering the News: A Social History of American Newspapers.* New York: Basic Books, 1978.
Schwantes, Carlos A. *Radical Heritage: Labor, Socialism and Reform in Washington and British Columbia, 1885-1917.* Seattle: University of Washington Press, 1979.
Scott, Charles L. "*Appeal to Reason:* A Study of the 'Largest Political Newspaper in the World.'" Master's thesis, Kansas State Teachers College, 1957.
Seretan, L. Glen. *Daniel DeLeon: The Odyssey of an American Marxist.* Cambridge: Harvard University Press, 1979.
Shannon, David A. "Eugene V. Debs Conservative Labor Editor." *Indiana Magazine of History* 47 (Dec. 1951): 141-46.
_____. "The Socialist Party before the First World War." *Mississippi Valley Historical Review* 38 (Sept. 1951): 279-301.
_____. *The Socialist Party of America: A History.* New York: Macmillan, 1955.
Sherburne, James Clark. *John Ruskin: or, The Ambiguities of Abundance: A Study in Social and Economic Criticism.* Cambridge: Harvard University Press, 1972.
Shoaf, George H.. "The Biggest Little Paper This Country Ever Knew." *Monthly Review* 3, 3 (July 1951): 88-98.
_____. "Debs and the *Appeal to Reason:* A Personal Memoir." *Progressive World,* Nov./Dec. 1975, pp. 13-17, and Jan./Feb. 1976, pp. 26-31.
_____. *Fighting for Freedom.* Kansas City, Mo.: Simplified Economics, [1953].
_____. *Love Crucified: A Romance of the Colorado War.* Girard, Kans.: Appeal Pub. Co., 1905.
Shore, Elliott. "Selling Socialism: The *Appeal to Reason* and the Radical Press in Turn-of-the-Century America." *Media, Culture and Society* 7 (1985): 147-68.
Silverman, Henry Jacob. "American Social Reformers in the Late Nineteenth and Early Twentieth Century." Ph.D. diss., University of Pennsylvania, 1963.
Simons, Algie Martin. "J. A. Wayland, Propagandist." *Metropolitan Magazine* 32 (Jan. 1913): 25-26, 62.
_____. *Our Bourgeois Literature: The Reason and the Remedy.* Chicago: Kerr, 1904.
Sinclair, Upton. *The Autobiography of Upton Sinclair.* New York: Harcourt, Brace & World, 1962.
_____. *The Brass Check.* Pasadena: the Author, 1920.
Smith, Harold Sherburn. "William James Ghent: Reformer and Historian." Ph.D. diss., University of Wisconsin, 1957.
Smythe, Ted Curtis. "The Reporter, 1880-1900: Working conditions and Their Influence on the News." *Journalism History* 7, 1 (Spring 1980): 1-10.
Social Democracy Red Book. Terre Haute, Ind.: Debs Publishing Co., 1900.
Socialist Party, National Committee. *National Convention of the Socialist Party, Chicago, 1904.* Stenographic report, edited by William S. Mailly. Chicago: Socialist Party, 1904.
Sombart, Werner. *Why Is There No Socialism in the United States?* Translated by Patricia M. Hockins and C. T. Husbands. White Plains, N.Y.: International Arts and Sciences, 1976.
Steffens, Lincoln. "Eugene V. Debs on What the Matter Is in America and What to Do About It." *Everybody's Magazine* 19 (Oct. 1908): 455-69.
Stevens, Errol Wayne. "Heartland Socialism: The Socialist Party of America in Four Midwestern Communities, 1898-1920." Ph.D. diss., Indiana University, 1978.
Tarbell, Ida Minerva. *The Nationalizing of Business, 1878-1898.* New York: Macmillan, 1936.
Thompson, Carl D. *What to Read and What to Give Others to Read on Socialism and Price List of Socialist Books.* Milwaukee, Wis.: Social-Democratic Publ. Co., n.d.

Tierney, Kevin. *Darrow: A Biography.* New York: Thomas Y. Crowell, 1979.

Trout, Harold A. "The History of the *Appeal to Reason:* A Study of the Radical Press." M.A. thesis, Kansas State Teacher's College, 1934.

Turner, John Kenneth. *Barbarous Mexico.* Chicago: Kerr, 1910; 2d ed., Austin: University of Texas Press, 1969.

Untermann, Ernest. *How to Get Socialism.* Girard, Kans.: J. A. Wayland, 1903.

_____. *Marxian Economics: A Popular Introduction to the Three Volumes of Marx's "Capital."* Chicago: Kerr, 1907.

Vincent, Henry. *Wayland: The Editor with a Punch, An Appreciation.* Massilon, Ohio: the Author, 1912.

Walden, Daniel. "W. J. Ghent: The Growth of an Intellectual Radical, 1892–1917." Ph.D. diss., New York University, 1964.

Walker, Ryan. *The Red Portfolio: Cartoons for Socialism.* Girard, Kans.: Coming Nation, n.d.

Warren, Fred D. *The Appeal's Arsenal of Facts.* 13th ed., rev. Girard, Kans.: Appeal to Reason, 1911.

_____. *The Boytown Railroad.* N.p., 1935.

_____. *The Catholic Church and Socialism.* Girard, Kans.: Appeal to Reason, 1914.

_____. *Freeman or Slave? A Book of Suppressed Information.* Girard, Kans.: Appeal to Reason, n.d.

_____. "The Little Old Appeal." Ms., Sinclair Papers, Lilly Library, [1950?].

_____. *The People's College Vest-Pocket Edition of the Report of the Industrial Relations Commission.* Fort Scott, Kans.: People's College, [1915].

Wayland, Julius Augustus. *Leaves of Life: A Story of Twenty Years of Socialist Agitation.* Girard, Kans.: Appeal to Reason, 1912; Westport, Conn.: Hyperion Press, 1975.

_____. *The Story of "The Appeal to Reason" and "The Coming Nation."* Girard, Kans.: Appeal to Reason, 1904.

_____. *Wayland's Undelivered Address and Ben Wilson's Funeral Oration.* Girard, Kans.: Appeal to Reason, 1913.

Weinstein, James. *The Decline of Socialism in America, 1912–1925.* New York: Monthly Review Press, 1967; Vintage, 1969.

Whitaker, Milo Lee. *Pathbreakers and Pioneers of the Pueblo Region.* N.p.: Franklin Press, 1917.

Who's Who in Socialist America for 1914. Girard, Kans.: Appeal to Reason, 1914.

Wilshire, Henry Gaylord. *Socialism: A Religion.* New York: Wilshire's Magazine, 1903.

_____. *Why a "Workingman" Should be a Socialist.* New York: Wilshire's Magazine, 1903.

Winstead, Ralph. "Social Structures." *One Big Union Monthly* 2, 9 (Sept. 1920): 23–25.

Work, John M. *What's So and What Isn't.* Girard, Kans.: Wayland, 1905.

Wright, James Edward. *The Politics of Populism: Dissent in Colorado.* New Haven, Conn.: Yale University Press, 1974.

Young, James Harvey. *The Toadstool Millionaires: A Social History of Patent Medicines in America before Federal Regulation.* Princeton, N.J.: Princeton University Press, 1961.

Index